D1109975

Alcoholism

A GUIDE TO DIAGNOSIS, INTERVENTION, AND TREATMENT

Donald M. Gallant, M.D. is Professor of Psychiatry and Adjunct Professor of Pharmacology and Director of Medical Student Education in Psychiatry, Tulane University School of Medicine, New Orleans, Louisiana; Medical Director of the Alcohol and Drug Abuse Unit (ADU) of Southeast Louisiana Hospital, Mandeville; and Chief of the Alcohol Dependence Treatment Program (ADTP), Veterans Administration Medical Center, New Orleans.

A NORTON PROFESSIONAL BOOK

Alcoholism

A GUIDE TO DIAGNOSIS, INTERVENTION, AND TREATMENT

Donald M. Gallant

W. W. NORTON & COMPANY • *NEW YORK* • *LONDON*

CREDITS

The following are reprinted with permission:

Table 1.2 from the National Council on Alcoholism.

Table 2.2 from J. Mayer and W. J. Filstead, The Adolescent Alcohol Involvement Scale: An Instrument for Measuring Adolescents' Use and Misuse of Alcohol, *Journal of Studies on Alcohol, 40*: 291–300, 1979.

Table 5.1A from C. L. Whitfield, J. E. Davis, and L. R. Barker, Addendum to the MAST. In: L. R. Barker, J. R. Burton, and P. Ziene (Eds.), *Principles of Ambulatory Medicine*. Baltimore: Williams & Wilkins, 1986.

Figure 2.1 from D. Kandel, Stages in Adolescent Drug Use, *Science, 190*: 912–914, 1975. Copyright 1975, AAAS.

Parts of Chapter 10 appeared originally in D. M. Gallant, Use of Psychopharmacologic Medications in the Treatment of Alcoholism, *Substance Abuse, Spring Issue*, 35–47, 1986.

Copyright © 1987 by Donald M. Gallant
All rights reserved.
Published simultaneously in Canada by Penguin Books Canada Ltd,
2801 John Street, Markham, Ontario L3R 1B4

Library of Congress Cataloging-in-Publication Data

Gallant, Donald M., 1929–
   Alcoholism: a guide to diagnosis, intervention,
and treatment.

   "A Norton professional book." — P. facing t.p.
   Includes bibliographies.
   1. Alcoholism. I. Title. [DNLM: 1. Alcoholism.
WM 274 G163a]
RC565.G33 1988   616.86′1   87-23966

ISBN 0-393-70043-7

W. W. Norton & Company, Inc. 500 Fifth Avenue, New York, N. Y. 10110

W. W. Norton & Company, Ltd. 37 Great Russell Street, London WC1B 3NU

   2   3   4   5   6   7   8   9   0

Foreword

THE APPEARANCE OF THIS BOOK is a fortunate event for the student and practitioner of alcoholism treatment, as this sophisticated but practical guide fills a troublesome void in our field. We have only recently moved toward a consensus of what options are available for the rehabilitation of alcoholism, and how they emerge from the underlying psychology and pathophysiology of this ubiquitous illness. What has been needed is a work that brings such a synthesis to the practitioner, to serve as an educational guide and practical reference. In this volume, this goal is effectively attained for physicians and allied health professionals.

Education of the physician in alcoholism treatment has only recently begun to gain the attention necessary to assure that alcoholic patients get proper care. As recently as 1972, for example, a position paper of the American Medical Association pointed out that the need for effective medical education about this illness had reached "a point of urgency." That same year, because of a similiar awareness, the federal government funded the first of 60 medical career teachers for alcoholism and addiction, and the year after it established a National Institute to address the problem of alcoholism. Altogether, this movement had a considerable impact. By 1987, for example, 735 graduate physicians were certified for expertise in alcoholism and other drug dependencies, in the first year of a process established to define specialized medical knowledge is the field.

The medical community, however, has not always been in the forefront of addressing this problem. The impact of Alcoholics Anonymous on the treatment system has, for example, been of singular importance in providing care. The establishment of AA 52 years ago was due in good part to a virtual absence of professional care at that time. AA spurred the emergence of large numbers of certified alcoholism counselors, some with a background in their own recovery from alcoholism and others with traditional professional experience; it provided important training exposure for physicians, too. The model these workers espoused, primarily oriented toward social influence and the channeling of patients into membership in AA, has come to be the predominant one among practitioners of alcoholism rehabilitation.

What has been lacking, however, is a comprehensive text and guide which offers the clinician the full body of experience of both the biomedical tradition and the experience emerging from the nonmedical community. The former now provides considerable insight into areas such as pathophysiology, genetics, and natural course of the illness; traditional diagnostic techniques and pharmacotherapy, too, are essential to effective management. On the other hand, the nonmedical approach, allied with the AA tradition, has provided techniques such as early intervention with the recalcitrant alcoholic, approaches to instituting abstinence, and ways of providing social support to prevent relapse.

This book offers an effective synthesis of both perspectives. For example, it lays out a sophisticated model of the pharmacologic underpinnings of alcohol addiction; even the most recent findings on the role of benzodiazepine receptor antagonists are explored. Similarly, it elucidates the genetics underlying the emergence of alcoholism and how this model can be made useful to the patients.

Conversely, this volume also draws on the tradition of AA and social intervention. It presents numerous rich examples of how abstinence is introduced into the clinical setting by interpersonal exchange in individual treatment, and ward milieu, and couples groups. The book offers a cogent and comprehensive compendium of useful intervention techniques gleaned from work with practitioners of this background.

Marc Galanter, M.D.
Professor of Psychiatry,
New York University
Medical Center

Contents

Foreword by Marc Galanter   v

Acknowledgments   x

Introduction   xi

Chapter 1. Definition and Diagnosis   1
  The Problem of Definition   1
  Medical Diagnostic Criteria   3
  Personality Types: The Problem   11

Chapter 2. Incidence of Alcoholism and Alcohol-Related
           Morbidity and Mortality   13
  Problems in Surveying the Incidence of Alcoholism   13
  Surveys for Alcoholism in the General Population   14
  Alcohol Misuse in the Adolescent Population   15
  Incidence of Alcohol Abuse in the Aging Population   21
  Alcohol-Related Morbidity and Mortality   21

Chapter 3. Pharmacology of Alcohol and Alcoholism   26
  Metabolic Pathways   27
  *Concepts of Alcohol Tolerance, Addiction, and
     Opiod Receptor Systems*   29
  *Biochemical Relationships Between Alcohol and
     Non-Opiod Receptor Systems*   31

Chapter 4. Psychologic, Cultural, and Genetic Aspects of
           Alcoholism   35
  *Psychodynamic and Psychologic Mechanisms
     Contributing to the Development of Alcoholism*   35
  Psychological Consequences of Alcoholism   40
  Variations and Effects of Cultural Attitudes   41
  Genetic Aspects of Alcohol and Drug Abuse   42

Chapter 5. Early Diagnosis of Alcoholism   47
    The Interview Process   47
    Early Symptoms and Signs of Alcohol Abuse   54
    Differential Diagnosis   58
    Indications for Referral for Psychiatric Consultation or to
      Specialized Treatment Programs   59

Chapter 6. Early Intervention Techniques   63
    The Importance of Early Intervention   63
    The Therapeutic Relationship   64
    The Techniques of Early Intervention   65
    Four Case Histories of Intervention   70
    A Modification of the Intervention With Adolescents   82
    Other Intervention Techniques   83

Chapter 7. Medical Consequences of Alcoholism   86
    Effects of Ethanol on the Nervous System   87
    Effects of Ethanol on Other Organ Systems   98

Chapter 8. Management of Acute Alcohol Intoxication and
    Alcohol Withdrawal (Detoxification)   105
    Management of Acute Alcohol Intoxication   107
    Management of the Acute Withdrawal Syndromes   108
    Management of Alcoholics Who Are Multiple Drug Abusers   116

Chapter 9. Inpatient Rehabilitation Treatment   119
    Problems in Evaluating Success Rates of Alcoholism
      Rehabilitation Programs   119
    Description of the Alcohol and Drug Abuse Unit (ADU)
      Treatment Program   121
    Special Treatment Problems   158
    Other Special Treatment Groups   163

Chapter 10. The Use of Psychopharmacologic Medications in
    Alcoholism   170
    Antabuse (disulfiram)   170
    Lithium   176
    The Role of Antidepressant Agents   178
    Use of Anxiolytic Agents   180
    The Role of Vitamins   182

Chapter 11. Outpatient Treatment   187
    The Intake or Initial History-Taking   187
    Couples Group Psychotherapy   193
    Family Therapy   199
    Other Special Treatment Modalities   211

Using the Clinic During the Waiting Period Before
   *Admission to a Rehabilitation Unit*214
*Use of Other Community Resources*216

Chapter 12. Prevention221
*Primary Prevention*221
*Secondary Prevention*238

Index246

Acknowledgments

I WANT TO EXPRESS my appreciation to Lola Adeola for typing the manuscript and to Fran Corbitt, who prepared all of the tables and figures. I especially wish to thank Susan E. Barrows, who edited the manuscript, for her careful eye, her meticulous attention to detail, and her continuing support throughout the preparation of the manuscript.

I particularly want to acknowledge the help and support I have received over a period of many years from the staff members of the Alcoholism and Drug Abuse Unit (ADU) of Southeast Louisiana Hospital, Mandeville, Louisiana, the staff of the New Orleans Substance Abuse Clinic, and the personnel at the Veterans Administration Alcoholism Dependence Treatment Program (ADTP). The dedicated workers at these facilities have made recovery possible for innumerable alcoholic patients who have moved through these services over the last 27 years.

Finally, I want to express my appreciation to the many patients I have treated throughout the years, whose strength, courage, and sense of humor in their fight against alcoholism have been nothing short of remarkable. Many of these patients are extraordinary human beings who have given me every bit as much, perhaps more, than I have been able to give them. It is these patients to whom I dedicate the book.

Introduction

ALCOHOL DEPENDENCE IS THE MOST COMMON medical and psychiatric problem in the United States today. An unprecedented government-supported study by the National Institute of Mental Health (NIMH) on the lifetime prevalence of specific psychiatric disorders in about 17,000 respondents over the age of 18 years showed that alcohol abuse or dependence affects 11% to 16% of the population (Robins et al., 1984). Only 10% of these alcohol dependent patients saw a mental health specialist. Another survey by the National Institute on Alcohol Abuse and Alcoholism found that 10% of the adult population exhibited symptoms of loss of control while drinking or dependency on alcohol during the year of the survey (Kamerow et al., 1986). In 1983, the cost for direct treatment and support of alcoholism in the U.S. was 14.9 billion dollars, almost 5% of the national health care expenditures. These direct costs combined with the indirect costs of productivity loss and property damage were estimated to be 116.7 billion dollars in a single year (Kamerow et al., 1986).

The enormity of this medical problem is further emphasized by the very high rate of alcoholism seen in hospital walk-in clinics (28%), emergency rooms (38%) (Zimberg, 1979), and general hospital wards (32% in males and 8% in females in one study) (Barcha et al., 1968). Even more impressive data are available from a prospective study of the association between alcohol abuse and mortality rate in an unselected population of 7,725 middle-aged males (Petersson et al., 1982). In the follow-up period (mean of three years) of this group, 30% of the deaths were classified as alcohol-related, a more frequent cause of death than cancer or cardiovascular diseases. The authors of this report were conservative in their application of statistics to other alcohol-related deaths, excluding deaths from cancer and stroke, although alcohol is recognized as one of the etiologic factors in these diseases.

In the myriad of medical and psychologic problems encountered by the

practicing physician, psychologist, social worker and substance abuse therapist, alcoholism is one of the illnesses that requires immediate attention
because of the shockingly high suicide rate associated with this disease. In a
valuable 30-year prospective study of 1,312 alcoholics, 88 (16%) of the 537
patients who died were definite suicides — a suicide rate more than 200 times
higher than would be expected in a non-alcoholic population (Berglund,
1984). Suicide, which occurs in younger age groups more often than a
number of potentially fatal medical illnesses, is the sixth leading cause of
lost years of productivity (Kamerow et al., 1986).

There are no signs that the national problem of alcohol abuse and alcoholism is going away. A recent report by the National Institute on Alcohol
Abuse and Alcoholism (NIAAA) showed that drinking intensity (or days of
intoxication) is increasing among high school seniors; other studies show
that alcohol abuse is not only a strong factor in teenage automobile-related
deaths but also a serious problem in adolescents seen in hospital emergency
rooms (Niven, 1984; Reichler et al., 1983).

Not only is education on alcoholism the most neglected topic in medical
schools today, but many other health care professionals, such as social
workers, psychologists, and nurses, feel that the teaching in their disciplines
is similarly lacking (Pokorny & Solomon, 1983). Despite the disturbingly
high incidence of alcoholism, a nationwide survey revealed that less than 1%
of the medical school curriculum is devoted to the subject of alcoholism
(Pokorny & Solomon, 1983). Since the incidence of alcoholism is two to two
and a half times greater among physicians than in the general population, it
is important that medical students be exposed to adequate teaching on the
subject of alcoholism, not only to prepare them for treating future patients
but also as a preventative measure for themselves (Murray, 1976; Vaillant et
al., 1972).

In private outpatient settings, a survey of family practitioners demonstrated that alcoholism was among the three most common psychiatric problems encountered in medical practice and was also rated as the most difficult
to diagnose and treat because of inadequate knowledge about the subject
(Werkman et al., 1976). At least 10% of all adults entering a physician's
office have an alcohol problem, but few are diagnosed (Kamerow et al.,
1986). In a recent study conducted by the American Medical Association
(AMA), 71% of physicians surveyed described themselves as not competent
to treat alcoholism (AMERSA, 1986). It has been shown that the alcoholic's
family may delay seeking help for more than seven years after the first
obvious occurrence of problem drinking; even then, the diagnosis is frequently missed by the physician or the social worker (Gorman & Rooney,
1979). Delay of diagnosis and treatment of this illness can only lead to severe
medical consequences. I strongly believe that physicians, psychologists, and

social workers in clinical practice should be capable of diagnosing and treating the great majority of alcoholics without having to refer them to specialized treatment programs. With these individuals in mind, I have nine specific objectives for the reader:

1. To learn to empathize with the alcoholic and offer an optimistic expectation of treatment success when trying to help this patient.
2. To be able to identify the major psychodynamic mechanisms, psychologic symptoms, cultural attitudes, and genetic predispositions that may subsequently lead to alcohol abuse or alcoholism.
3. To know how to diagnose the early phases of alcoholism; to be able to decide which patients can be treated as outpatients and which patients require referral to a psychiatrist or to specialized rehabilitation programs.
4. To define the essential elements of the doctor-patient or therapist-patient relationship and to learn the techniques of early intervention and treatment.
5. To become knowledgeable about a variety of treatment techniques, including detoxification for the acute phase of alcoholism, counseling and psychopharmacology (including Antabuse) for the chronic phase; to be able to use specific techniques to improve the quality of the alcoholic's life while helping the patient remain abstinent.
6. To feel comfortable working with staff of other disciplines and lay personnel (e.g., Alcoholics Anonymous, Al-Anon, and Al-Ateen).
7. To learn how to aid in the intervention and treatment of one's professional peers who are disabled by alcoholism.
8. To be able to diagnose and treat alcoholism-induced organic mental disorders; to learn techniques that will enable the brain-damaged patient to function more adequately at home, thus avoiding the need for chronic institutionalization.
9. To understand the various methods of prevention of alcoholism within a community; to become a resource person for the genetic sociologic, economic, and legal problems that may increase the incidence of alcohol abuse and alcoholism in the community; and to be able to deal effectively with alcohol problems in minority groups.

Recently there has been an explosion in new research data in the field of alcohol abuse and alcoholism, such as new psychotherapeutic intervention techniques and psychosocial treatment modalities, controlled psychopharmacologic research, and advances in basic biochemistry and genetics. It is essential that this important new information be disseminated to medical students, as well as to practicing physicians, psychologists, and social workers who did not have the opportunity to be exposed to this material while in graduate school. This book is intended to present this new information to the reader and to provide help in understanding the problem of alcoholism and the practical aspects of its treatment.

REFERENCES

AMERSA news release (1986). Brown University. Providence, R. I.

Barcha, R., Stewart, M. A., & Guze, S. B. (1968). The prevalence of alcoholism among general ward patients. *American Journal of Psychiatry, 125,* 681–685.

Berglund, M. (1984). Suicide in alcoholism. *Archives of General Psychiatry, 41,* 888–891.

Gorman, J. M., & Rooney, J. F. (1979). Delay in seeking help and onset of crises among Al-Anon wives. *Journal of Drug and Alcohol Abuse, 6,* 223–233.

Kamerow, D. B., Pincus, H. A., & Macdonald, D. I. (1986). Alcohol abuse, other drug abuse, and mental disorders in medical practice. *Journal of the American Medical Association, 225,* 2054–2057.

Murray, R. N. (1976). Alcoholism amongst male doctors in Scotland. *Lancet, 2,* 729–731.

Niven, R. (1984). Personal communication. 1974–1984 National Institute of Drug Abuse Report: Monitoring the Future Study. Binge drinking among high school seniors.

Petersson, B., Kristenson, H., Krantz, P., Trell, E. & Sternby, W. H. (1982). Alcohol-related death: A major contributor to mortality in urban middle-aged men. *Lancet, 2,* 1088–1090.

Pokorny, A. D., & Solomon, J. (1983). A follow-up survey of drug abuse and alcoholism teaching in medical schools. *Journal of Medical Education, 58,* 316–321.

Reichler, B. D., Clement, J. L., & Dunner, D. L. (1983). Chart review of alcohol problems in adolescent psychiatric patients in an emergency room. *Journal of Clinical Psychiatry, 44,* 338–340.

Robins, L. N., Heltzer, J. E., Weissman, M. M., Orvaschel, H., Gruenburg, E., Burke, J. D., & Reiger, D. A. (1984). Lifetime prevalence of specific psychiatric disorders in three sites. *Archives of General Psychiatry, 41,* 949–958.

Vaillant, G. E., Sabowale, N. C., & McArthur, C. (1972). Some psychologic vulnerabilities of physicians. *New England Journal of Medicine, 287,* 372–375.

Werkman, S. L., Mallory, L., & Harris, J. (1976). The common psychiatric problems in family practice. *Psychosomatics, 17,* 119–122.

Zimberg, S. (1979) Alcoholism: Prevalence in general hospital emergency room and walk-in clinic. *New York State Journal of Medicine, 79,* 1533–1536.

Alcoholism

*A GUIDE TO DIAGNOSIS,
INTERVENTION, AND
TREATMENT*

CHAPTER 1

Definition and Diagnosis

THE PROBLEM OF DEFINITION

DEFINITION IS CONCERNED with the meaning of a word or term, while medical diagnosis should identify a disease from the patient's signs and symptoms. Ideally, the diagnosis should indicate the etiology or specific pathologic changes, the prognosis, and the therapeutic implications. With many medical illnesses, such as pneumococcal pneumonia or hyperparathyroidism, the diagnosis is clear-cut, the etiology or pathologic abnormality, prognosis, and treatment are known, and no preexisting public or medical concepts interfere with the scientific identification of the illness. Such is not the case with alcoholism, a heterogeneous condition with signs and symptoms of unknown etiologies, consisting of different subgroups showing significantly different treatment responses to a variety of therapeutic modalities (Gallant, 1982; Gallant et al., 1973), with the results frequently based on self-reports of an unreliable patient population (Duffy & Waterton, 1984; Orrego et al., 1979).

These problems are compounded by long-standing public prejudices and moral attitudes about excessive alcohol use and "public drunkenness," as well as by discontent with the American Psychiatric Association nomenclature for Alcohol Abuse and Alcohol Dependence in its *Diagnostic and Statistical Manual, Third Edition* (*DSM-III*, 1980; Donovan, 1986; Schuckit et al., 1985). This third edition has been revised and is now available (DSM-III-R, 1987). It is likely that this revision will be only temporary, since the rapid explosion of new knowledge in the field of alcoholism should result in additional changes within the near future. Therefore, before listing the present APA criteria and the National Council on Alcoholism (NCA) criteria for the diagnosis of alcoholism, let me offer a definition of this disorder

1

which may be helpful to the therapist or family when reviewing the patient's presenting alcohol-related problems.

The following clinical definition, which is not intended for diagnostic or research purposes, is based on guidelines which stress a *pattern of impairment of functioning*. A drinking problem which may require treatment exists if the use of alcohol continues despite significant interference in any *one* of the five following major areas of a person's life:

1. employment or a student's work, for example, hangovers;
2. marital, family, or living-in companion relationship, with these individuals complaining about this problem on a number of occasions;
3. interpersonal relationships, resulting in a situation in which most social relationships are with heavy drinkers, thus indicating that the alcohol is controlling the person's choice of friends;
4. legal problems, such as charges of driving while intoxicated (DWI) or arrests for child abuse or spouse battering; and
5. medical complications, such as liver damage, alcohol-related essential hypertension, and pancreatitis. Medical complications are problems that occur late in the development of alcoholism, problems that should have been treated many years earlier.

Using this definition of alcoholism may enable the family to gain more confidence about the need for treatment of the alcohol problem and may make it easier for the alcoholic to accept the fact that a drinking problem does exist. Because it is extremely difficult to penetrate the alcoholic's denial, a diagnosis with complicated criteria can sometimes allow the patient to further minimize the problem. Such general terms as "pathological use," "loss of control," and "physiological dependency" may enable the alcoholic patient, preoccupied with rationalizations for continuing the intake of alcohol, to avoid confronting the problem.

Other attempts have been made to simplify the diagnosis and provide a rapid screening method for alcoholism. In one study (Woodruff et al., 1976), three questions, derived from the Michigan Alcoholism Screening Test (MAST), were used for the diagnosis of alcoholism in a research clinic population of 1,350 consisting of 500 psychiatric patients and 850 relatives. Of these 1,350 subjects, 151 were definite or probable alcoholics. Ninety-six percent of these definite or probable alcoholics were identified as alcoholic if the answer was "yes" to *only one* of the three key questions. Only 10% of those diagnosed as alcoholics were misidentified. The three questions are simple and easy to remember:

1. Has your family ever objected to your drinking?
2. Did you ever think you drank too much in general?
3. Have others (such as friends, physicians, clergy) ever said you drink too much for your own good?

In this research clinic report, the questions provide a highly reliable index of the presence of alcoholism. If this type of study can be replicated in a general population survey, this knowledge should enable health professionals to be more accurate in screening for alcoholism among all of their patients, an effort which could result in early diagnosis, with better chances for successful treatment.

MEDICAL DIAGNOSTIC CRITERIA

DSM-III-R Criteria

The arbitrary separation of Alcohol Abuse and Alcohol Dependence as defined in *DSM-III* has been questioned by many professionals in the field of substance abuse. Results of an evaluation of the clinical significance of this distinction between abuse and dependence showed no clinically significant prognostic differences between these two groups (Schuckit el al., 1985). In this study, 406 primary alcoholic patients admitted to a Veterans Administration Medical Center were separated into Alcohol Abuse and Alcohol Dependence subgroups and reevaluated at a 12-month follow-up period. The groups were almost identical as to family history of alcoholism (50% versus 48%) and drug abuse, family histories of psychiatric problems, rate of early life antisocial problems, past and present drug- and alcohol-related social problems, employment rate, and death rate. The two groups did show significant differences in drinking patterns and alcohol-related medical problems; the alcohol-dependent group reported a greater number of drinks per day during the preceding six months and were more likely to have been hospitalized for alcohol problems. These data would be expected since the definition of alcohol dependence reflects the presence of withdrawal symptoms and/or tolerance, symptoms which relate to the quantity of ingested alcohol. Nevertheless, it is worth emphasizing that the results showed no significant prognostic differences between patients with the labels of Alcohol Abuse and Alcohol Dependence in this study population of male VA inpatients. In another field trial of *DSM-III-R* psychoactive substance dependence disorders, the "overwhelming majority" of substance abusers were found to meet the *DSM-III-R* criteria for dependency (Rounsaville et al., 1987). Since these two diagnoses do not represent any meaningful differ-

TABLE 1.1
DSM III-R Criteria for Alcoholism (1987)

PSYCHOACTIVE SUBSTANCE ABUSE DISORDERS
A. A maladaptive pattern of substance use is indicated by at least one of the following:
  (1) continued use despite a persistent social, occupational, psychological, or phys-
      ical problem that is caused or exacerbated by use of the substance
  (2) recurrent use in situations when use is hazardous (e.g., driving while intoxicat-
      ed).
B. Some symptoms of disturbance have persisted for at least one month or have
   occurred repeatedly over a longer period of time.
C. Patient has never met the criteria for psychoactive substance dependence for this
   substance.

Note: This category was included to allow the diagnosis for those with comparatively
      mild disorders or who had only recently started to use a given type of psy-
      choactive substance. It is conceived of as a residual category to be used only for
      those who have dysfunctional or hazardous substance use without other symp-
      toms of dependence.

Reprinted with permission from the *Diagnostic and Statistical Manual of Mental Disorders,* Third Edition,
Revised. Copyright, 1987 American Psychiatric Association.

ences in etiology, prognosis, or treatment, differential diagnosis of these two
categories may be of no practical clinical significance.

The new *DSM-III-R* criteria for the diagnoses of Alcohol Abuse and
Alcohol Dependence are found in Table 1.1.

National Council on Alcoholism (NCA) Criteria

The Criteria Committee of the NCA published its recommendations for
the diagnosis of alcoholism in 1972. The goals of the committee were to
establish criteria which would promote early diagnosis, provide a uniform
nomenclature, and prevent overdiagnosis. The criteria were to be used to
identify individuals at multiple levels of dependency. The definition of alcoholism as a "pathological dependency" was unanimously adopted by the
committee and derived from *DSM-II* (APA, 1968). The committee assem-
bled the data into two tracks. Track I consisted of physiological and clinical
signs and symptoms; Track II included behavioral, psychological and attitudinal items. The manifestations of the symptoms were divided into early,
middle, and late phases, and each item was graded according to its "degree
of implication for the presence of alcoholism," with a weighting from 1
(most significant and a classical symptom of alcoholism) to 3 (may arouse
suspicion and is only a possible symptom). The NCA major and minor
criteria are listed in Table 1.2.

TABLE 1.2
NCA Criteria for the Diagnosis of Alcoholism (1972)

CRITERION	DIAGNOSTIC LEVEL

Major Criteria

TRACK I. PHYSIOLOGICAL AND CLINICAL

A. Physiological Dependency
  1. Physiological dependence as manifested by evidence of a withdrawal syndrome (1), when the intake of alcohol is interrupted or decreased without substitution of other sedation*. It must be remembered that overuse of other sedative drugs can produce a similar withdrawal state, which should be differentiated from withdrawal from alcohol.

a) Gross tremor (differentiated from other causes of tremor)	1
b) Hallucinosis (differentiated from schizophrenic hallucinations or other psychoses)	1
c) Withdrawal seizures (differentiated from epilepsy and other seizure disorders)	1
d) Delirium tremens. Usually starts between the first and third day after withdrawal and minimally includes tremors, disorientation, and hallucinations (1)	1

  2. Evidence of tolerance to the effects of alcohol. (There may be a decrease in previously high levels of tolerance late in the course.) Although the degree of tolerance to alcohol in no way matches the degree of tolerance to other drugs, the behavioral effects of a given amount of alcohol vary greatly between alcoholic and non-alcoholic subjects.

a) A blood alcohol level of more than 150 mg without gross evidence of intoxication	1
b) The consumption of one-fifth of a gallon of whiskey or an equivalent amount of wine or beer daily, for more than 1 day, by a 180-lb. individual	1

  3. Alcoholic "blackout" periods. (Differential diagnosis from purely psychological fugue states and psychomotor seizures) — 2

B. Clinical: Major Alcohol-Associated Illnesses
  Alcoholism can be assumed to exist if major alcohol-associated illnesses develop in a person who drinks regularly. In such individuals evidence of physiological and psychological dependence should be searched for.

Fatty degeneration in absence of other known cause	2
Alcoholic hepatitis	1
Laennec's cirrhosis	2
Pancreatitis in the absence of cholelithiasis	2
Chronic gastritis	3
Hematological disorders:	
Anemia—hypochromic, normocytic, macrocytic, hemolytic with stomatocytosis, low folic acid	3
Clotting disorders—prothrombin elevation or thrombocytopenia	3
Wernicke-Korsakoff syndrome	2
Alcoholic cerebellar degeneration	1

*Some authorities term this "pharmacological addiction."

(continued)

TABLE 1.2
Continued

CRITERION	DIAGNOSTIC LEVEL
Cerebral degeneration in absence of Alzheimer's disease or arteriosclerosis	2
Central pontine myelinolysis Marchiafava-Bignami's disease diagnosis only possible at postmortem	2
Peripheral neuropathy (see also beriberi)	2
Toxic amblyopia	3
Alcohol myopathy	2
Alcoholic cardiomyopathy	2
Beriberi	3
Pellagra	3

TRACK II. BEHAVIORAL, PSYCHOLOGICAL, AND ATTITUDINAL

All chronic conditions of psychological dependence occur in dynamic equilibrium with intrapsychic and interpersonal consequences. In alcoholism, similarly, there are varied effects on character and family. Like other chronic relapsing diseases, alcoholism produces vocational, social and physical impairments. Therefore, the implications of these disruptions must be evaluated and related to the individual and his pattern of alcoholism. The following behavior patterns show psychological dependence on alcohol in alcoholism.

1. Drinking despite strong medical contraindication known to patient	1
2. Drinking despite strong, identified social contraindication (job loss for intoxication, marriage disruption because of drinking, arrest for intoxication, driving while intoxicated)	1
3. Patient's subjective complaint of loss of control of alcohol consumption	2

Minor Criteria

TRACK I. PHYSIOLOGICAL AND CLINICAL

A. Direct Effects (ascertained by examination)

1. Early	
Odor of alcohol on breath at time of medical appointment	2
2. Middle	
Alcoholic facies	2
Vascular engorgement of face	2
Toxic amblyopia	3
Increased incidence of infections	3
Cardiac arrhythmias	3
Peripheral neuropathy (see also Major Criteria, Track I, B)	3
3. Late (see Major Criteria, B)	

B. Indirect Effects

1. Early	
Tachycardia	3
Flushed face	3

(continued)

TABLE 1.2
Continued

CRITERION	DIAGNOSTIC LEVEL
Nocturnal diaphoresis	3
2. Middle	
Ecchymoses on lower extremities, arms, or chest	3
Cigarette or other burns on hands or chest	3
Hyperreflexia or, if drinking heavily, hyporeflexia (permanent hyporeflexia may be a residuum of alcoholic polyneuritis)	3
3. Late	
Decreased tolerance	3
C. Laboratory Tests	
1. Direct	
Blood alcohol level at any time of more than 300 mg/100 ml or level of more than 100 mg/100 in routine examination	1
2. Indirect	
Serum osmolality (reflects blood alcohol levels): every 22.4 increase over 200 mOsm/litre reflects 50 mg/100 ml alcohol	2
Results of alcohol ingestion:	
Hypoglycemia	3
Hypochloremic alkalosis	3
Low magnesium level	2
Lactic acid elevation	3
Transient uric acid elevation	3
Potassium depletion	3
Indications of liver abnormality:	
SGPT elevation	2
SGOT elevation	3
BSP elevation	2
Bilirubin elevation	2
Urinary urobilinogen elevation	2
Serum A/G ration reversal	2
Blood and blood clotting:	
Anemia—hypochromic, normocytic, macrocytic, hemolytic with stomatocytosis, low folic acid	3
Clotting disorders—prothrombin elevation, thrombocytopenia	3
EEG abnormalities:	
Cardiac arrhythmias; tachycardia; T waves dimpled, cloven, or spinous; atrial fibrillation, ventricular premature contractions; abnormal P waves	2
EEG abnormalities:	
Decreased or increased REM sleep, depending on phase	3
Loss of delta sleep	3
Other reported findings	3
Decreased immune response	3
Decreased response to Synacthen test	3
Chromosomal damage from alcoholism	3

(continued)

TABLE 1.2
Continued

CRITERION	DIAGNOSTIC LEVEL

TRACK II. BEHAVIORAL, PSYCHOLOGICAL AND ATTITUDINAL

A. Behavioral
  1. Direct effects
    Early

Gulping drinks	3
Surreptitious drinking	2
Morning drinking (assess nature of peer group behavior)	2

    Middle

Repeated conscious attempts at abstinence	2

    Late

Blatant indiscriminate use of alcohol	1
Skid row or equivalent social level	2

  2. Indirect effects
    Early

Medical excuses from work for variety of reasons	2
Shifting from one alcoholic beverage to another	2
Preference for drinking companions, bars, and taverns	2
Loss of interest in activities not directly associated with drinking	2

    Late

Chooses employment that facilitates drinking	3
Frequent automobile accidents	3
History of family members undergoing psychiatric treatment; school and behavioral problems of children	3
Frequent change of residence for poorly defined reasons	3
Anxiety-relieving mechanisms, such as telephone calls inappropriate in time, distance, person, or motive (telephonitis)	2
Outbursts of rage and suicide gestures while drinking	2

B. Psychological and Attitudinal
  1. Direct effects
    Early

When talking freely, makes frequent reference to drinking alcohol, people being "bombed," "stoned," or admits drinking more than peer group	2

    Middle

Drinking to relieve anger, insomnia, fatigue, depression, social comfort	2

    Late

Psychological symptoms consistent with permanent organic brain syndrome (see also Major Criteria, Track I, B)	2

  2. Indirect effects
    Early

Unexplained changes in family, social, and business relationships; complaints about wife, job, and friends	3
Spouse makes complaints about drinking behavior, reported by patient or spouse	2

(continued)

TABLE 1.2
Continued

CRITERION	DIAGNOSTIC LEVEL
Major family disruptions, separation, divorce, threats of divorce	3
Job loss (owing to increasing interpersonal difficulties), frequent job changes, financial difficulties	3
Late	
Overt expression of more regressive defense mechanisms: denial, projection, and so on	3
Resentment, jealousy, paranoid attitudes	3
Symptoms of depression; isolation, crying, suicidal preoccupation	3
Feelings of "losing one's mind"	2

According to this committee, the diagnosis of alcoholism can be established if one or more of the major criteria are satisfied or if several of the minor criteria in Tracks I and II are present. The committee emphasized that the history, physical examination, and laboratory data "must fit into a consistent whole to ensure a proper diagnosis."

The complexity of this diagnostic classification apparently has hindered its widespread acceptance and use in the majority of alcoholism treatment programs. In addition, the NCA criteria were deficient in genetic, developmental, psychosocial and psychodynamic predisposition, and environmental factors. Therefore, guidelines for treatment modality or prognosis were not established, although the committee did state that indications for different treatment modalities were "beyond the scope of its mandate" and that "at present the prognosis for alcoholism is obscure."

Jellinek's concepts

In 1960, E. M. Jellinek's significant book on alcoholism was published. At that time, alcoholism was still not accepted by the majority of professionals or laymen as a medical problem. The public still perceived this disorder as a moral illness. This book was a major impetus in changing professional and public attitudes towards the alcoholic patient. Although Jellinek's criteria and alcoholism subtypes are no longer widely used, the historical importance of his contributions should be noted. E. M. Jellinek used the following operational definition of alcoholism: "any use of alcohol beverages that causes any damage to the individual or society or both"

(Jellinek, 1960). Realizing how broad an area of behavior this definition encompassed and the vagueness of this concept, Jellinek proceeded to define the following subgroups of alcoholism:

1. Alpha alcoholism: The alcoholic has "undisciplined" psychological, continual dependence upon the effect of alcohol to relieve emotional pain, without the "loss of control or inability to abstain." This type of alcoholism can result in interference with interpersonal relations and employment but is not associated with physiologic dependence leading to withdrawal symptoms. Nor are there any signs of a progressive process. Alpha alcoholism may develop into gamma alcoholism.
2. Beta alcoholism: In this type of alcoholism, such medical complications of alcohol as polyneuropathy, gastritis, and cirrhosis of the liver may occur without the development of physical dependence or withdrawal symptoms. Beta alcoholism may also develop into gamma or delta alcoholism.
3. Gamma alcoholism: The patient displays increased tissue tolerance to alcohol with "loss of control" and subsequent development of withdrawal symptoms, "craving," and physical dependence. This type of alcoholism results in the most serious kinds of damage to interpersonal relationships, health, and socioeconomic status.
4. Delta alcoholism: In this type of alcoholism the patient is unable to abstain from alcohol for even a day or two without the development of withdrawal symptoms. According to Jellinek, this patient, despite the severity of the alcoholism, is still able to control the amount of intake on any given occasion.
5. Epsilon alcoholism: This term is used for periodic alcoholism or binge drinking, which can lead to serious physical and interpersonal damage.

Although Jellinek did suggest that different constitutional vulnerabilities exist for each of these groups, he did not attempt to relate these proposed clinical types to specific etiology, nor did he evaluate the possible differences in psychologic and interpersonal backgrounds that might indicate different treatment modalities. However, the definitions of these five types of alcoholism did suggest differences in prognosis. One of the shortcomings of this diagnostic classification is that it is almost a pure description of drinking behavior without adequate attention devoted to the psychologic, interpersonal, sociocultural, and genetic backgrounds.

PERSONALITY TYPES: THE PROBLEM

In studies which attempt to identify personality subtypes or an underlying alcoholic personality, the relative lack of controls for such variables as age, socioeconomic status, education, pattern of drinking and genetic backgrounds has led to confusion among researchers as well as clinicians (Gallant, 1983). In a review of 29 studies that attempted to identify personality subtypes among alcohol abusers, Skinner (1982) reported that the investigators mainly used personality profiles or measurements of psychopathology such as the Minnesota Multiphasic Personality Inventory (MMPI), neglecting the patterns of alcohol use. Using psychopathology measurements, he reported four personality subtypes which were found equally among alcoholics, prison inmates, psychiatric patients, and college students. These data raised additional doubts about the supposedly unique psychopathologic syndrome presented by alcoholics.

At this time, the available research data demonstrate the existence of multiple syndromes of alcohol use. Future research on classification of alcoholism should focus on integrating the cluster syndrome typologic approach (personality traits) and the substance use pattern (e.g., alcohol dependence syndrome, continuous versus episodic pattern) in regard to diagnosis, prognosis and possible differential treatment approaches. In addition, any attempts to integrate typological and dimensional (such as severity of withdrawal symptoms) statistical approaches for the classification of alcoholism should incorporate the important genetic variable as one of the factors. The diagnostic differentiation between primary and secondary alcoholism will be addressed in the chapters on inpatient treatment and on the use of psychopharmacologic agents in the treatment of alcoholism (Schuckit, 1985).

Until a satisfactory definition of Alcoholism Dependence is finally formulated by research and clinicians, the following definition which stresses impairment of functioning should be of help to the therapist in establishing a therapeutic bridge to the patient and penetrating the denial mechanism. A drinking problem exists and requires treatment if the use of alcohol continues despite significant interference in any *one* of the five following major areas of a person's life: job or studies, relationships within the home, social relationships, legal problems, or medical complications.

REFERENCES

American Psychiatric Association (1968). *Diagnostic and statistical manual of mental disorders (2nd ed.)*. Washington, DC: Author.

American Psychiatric Association (1980). *Diagnostic and statistical manual of mental disorders (3rd ed.)*. Washington, DC: Author.

American Psychiatric Association (1987). *Diagnostic and statistical manual of mental disorders (3rd. ed.-R)*. Washington, DC: Author.

Donovan, J. M. (1986). An etiologic model of alcoholism. *American Journal of Psychiatry, 143*, 1–11.

Duffy, J. C., & Waterton, J. J. (1984). Under-reporting of alcohol consumption in sample surveys: The effect of computer interviewing in fieldwork. *British Journal of Addiction, 79*, 303–308.

Gallant, D. M. (1982). *Alcohol and drug abuse curriculum guide for psychiatry faculty* (p. 30). Rockville, MD: DHHS Publication No. (ADM) 82-1159.

Gallant, D. M. (1983). Classification of alcohol and drug addiction. The problem. *Alcoholism: Clinical and Experimental Research, 7*, 343–344.

Gallant, D. M., Bishop, M. P., Mouledoux, A., Faulkner, M. A., Brisolara, A., & Swanson, W. A. (1973). The revolving door alcoholic. *Archives of General Psychiatry, 28*, 633–635.

Jellinek, E. M. (1960). *The Disease Concept of Alcoholism*. New Haven, CT: Hillhouse.

National Council on Alcoholism (1972). Criteria for the diagnosis of alcoholism. *Annals of Internal Medicine, 77*, 249–258.

Orrego, H., Blendis, L. M., Blake, J. E., Kapur, B. M., & Israel, Y. (1979). Reliability of alcohol intake based on personal interviews in a liver clinic. *Lancet, 2*, 1354–1356.

Rounsaville, B. J., Kosten, T. R., Williams, J. B. W., & Spitzer, R. L. (1987). A field trial of *DSM-III-R* psychoactive substance dependence disorders. *American Journal of Psychiatry, 144*, 351–355.

Schuckit, M. A. (1985). The clinical implications of primary diagnostic groups among alcoholics. *Archives of General Psychiatry, 42*, 1043–1049.

Schuckit, M. A., Zisook, S., & Mortola, J. (1985). Clinical implications of *DSM-III* diagnoses of alcohol abuse and alcohol dependence. *American Journal of Psychiatry, 142*, 1403–1408.

Skinner, H. A. (1982). Statistical approaches to the classification of alcohol and drug addiction. *Alcoholism: Clinical and Experimental Research, 77*, 259–273.

Woodruff, R. A., Clayton, P. J., Cloninger, C. R., & Guze, S. B. (1976). A brief method of screening for alcoholism. *Diseases of the Nervous System, 37*, 434–435.

CHAPTER 2

Incidence of Alcoholism and Alcohol-Related Morbidity and Mortality

PROBLEMS IN SURVEYING THE INCIDENCE OF ALCOHOLISM

A VARIETY OF DATA has been used to estimate the incidence of alcoholism — deaths resulting from cirrhosis of the liver, frequency of alcohol intake, total alcohol consumption during a specified period of time, and population responses to diagnostic interviewer instruments. However, there are limitations to these measures. For instance, although the incidence of cirrhosis of the liver in the United States roughly parallels the consumption of alcohol, many chronic heavy drinkers do not develop liver disease. There are many causes of cirrhosis, with the etiologies varying in incidence in different countries (Jeffries, 1979). Using alcohol-related cirrhosis deaths to determine the incidence of alcoholism may result in an underestimation of the problem, since many alcoholics die from suicide, automobile accidents, or other causes before cirrhosis develops.

Interview surveys dealing with sensitive problems such as alcoholism may be associated with increased respondent errors since the subject may unrealistically feel that confidentiality is threatened. Sample surveys of alcohol consumption have been used to estimate the incidence of drinking problems; many of these surveys have relied on self-reporting estimates elicited from questions about the quantity of alcohol consumed within a certain period of time. Estimates of the total amount of alcohol consumed by the population being surveyed by this method are 30 to 60% lower than the known total alcohol consumption derived from government data in taxation and sales (Duffy & Waterton, 1984). Further, this known total consumption may be an

13

underestimation since it does not include alcohol beverages derived from illegal sources.

In an attempt to increase the reliability of the interviewer survey for alcohol consumption, Duffy and Waterton (1984) used an impersonal computer program. Two matched samples of 320 subjects were randomly contacted for computer interviews or direct personal interviews. The format for the computer interview consisted of the interviewer's beginning with some demographic questions and then asking if the subject had consumed any alcoholic beverages in the 7 days prior to the interview. If the answer was positive, the use of the computer was explained to the respondent, and the interviewer then withdrew to a place in the room where the display screen with the respondent's answers would not be visible to him. The interviewers conducting the direct survey were instructed to reproduce the wording of the questions exactly as they were asked by the machines and not to offer memory suggestions, so as to maintain "comparability" with the computer interview. The results showed that the overall amount of consumed alcohol reported to the computer was 33% higher than that obtained by direct questioning.

Other studies have shown that there is considerable underreporting of alcohol consumption by patients who have already been diagnosed as alcoholics. One such study was performed in alcoholics whose urines were assayed for alcohol while they were visiting a medical clinic; 52% of their reports on drinking were unreliable (Orrego et al., 1979). Since these patients did not realize that their urines were being evaluated for alcohol, many of them denied any alcohol intake during the preceding 24 hours. Such data should make the reader aware that routine self-reporting on alcohol (and other drug) consumption is suspect. The embarrassment and stigma still associated with alcoholism, as well as the denial mechanism, lead to the subject's minimizing the reported alcohol intake. These reports should be kept in mind as the reader reviews the data in the succeeding sections.

SURVEYS FOR ALCOHOLISM IN THE GENERAL POPULATION

In a U.S. government supported study of the lifetime prevalence of specific psychiatric disorders, alcohol abuse/dependence was found to be the most common illness (Robins et al., 1984). Seventeen thousand subjects over the age of 18 years, living in five different communities (Baltimore, New Haven, Durham, St. Louis, and Los Angeles), were interviewed, and the initial results from three of these sites were reported. This Epidemiologic Catchment Area (ECA) survey was a collaborative effort to apply common diagnostic instruments (Diagnostic Interview Scale, DIS) at six-month intervals to large general population samples, including both persons in house-holds and those still institutionalized.

The lifetime prevalence rates of 15 *DSM-III* diagnoses in the metropoli-tan areas of New Haven (3,058 responders), Baltimore (3,481), and St. Louis (3,004) were reported. The lifetime prevalence of a disorder is defined as the proportion of persons in a representative sample of the population who have ever experienced that disorder up to the date of assessment ("proportion of survivors affected"). In considering the survey results, it should be noted that the DIS does not distinguish among the various organic mental disor-ders, since a physical examination or laboratory test results may be required. Also, since alcoholism carries an increased risk of death as the subjects age, rates in the older population in this study may have been reduced by mortali-ty (Gallant, 1983b). Thus, the incidence of alcohol-related illnesses in this study, although impressively high, might still be underestimated.

In each of the three sites, 29 to 38% of the sample had experienced at least one of the 15 diagnostic disorders in their lifetimes. Rates differed by only 2.1% between St. Louis and New Haven; Baltimore's rate was signifi-cantly higher. In all three sites, alcohol abuse or dependence affected be-tween 11 and 16% of the population. Thus, alcoholism accounted for ap-proximately one-third of all the psychiatric disorders. A significantly higher incidence of alcohol abuse/dependence was found in the inner city (19.4% in St. Louis central city) than the rural area (14.0% in a small town adjacent to St. Louis). If the final report of this impressive epidemiologic investiga-tion confirms this surprisingly high incidence of alcohol abuse and depen-dence, then a nationally organized public health policy for this very prevent-able illness should be obligatory (Gallant, 1983a).

Other surveys of the incidence of alcoholism have reported lower figures than the ECA study. The incidence rates have varied from 4% of the popula-tion over 18 years of age (Westermeyer, 1976) to 10% of males and 5% of females in this same age range (Weissman et al., 1980; Schuckit, 1984).

ALCOHOL MISUSE IN THE ADOLESCENT POPULATION

Surveys in the General Adolescent Population

Although it is not unusual to see a "full-blown" adolescent alcoholic who meets all of the criteria for the diagnosis of alcohol dependence in the *DSM-III-R*, the fewer available years for drinking should result in a lower inci-dence of alcohol dependence in this age group. However, the increased presence of traits such as impulsivity, emotional intensity and lability, as well as the tremendous impact of adolescent peer pressure—all part of normal adolescent development—can lead to increased destructive behavior

TABLE 2.1
Trends in Prevalence of Alcohol Use in High School Seniors

Class of Approx N (in thousands)	1975 (9.4)	1976 (15.4)	1977 (17.1)	1978 (17.8)	1979 (15.5)	1980 (15.9)	1981 (17.5)	1982 (17.7)	1983 (16.3)	1984 (15.9)
Percentage who used in past 12 months	84.8	85.7	87.0	87.7	88.1	87.9	87.0	86.8	87.3	86.0
Percentage who used in last 30 days	68.2	68.3	71.2	72.1	71.8	72.0	70.7	69.7	69.4	57.2
Percentage who used daily	5.7	5.6	6.1	5.7	6.9	6.0	6.0	5.7	5.5	4.8
Drinking 5 or more drinks in a row (binges) at least once in past 2 weeks, (percentage error is ± 1.0)	37.0	37.2	37.8	40.0*	41.0*	41.0*	41.0*	40.2*	40.2*	40.0*

Abstracted from data in Personal Communication from Dr. Robert Niven, Director of the National Institute on Alcohol Abuse and Alcoholism (October, 1985).
*Significant increase from 1975–77

while under the influence of a disinhibiting drug such as alcohol. Thus, in addition to the adult criteria, data such as frequency of use, frequency of binge drinking, and alcohol-related automobile morbidity and deaths take on added importance when surveying adolescents. As seen in Table 2.1, although exposure to alcohol has remained about the same in the population of high school seniors from 1975 through 1984, the incidence of frequency of drinking has slightly decreased. However, the frequency of heavy *binge* drinking in 1984 still shows an increase compared to the years of 1975–78.

Other data-gathering instruments are needed to obtain a more adequate picture of alcohol abuse in adolescents. The Adolescent Alcohol Involvement Scale (AAIS), Table 2.2, has been used to define alcohol misuse and "alcoholism-like" illnesses in the adolescent population (Mayer & Filstead, 1979). In addition to obtaining data on frequency of use, this scale includes items on drinking behavior, source of alcohol beverages, effects of alcohol on interpersonal relationships, and adolescent attitudes about alcohol use and misuse.

Even though the AAIS may have practical applications, the authors designed this scale primarily as a research tool to aid in defining adolescents' alcohol misuse. Using the score of 42 as a cutoff point, these authors have undertaken studies to evaluate the hypothesis that all adolescents scoring above 42 are misusing alcohol.

This scale can also be used as an evaluation tool by social workers,

TABLE 2.2
Adolescent Alcohol Involvement Scale

1. How often do you drink?
   - a. never
   - b. once or twice a year
   - c. once or twice a month
   - d. every weekend
   - e. several times a week
   - f. every day

2. When did you have your last drink?
   - a. never drank
   - b. not for over a year
   - c. between 6 months and 1 year ago
   - d. several weeks ago
   - e. last week
   - f. yesterday
   - g. today

3. I usually start to drink because:
   - a. I like the taste
   - b. to be like my friends
   - c. to feel like an adult
   - d. I feel nervous, tense, full of worries or problems
   - e. I feel sad, lonely, sorry for myself

4. What do you drink?
   - a. wine
   - b. beer
   - c. mixed drinks
   - d. hard liquor
   - e. a substitute for alcohol—paint thinner, sterno, cough medicine, mouthwash, hair tonic, etc.

5. How do you get your drinks?
   - a. supervised by parents or relatives
   - b. from brothers or sisters
   - c. from home without parents' knowledge
   - d. from friends
   - e. buy it with false identification

6. When did you take your first drink?
   - a. never
   - b. recently
   - c. after age 15
   - d. at ages 14 or 15
   - e. between ages 10–13
   - f. before age 10

7. What time of day do you usually drink?
   - a. with meals
   - b. at night
   - c. afternoons
   - d. mostly in the morning or when I first awake
   - e. I often get up during my sleep and drink

8. Why did you take your first drink?
   - a. curiosity
   - b. parents or relatives offered
   - c. friends encouraged me
   - d. to feel more like an adult
   - e. to get drunk or high

9. How much do you drink, when you do drink?
   - a. 1 drink
   - b. 2 drinks
   - c. 3–6 drinks
   - d. 6 or more drinks
   - e. until "high" or drunk

(continued)

TABLE 2.2
Continued

---

10. Whom do you drink with?
    a. parents or relatives only   d. with older friends
    b. with brothers or sisters only e. alone
    c. with friends own age

11. What is the greatest effect you have had from alcohol?
    a. loose, easy feeling   d. became ill
    b. moderately "high"   e. passed out
    c. drunk   f. was drinking heavily and the next
                                 day didn't remember what happened

12. What is the greatest effect drinking has had on your life?
    a. none; no effect   e. have lost friends because of drinking
    b. has interfered with talking   f. has gotten me into trouble at home
       to someone   g. was in a fight or destroyed property
    c. has prevented me from   h. has resulted in an accident, an
       having a good time   injury, arrest, or being punished at
    d. has interfered with my   school for drinking
       school work

13. How do you feel about your drinking?
    a. no problem at all   d. I often feel bad about my drinking
    b. I can control it and set limits e. I need help to control myself
    c. I can control myself, but my   f. I have had professional help to
       friends easily influence me   control my drinking

14. How do others see you?
    a. can't say, or a normal   d. my family or friends tell me to get
       drinker for my age   help for my drinking
    b. when I drink I tend to   e. my family or friends have already
       neglect my family or friends   gone for help for my drinking
    c. my family or friends advise
       me to control or cut down
       on my drinking

Scoring Instructions: The highest total score is 79. An "a" response is scored 1 (except on questions 1, 2, 6, 12, 13 and 14, on which a = 0); b = 2; c = 3; and so on to h = 8. When more than one response is made, the one with the higher or highest score is used. An unanswered question is scored 0.

psychologists, nurses, pediatricians, or family physicians as one measure of degree of alcohol misuse in a community school. In association with this scale, extrapolating data from Kandel's 1975 study on the stages of adolescent drug use may help the community-oriented therapist to arrive at an educated estimate of the degree of drug misuse or illegal drug use in a local high school population.

As can be seen in Figure 2.1, legal drugs such as beer, wine, hard liquor,

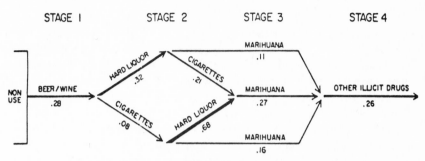

FIGURE 2.1
Major Changes of Adolescent Involvement in Drug Use
Probabilities of moving from one stage to another based on changes between Fall 1971 and Spring 1972 in a cohort of New York state high school students, 14 to 18 years old. Youths who started using more than one drug within the follow-up interval were distributed in a sequential order which reproduced the proportions of known exclusive starters of each drug. (From Kandel, 1975.)

and cigarettes are usually intermediates between abstinence and marijuana in adolescents (Kandel, 1975). Peer pressure plays a meaningful role in this transition. The therapist should never underestimate the importance of peer impact as one of the most important influences upon the adolescent's decision whether or not to use alcohol or other substances of abuse. Of course, other variables such as rebelliousness, resentment against authority figures, and impulsivity may be the underlying reasons for the adolescent choosing to join the substance-abusing group. One of the first steps in treatment is to encourage adolescent substance abusers to detach themselves from these deviant groups and find healthier social peer groups.

Alcohol Problems in Adolescent Psychiatric Patients

It is not unusual to find that recent alcohol ingestion in an adolescent is associated with the development of a severe psychological problem that may require emergency treatment. The importance of obtaining blood alcohol levels from adolescent psychiatric patients was emphasized by a study of 459 consecutive teenage patients seen for psychiatric evaluations in a general hospital emergency room during a one-year period (Reichler et al., 1983). If a patient had a suspected alcohol problem by history or presentation in the emergency room, blood alcohol levels were obtained. Of the 137 adolescent subjects who had blood drawn for alcohol levels, 76 (37 males; 39 females) had blood levels above 100 mg/dl and 61 showed values less than 100 mg/dl.

Evaluation of the 76 subjects whose alcohol blood levels were greater than 100 mg/dl revealed the following data: The mean age was 16 years;

mean blood levels for both males and females were greater than 215 mg/dl; and approximately half of these teenagers had *DSM-III* diagnoses, mainly depressive disorders and conduct disorders. The data indicated that the males with high blood alcohol levels were more likely to be white (92%), whereas the females with high levels were equally distributed according to race. Twenty-two of these 76 adolescent patients reported having an alcoholic parent, almost three times the anticipated rate.

In this study of consecutive teenage admissions, there were no sex-related differences in the incidence of alcohol abuse, mean blood levels, or referral for detoxification. Subsequent cultural and environmental effects and genetic differences may account for the development of a significantly greater incidence of alcoholism dependence in adult males, or perhaps these types of data are early evidence of the increasing problem of alcoholism in females.

These data show that alcohol abuse is a major problem among teenagers who require psychological treatment in an emergency room; the significant percentage of the subjects (16% of these patients) showing levels of alcohol greater than 300 mg/dl indicated the presence of tolerance.

The results of this study indicate the need for obtaining routine blood alcohol and urine drug levels from all adolescents using a general hospital emergency room. Further evaluation of alcohol use in these teenagers will contribute to understanding risk factors and more adequately defining adolescent alcoholism.

Adolescent Drinking and Traffic Mortality Rate

Well-documented reports reveal and confirm the consistent correlation between minimum legal drinking ages and traffic morbidity and mortality rates in young people with high blood alcohol concentrations at the time of the accident (Cohen, 1981; Wagenaar & Douglass, 1980). In 1972, Michigan reduced the minimum legal driving age from 21 to 18 years. A five-year follow-up report by the University of Michigan Highway Safety Institute showed an increase of 132% in 18-to-20-year-old drinking drivers involved in fatal accidents and a 217% increase in the same age group who were involved in nonfatal personal injury accidents. During this same five-year follow-up period, the number of 18-to-20-year-old licensed drivers increased by only 9% (Wagenaar & Douglass, 1980). Similar data are available from Massachusetts, where alcohol-related accidents in the 18-to-20-year-old group increased 176% after the minimum drinking age was lowered to 18 years, while fatal accidents in the total driving population during this same time period increased by 57% (Teendrinking . . . , 1980).

After the minimum drinking age was lowered from 21 to 18 years in 1971 in Ontario, Canada, the number of alcohol-related driving accidents in the 15-to-19-year-old group increased by 75% while there were no significant changes in the other age groups (Smart, 1971). These data show a "drifting down" effect, which indicates that decreasing the drinking age to 18 years probably provides increased drinking opportunities for those who are younger than 18. In association with these findings, the same author cited data which indicate that lowering the minimum drinking age to 18 years probably led to 29 additional deaths in Michigan, 28 in Ontario, and 13 in Wisconsin during the first year that the laws were in effect.

INCIDENCE OF ALCOHOL ABUSE IN THE AGING POPULATION

With the increasing size of the aged population, it is inevitable that the number of elderly alcohol abusers will also grow. Brody's (1982) objective evaluation of the data helps us to place this problem in its proper perspective. Using the arbitrary definition of the aged as 65 years and older, Brody estimates that there will be 32 million in this category by the year 2,000. At present, there are 150 females for every 100 males in this age group and 1.6 million males and 5.5 million females over the age of 65 living alone in the U.S. Only 20% of these men are working, and a devastatingly low 8% of women in this group are employed. Forty percent of this population have serious health problems which interfere with normal daily activities.

Reliable data about the incidence of drinking problems in the elderly residing in communities are not yet available; estimates have varied fivefold. However, most surveys do agree that there is a high incidence of alcoholism, varying from 10 to 15%, in the elderly who are hospitalized or institutionalized. This percentage may be too low, because denial of a drinking problem is likely to be more common in the elderly. Their lifetime exposure to very negative cultural attitudes about alcohol often results in embarrassment about drinking and a tendency to minimize the amount of alcohol consumed. By even the most conservative estimates, the U.S. will have more than three million alcoholics over the age of 65 by the year 2,000. More accurate surveys of the incidence of alcohol abuse in the aged are required if this country is to plan adequate prophylactic and treatment programs for the aged, who respond quite well to treatment (Rix, 1982).

ALCOHOL-RELATED MORBIDITY AND MORTALITY

Alcohol use is the most frequent cause of death in middle-aged males. The excessive number of alcohol-related accident deaths is well publicized by the media, and only a brief review of this data will be presented here before going on to alcohol-related medical deaths. According to the National Highway Traffic Safety Administration (NHTSA), approximately 55% of all fatal motor vehicle accidents in the U.S. are alcohol-related. During the 1979–1981 period, the NHTSA study noted 24,651 alcohol-related deaths, 56,000 alcohol-related serious injury accidents, and 389,000 mild to moderate automobile accident injuries per year (Drunk driving, 1985). In addition, approximately one-third of accidental private plane deaths and one-third to one-half of all drownings are associated with alcohol intake. Alcohol-related deaths and injuries at home are not included in this data.

In an extensive prospective study, Petersson et al. (1982) evaluated the association between excessive alcohol use and mortality rate in an unselected population of 7,725 men, ages 46 to 48 years. The follow-up period was a mean of three years (zero to six years). A subject was assigned to the alcohol-related death category if high alcohol consumption was the major underlying cause of death. The alcohol-related death subgroups were:

1. accidental deaths occurring as a result of an alcohol-intoxicated state;
2. deaths due to organic complications of alcoholism, e.g., cirrhosis, pancreatitis, cardiomyopathy, etc;
3. signs of intoxification at death, with a high level of alcohol in the blood or urine at necropsy and no other specific demonstrable causes of death;
4. pneumonia in a known alcoholic;
5. cause unknown in a known alcoholic;
6. suicide in a known alcoholic.

During the follow-up period, 199 men died. Sixty-one of the 199 deaths (30.7%) were classified as alcohol-related, a more frequent cause of death than cancer or cardiovascular disease. The death rate in subjects with a positive alcoholism history was 6.8 times the expected rate. The authors were conservative in their application of statistics to other alcohol-related deaths, excluding deaths from cancer (buccal cavity, upper gastrointestinal tract, etc., which are significantly higher in excessive drinkers) and stroke (hypertension is significantly higher among excessive drinkers, and alcohol has been shown to have a direct pressor effect on blood pressure) (Gallant, 1986; Puddey et al., 1985).

The suicide risk in known alcoholics is indeed frightening. In a valuable 30-year prospective study of 1,312 alcoholics, 88 (16%) of the 537 deaths were found to be definite suicides (Berglund, 1984). In this study senior psychiatrists at the department of psychiatry, University Hospital Lund, evaluated first-admission alcoholic patients, using a multidimensional diagnostic scale. These ratings were performed at discharge when the initial symptoms of alcohol intoxication or withdrawal were no longer present. The median follow-up was 18 years. "Uncertain suicides were included in the nonsuicidal group." Of the 537 deaths (2.6 times the expected rate), 88 were suicides (poisoning in 47 cases and hanging in 23); 98 other deaths were caused by violence, including 44 cases of "uncertain suicide." Thus, the number of suicides in this population may actually have been underestimated. Comparison of the suicidal and nonsuicidal deaths showed no significant differences in such variables as age at time of admission (42 versus 43 years), occupation, family history of alcoholism or suicide, presence of organic mental disorder, sleep disturbance, dependency traits, rigidity of personality, antisocial behavior, marital problems or economic circumstances. Male subjects, 91% of this population, had a suicide rate twice that of the female subjects. Surprisingly, contrary to previous reports, more suicidal patients were married at the time of first admission ($p < 0.05$). Severe primary major depression with psychomotor retardation was uncommon in both groups.

Four major positive findings occurred at a significantly higher rate in the suicide group: peptic ulcer ($p < 0.001$); lability of affect with explosiveness ($p < 0.01$); moderate depressive symptoms of dysphoria, depression, and irritability ($p < 0.05$); and personality features of hypersensitivity with "brittleness" ($p < 0.05$). Peptic ulcer showed no significant relationship with the other three factors and stood alone as an important suicide factor. The highest frequency of suicide was found during the years immediately following discharge. In the patients who met violent deaths other than suicides, the rate at which these four factors occurred was not significant. There were several data collection problems in this study: It was not possible to ascertain the exact time sequence of the appearance of alcohol abuse and peptic ulcer symptoms; the frequencies of primary and secondary depressions were not determined; and adequate descriptions of and possible differences in treatment modalities for these patients were not included.

The predictive value of risk for suicide was 9 to 13% (or approximately 300 times the anticipated rate for nonalcoholics) in patients presenting symptomatology of explosive behavior, depression, dysphoria, and "brittleness," and 18% (or 600 times the anticipated rate) if the alcoholic patient had a history of peptic ulcer. It is difficult to generalize about the supposed typical personality characteristics of peptic ulcer patients as having some bearing on the suicidal outcome, since no significant differences between the suicidal and nonsuicidal group were seen in such rating items as tenseness, anxiety, strain, personality rigidity, and responsibility conflicts.

This shockingly high suicide rate in the alcoholism population indicates that *every* alcoholism program should be required to conduct a thorough psychological, social, and medical history and examination of every alcoholic patient at the time of first admission to either an outpatient or inpatient treatment program. The history, physical, and psychological examination should specifically include the above suicidal prognostic items and be performed only after the alcoholic has been detoxified and is completely free of any withdrawal symptoms.

As one of the most common illnesses in the U.S. (Robins et al., 1984), alcoholism is one of the most frequent causes of emergency room admission for adolescents (Reichler et al., 1983) and is the most common cause of morbidity and mortality in middle-aged males (Petersson et al., 1982). It is becoming one of the major illnesses in the elderly population (Brody, 1982) and plays the major role in suicide (Berglund, 1984). It is hoped that policymakers in Washington will not only concentrate more financial support for research on and prevention of alcoholism, but also coordinate legislation (taxation as well as minimum age laws) with the available medical and socioeconomic knowledge to formulate an organized public health policy for this very preventable disease.

REFERENCES

Berglund, M. (1984). Suicide in alcoholism. *Archives of General Psychiatry, 41*, 888–891.
Brody, J. A. (1982). Aging and alcohol abuse. *Journal of the American Geriatric Society, 30*, 123–126.
Cohen, S. (1981). The one vehicle accident. *Drug and Alcoholism News, 10*, 1–3.
Drunk driving. (1985). *The Bottom Line, 26*, 23–24.
Duffy, J. C., & Waterton, J. J. (1984). Under-reporting of alcohol consumption in sample surveys: The effect of computer interviewing in fieldwork. *British Journal of Addiction, 79*, 303–308.
Gallant, D. M. (1983a). Taxation of alcohol as a public health measure. *Alcoholism: Clinical and Experimental Research, 7*, 342–343.
Gallant, D. M. (1983b). Alcohol abuse: The major cause of death in middle-aged males. *Alcoholism: Clinical and Experimental Research, 7*, 448–449.
Gallant, D. M. (1986). Hypertension and Alcohol Consumption, *Alcoholism: Clinical and Experimental Research, 10*, 358–359.
Jeffries, G. H. (1979). Diseases of the liver. In. P. B. Beeson, W. McDermott, J. B. Wyngaarden (Eds.). *Cecil textbook of medicine* (pp. 1637–1669). Philadelphia: W. B. Saunders.
Kandel, D. (1975). Stages in adolescent involvement in drug use. *Science, 190*, 912–914.
Mayer, J. & Filstead, W. J. (1979). The adolescent alcohol involvement scale. *Journal of Studies on Alcohol, 40*, 291–300.
Niven, R. (1985). Personal Communication. 1974–1984 National Institute of Drug Abuse Report: Monitoring the Future Study. Binge drinking among high school seniors.
Orrego, H., Blendin, L. M., Blake, J. E., Kapur, B. M., & Israel, Y. (1979). Reliability of alcohol intake based on personal interviews in a liver clinic. *Lancet, 2*, 1354–1356.
Petersson, B., Kristenson, H., Krant, P., Trell, E., & Sternby, W. H. (1982). Alcohol related deaths: A major contributor to mortality in urban middle-aged men. *Lancet, 2*, 1088–1090.
Puddey, I. B., Berlin, L. J., Vandongen, R., Rouse, I. L., & Rogers, P. (1985). Evidence for a direct effect of alcohol consumption on blood pressure in normotensive men. *Hypertension, 7*, 707–713.
Reichler, B. D., Clement, J. L., & Dunner, D. L. (1983). Chart review of alcohol problems in

adolescent psychiatric patients in an emergency room. *Journal of Clinical Psychiatry, 44*, 338–340.

Rix, K. J. B. (1982). Elderly alcoholics in the Edinburgh Psychiatric Services. *Journal of the Royal Society of Medicine, 75*, 177–180.

Robins, L. N., Helzer, J. E., Weissman, M. M., Orvaschel, H., Gruenberg, E., Burke, J. D., & Reiger, D. A. (1984). Lifetime prevalence of specific psychiatric disorders in three sites. *Archives of General Psychiatry, 41*, 949–958.

Schuckit, M. A. (1984). *Drug and alcohol abuse: Clinical guide to diagnosis and treatment.* New York: Plenum.

Smart, R. G. (1971). *The New Drinkers*. Ontario, Canada: Addiction Research Foundation.

Teen drinking patterns affected by law changes (1980). *The Bottom Line, 3*, 2–10.

Wagenaar, A. C., & Douglass, R. K. (1980). An evaluation of changes in the legal drinking age. *The Bottom Line, 4*, 16–17.

Weissman, M. M., Myers, J. K., & Harding, P. S. (1980). Prevalence and psychiatric heterogeneity of alcoholism in a US urban community. *Journal of Studies of Alcoholism, 41*, 672–681.

Westermeyer, J. (1976). *A primer on chemical dependency.* (pp. 82–83). Baltimore, MD.: Williams & Wilkins.

CHAPTER 3

Pharmacology of Alcohol and Alcoholism

THE BIOCHEMICAL ASPECTS of alcoholism may seem very technical and at times tedious to the reader with a background in a discipline other than biochemistry or medicine. Unfortunately, there are no substitutes for the tongue-twisting medical terms and chemical formulae that specifically explain the metabolic steps for the conversion of alcohol. Such technical information is necessary to provide the reader with a framework for understanding the physical basis of alcoholism, which will be discussed in subsequent chapters, particularly the genetic-biochemical aspects of alcoholism in Chapter 4 and the medical consequences of alcoholism in Chapter 7.

Ethanol (ethyl alcohol) is a hydrophilic molecule which easily combines with water. Due to its chemical simplicity and small size, the ethanol molecule can cross cell membranes with great facility and can distribute itself widely throughout the body. Peak blood ethanol levels are usually achieved about 70 to 100 minutes following ingestion, but the rate of absorption is retarded by food in the stomach, high concentrations of ethanol, or presence of other drugs such as antidepressants, all of which delay gastric emptying. The absorbed ethanol is carried to the liver from the gastrointestinal tract via the portal vein; 90 to 97% is mainly catabolized in the liver. Excess ethanol spills over into the hepatic vein and enters the systemic circulation where it is distributed rapidly to tissues that have a good blood supply but less so to fatty depots. Thus, obese persons or people with unusual excessive fat depots will display central nervous system effects more rapidly and with more intensity than lean muscular people of equal weight. The average person metabolizes 10–20 mg/100 ml per hour or one typical drink (can of beer or 1 1/2 oz. of liquor) within 1–2 hours after consumption.

METABOLIC PATHWAYS

The principal pathway for normal ethanol metabolism appears to be oxidation in the liver by an enzyme, alcohol dehydrogenase (ADH), to form acetaldehyde, a process which is limited by the amount of ADH. The acetaldehyde is then catabolized to acetate by another enzyme, aldehyde dehydrogenase (Ald DH), which is primarily located in the mitochondrial and cytosol fractions of the hepatocytes. Antabuse (disulfiram) a medication that is associated with a severe physical reaction of nausea, flushing, and shortness of breath if alcohol is ingested, inhibits Ald DH, which causes a rapid rise in acetaldehyde. Other drugs that block Ald DH are listed in Table 3.1.

There are 2 secondary metabolic pathways for oxidation of ethanol: the microsomal ethanol oxidizing system (MEOS) and the catalase system (Figure 3.1). Chronic ingestion of ethanol (ethyl alcohol) results in the enhanced activity of the hepatic microsomal ethanol oxidizing system (MEOS), with an associated increase in the smooth endoplasmic reticulum (SER) in the liver. This enhanced MEOS appears to become a major pathway for the clearance of higher ethanol concentrations. Thus, when a patient starts to drink excessive amounts of ethanol, metabolic tolerance develops as ethanol is more rapidly metabolized. As metabolic tolerance develops, some heavy drinkers can considerably increase the amount of ethanol that they ingest without appearing obviously intoxicated to the people around them. The increase in the activity of the MEOS can accelerate ethanol elimination from the blood by as much as 50 to 70%. This same MEOS is responsible for the increased tolerance that develops with the chronic administration of other hypnotic-sedative drugs.

TABLE 3.1
Drugs Which Block Aldehyde Dehydrogenase

disulfiram (Antabuse)
metronidazole (Flagyl)
phentolamine (Regitine)
tolbutamide (Orinase)
furazolidine (Furoxone)
nitroglycerine
citrated calcium carbimide (Temposil)
chloramphenicol (Chloromycetin)
griseofulvin (Fulvicin)
chlorpropamide (Diabinese)
quinacrine (Atabrine)
isosorbid dinitrate (Isordil)

From Liepman et al., 1982

FIGURE 3.1
Hepatic Ethanol Metabolism

$$\text{1.} \quad \underset{\text{ethanol}}{CH_3CH_2OH} + NAD^+ \xrightarrow[]{\overset{\text{hepatic}}{\underset{}{*ADH}}} \underset{\text{acetaldehyde}}{CH_3CHO} + NADH + H^+$$

$$CH_3CHO + NAD^+ + H_2O \xrightarrow{\text{Ald DH}} \underset{\text{acetate}}{CH_3COOH} + NADH + H^+$$

$$\text{2.} \quad CH_3CH_2OH + NADPH + H^+ + O_2 \xrightarrow{**MEOS} CH_3CHO + 2H_2O + NADP^+$$

$$\text{3.} \quad CH_3CH_2OH + H_2O_2 \xrightarrow{\text{catalase}} CH_3CHO + 2H_2O$$

*ADH plays a major role in normal ethanol oxidation

* *MEOS may play the major role at higher ethanol
    concentrations

NAD = nicotinamide adenine dinucleotide

NADP = NAD phosphate; NADPH = reduced NADP

Chronic ingestion of ethanol can produce the following metabolic problems: enhancement of the mitochondrial enzyme delta aminolevulinic acid synthetase (ALAS) and P-450 activity, which can increase urinary porphyrins and exacerbate symptoms in porphyria patients; stimulation of the hepatic cholesterol synthesis, which can contribute to cholesterol accumulation in the liver; displacement of the fatty acids as a source of hydrogen for oxidation, thus increasing fat deposition in the liver (the fatty liver that is so common in alcoholics); and stimulation of the hepatic lipoprotein production, which is associated with hyperlipemia (Lieber et al., 1971). Of course, continued excessive chronic alcohol intake can damage the mitochondria with a resultant decrease in rate of ethanol metabolism and tolerance. This decrease in the functioning of enzyme systems resulting from liver damage can lead to a decreased tolerance of ethanol in the elderly chronic alcoholic.

The acetaldehyde formed from ethanol is further oxidized by aldehyde dehydrogenase (Ald DH) to form acetate and acetyl-coenzyme A. These metabolic processes are depicted in Figure 3.1 and will be referred to in subsequent discussions of theories of alcohol addiction, the genetic vulnerability of offspring of alcoholics, and the medical complications of alcoholism.

ADH exists in at least two different forms with somewhat different properties. "Atypical ADH," which is common in Oriental populations, has an active catalytic rate three to four times greater than the typical ADH found in most Caucasians (Li, 1983). Thus, acetaldehyde, a toxic metabolite of ethanol, accumulates more rapidly in Orientals. Ald DH also exists in more than one form (isozymes) and deficiency in one of these isozymes, low km Ald DH, in Orientals appears to be associated with flushing and reduced tolerance to ethanol effects.

The possibility exists that severely alcoholic patients may metabolize ethanol by a different pathway than nonalcoholic control subjects (Rutstein et al., 1983). Impressed by experimental evidence that ethanol can be metabolized in rats to produce 2,3-butanediol, these investigators evaluated the concentrations of 2,3-butanediol and 1,2 propanediol in volunteer male alcoholics and a control group of social drinkers before and after they had consumed "self-selected alcohol beverages." Only those subjects who reported consumption of distilled spirits, which contain neither butanediol nor propanediol, were evaluated in the final data collection. The results showed that serum 2,3-butanediol in concentrations $\geq$ 5 umol/l was present in 15 of the 19 alcoholics and in only 1 of 22 controls, and there was no significant linear correlation between serum ethanol and the 2,3-butanediol levels. In this study, the patients and the comparison groups could not be controlled as to quantity and type of alcohol consumed, and the investigators depended on the reports of the subjects as to which alcohol beverages were ingested. If the subjects' self-reporting was unreliable, then the results could be confusing, since beer and wine do contain propanediol and butanediol. Nonetheless, this study warrants serious attention; it is important for other researchers to replicate these results in carefully controlled studies and to undertake investigations to evaluate possible differences in 2,3-butanediol metabolism in alcoholic and nonalcoholic offspring of the families of alcoholics.

CONCEPTS OF ALCOHOL TOLERANCE, ADDICTION, AND OPIOID RECEPTOR SYSTEMS

The concept of tolerance is sometimes confusing because the word may have different meanings to clinicians and basic scientists. The tolerance that develops from enhanced MEOS activity in chronic ethanol intake results in more rapid metabolization of the ethanol. The tolerance that develops when a person requires higher blood alcohol levels to attain the same clinical effects (e.g., relaxation or euphoria) is more directly related to CNS neuronal cell adaptation and, if continued, may result in the hyperactive addictive phenomena that occur with sudden alcohol withdrawal.

Some interesting theories have been proposed regarding the addictive properties of the metabolic by-products of alcohol (Cohen & Collins, 1970; Davis & Walsh, 1970; Hsu, 1976). The majority of alcohol abusers and alcohol-dependent patients seen in clinical practice do not display the classical symptoms of withdrawal upon abrupt cessation of alcohol. However, a not inconsiderable minority of severe alcohol-dependent subjects shows a typical addictive type of drinking evidenced by an inability to stop after the first or second drink, followed by a severe withdrawal syndrome upon abrupt cessation. It is these severely alcohol-dependent patients to whom the concepts of metabolic addiction may apply. Davis and Walsh, in their "in vitro" studies of alcohol and dopamine (DA), reported the metabolic diversion of DA to tetrahydropapaveroline (THP) instead of conversion to norepinephrine (NE). Acetaldehyde, the primary metabolite of alcohol, competitively inhibits nicotinamide-adenine dinucleotide (NAD)-linked Ald DH and thus increases the formation of THP from DA. THP can be converted to normorphan, an addicting compound which can have an affinity for the opioid receptors. The researchers suggested that this process may be one of a series of metabolic events in cerebral tissue that could lead to physical dependence on ethanol. Similar results have been reported with tetrahydro-β-carbolines (THBC), which may be related to the benzodiazepine (BZ) receptors. These data have been replicated in a laboratory where alcohol drinking was induced by injection of these amine-aldehyde condensation products into the brains of rats (Myers, 1983). In association with these findings, Myers also reported that opiate antagonists such as naloxone and naltrexone have reduced ethanol intake in rats and monkeys.

These theories that link alcohol addiction to the opioid receptors emphasize that the metabolic ethanol product acetaldehyde is one of the chemicals necessary for the development of this biochemical occurrence. The importance of these theories has been indirectly enhanced by a study of a possible defect of acetaldehyde metabolism in man. In 1982, Thomas and his associates conducted two studies in an evaluation of hepatic acetaldehyde metabolism in male alcoholics who showed no evidence of cirrhosis. In the first evaluation of 15 alcoholic patients, biopsied within five days after admission to a rehabilitation unit, all of the subjects showed only fatty livers with no evidence of hepatitis or cirrhosis. Six subjects with normal livers were used as controls. In a second study of other alcoholics, biopsies were performed at admission and after a mean abstinence period of 15 weeks. By the time of the second biopsy, almost all of the liver tests had returned to normal and a decrease in stainable lipid (fatty liver) was observed in all patients.

The overall results of these two studies showed that the activity of cytosolic aldehyde dehydrogenase (Ald DH) in the 15 alcoholics was significantly lower than that in the six controls, whereas the activity of the mitochondrial Ald DH showed only a trend toward decrease in the alcoholic subjects. The follow-up biopsies in the second study showed that the cytosol Ald DH remained at a significantly low level while ADH returned to normal limits. This low Ald DH activity may explain the relatively high acetaldehyde levels reported in male offspring of alcoholics after they ingest alcohol. These high acetaldehyde levels "in vivo" may affect the metabolism of DA in humans as well as "in vitro," as shown by Davis and Walsh. Of course, the small number of patients and controls in the study indicates the need for additional studies to replicate the findings before we can agree with Thomas et al.'s statement that " . . . the demonstration of a persistent enzymatic abnormality in alcoholic subjects argues against the possibility that alcoholic patients may successfully return to social drinking."

BIOCHEMICAL RELATIONSHIPS BETWEEN ALCOHOL AND NON-OPIOID RECEPTOR SYSTEMS

In one well designed animal study, it was reported that two lines of mice, an ethanol reactive long-sleep (LS) group and an ethanol insensitive short-sleep (SS) group, with distinct sensitive reactions to ethanol depressant effects, differed significantly in their behavioral responses to both an adenosine receptor agonist and an adenosine receptor antagonist (Proctor & Dunwiddie, 1984). On all behavioral tests, the ethanol sensitive LS mice showed significantly greater sensitivity to an adenosine receptor agonist than did the SS mice. The results of this study showed that mice which are slectively bred for differential sensitivity to the soporific effects of ethanol differ markedly in their behavioral and physiological responses to drugs which act on the adenosine receptors. These results suggest that significant differences in endogenous levels of brain adenosine or in adenosine receptors may relate to sensitivity to alcohol. It is possible that the adenosine receptor system may be an important mediator of responses to alcohol, as well as to caffeine.

Another biochemical concept involves the gamma aminobutyric acid (GABA) system. In an attempt to replicate previous results of studies of plasma GABA, Coffman and Petty (1985) evaluated 85 consecutively admitted, male patients in a Veterans Administration (VA) alcoholism program. Forty-two normal control subjects were used. The mean plasma GABA level of the chronic alcoholics was 14.3 ± 7.3 ng/ml and that of the control subjects was 57.5 ± 12.0 ng/ml with virtually no overlap between the two groups. These researchers speculated that reduction in GABA-ergic activity may be an alcoholic trait and that the lower levels of inhibitory function may lead to a higher arousal level, with a greater tolerance for the effects of alcohol.

Another study which indirectly linked the GABA system to chronic alcohol ingestion was an evaluation of alcohol and diazepam in rats (Deutsch & Walton, 1977). In this study, rats, after exposure to forced intragastric intubation of alcohol, showed a greatly increased tendency to self-administer alcohol in a setting which offered a free choice between alcohol and water. When diazepam, 5 mg/kg, was used during the period of withdrawal, it served to maintain the preference for alcohol. Without the use of diazepam during the withdrawal phase, the tendency to self-administer alcohol returned to control baseline levels. This relationship between diazepam and the maintenance of preference for alcohol suggests the possibility that both drugs share some common characteristics in relation to the GABA receptor complex. The importance of the GABA receptor complex in alcoholism is further underscored by a recent research report from the National Institute of Mental Health. These investigators have successfully demonstrated the existence of a selective benzodiazepine antagonist of ethanol in rats (Suzdak et al., 1986).

It should be noted that diazepam is an effective drug in the prevention and control of the withdrawal syndrome (Guerrero-Figueroa et al., 1970). In cats with implanted subcortical electrodes, chronic alcohol administration for 30 days followed by abrupt cessation resulted in an increase of electroencephalographic (EEG) slow-wave background activity associated with activation of epileptiform discharges and an increase in amplitude of the local evoked potentials (LEP). Diazepam, injected 6 hours after the last administration of alcohol, completely eliminated these EEG and LEP changes of CNS excitement and inhibited the clinical withdrawal syndrome.

Other theories of addiction involve norepinephine (NE) metabolism. Adaptive responses to chronic ethanol exposure may involve changes in "rebound" phenomena of NE turnover during the intoxication and withdrawal phases (Tabakoff & Rothstein, 1983). In discussing the amelioration of some of the withdrawal symptoms by β-blockers, these authors consider the possible relationship between NE metabolism and physical dependence.

Some investigators have attempted to explain the development of tolerance and withdrawal in terms of state-dependent learning (Cicero, 1978). When alcohol is ingested, performance decrement occurs. However, in a state-dependent model, practice during the intoxicated state may enable the patient to perform satisfactorily again; learned tolerance has then occurred. Abrupt withdrawal of alcohol, shifting the patient to an abstinent state, results in the recurrence of the performance deficit; some investigators would interpret this deterioration as the withdrawal syndrome. However, such withdrawal symptoms as convulsions or hallucinations cannot be completely explained by this state-dependent explanation of the withdrawal stage.

For the reader who is interested in a more detailed discussion of the biochemical aspects of alcoholism, I would recommend the book by Tabakoff et al., *Medical and Social Aspects of Alcohol Abuse*, published in 1983.

REFERENCES

Cicero, T. J. (1978). Tolerance to and physical dependence on alcohol: Behavioral and neurobiological mechanisms. In M. A. Lipton, A. Dimascio, & K. F. Killam (Eds.). *Psychopharmacology: A generation of progress*. New York: Raven Press.

Coffman, J. A., & Petty, F. (1985). Plasma levels in chronic alcoholics. *American Journal of Psychiatry, 142*, 1204–1205.

Cohen, G., & Collins, M. (1970). Alkaloids from catecholamines in adrenal tissue: Possible role in alcoholism. *Science, 167*, 1749–1751.

Das, I. (1986). Ph.D. disseration on alcohol metabolism. Department of Biochemistry, Tulane Medical School, New Orleans, La.

Davis, V. E., & Walsh, M. J. (1970). Alcohol, amines, and alkaloids: A possible biochemical basis for alcohol addiction. *Science, 167*, 1005–1007.

Deutsch, J. A., & Walton, N. Y. (1977). Diazepam maintenance of alcohol preference during alcohol withdrawal. *Science, 198*, 307–310.

Guerrero-Figueroa, R., Rye, M. M., Gallant, D. M., & Bishop, M. P. (1970). Electrographic and behavioral effects of diazepam during alcohol withdrawal stage in cats. *Neuropharmacology, 9*, 143–150.

Hsu, L. L. (1976). Formation of 1, 2, 3, 4-tetrahydro-β-carboline and methylene-β-phenethylamine from 5-methyltetrahydrofolate and amines in tissues from developing rat brain. *Life Sciences, 19*, 493–496.

Li, T.-K. (1983). The absorption, distribution, and metabolism of ethanol and its effects on nutrition and hepatic function. In Tabakoff, B., Sutker, P. B., & Randall, C. L. (Eds.). *Medical and social aspects of alcohol abuse*. New York: Plenum Press.

Lieber, C. S., Rubin, E., & DeCarli, L. M. (1971). Chronic and acute effects of ethanol on hepatic metabolism of ethanol, lipids, and drugs: Correlation with ultrastructional changes. In N. K. Mello & J. H. Mendelson (Eds.). *Recent advances in the study of alcoholism*. (pp. 3–41). Washington, DC.: NIMH.

Liepman, M. R., Anderson, R. C., & Fisher, J. V. (1982). *Family medicine curriculum guide to substance abuse*. Kansas City, MO: Society for Teachers of Family Medicine.

Myers, R. D. (1983). Alkaloid metabolites and addiction drinking of alcohol. In N. C. Chang & H. M. Chao (Eds.). *Early identification of alcohol abuse*. (pp. 268–284). Rockville, MD: DHHS-PHS.

Proctor, W. R., & Dunwiddie, T. V. (1984). Behavioral sensitivity to purinergic drugs parallels ethanol sensitivity in selectively bred mice. *Science, 224*, 519–521.

Rutstein, D. D., Nickerson, R. J., Vernon, A. A., Kishore, P., Veech, R. L., Felver, M. E., Weedham, L. L., & Thicken, S. B. (1983). 2,3-Butanediol: An unusual metabolite in the serum of severely alcoholic men during acute intoxication. *Lancet, 2*, 534–537.

Suzdak, P. D., Glowa, J. R., Crawley, J. N., Schwartz, R. D., Skolnick, P., & Paul, S. M. (1986). A selective imidazobenzodiazepine antagonist of ethanol in the rat. *Science, 243*, 1243–1297.

Tabakoff, B., & Rothestein, J. D. (1983). Biology of tolerance and dependence. In Tabakoff,

B., Sutker, P. B., & Randall, C. L. (Eds.). *Medical and social aspects of Alcohol Abuse.*
New York: Plenum Press.

Tabakoff, B. Sutker, P. B., & Randall, C. L. (Eds.) (1983). *Medical and social aspects of
Alcohol Abuse.* New York: Plenum Press.

Thomas, M., Halsall, S. & Peters, S. J. (1982). Role of hepatic acetaldehyde dehydrogenase in
alcoholism: Demonstration of persistent reduction of cytosolic activity in abstaining patients. *Lancet, 2*, 1057–1059.

CHAPTER 4

Psychologic, Cultural, and Genetic Aspects of Alcoholism

PSYCHODYNAMIC AND PSYCHOLOGIC MECHANISMS CONTRIBUTING TO THE DEVELOPMENT OF ALCOHOLISM

THERE IS NO SINGLE psychodynamic formulation or specific type of personality disorder that can explain the development of alcoholism (Knox, 1978; Westermeyer, 1976a). However, in most cases, the *denial mechanism* plays a major role. The use of analogies may be helpful in illustrating the denial mechanism; for example, we might compare the patient with a pathologic denial mechanism to a race horse wearing blinders to decrease the excitement generated by the other horses and the crowd so that his concentration will be focused on the one goal of crossing the finish line first. In the case of the person with a drinking problem, the denial mechanism represents the patient's blinders, which serve to ward off any insights that may interfere with the major goal of going on to the next drink. Another analogy that comes to mind is the ostrich with its head in the ground. Just as the ostrich is unaware of its exposure to the rest of the world, so is the alcoholic convinced that no one is aware of his excessive drinking. Minimizing the severity of the drinking problem becomes an essential part of the alcoholic's orientation to the environment.

When explaining the denial mechanism to the patient, I might say, "Here you are, a mentally competent person who is certainly not stupid. So you have to deceive or 'con' yourself tremendously in order to let yourself go on or return to your drinking. You may tend to fool yourself or minimize the seriousness of your drinking problem, but above all else, you have to deceive yourself. All of us fool ourselves every now and then it's a perfectly human thing to do, but you're doing something more. You have to be an expert with the defense mechanism in order to allow the alcohol to dominate your life. You may have to deny the fact that you have a drinking problem until it is too late, having lost your family, job, and self-respect." This explanation of the denial system or mechanism is also reviewed with family members and friends during subsequent family sessions and in the intervention technique discussed in Chapter 6.

An example of the denial mechanism in its most overt form occurred during one of the family meetings on our inpatient alcohol rehabilitation unit. We were reviewing the patient's recent drinking history in the presence of his wife and several other families. During the year prior to admission, the patient's drinking episodes had been responsible for his beating his wife on two separate occasions and being arrested for drunk driving twice, the second conviction resulting in a six-month jail sentence. Previously, he had been treated in two other alcoholism programs with no significant periods of abstinence afterwards. When he was sober, he had not had any serious problems with his marriage or job. He said that he loved his wife and four-year-old daughter very much and the reason he sought treatment was because he did not want to lose them or ever be separated from them by another alcohol-related jail sentence. He seemed very serious when he discussed his motives for treatment.

At the end of this part of the discussion, I explained the benefits and risks of Antabuse and told him that Antabuse, in association with follow-up at AA meetings and couples therapy, would be good insurance for both him and his family. We reviewed some research data on Antabuse which showed its efficacy and relative lack of side effects. At this point, his facial muscles became a bit rigid and his eyes intense, as he said in a flat tone, "I don't need the Antabuse. I can make it on my own. I still think I can be a social drinker." The statement was made in such a manner that it seemed he had emotionally separated himself from the history that had been presented during the previous 30 minutes. All of the other families, the wife, and I were shocked. The patient could not understand our reaction and our lack of trust in his judgment about his ability to control his alcohol intake.

One fascinating aspect of how a patient's denial mechanism can result in conscious distortion is highlighted by a research survey on cigarette smoking (Kozlowski, 1980). Although 63% of highly motivated cardiac patients in one study reported that they no longer smoked as long as 18 months after their last heart attack, urine assays showed that one-fifth of these patients were still smoking. A similar study of alcoholics whose urines were assayed for alcohol while they were visiting a medical clinic showed that 52% of their self-reports on drinking were unreliable (Orrego et al., 1979). These patients, who did not realize that their urines were being evaluated for alcohol, denied any alcohol intake during the preceding 24 hours. Instructions on how to approach the denial mechanism in a sensitive manner while taking an adequate psychosocial history will be described in detail in Chapter 6.

The *learning theory of chemical dependency* stresses the concept of anxiety leading to alcohol use, with a subsequent reduction in anxiety. The relief of anxiety (and subsequent positive reinforcement) by alcohol may be immediate, as contrasted with other adaptive techniques for relieving anxiety, and repetitive practice can result in overlearning this habit. This conditioned response is maladaptive and may result in negative, anxiety-perpetuating responses by family, employer, and other social contacts, leading to a cycle of anxiety increase→alcohol increase→relief of anxiety by excessive alcohol intake→social disapproval→anxiety (see Figure 4.1). For those patients displaying this model of the development of alcoholism, it is important to interrupt this negative cycle at the earliest possible stage. For example, the treatment team should teach the patient behavior modification or assertiveness training techniques to cope with the initial increase in anxiety and to thus substitute for the alcohol.

The *psychodynamic formulation* of the overindulgent mother and the resultant, excessively demanding child does apply to some patients. In infancy, immediate soothing of the child could produce an impulsive individual who later reacts with frustration and anger to any attempts at delay of gratification. The use of alcohol to pacify the discontent may also be interpreted as a hostile act to spite family members and friends. From the viewpoint of some psychoanalysts, the subsequent alcoholic debasement satisfies the drinker's guilt about his hostile acts against the people who interfere

FIGURE 4.1
Learning Theory of Chemical Dependency

ANXIETY

SOCIAL
DISAPPROVAL

INCREASED
ALCOHOL USE

RELIEF
OF ANXIETY

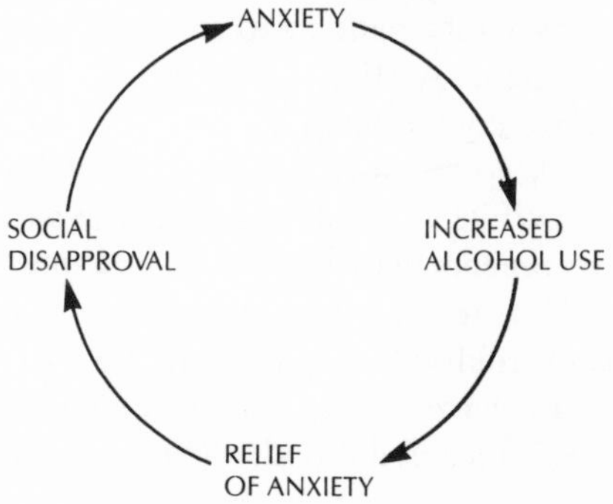

with his immediate gratification. Although this type of formulation does not apply to many alcohol abusers, it can serve as a therapeutic guideline for those patients who fit the description.

For instance, I recently treated a 27-year-old black male who had been reared by his mother in a ghetto area. The mother's income was minimal; she was a welfare recipient, with one son and two young daughters as her responsibility, while the husband was in prison for crimes related to heroin. The mother worked very hard at menial jobs to support herself and the three children. From her viewpoint, the son could never do any wrong and she could never do enough for him. By the time he was nine or ten years old, she had begun buying $50 shoes and designer pants for her son, with money she could not really afford to spend. The patient described himself to me as having been "spoiled—I could get anything I asked for. I could do no wrong." The father returned from prison when the boy was 11 years old. He deeply resented the father's presence because he came between him and his mother. In this rather classical case of oedipal conflict, the boy instigated terrible conflicts between the father and mother. When he caught the father smoking "weed," he would "snitch" to the mother and lead the mother to believe that her husband was "running around." These desperate maneuvers were intended to maintain the intense relationship between the patient and his mother. Later, after his marriage, he always stopped by to see his mother after work and gave her a significant part of his paycheck before going to his own household. He had tried three other inpatient treatment programs before being admitted to our unit. He had signed out of two and been expelled from the third.

On our alcohol rehabilitation ward, the patient began his stay by expecting his roommate to wake him after his daily morning nap and by alienating several of other patients with his self-indulgent behavior. After each disagreement, he concluded that everyone else was wrong and he was right. The patient did agree to allow us to videotape a confrontation between him and several patients in his group and promised to review the film with us the following week. During the taping, I reviewed the highlights of the maternal relationship and then asked the patients to confront him with individual lists of his narcissistic behavior. At first, as expected, he rejected all of their opinions. In fact, he was contemplating signing out against medical advice. However, he agreed to keep his word and first review the videotape with the patients and the staff. While watching the tape, the patient started to laugh at some of his own comments denying that he was spoiled and self-centered or that he was responsible for alienating the people around him. The visual impact of seeing his overindulgent, narcissistic behavior apparently started to penetrate the denial mechanism, as well as his obvious oedipal problem, which had been fixated since childhood. We have found this type of video confrontation to be much more effective than other forms of treatment for this type of self-indulgent alcoholic patient.

Lack of family cohesiveness has also been shown to be associated with an increase in alcohol abuse. In a study of alcohol abuse in adolescents, Burnside et al. (1986) reported a direct correlation between disruption of families (early death or divorce or separation of parents) and the incidence of alcohol-related problems in the offspring. (Exploration of the family dynamics are detailed in Chapter 11.)

Some of the older theories relating alcoholism and personality, such as the theory that passive-dependent or narcissistic personalities are more likely to develop problems with chemical dependency, have not been confirmed, despite a number of studies of these patients (Westermeyer, 1976b). However, some psychological factors do appear more frequently in substance-abusing groups, even 15 to 20 years before admission to treatment centers. In an interesting study published in 1974, Hoffman and his associates evaluated a group of substance abusers and a control group; both groups were tested with the Minnesota Multiphasic Personality Inventory (MMPI) during their college years. No consistent personality patterns were more apparent in the drug-abusing group than in the control group. However, compared to their control peers, the students who later became substance abusers were likely to identify with groups who shared alcohol and drugs during adolescence (G), were more impulsive (I), and were more likely to display evidence of adolescent independent rebelliousness or to be nonconforming (N). These letters, GIN, can serve as a mnemonic in predicting which adolescents are more likely to develop future alcohol or drug abuse problems. It should be remembered, however, that these subjects showed no more serious maladjustment at the time of testing than their comparative peer groups.

Similar findings have been reported in heavy drug users (Goldstein & Sappington, 1977). A follow-up study of MMPI profiles, which had been administered to all entering freshmen prior to any significant drug use, compared later, heavy users of marijuana and hallucinogenic drugs with the non-drug-using group. Those who later became drug users appeared to have been more impulsive, more rebellious and resistant to authority, less likely to learn by experience, and less reserved than the control group. However, neither group showed any significant deviations on the MMPI profiles, and both groups were considered to be within normal limits. It would appear that many substance-abusing patients, when abstinent, are not that different from the remainder of the population (except for the behavioral characteristics of impulsivity and rebelliousness); therefore, it may not be appropriate to generalize about the "antisocial" personalities of substance abusers.

It does appear that alcoholism and depression quite frequently are related. This is important in treatment planning (Wester et al., 1979). One of the most difficult clinical problems in alcoholism is differentiating primary from secondary depression. Alcoholics have a very high incidence of depressive symptomatology secondary to the depressant effects of alcohol, the deterioration of life-style, the loss of meaningful relationships, and other failures related to prolonged excessive drinking. Theoretically, this secondary depression should significantly decrease with abstinence and attention to environmental problems. In alcoholic patients with a primary depression, the depressive symptomatology has preceded the onset of alcohol abuse or has developed during prolonged periods of abstinence. In these individuals, there may be a strong family history of depression and possibly of panic disorder. These patients may be using alcohol in an attempt to alleviate or temporarily obliterate the dysphoric symptoms. It is absolutely essential to treat the depressive symptomatology; otherwise the patient is quite likely to return to drinking. Appropriate use of antidepressant drug therapy in addition to counseling or insight psychotherapy must be an integral part of the patient's treatment. Since the suicide rate is more than 200 times higher in this patient group than in the general population, it may be wise to initiate treatment on an inpatient rehabilitation treatment service. The therapeutic importance of delineating these two types of depression has been summarized by Schuckit (1980).

PSYCHOLOGICAL CONSEQUENCES OF ALCOHOLISM

Not only may psychological problems contribute to the development of alcoholism, but they also may occur as a consequence of alcohol abuse. Thus, some of the patient's current personality characteristics and psychologic problems may not have been present at the outset of the alcohol problem. The best example of this change can be seen in the severe personality deterioration of chronic alcohol abuse in the skid-row or revolving-door alcoholic (Brisolara et al., 1968). After many years of alcohol abuse and many arrests for drunkenness, this individual has developed pathologically low self-esteem, an inability to identify with any segment of society except his fellow "bottle" companions, pitiful, unrealistic optimism about the future, and increased distrust or emotional isolation, as measured by the Psychiatric Evaluation Profile (PEP). Many of these alcoholics have no difficulty in admitting their drinking problem, but the denial mechanism may operate in regard to future plans and expectations. This unrealistic outlook is frequently exacerbated by the presence of alcohol-induced organic mental disorders in this population.

The cultural environment of skid-row alcoholics promotes a mistrust of the world. These homeless people are frequently picked up by the police and incarcerated even when they are not disobeying the law (Brisolara et al.,

1968). Sometimes other inhabitants of the skid-row areas rob these alcoholics while they are lying in the street in a drunken stupor. At other times, they are mishandled by the police. As a result, it is not unusual to find deteriorated alcoholics displaying a manipulative personality and a suspicious attitude toward the typical representatives of society, including physicians. If one regards trust as the cornerstone of the therapeutic relationship, the difficulty in treating these patients becomes apparent.

In the great majority of alcoholics, chronic excessive alcohol intake invariably leads to failures within the family, interpersonal relationships, and/or employment. The subsequent feelings of inadequacy, frequently associated with temporary guilt, result in a negative cycle, with the patient using more alcohol in an attempt to obliterate these uncomfortable feelings. Additional failures then result from the return to alcohol, followed by increasing feelings of inadequacy and plummeting self-esteem and self-confidence. Some patients may develop reaction formations to this sense of failure, adopting a grandiose attitude toward the people around them. Others may retreat from the environment as part of a depressive reaction to their loss or sense of failure. At times it may be quite difficult to separate the psychologic problems present prior to the drinking problem from those that have developed consequently.

VARIATIONS AND EFFECTS OF CULTURAL ATTITUDES

Cultural attitudes play an important role in the acceptance or rejection of alcohol. While cultural approval may increase the accessibility to alcohol, ritualistic use of the drug by the culture may help to inhibit the abuse or overuse of the drug (Westermeyer, 1976b). Other cultural influences that may tend to lower the incidence of alcohol abuse are the labeling of solitary use as deviant and of intoxication as shameful. The low rate of alcoholism among Jewish people and the high rate of opiate abuse but low rate of alcoholism in the Meo of Southeast Asia may be examples of cultural effects. However, growth of mass media, increased migration, and rapid social changes during the past several decades have been associated with the assimilation of some cultures and have blurred the distinction between other cultural groups. Thus, traditional concepts about cultural effects, such as the belief that societies with ritualistic alcohol use consistently have a very low incidence of alcoholism, may have to be modified. For example, Jewish Yemenite immigrants to Israel have a higher incidence of alcohol abuse than either "nonimmigrant" Yemenites or native Israelis; also, first-generation Irish immigrants to the United States have a higher rate of alcoholism than "nonimmigrant" Irish (Westermeyer, 1976b). Apache Indians, who traditionally had few problems with alcohol abuse, have developed increasing rates of problem drinking, while the Sioux and Navajo have shown an increased rate of death from cirrhosis of the liver and other alcohol-related illnesses as they have moved from their ancestral tribal areas to "integrated White-Indian" towns (Westermeyer, 1976b). Cultural identity and cultural change always have to be considered when evaluating alcoholic patients and planning treatment goals with them.

The incidence of alcohol abuse also depends upon such cultural factors as peer impact, laws concerned with consequences of alcohol use, and family dynamics, as well as biological factors. There recently has been a resurgence of anti-alcohol attitudes in the U.S., seen in such actions as the formation of vociferous groups against drunk driving, laws raising the legal minimal drinking age, and a decrease in the population's liquor consumption habits (Okula, 1986). Extensive publication of morbidity and mortality data, as well as publicity about the relationship between a lowered legal drinking age and an increase in adolescent driving accidents and about such groups as Mothers Against Drunk Driving, have played a strong role in affecting cultural attitudes and subsequent changes in the law. Thus, the federal government was compelled to require states to raise the minimal drinking age to 21 years through an indirect form of blackmail by eliminating highway transportation funds for those states that did not comply with this request by 1989.

The forces opposing this anti-alcohol drive are represented by such groups as the alcohol beverage industry and barroom owners. The alcohol beverage industry saturates college newspapers with advertisements for its products, making up more than one-half of all national advertisements in such publications. The majority of these advertisements seek to increase peer pressure on students to join in drinking (Defoe & Breed, 1979). In a sample of nationwide college newspapers, alcohol advertisements were found to ridicule studying, graduation, and education by picturing serious students as being "square."

GENETIC ASPECTS OF ALCOHOL AND DRUG ABUSE

In a 1974 review of the genetic studies of alcoholism, Goodwin et al. suggested that one subgroup be categorized "familial alcoholism"; it is characterized by an early onset of loss of control, high tolerance for alcohol, and absence of significant psychiatric pathology. Goodwin et al.'s suggestion is supported by a number of adoption studies.

In an attempt to decrease the impact of environmental influences as a factor in the development of various diseases, adoption studies include only those adoptees separated shortly after birth from their blood parents. Comparison is then made between the adoptees whose blood parents have the disease and those adoptees whose blood parents do not. In one study, although the index adoptees of alcoholic parents and control adoptees were interviewed at a mean age of only 30 years, the index adoptees already had developed more than three times the incidence of alcoholism, a significant difference (Goodwin et al., 1973).

The genetic influence of an alcoholic parent was also demonstrated in a study of half-siblings (Schuckit et al., 1972). Children of alcoholic biological parents reared by either alcoholic or non-alcoholic parents had the same incidence of alcoholism. Children of alcoholic biological parents raised by nonalcoholic foster parents developed a significantly higher incidence of alcoholism than offspring of nonalcoholic biological parents raised by alcoholic foster parents. Children of both alcoholic and nonalcoholic biologic parents who shared their home with an alcoholic proband showed no greater evidence of alcoholism than did those individuals who did not share their childhood home with an alcoholic. The history of an alcoholic biological parent was the only predictor of alcoholism.

Further validation of genetic impact on the development of alcoholism was reported in two impressive Swedish studies (Bohman et al., 1981; Cloninger et al., 1981). In the first study they carefully followed 913 Swedish female adoptees. The criteria for inclusion were adoption by nonrelatives and being younger than three years at the time of adoption. Most of the subjects had been separated from their parents during infancy, with an average age at final placement of eight months. Statistical analyses of the variables of the foster homes showed that the extent of non-random assignment was insignificant. The age range of the adoptees at time of follow-up was 23 to 43 years. In evaluating their results, the authors used a meticulous cross-fostering analysis by subdividing the adoptees according to both characteristics of their biological parents and characteristics of their adoptive parents. This technique explores each possible combination of congenital background and postnatal foster environment. The results showed a threefold increase in alcoholism in the adoptive daughters of alcoholic biological mothers (p < 0.01), compared with adoptees of nonalcoholic mothers. The presence of alcoholism in adoptive parents had no influence on the incidence of alcohol abuse in the female adoptees.

In the second study the same research team reported a cross-fostering analysis of Swedish adoptive men (Cloninger et al., 1981). The incidence of alcoholism in the male offspring of male alcoholics was more than seven times the incidence in male adoptees from nonalcoholic biological parents. The incidence of alcoholism in the daughters was no higher than in the female adoptees of nonalcoholic parents. Thus, there appears to be a sex-linked transmission of this possibly genetic defect in a particular subgroup of alcoholics — particularly young, male alcoholic patients.

In my clinical experience, the following generalization has been quite consistently supported: The more heavily weighted or the stronger the paternal alcoholism history of the male alcoholic, the earlier the onset of blackouts and loss of control after social drinking has been initiated.

If a genetic substrate does exist for a specific group of alcoholics, it may relate to acetaldehyde levels. Blood acetaldehyde concentrations have been reported to be significantly elevated ($p < .004$) after a single dose of ethanol (0.5 ml/kg) in 20 young, non-alcoholic males with alcoholic parents or siblings, as compared with 20 young, non-alcoholic male offspring with no family history of alcoholism (Schuckit & Vidamantas, 1979). These elevated acetaldehyde levels could result in a tetrahydroisoquinoline product from catecholamine condensation, a compound that may be related to the development of addiction.

If significantly elevated acetaldehyde levels after alcohol ingestion do play a role in the genetic subgroup of alcoholism, then acetaldehyde dehydrogenase deficiency may account for this clinical phenomenon (Thomas et al., 1982). Liver biopsy specimens obtained from 15 alcoholic patients and six control subjects showed that the cytosolic component of the hepatocyte in alcoholics was selectively depleted of aldehyde dehydrogenase (Ald DH), a finding that could be directly related to the genetic defect. In this study, the cystosol Ald DH remained at a significantly low level during alcohol administration and after a relatively long period of abstinence.

Physiologic studies have indicated that the male offspring of alcoholics, as compared with male offspring of non-alcoholics, have a decreased intensity of reaction to ethanol, may demonstrate a decreased P300 amplitude brain wave, appear to have a relatively poorer vocabulary, and perform worse on tests of categorizing ability, organization and planning (Drejer et al., 1985; Schuckit et al., 1985). It is difficult to estimate the relative importance of the genetic, prenatal, and environmental factors that affect these reported physiologic differences.

In therapy, we give copies of the reports of the two Swedish studies (Bohman et al., 1981; Cloninger et al., 1981) to all of our patients whom we consider to be primary alcoholics with a strong genetic family history. This is part of a much needed educational effort to decrease or eliminate alcohol consumption in the offspring of alcoholics.

While these genetic, pathologic, and physiologic studies point to the existence of a genetic subgroup of alcoholics, it should be emphasized that the majority of offspring of alcoholics never develop alcoholism, and a significant number of alcoholics have no family history of alcoholism. Alcoholism is such a complex illness that it would be presumptuous to conclude that it is strictly a genetic problem. Other factors discussed in this chapter — the psychologic mechanism of denial, other personality problems, family disruption, and cultural factors — all play a role in association with the genetic predisposition in one possible subgroup of alcoholics, leading to the final common pathway of the illness of alcoholism.

REFERENCES

Bohman, M., Sigvardsson, S., & Cloninger, C. R. (1981). Maternal inheritance of alcohol abuse: Cross-fostering analysis of adopted women. *Archives of General Psychiatry, 38*, 965–969.

Brisolara, A., Bishop, M. P., Bossett, J. R., & Gallant, D. M. (1968). The New Orleans revolving-door alcoholic: Degree of severity of illness and financial expense to the community. *Journal of the Louisiana State Medical Society, 120*, 397–399.

Burnside, M. A., Baer, P. E., McLaughlin, R. J., & Pokorny, A. D. (1986). Alcohol use by adolescents in disrupted families. *Alcoholism: Clinical and Experimental Research, 10*, 274–278.

Cloninger, C. R., Bohman, M., & Sigvardsson, S. (1981). Inheritance of alcohol abuse: Cross-fostering analysis of adopted men. *Archives of General Psychiatry, 38*, 861–868.

Defoe, J. R., & Breed, W. (1979). The problem of alcohol advertisements in college newspapers. *Journal of the American College Health Association, 27*, 195–199.

Drejer, K., Theilgaard, A., Teasdale, T. W., Schulsinger, F., & Goodwin, D. W. (1985). A prospective study of young men at high risk for Alcoholism: Neuropsychological assessment. *Alcoholism: Clinical and Experimental Research, 9*, 498–502.

Goldstein, J. N., & Sappington, J. T. (1977). Personality characteristics of students who become heavy drug users: An MMPI study of an avant-garde. *American Journal of Alcohol and Drug Abuse, 4*, 401–412.

Goodwin, D. W., Schulsinger, F., Herman, L., Guze, S. B., & Winokur, G. (1973). Alcohol problems in adoptees raised apart from alcoholic biological parents. *Archives of General Psychiatry, 28*, 238–245.

Goodwin, D. W., Schulsinger, F., Muller, N., Herman, L., Winokur, G., & Guze, S. B. (1974). Drinking problems in adopted and nonadopted sons of alcoholics. *Archives of General Psychiatry, 31*, 164–169.

Hoffman, H., Loper, R. G., & Kammier, M. L. (1974). Identifying future alcoholics with MMPI alcoholism scales. *Quarterly Journal of Studies on Alcohol, 35*, 490–498.

Knox, W. (1978). Objective psychological measurements in alcoholism: Survey of the literature — 1973. *Psychological Reports, 42*, 439–480.

Kozlowski, L. T. (1980). What researchers make of what cigarette smokers say: Filtering smokers' hot air. *Lancet, 1*, 699–700.

Okula, S. (1986, March 23). Anti-alcohol feeling makes resurgence. *The Times Picayune*, New Orleans. (p. A-2).

Orrego, H., Blendis, L. M., Blake, J. E., Kapur, B. M., & Israel, Y. (1979). Reliability of alcohol intake based on personal interviews in a liver clinic. *Lancet, 2*, 1354–1356.

Schuckit, M. A. (1980). Alcohol and depression. *Advances in Alcohol, 1*, 1–3.

Schuckit, M. A., Goodwin, D. W., & Winokur, G. (1972). A study of alcoholism in half-sibs. *American Journal of Psychiatry, 128*, 1132–1136.

Schuckit, M. A., & Vidamantas, R. (1979). Ethanol injection: Differences in blood acetaldehyde concentrations in relatives of alcoholics and controls. *Science, 203*, 54–55.

Schuckit, M., Li, T. K., Cloninger, R., & Dietrich, R. A. (1985). Genetics of alcoholism. *Alcoholism: Clinical and Experimental Research, 9*, 475–492.

Thomas, M., Halsall, S., & Peters, T. J. (1982). Role of hepatic acetaldehyde dehydrogenase in alcoholism: Demonstration of persistent reduction of cytosolic activity in abstaining patients. *Lancet, 2*, 1057–1059.

Wester, R., Atchison, B., Kleinman, R., Gallant, D. H., & Gallant, D. M. (1979). A study of depression in alcoholic patients. *Journal of the Louisiana State Medical Society, 131*, 259–261.

Westermeyer, J. (1976a). Models for chemical dependency. In J. Westermeyer, *Primer on chemical dependency* (pp. 1–22). Baltimore: Williams & Wilkins.

Westermeyer, J. (1976b). Predisposing factors. In J. Westermeyer, *Primer on chemical dependency* (pp. 23–29). Baltimore: Williams & Wilkins.

CHAPTER 5

Early Diagnosis of Alcoholism

THE INTERVIEW PROCESS

As WITH OTHER MEDICAL and psychologic illnesses, the earlier the therapist establishes the diagnosis of alcoholism and begins treatment, the better the prognosis. Learning how to sensitively interview the patient in order to obtain a reliable history is one of the most important goals for a therapist in the field of alcoholism.

It is important to recognize several problems that may interfere with the interview process. The beginning therapist may have already developed pre-existing attitudes about alcoholism patients; these may be a barrier to effective care. In addition, the patient's attitudes about alcoholism may interfere with the interview. The patient's sense of stigma about having to be seen by a mental health professional and embarrassment about discussing the possibility of alcoholism can hinder the development of the therapist-patient relationship and result in an unreliable history and a misdiagnosis. The strength of the defense mechanism of denial, described in Chapter 4, creates an additional problem in making an early diagnosis of alcoholism.

A sensitively performed clinical history is essential if the therapist is to diagnose alcoholism before obvious evidence of chronic alcohol-induced damage develops. The history of chemical use should begin with questions about the least threatening subjects. The interviewer should begin with substances that are legal or culturally acceptable, such as the number of cups of caffeinated beverages per day, progress to the number of cigarettes filtered or unfiltered, and then to the daily number of glasses of wine and beer and/or ounces of liquor. In addition to ascertaining the type and amount of drug, the interviewer should try to assess the pattern of usage. After each specific drug is discussed, the patient should be asked a question about the effects of drug behavior upon other people, starting with caffeinated coffee, e.g., "Does your spouse or do your fellow employees ever comment that you may be drinking too much coffee?" If the answer is yes, a subsequent question should be, "Do you become more irritable after 4 or 5 cups?" The same questions can be asked about cigarettes and then about wine, beer, or other drugs as each substance is reviewed in the history.

The interviewer must be very sensitive in handling the transition to questions about marijuana and then to the "more illegal" drugs, since polydrug misuse has become more common in alcoholic patients and can confuse the clinical presentation as well as the formulation of a treatment plan (Gallant, 1982a). Attention to type, amount, and pattern of drug usage will result in a more reliable assessment.

It is helpful to introduce these subjects by saying something like, "I do have to ask these questions because some of these drugs can cause changes in a person's behavior or affect the action of other drugs." This kind of approach may help to smooth the path. These questions must be asked in a nonjudgmental manner, and labels such as "alcoholic" or "addict" should be avoided. At the beginning of a therapeutic relationship, the therapist should never attack the denial mechanism but instead work around it, without allowing the mechanism to prevent him or her from obtaining a reliable substance abuse history.

The clinical history interview should cover both social functioning and psychological functioning, including a review of such problems as mood disturbances, suicide (see the discussion of significant risk in alcoholics in Chapter 2), impulse control, violence potential, conditioned responses to seductive alcohol cues in the environment, thought disorders, and sexual functioning. In addition, the family history should be elicited in order to estimate the patient's genetic vulnerability to the development of alcoholism. Carefully worded questions about chemical use by other family members may yield additional helpful information. Such questions may be more easily accepted by the patient who is told that 22% of U.S. families have a problem related to alcohol (Gallup, 1981).

With the increased incidence of polydrug misuse or abuse in alcoholic patients, it is important for the therapist to obtain a comprehensive history of all drug use. It is not unusual for some alcoholics or abusers of other drugs to be unaware that there is a problem. Here are several common examples which should be kept in mind:

1. A person who uses amphetamines to lose weight and continues their use for prolonged periods develops a tolerance to the anorexigenic effect. Still, each time the person attempts to stop using the medication something "doesn't feel right."
2. A chronic user of sleeping pills becomes tolerant to the hypnotic

effect; yet, if the patient fails to take the pills, he or she suffers from vivid nightmares, insomnia, and anxiety. The patient may even take the pills during the day in an attempt to reduce anxiety and depression.

3. Chronic use of anxiolytics can result in drug dependence. Diazepam, for instance, may lead to varying degrees of psychological and/or physical dependence, even at recommended daily dosages.
4. Patients may begin to take a prescribed analgesic narcotic for general discomfort and nervousness although the prescription was initially prescribed to combat chronic pain.
5. Habit-forming analgesics (e.g., Darvon) may seem necessary to a patient's well-being because of withdrawal symptoms, even though the original need for an analgesic no longer exists.

There are also many patients who do not realize that alcohol or drug abuse is responsible for their medical problems. A patient with complaints such as pancreatitis or insomnia may have a history of alcohol abuse which has caused these problems. This point should be stressed, since many patients are relatively naive about the effects of excessive alcohol intake and drugs and are unaware of the relationship between the use of alcohol and drugs and their deteriorating health.

Assessments of current social functioning are important in providing both essential information about the severity of the illness and a baseline for evaluating treatment outcome. *These social items, as well as evaluations of psychological functioning, require outside corroboration, e.g., getting information from family or friends.* In obtaining the outside corroborative material, the therapist must remember not to violate the rules of confidentiality; the patient's permission must be granted before family members or friends are contacted. The therapist should make inquiries into the patient's employment history and reasons for job changes, educational background, possible current and past legal problems, family life, social activities, and previous enrollment in other types of treatment programs. All these factors are important elements of social functioning.

An adequate psychological evaluation is necessary not only for early diagnosis but also for treatment planning. A severe psychological disturbance is one important reason why patients fail in alcohol abuse treatment. However, presence of a severe psychological disturbance does not mean that the patient is untreatable, but rather that the usual alcohol treatment plan must be modified to take the disturbance into account. Effective treatment is available for many types of psychological disturbances (e.g., depression and psychosis); if these problems are successfully treated through psychotherapy and/or psychopharmacology, the patient can frequently stay in a traditional alcohol treatment program. The therapist should also be aware that certain psychological impairments are organic consequences of alcoholic abuse; these abnormalities may show significant improvement if abstinence is maintained.

Instruments have been developed to assess early symptoms of alcoholism as well as the psychological and social functioning of the alcoholic patient. The MacAndrew Alcoholism Scale, derived from the Minnesota Multiphasic Personality Inventory (MMPI), has been used as a detection instrument (Babor & Kadden, 1983). However, its 49 items may be employed only as an indirect screening procedure, since few of the items deal specifically with drinking. Apparently this subtest taps an underlying tendency toward acting-out behaviors common to drug abusers and alcohol abusers, as well as to impulsive, rebellious individuals without substance abuse problems.

A number of brief questionnaires have been suggested as useful additions to the interview process. The CAGE 4-item questionnaire includes questions relating to a history of attempting to cut down on alcohol intake (C), annoyance over criticism about alcohol (A), guilt about drinking behavior (G), and drinking in the morning to relieve withdrawal anxiety, sometimes known as an "eye opener" (E). This is a reliable instrument if a friend or relative is available to corroborate the patient's history. The most researched diagnostic instrument is the self-administered Michigan Alcoholism Screening Test (MAST) (Table 5.1 and 5.1A), which was originated by Selzer in 1971. This test consists of 25 true or false statements describing medical, social, and behavioral events associated with excessive drinking. The test has demonstrated a degree of validity in distinguishing between known groups of alcoholics and nonalcoholics (Babor & Kadden, 1983).

As mentioned in Chapter 1, Woodruff et al. (1976) abstracted three questions from the MAST to quickly diagnose alcohol problems:

1. Has your family ever objected to your drinking?
2. Did you ever think you drank too much in general?
3. Have others ever said you drink too much for your own good?

These are a worthwhile addition to the interview and can easily be incorporated at the end of the interview process.

In 1982 Bernadt et al. reported a study comparing the efficacy of three short alcoholism questionnaires to eight laboratory tests for the detection of alcoholism in 385 psychiatric patients. Of the laboratory tests used, the serum gamma-glutamyl-transpeptidase (GGTP) was the most reliable, but this test identified less than two-thirds of the excessive drinkers. The three interview questionnaires, the MAST, CAGE, and Reich Test, were much more sensitive, identifying almost 90% of the alcoholics and having a rea-

TABLE 5.1
Michigan Alcohol Screening Test (MAST)

POINTS	QUESTIONS
(0)	1. Do you enjoy a drink now and then?
(2)	2. Do you feel you are a normal drinker?*
(2)	3. Have you ever awakened the morning after some drinking the night before and found that you could not remember a part of the evening before?
(1)	4. Does your spouse (or parents) ever worry or complain about your drinking?
(2)	5. Can you stop drinking without a struggle after one or two drinks?*
(1)	6. Do you ever feel bad about your drinking?
(2)	7. Do friends and relatives think you are a normal drinker?*
(0)	8. Do you ever try to limit your drinking to certain times of the day or to certain places?
(2)	9. Are you always able to stop drinking when you want to?*
(4)	10. Have you ever attended a meeting of Alcoholics Anonymous (AA)?
(1)	11. Have you gotten into fights when drinking?
(2)	12. Has drinking ever created problems with you and your spouse?
(2)	13. Has your spouse (or other family member) ever gone to anyone for help about your drinking?
(2)	14. Have you ever lost friends or girl/boy friends because of drinking?
(2)	15. Have you ever gotten into trouble at work because of drinking?
(2)	16. Have you ever lost a job because of drinking?
(2)	17. Have you ever neglected your obligations, your family, or your work for 2 or more days because you were drinking?
(1)	18. Do you ever drink before noon?
(2)	19. Have you ever been told you have liver trouble? Cirrhosis?
(2)	20. Have you ever had delirium tremens (DTs), severe shaking, heard voices or seen things that weren't there after heavy drinking?
(4)	21. Have you ever gone to anyone for help about your drinking?
(4)	22. Have you ever been in a hospital because of drinking?
(0)	23. (a) Have you ever been a patient in a psychiatric hospital or on a psychiatric ward of a general hospital?
(2)	(b) Was drinking part of the problem that resulted in hospitalization?
(0)	24. (a) Have you ever been seen at a psychiatric or mental health clinic, or gone to any doctor, social worker, or clergyman for help with an emotional problem?
(2)	(b) Was drinking part of the problem?
(2)	25. Have you ever been arrested, even for a few hours, because of drunk behavior?
(2)	26. Have you ever been arrested for drunk driving after drinking?

*Negative responses are "alcoholic" responses.

Scoring: A total of 4 or more points is presumptive evidence of alcoholism, while a 5-point total would make it extremely unlikely that the individual was not alcoholic. However, a positive response to 10, 23b, or 24b would be diagnostic; a positive response indicates alcoholism.

TABLE 5.1A
Addendum to the MAST[a]

In patients in whom a drinking problem is suspected, yet who score 9 points or less and especially those who score 4 points or less, one may ask seven additional yes-no questions[b]:

1. Have you ever consciously stopped drinking for a period of time?
2. Can you or could you at any time in your life drink more than other people without showing it?
3. Did either of your parents ever have a problem with drinking?
4. Have you ever been stopped while driving or apprehended by a law officer for any reason while you were drinking, yet you did not get arrested or receive a citation, but probably should have?
5. Have you ever gone to a doctor for a medical problem, other than liver disease or cirrhosis, that you or he suspected was caused by drinking?
6. Have you ever been dependent upon or ever had recurring problems with using a drug other than alcohol?[c]

    (A "Yes" answer to any of these questions should be scored two points. For question 3, if the answer is "Yes" for both parents, score 4 points.)

7. Did you often have hangovers (feeling bad or sick after drinking) during the first few years of your heavy drinking?

    (A "No" answer to question 7 should be scored 2 points.)

Three additional observations can be helpful, and these are to be answered by the clinician.

8. Does the patient display any "red flags" during the taking of the drinking history? (e.g., glibness, avoiding, anger, defensiveness) ("Yes" answer = 3 points)
9. At any time during the interview did the patient say "I can quit anytime," "I don't need it," "I can take it or leave it," or the like? ("Yes" answer = 3 points)
10. If there is a blood alcohol level available, does it fulfill any of the following criteria?
    a. 100mg/100 ml at any office visit
    b. 150mg/100 ml without gross evidence of intoxication
    c. 300mg/100 ml at anytime
    ("Yes" answer to any one of a, b, or c = 5 points)

Although these ten questions are not a part of the standardized MAST, Whitfield finds them to be of value in patients with doubtful or negative MAST scores. They can provide up to 27 additional points.

Rarely, patients who are alcoholic will score 3 points or less on the standard MAST. In these patients, the clinician can usually find other information that indicates that the patient may be or is alcoholic. It may also be helpful to give the MAST and the Addendum to a family member, such as the spouse, to answer for the patient, as though the patient were answering truthfully. In such a case the MAST score will be as accurate as if the patient answered it honestly. In recording the patient's score, the MAST score should be listed first, followed by the sum of both the MAST and the Addendum, e.g., 15/22(MAST/MAST and Addendum).

Explanation for MAST Addendum
Answers by the patient/client
Question
1. Normal drinkers normally do not consciously stop drinking. Any person who consciously stops drinking is giving evidence that he has found drinking to be a

(continued)

52

TABLE 5.1A
Continued

negative experience. Alcoholics usually stop drinking periodically toward the middle and advanced stages of their alcoholism. Consciously stopping drinking usually indicates that the person has some form of struggle with drinking.

2. This demonstrates tolerance to alcohol, either acquired or congenital. Alcoholics commonly manifest one or both of these.

3. About two-thirds of alcoholics have a family history of a drinking problem in a parent. If you are now seeing a person for suspicion of an alcohol problem who discloses that his/her parent was an "alcohol abuser" or that he was concerned about the parent's drinking, or that the parent was a heavy drinker, this is further evidence of either risk or an actual problem. For those people with both parents having had a drinking problem, there is probably an even higher risk of being or becoming alcoholic. If the person has some doubt about a parent's alcoholism, taking the MAST for the parent as though the parent were answering honestly is usually helpful and can help remove the doubt.

4. This can be called a "near arrest." It commonly occurs in women and VIP drunk drivers, where the law officer often does not issue a citation because, for example, the woman cries or the VIP uses other influence.

5. This questions a medical consequence of alcoholism other than liver disease or cirrhosis. Any person who has such should be suspected of having alcoholism.

6. People with drug dependence to one type of drug tend to develop dependence to other types of psychoactive drugs. Alcoholism is the most common drug dependence. Thus, having another type of drug dependence places a person at a higher risk of becoming or being alcoholic.

7. In a pilot survey by Whitfield, from 25 to 65% of 400 people who identified themselves as recovering alcoholics said that they rarely, if ever, experienced a hangover after heavy drinking during the first few years of their alcoholism, contrasted to less than 5% of a smaller non-alcoholic population so surveyed.

Observations by the Clinician

8. These responses indicate struggle, similar to question 1.

9. These statements or the like also indicate struggle. Normal drinkers do not make this type of statement. Some alcoholism experts consider this to be almost diagnostic of alcoholism.

10. These blood alcohol levels are those set forth by the National Council on Alcoholism's expert committee on the diagnosis of alcoholism. Any one of these is considered to be a major diagnostic criterion and, therefore, is diagnostic of alcoholism.

---

a. The authors have developed these additional questions to facilitate diagnosis in patients with low MAST scores. While the authors have found them to be helpful over about 5 years of experience with hundreds of patients, these questions have not been standardized.

b. These questions may also be asked of those who score above 9 points on the MAST to provide additional data.

c. If the patient answers "No" to this question, yet the clinician knows that the patient has or had a drug problem, 2 points should be scored. This principle also applies to other questions on the MAST and this addendum as well.

*From Whitfield et al., 1986

sonable specificity with misdiagnosis of less than 10%. The reliability and sensitivity of these three tests compare favorably with the figures obtained with the three-item Woodruff test.

The Diagnostic Questions for Early or Advanced Alcoholism (DQEAA) (Table 5.2) and the MAST (Table 5.1) may be used early during the interview process, at the end of either the first or second sessions. After the initial relationship with the patient has been established, answering the questionnaires may enable the patient to take a more honest look at himself or herself, particularly if there is a family member or friend present during this part of the interview. The DQEAA is somewhat more subtle than the MAST. Before reading the last paragraph of this questionnaire to the patient, the interviewer should first have the patient respond to the questions, with corroboration by family members or a close friend if possible. At times I have found this approach to be quite successful in helping the patient to decrease the denial mechanism and take a more honest look at his or her drinking behavior.

EARLY SYMPTOMS AND SIGNS OF ALCOHOL ABUSE

Frequent headaches, recurrent gastrointestinal complaints, recent absence from work based on vague physical complaints, or sudden unexplained mood changes are all possible early symptoms of alcohol abuse. More advanced symptoms may include the continued use of alcohol in the same amounts even after having sustained injuries while using alcohol or after being charged with driving while intoxicated (DWI). Increased frequency of use despite "blackouts," antisocial or belligerent behavior while under the influence of alcohol, or confrontations by spouse or friends about use are often symptoms of loss of control. Frequent injuries or cigarette burns due to drowsiness may be other symptoms of alcohol misuse. In order to validate the diagnosis in some suspected cases, the physician may ask the patient if a close family member could accompany him or her during a subsequent visit.

In adolescents and young adults, an unexplained drop in grades, chronic tardiness, increased absenteeism, deterioration in personal hygiene, and decrease in physical and recreational activities are all possible symptoms of increased alcohol use or possible abuse of other types of drugs. Personality traits such as impulsivity and rebelliousness may be early warning signs of future alcohol or drug misuse (Goldstein & Sappington, 1977). A combination of *two* or more of the following symptoms in college or graduate students may be a predictor of present or future alcohol or drug misuse: failure in any area of education; difficulty in social functioning; failure to find humor in one's role as a student; frequent use of alcohol to relieve

TABLE 5.2
Diagnostic Questions for Early or Advanced Alcoholism

1. Do I get drunk when I intended to stay sober?
   This question speaks to early loss of control over one's drinking. The inability to stop, once drinking has commenced, is an ominous sign. *Even an occasional loss of control may* be a warning signal.

2. When things get rough, do I need a drink or two to quiet my nerves?
   Using alcohol as a tranquilizer can be precarious because the dose is difficult to adjust, and no other person is supervising the medication.

3. Do other people say I'm drinking too much?
   If the negative effects of drinking are evident to more than one person on a number of occasions, this means that one's behavior is exceeding the social limits. It would be well to listen to such comments, remembering that most people are usually reluctant to talk about the drinking troubles of their friends and relatives.

4. Have I ever had a "DWI" (Driving While Intoxicated) charge?
   Being arrested even once means that one has a 50% chance of already having a drinking problem.

5. Is it not possible for me to stop drinking for a month or more?
   Resolving to stop and not being able to carry it off would indicate a definite psychological or physical dependence and reflect a serious future outlook. Being able to stop is encouraging, but does not eliminate the possibility of binge or other types of destructive drinking. It is not being able to stop that is indicative of a dangerous situation.

6. Do I sometimes not remember what happened during a drinking episode?
   Blackouts due to alcohol consist of variable periods of *amnesia* for what happened during the drinking bout. They are to be differentiated from passing out into unconsciousness, which is the end state of intoxication. Blackouts strongly suggest the problem of alcoholism. Passing out is an unfavorable sign.

7. Has a doctor ever said that my drinking was impairing my health?
   By the time a medical examination reveals abnormalities attributable to alcohol, it is clear that continuing to drink as previously will seriously damage one's health. Abnormalities of amino acid ratios, plasma lipoproteins, or hepatic enzymes are signals that too much ethanol is being ingested for the liver to cope with.

8. Do I take a few drinks before going to a social gathering in case there won't be much to drink?
   Assuring oneself of a sufficient supply of alcohol, just in case, is evidence of an unhealthy preoccupation with such beverages and speaks for a need to feel "loaded" on social occasions and of the presence of a drinking problem.

(continued)

TABLE 5.2
Continued

9. Am I impatient while awaiting my drink to be served?
   The urgency to obtain a drink reflects a craving. Gulping drinks is another sign of overinvolvement with alcohol.

10. Have I tried to cut down but failed?
    As with the inability to stop drinking for periods of time, the inability to cut down is a warning that dependence is present or impending. Cutting down successfully but eventually slipping back up is another sign of possible future trouble.

11. Do I have a drink in the morning because I feel queasy or have the shakes?
    The relief obtained from a drink after arising is apparently the relief of early, mild withdrawal symptoms. Therefore, a degree of physical dependence is already present, and this symptom suggests that alcoholism is now a severe problem.

12. Can I hold my liquor better than other people?
    Being able to hold one's liquor is not necessarily evidence of manliness or freedom from complications of drinking. It may indicate the development of tolerance due to the presistent consumption of large quantities. Although social disabilities may be avoided by holding one's liquor, physical impairment due to the amount consumed is inevitable.

13. Have many members of my family been alcoholics?
    There is a genetic component to some instances of alcoholism. People whose parents or siblings had serious problems with alcohol have reason to be extra careful of drinking habits.

The 13 indicatives mentioned above are early or somewhat advanced signs of alcoholism. They should be assessed seriously by the individual concerned or by the health professional who is evaluating him or her. The recognition that a threat to one's future exists is a first step. The second step is taking realistic action on the basis of the threat. The third step is sustaining the new behavior. These steps are the critical blocks to altering the course of destructive drinking: refusal to accept the information, refusal to do anything about it, and refusal to maintain a corrective course of action.

If any 2 of these 13 indicators are present, the problem drinker and the family should probably seek immediate help and guidance from AA and Al-Anon as well as the nearest available alcoholism treatment clinic.

uncomfortable moods; irregular class attendance; and friction with more than one professor.

Of course, the simplest test for alcohol abuse may be measurement of the blood alcohol (Dubach & Schneider, 1980). Of 1,476 patients screened at the University Hospital of Basel, 12% of admissions to the surgical service, 9% of admissions to the medical service, and 2% of the outpatients had blood alcohol levels higher than 100 mg% (100 mg/dl). Any patient who can tolerate a blood level of alcohol of 100 mg% or 150 mg% without the appearance of intoxication should be strongly suspected of having a drinking problem.

The importance of obtaining alcohol blood levels from adolescent patients is emphasized by another study that evaluated 459 consecutive teenage patients seen for psychiatric evaluations in a general hospital emergency room (ER) during a 1-year period (Reichler et al., 1983). (Please see Chapter 2 for details of this study.)

One detailed study reported other laboratory tests which were indicators of early signs of alcoholism: an increase of gamma-glutamyl transpeptidase (GGTP) was positive in 63% of middle-class excessive drinkers; serum glutamic-oxalecetic transaminase (SGOT) increase in 48%; macrocytosis without anemia in 26%; elevated serum triglyceride in 28%; alkaline phosphatase in 16%; bilirubin increase in 13%; and an increased uric acid in 10% of these patients (Morse & Heest, 1979). In another investigation, routine physical examinations and lateral chest X-rays showed rib and/or thoracic vertabral fractures in as many as 30% of alcoholic male patients, whereas non-alcoholic male patients showed only a 2% incidence (p < 0.001) (Israel et al., 1980). Thus, if a patient shows a relative macrocytosis without an anemia and a fracture of a rib and/or thoracic vertebra on the routine CBC and chest X-ray, the odds are very great that this individual is an alcoholic.

In one study in which the subjects were followed from 4 to 6 years, a more sensitive liver enzyme test, serum gamma-glutamyl-transferase (GGT), was used as a screening device for detecting alcoholism in its early phases and then incorporated into an intervention program. This resulted in significant reductions in illness-related days absent from work (80%), hospitalization days (60%), and mortality rate (50%), compared to a control group (Kristenson et al., 1983). In screening patients who may have stopped drinking several days ago, the GGT is very helpful, since its level rises so high above baseline (up to 20 times) and its return to baseline may take two or three weeks after a drinking binge (Liepman et al., 1982). This laboratory test intervention was conducted in Malmo, Sweden, as part of a voluntary population screening program to decrease the major middle-aged health risks related to cardiovascular disease, diabetes, and heavy drinking.

A more complex evaluation of laboratory data, analyzing multiple tests, was reported by Ryback et al. in 1980. Using the SMA-12 laboratory test, the SMA-6 and CBC, this research team was able to identify correctly 86% of a group of alcoholics in medical ward and treatment programs and 100% of medical inpatient controls who were not alcoholic, including 12 patients with non-alcoholic liver diseases which were verified by biopsy. The statistical use of these laboratory data also helped to identify 23 supposed non-alcoholic patients whose drinking behavior surpassed the specific criteria for inclusion in the non-alcoholic group but who claimed to have had no drinking problems. After further evaluation, 16 of these 23 patients were placed in the alcoholic group. This statistical evaluation of the three laboratory procedures was not valid in people over 65 years; the percentage of misdiagnosis in this age group was 50%. All subjects in this study were males in a V.A. hospital; since many standard laboratory values for females do vary from male data, it would be important to perform similar laboratory correlation studies in patients of both sexes admitted to large general hospitals.

DIFFERENTIAL DIAGNOSIS

Because of the widespread use of alcohol in our society, physicians as well as laymen are frequently too hasty in attributing to alcohol any unusual behavior or difficulty with coordination. When a patient arrives in a therapist's office or an emergency room with symptoms of slurred speech, difficulty with coordination, ataxia, loquaciousness, and difficulty with attention, there may be a natural tendency for the professional to attribute the patient's symptoms to alcohol intoxication. However, it is important to note that similar symptoms may be caused by certain neurological diseases, such as multiple sclerosis of cerebellar dysfunction, or by intoxication due to other sedative substances (e.g., barbiturates or benzodiazepines such as Valium or Librium). Metabolic diseases such as diabetes mellitis may also be associated with impairment of central nervous system function and result in the development of these signs and symptoms. Even if the diagnostic impression is supported by a relatively high blood level of alcohol, it would be wise for the physician or therapist to follow the patient carefully in order to be sure that these symptoms clear as the alcohol disappears from the blood. It should be emphasized that the alcohol intoxication may be masking underlying physical sequelae of alcoholism, such as a subdural hematoma.

If the patient is cooperative, careful inquiry into recent meals and the amount of alcohol ingested may help the therapist to formulate an educated guess about the present level of blood alcohol, since food does inhibit alcohol absorption. If the patient had started drinking less than 1 hour after his last heavy meal, the blood alcohol level should be somewhat modified, as compared to if he started drinking on an empty stomach (Lin et al., 1976). The blood alcohol peaks within 50 minutes to three hours after rapid drinking ceases. Each ounce of whiskey, glass of wine, or a 12-ounce beer raises the blood alcohol level by approximately 15 to 25 mg%. Table 5.3 outlines the clinical manifestation of blood alcohol levels.

Severity of the symptoms of intoxication depends upon the rapidity of the blood alcohol level ascent and upon the peak level of blood alcohol concentration attained, as well as the patient's acquired tolerance and the presence of other drugs. It has been demonstrated that women become

TABLE 5.3
Clinical Manifestations of Blood Alcohol Levels in Nontolerant Drinkers

BAL	CLINICAL STATUS
50 mg/dl	mild reduction of inhibitions, impaired thought and judgment
100 mg/dl	ataxia, impaired sensory discrimination, slow reflexes, exaggerated emotion and behavior, denial of impairment, legally intoxicated
150 mg/dl	clumsy, belligerent
200 mg/dl	lethargic, emotional outbursts, motor retardation
300 mg/dl	confusion, stupor
400 mg/dl	disorientation, coma
500 mg/dl	respiratory and vasomotor depression, death

intoxicated more rapidly than men, exhibiting an increase of blood levels 20% to 45% higher than men after receiving the same amount of alcohol per unit of weight, regardless of body build (Jones & Jones, 1975; Sutker et al., 1983). It appears that the differences in the peak levels of blood alcohol may be explained by differences in body water content between the sexes. Evaluation of women ingesting alcohol during their premenstrual phase indicates that peak levels of alcohol may occur even more rapidly during this time, with higher absorption rates as compared to other phases of their menstrual cycle (Jones & Jones, 1975). It should be noted that oral contraceptives contain compounds such as estrogen that inhibit the metabolism of alcohol, resulting in higher peak levels and more sustained blood levels (Hatcher & Jones, 1977).

If the patient does not show typical signs and symptoms of alcohol intoxication at blood levels of 150 mg%, this indicates a very high tolerance and a strong possibility of alcohol dependence. If the blood alcohol level is 300 mg% and the patient is still ambulatory, the therapist can be fairly certain of the diagnosis of alcohol dependence.

INDICATIONS FOR REFERRAL FOR PSYCHIATRIC CONSULTATION OR TO SPECIALIZED TREATMENT PROGRAMS

It is my opinion that most clinical psychiatric social workers, physicians in primary care practice, clinical psychologists, and substance abuse counselors should be capable of managing the treatment of the great majority of alcoholic patients. With the help of a spouse and family, if available, and with the aid of AA, Al-Anon, NA, Pills Anonymous (PA), and other community resources, the therapist may be able to treat the patient without psychiatric referral or specialized inpatient therapy. However, those alcoholics who have episodes of non-drug-related psychotic reactions, such as schizophrenic disorders, paranoid disorders, or biopolar disorders (as described in *DSM-III* and *DSM-III-R*) should be referred for psychiatric management. Patients with severe recurrent major depression when abstinent should also be referred for psychiatric consultation and possible antidepressant drug management by a consultant who is experienced in the psychopharmacologic treatment of the alcoholic patient with a major depression. If the patient has a serious long-standing marital or sexual problem that presents during abstinence, then a referral to a psychiatrist or marital and/or sex therapist would be appropriate. However, it is not unusual to see many of the alcoholic patient's psychologic problems and interpersonal difficulties gradually resolve themselves as the duration of abstinence increases, since many of the psychological problems associated with alcoholism are consequences of the life-style.

Specialized rehabilitation programs can help by temporarily immersing patients in an inpatient program totally concerned with their alcoholism and personality problems. These programs are particularly useful for the patient who has an extremely rigid denial mechanism and who may be only temporarily cooperating with abstinence treatment because of recent environmental or legal pressures. The very depressed patient and the patient who has recently undergone a very severe blow, such as the loss of job because of alcoholism, can also profit from such a program, since it helps the alcoholic stop and reexamine his lifestyle and future goals.

It has been our experience that those patients who have grown up in very isolated or very abusive families and have never had the opportunity to experience any healthy living experiences with other human beings can also profit from an inpatient rehabilitation program where the staff are sincerely concerned about the patient, can listen to him with an "open ear," and can be honest both in treating the patient and in relating to him as a fellow human being. This enables the patient to begin trusting a few key people in the environment. This trust will help him to open up about his emotional problems and feel comfortable with these few people. The patient may be able to apply the lessons learned in this healthy live-in environment to the outside world after discharge from the hospital. This type of patient with no basis of trust is extremely difficult to treat on a one-to-one basis in an outpatient setting, where the therapist may have the opportunity to see him only once or twice a week or perhaps even less frequently if the outpatient staff is overburdened with an unusually large patient load.

Many patients who have recently undergone a severe withdrawal reaction from alcohol addiction show some symptoms of the protracted withdrawal syndrome: short-lived episodes of anxiety, anger, or depression for no apparent reason, lability of blood pressure and pulse rate, lability of affect, and sensations of being on a "dry drunk." Such patients may benefit considerably from continued inpatient treatment in a specialized rehabilitation unit.

It is important to emphasize that many alcoholics or problem drinkers do not like to view themselves as "real alcoholics," "psychiatric patients," or "real addicts." Outpatient treatment may be more acceptable to these patients, particularly in the early phase of therapy while the denial mechanism is still strong. A premature suggestion or too early a referral of the patient to specialized treatment facilities or to a psychiatrist may only result in termination of the relationship with the physician or therapist, who is just starting to make headway with the alcoholism problem (Gallant, 1982b).

REFERENCES

American Psychiatric Association (1980). *Diagnostic and statistical manual of mental disorders (3rd ed.)*. Washington, DC: Author.

American Psychiatric Association. *Diagnostic and statistical manual of mental disorders (3rd ed.-R)*. Washington, DC: Author.

Babor, T. F., & Kadden, R. (1983). Screening for alcohol problems: Conceptual issues and practical considerations. In N. C. Chang & H. M. Chao (Eds.). *Early identification of alcohol abuse*. (pp. 1–30). Washington, DC: DHHS Pub. No. (ADM) 85–1258.

Bernadt, M. W., Taylor, C., Mumford, J., Smith, B., & Murray, R. M. (1982). Comparison of questionnaire and laboratory tests in the detection of excessive drinking and alcoholism. *Lancet, 1*, 325–328.

Dubach, U. C. & Schneider, J. (1980). Screening for alcoholism. *Lancet, 2*, 1374–1375.

Gallant, D. M. (1982a). The new breed of alcoholics. *Alcoholism: Clinical and Experimental Research, 6*, 536–537.

Gallant, D. M. (1982b). *Alcohol and drug abuse curriculum guide for psychiatry faculty*. (pp. 16–17). Washington: DHHS Pub. No. (ADM) 82–1159.

Gallup, G. (1981, February 8). Gallup poll on alcohol use. *The New Orleans Times Picayune*. (p. 4).

Goldstein, J. N., & Sappington, J. T. (1977). Personality characteristics of students who become heavy drug users: An MMPI study of an avant-garde. *American Journal of Alcohol and Drug Abuse, 4*, 401–412.

Hatcher, R. & Jones, B. M. (1977). Inhibition of alcohol dehydrogenase with estrogen. *Alcoholism Technical Reports, 6*, 39–41.

Israel, Y., Orrego, H., Holt, S., McDonald, M., & Meema, H. (1980). Identification of alcohol abuse: Thoracic fractures on routine chest x-ray as indicators of alcoholism. *Alcoholism: Clinical and Experimental Research, 4*, 420–422.

Jones, B. M., & Jones, M. K. (1975). Alcohol effects in women during the menstrual cycle. *Annals of the New York Academy of Science*, 576–587.

Kristenson, H., Ohlin, H., Hulten-Nosslin, M-J., Trell, F., & Hood, B. (1983). Identification and intervention of heavy drinking in middle aged men: Results and follow-up of 24–60 months of long term study with randomized controls. *Alcoholism: Clinical and Experimental Research, 7*, 203–209.

Liepman, M. R., Anderson, R. C., & Fisher, J. V. (1982). *Family medicine curriculum guide to substance abuse.* Kansas City, MO: Society for Teachers of Family Medicine.

Lin, Y-J., Weidler, D. J., & Garg, D. C. (1976). Effects of solid foods on blood levels of alcohol in man. *Research and Communications in Chemistry and Pathology, 13,* 713–722.

Morse, R. M., & Heest, R. D. (1979). Screening for alcoholism. *Journal of the American Medical Association, 242,* 2628–2690.

Reichler, B. D., Clement, J. L., & Dunner, D. L. (1983). Chart review of alcohol problems in adolescent psychiatric patients in an emergency room. *Journal of Clinical Psychiatry, 44,* 338–340.

Ryback, R. S., Eckardt, M. J., & Pautler, C. P. (1980). Biochemical and hematological correlates of alcoholism. *Research Communications in Chemistry, Pathology, and Pharmacology, 27,* 533–550.

Selzer, M. L. (1971). The Michigan Alcoholism Screening Test: The quest for a new diagnostic instrument. *American Journal of Psychiatry, 127,* 1653–1658.

Sutker, P. B., Tabakoff, B., Goist, K. C., & Randall, C. L. (1983). Acute alcohol intoxication, mood states, and alcohol metabolism in women and men. *Pharmacology, Biochemistry, and Behavior, 18,* 349–354.

Whitfield, C. L., Davis, J. E., & Barker, L. R. (1986). Alcoholism. In L. R. Barker, J. R. Burton, & P. Ziene (Eds.). *Principles of ambulatory medicine.* Baltimore, MD: Williams & Wilkins.

Woodruff, R. A., Clayton, P. J., Cloninger, C. R., & Guze, S. B. (1976). A brief method of screening for alcoholism. *Diseases of the Nervous System, 37,* 434–435.

CHAPTER 6

Early Intervention Techniques

THE IMPORTANCE OF EARLY INTERVENTION

Objective research data show that alcohol abuse is the major cause of death in middle-aged males and that alcoholics have a suicide rate 300 to 600 times higher than non-alcoholics (Berglund, 1984; Petersson et al., 1982). These should convince us of the need for intervention in the early or middle phases of this illness. In addition, computerized tomographic scans (CT) have vividly shown both alcoholic brain damage and its potential reversibility, reinforcing the importance of interrupting the devastating illness of alcoholism even in its later stages. In one CT evaluation of alcohol-induced brain damage, the alcoholic subjects showed greater cerebral atrophy than aged-matched neurological controls (Carlen et al., 1986). However, the cerebral atrophy reversed in some subjects with maintained abstinence.

Computerized assessment of cerebral spinal fluid volume (CSF), an indicator of cerebral atrophy, and mean cerebral density showed decreased CSF volume and increased cerebral density with maintained abstinence over a period as short as 4 weeks in a group of 20 alcoholics. In association with the decrease in brain damage, the patients showed an improvement in thought processes and memory functions. These data emphasize the point that intervention at any phase of alcoholism can be worthwhile; of course, the earlier intervention takes place, the greater the retention of human resources for maintaining a worthwhile life-style.

Delayed treatment of alcoholism can only result in greater tragedies for the patients, their families and friends. One report detailing the delay in seeking help for alcoholism merits attention. In this study, a survey of 123 Al-Anon wives showed that these spouses of alcoholics delayed seeking help for an average of more than seven years after the first obvious occurrence of problem drinking (Gorman & Rooney, 1979). Reviewing other studies as well as their own, Gorman and Rooney cite such reasons for delay in seeking help as lack of knowledge of the true nature of alcoholism (i.e., believing that the problem is temporary), embarrassment over the perceived stigma, guilt and feelings of responsibility for the husband's alcoholism, and fear of repeated confrontations.

In this study, the majority of the subjects were white, middle-to-upper-middle-class suburbanites in the Washington, D.C., area; the mean age was 44 years, with an average marriage duration of 20 years. At the time of the survey, 37% of the husbands were still drinking, 28% had been sober less than one year, and 15% had been sober more than one year. Such events as beating their wives or other family members, staying out all night, and being arrested for alcohol-related incidents occurred from a mean of 5.4 to 7.2 years before the wives sought help. Pressure from family or friends or confrontation by the family physician about serious health impairment from alcohol occurred about 2.7 years before the spouse contacted Al-Anon or sought professional counseling. One of the several tragic statistics in this study was the finding that 60% of the wives had reached the point of hating their alcoholic husbands by the time they sought help.

One of the shortcomings of this study was the relative homogeneity of the economic class to which these Al-Anon members belonged. Lemert (1965) has reported that lower-class families seek help earlier, since they experience greater economic deprivation relatively early in the course of the husband's alcoholism (Lemert, 1965). The report by Gorman and Rooney, while not representative of the spouses of male alcoholics in general, is still an extremely important indicator of the many years of suffering endured by such spouses before they seek help.

THE THERAPEUTIC RELATIONSHIP

Before detailing the techniques of early intervention, let me turn to the essential elements of the therapeutic relationship. Trust is the essence of the therapist-patient relationship, as well as of other human relationships. Without this trust, the best efforts of a brilliant therapist or physician may be useless when it comes to helping a patient. As distrust enters the relationship, patient noncompliance will assuredly increase, as will the dropout rate.

A sensible division of the three important elements of a therapeutic relationship has been put forth by Truax and Carkhuff (1967). The concepts of nonpossessive warmth (showing the patient that you care without "suffocating" him or her), accurate empathy (conveying to the patient that you understand his or her feelings), and genuineness (conveying honesty to the patient and being able to admit your mistakes in an appropriate manner) are the foundation for the therapeutic relationship. When the therapist is able to incorporate these three elements into the relationship with the patient, a bond of trust is established and true therapy begins. Without the factors of caring, empathy, and honesty, the patient's symptoms may actually worsen (Traux & Carkhuff, 1967). When these three factors are present to a high degree, then the patient will show greater evidence of constructive personality change. It is essential for all therapists to develop and improve these positive attitudes.

THE TECHNIQUES OF EARLY INTERVENTION

All therapists involved in the treatment of alcoholics should be exposed to the techniques of early intervention, since a delay of treatment will frequently result in tragedy. In many cases, early intervention may save years of hardship for the family and friends, as well as for the patient. Early intervention with the alcoholic compresses the past crises caused by the misuse of alcohol into one dramatic confrontation, in order to brush aside the denial mechanism and get the patient to agree to seek help. It is a therapeutic maneuver designed to help the patient *now*, an alternative to waiting interminably for the alcoholic to "hit bottom," to lose or destroy his or her family, health, or job; if we wait, it may be too late. For example, it is not unusual in the field of alcoholism to treat a severe, chronic alcoholic successfully and then to see the patient develop cancer of the esophagus (the rate of this cancer is significantly increased with chronic heavy alcohol intake) or later to learn that the patient hemorrhaged to death from esophageal varices 6 to 12 months after he stopped drinking. The help, although successful, came too late. Some AA and Al-Anon members are reluctant to recommend intervention because they have the opinion that alcoholics should "hit bottom" and make the decision for themselves while the family attempts to stay detached. However, I believe that early intervention, when used with adequate preparation and sensitivity, may save the patient and the family many years of suffering and in some cases prevent the breakup of the marriage (Gallant et al., 1970).

There are a number of different intervention approaches (Gallant, 1982; Johnson, 1973). Each therapist modifies his or her technique according to the available human resources, treatment facilities, and attitudes about confrontation techniques. For example, in the Johnson Institute technique, the patient may be given a choice between hospitalization and temporary separation from the family or other important relationships. In our intervention approach at Tulane Medical School, the options are inpatient *or* outpatient therapy with disulfiram used as needed *or* temporary separation from the family. Offering several options is an attempt to influence the drinker to select a therapy without "backing the patient into a corner."

Adequate preparation, sensitivity, and experience are required for this therapeutic intervention. The following steps describe the approach that I have adopted. Usually, it is the alcoholic's spouse who calls saying that he or she is upset and feels hopeless because the drinker refuses to see the problem or the need for help. There is an initial interview with the spouse to identify the key people in the environment who have the most influence on the alcoholic. The therapist explains to the spouse that she or he is the patient because this spouse is the person who is seeking help, and thus the confidentiality of the alcoholic is not involved.

The next meeting includes the alcoholic's teenage or adult children and possibly one or two close friends whose attendence is requested in order to validate the spouse's history as well as to educate them about alcoholism. They are asked to assume a nonjudgmental attitude and make a list of three to five painful or embarrassing events associated with the *behavior* of the alcoholic while intoxicated; they are cautioned to avoid labels and name-calling in describing these upsetting situations. During this session, the three key attitudes are emphasized:

1. Always express genuine concern to the alcoholic.
2. Maintain a nonjudgmental attitude.
3. Be honest.

The spouse is told to inform the alcoholic about each meeting and to invite him or her to attend, since the specific goal of the intervention is to have the alcoholic come in to see the therapist for at least one visit. It is then the therapist's job to convince the alcoholic to begin treatment.

The spouse should also explain to the alcoholic that the children and friends were included at the request of the therapist, not through the spouse's choice, so that some of the anger will be directed toward the therapist. There is already more than enough anger in the household. Nothing is done behind the back of the alcoholic; this method is considered to be safer than a surprise confrontation and less likely to precipitate unexpected tragic events such as a sincere or manipulative suicide attempt.

Having prepared their lists of significant events, the members of the newly composed intervention team (spouse, children, friends) should rehearse part of the confrontation with the therapist in order to avoid disagreements during the actual confrontation and to eliminate any individuals who may tend to overprotect the alcoholic. This rehearsal is helpful in several ways: (1) identifying unexpected problems; (2) enhancing the ability to be concise and work together; (3) exploring resistance; and (4) increasing the confidence of the intervention team.

The time of the actual confrontation must be carefully planned to be sure that the drinker will be alcohol-free; a confrontation with an intoxicated person will be ineffective. This is the only session that is conducted without warning the alcoholic. Usually, I enlist the aid of another couple who has had a successful intervention and ask this couple join the intervention meeting. Their presence helps to defuse the situation by offering the person being confronted an opportunity to identify with someone else who has gone through the same painful process.

Finally, it should be emphasized that there must be a commitment by the entire intervention team, with the realization that there is a great deal at stake if the alcoholic refuses the treatment options of the intervention. It is unusual for the alcoholic to reject the confrontation and the treatment options, but the intervention team should be prepared for the worst. For example, after the lists describing the alcoholic's behavior are read, the spouse may have to end the discussion by saying, "If you do not follow up with (the therapist's name) at least once, then we will be separating until you do so." With the scales weighted so heavily, separation versus one visit to the therapist, it is easy to see why it would be unlikely for the person to refuse one session. Possibly, one of the reasons why this type of technique rarely fails is that the alcoholic has *not* been pushed into a corner without options. The threat of separation is quite severe compared to the alternative of seeing a therapist for one visit.

It is important that the intervention team realize that rash but empty threats will be useless in the intervention process. These threats only increase the patient's denial. Another reason for the success of this approach is that, before the massive intervention or confrontation, the alcoholic was able to keep his head in the ground like an ostrich; angry, individual accusations about the alcoholic's behavior only made him more defensive with his denial. Now, his head has suddenly been plucked out of the ground, and he is forced to look at the effects of his alcoholic behavior on the people whom he loves and on himself; thus, he has to abandon at least a small piece of his denial. Even if the alcoholic refuses to return to the therapist after the follow-up session, he or she still has been forced to look at his behavior, and the entire family problem can now be handled in a more realistic manner. Table 6.1 outlines the technique for intervention and confrontation of alcoholics.

Treatment contracts with the patient may also be a part of early intervention. Optional contracting may be utilized as one follow-up of the confrontation process. During the confrontation, the alcoholic can be offered the choice of a visit with the therapist for an initial interview, commitment to ongoing outpatient treatment, or referral to an inpatient service. In the great majority of the cases, the patient will select the choice of seeing the therapist for one visit. During the initial visit, contracting on disulfiram (Antabuse)

TABLE 6.1
Outline of Technique for Intervention and Confrontation of Alcohol Abusers

The concept behind the intervention technique is that substance habituation is usually a progressive illness and very rarely goes into remission without outside help. The following technique is only one of several approaches.

1. THREE KEY ATTITUDES FOR INTERVENTION
    a. Express genuine concern.
    b. Maintain a nonjudgmental approach.
    c. Be honest.

2. GOALS OF AN INTERVENTION
The goal of the intervention is to bring the substance-abusing person into treatment by using a dramatic confrontation to help penetrate his or her denial mechanisms.

3. THE TEAM APPROACH
In most cases, the family and/or friends have previously tried unsuccessfully to get the substance abuser to cut down or stop chemical use; usually these attempts have failed because:
    a. The approach was made in a inflammatory and accusatory fashion that placed the chemically dependent person on the defensive and only increased the denial mechanisms.
    b. These concerned persons were uninformed about the diagnosis and proper treatment of chemical dependency.
    c. Each attempt was made at a different time. Consequently, the chemically dependent person was able to use his denial mechanism in an effective manner. Also, at times an available "enabler" may have helped him to further resist help (e.g., after his wife threw him out of the house, his mother took him in). This type of person is called an "enabler" because such relatives or friends enable the chemically dependent person to continue the pattern of abuse; without the enabler, the substance abuser may be forced to stop.

4. TECHNIQUES
    a. A concerned person seeks help for a problem related to the chemical dependency of the person he or she cares about. (The concerned person is usually a spouse but may be a child, employer, or friend.) Keep the process in the open and have the spouse inform the substance abuser about the meetings. Be sure the substance abuser is informed that the therapist (not the concerned person) has invited the participants. This procedure describes the reality of the situation and directs the anger away from the concerned person.
    b. This person is enlisted to gather other significant persons into a meeting about the intervention process. This group will be organized into an intervention team.
    c. Team members are educated about the chemical dependency, the treatment, and the intervention process. This includes discussion of the denial or sincere self-deception of the substance abuser, symptoms of the illness, prognosis, and so on.
    d. Each team member is asked to make a list of three to five significant events in the relationship in which he or she was hurt in some way by the chemically dependent person. The lists should be specific as to time, place, and circumstances,

(continued)

TABLE 6.1
Continued

and nonjudgmental, avoiding labels and sticking to detailed descriptions of and reactions to the behavior.

e. Each event should be presented in a way that emphasizes the connection between the use of chemicals and the event (e.g., "You came late to my school play. You were drinking and made a scene in the audience. The principal finally asked you to leave. I was *so* embarrassed, Dad.") Note that the statement should include the team member's feelings: "I felt helpless, scared, frustrated, angry," etc.

f. All team members are cautioned to temporarily suspend past quarrels among themselves for the benefit of the team effort. It is important to present a united front with a consistent message: "We are concerned about your drinking (or drug-taking) and its effects on your behavior. We can no longer stand helplessly in the wings while you destroy yourself and us. You need treatment."

g. A chairperson is selected to serve as coordinator, keeping the team together and on target. This person may be a professional in the field of alcoholism, a physician, or one of the interveners (i.e., spouse, brother, or neighbor).

h. If some members of the team feel unable to carry through with their roles, they are encouraged to share that feeling and exclude themselves from the intervention. They may plan with the team how they will be involved in the future.

i. *Treatment options* are discussed, selected, and arranged prior to the intervention.

5. COMMITMENT OF THE TEAM

a. If the chemically dependent person rejects the intervention team (this is rare), the team must be ready to assert itself by honestly stating what is at stake if there is no treatment.

b. Each team member must have thought out what he or she is prepared to do if the person refuses to see the therapist. The power of this strategy is consolidating all of the consequences into a single time frame and making it very clear that the only remedy is treatment as defined by the team (e.g., "If you refuse to see Dr. _____, you can't come home.").

c. Each team member must be ready to present the ultimatum in a clear and unyielding fashion. If a team member falters on the commitment, the team must rally to hold that member to the commitment. Because of this possibility, it is very important that step b is carefully thought out and understood by all team members. Rash but empty threats will be of no use in the intervention process. These threats only increase the denial mechanism.

6. REHEARSAL

Having reviewed the above material and prepared their lists of "significant events," the team stages a practice session of the intervention. This is helpful in:

a. Identifying unexpected problems.

b. Enhancing ability to be concise and work together.

c. Exploring resistance.

d. Increasing the confidence of the treatment team.

In summary, the intervention technique attempts to telescope or compress the events associated with substance abuse into an early therapeutic confrontation in order to precipitate a crisis in the present rather than waiting for years of suffering to take place and risking the future loss of family, job, or other important life factors.

can be used, with the alcoholic patient's agreeing to take the medication if he or she drinks again. If the patient is a multiple drug abuser as well as an alcoholic, the patient and therapist can make a contract specifying that the patient will enter an inpatient service for detoxification if tests reveal a "dirty urine." Contracting should always offer the patient a choice of treatment modalities, each one leading to a more controlled treatment setting if the patient fails in the initial treatment arrangement. In this manner the patient is not backed into a corner with no way out except angry denial. It should be stressed that it is highly unusual for the patient to reject the intervention confrontation totally (unless there are no team members to participate except the spouse), and very rarely does the alcoholic refuse the contracting options under these circumstances (Johnson, 1973).

FOUR CASE HISTORIES OF INTERVENTION

MR A.: A TYPICAL INTERVENTION

The caller, Mrs. A., was a 40-year-old woman who was married to a successful 44-year-old maritime executive. His drinking behavior had progressed to the point that he was almost totally intoxicated by the time he reached home at the end of the day. Their 14-year-old son had been doing well at school and on the football team, but six months before Mrs. A.'s phone call his grades had dropped significantly and he had quit the football team. Recently, he had started staying out late at night and hardly talked to either of his parents. The second child was an 11-year-old daughter who apparently was depressed and spent most of her time sulking around the house. She was described as negative and rebellious. It had become increasingly difficult for her mother to control the girl's behavior, especially when she returned home after having been with her friends. The initial appointment was scheduled with Mrs. A.

During our first meeting, she told me that the early years of their marriage had been quite good. However, Mr. A.'s drinking was now seriously interfering with their relationship. She said that her husband apparently did most of his drinking while at work. During lunch and toward the end of the day he increased his intake of vodka. At the end of the day, he often invited some of the men who worked for him to a local bar, where he continued to drink until he reached a state of severe intoxication. He had developed a habit of then stopping off at the homes of one or two of his best friends in an attempt to sober up before going home. He drank very little at his friends' homes but was still not able to reach a sober state by the time he arrived at his house. There would be very little conversation on arrival; Mr. A. would quickly undress, eat a little, and then retire to the bedroom and go to sleep. He was described as not being physically or verbally abusive, but the relationship between him and his family was practically nonexistent. Occasionally, he would become quite abrupt and irritated if any of his children's friends were visiting or if they were playing records or engaged in other adolescent activities. I suggested to Mrs. A. that we have the two children join us for the next session.

During the second session, the children validated Mrs. A.'s history and related several embarrassing situations that had occurred as a result of their father's drinking. One typical incident was described by the daughter. The graduation of her piano class was taking place in a local auditorium where a bar had been set up in the back of the room. Her father had been steadily drinking at the bar while the ceremony proceeded, and by the end of the graduation exercise he was totally intoxicated. When his daughter tried to introduce some of her friends to him, he made some obscene remarks which she found impossible to forget. She was still intensely embarrassed as she related this episode, which had occurred more then six months earlier. On the day following the graduation, when she confronted her father at home, he could not remember the event. I explained to the family that he had an alcoholic blackout during that period.

The son discussed his discouragement about the family situation. He talked about his father's never attending any of the football games and never giving him approval for his performance in school or on the football field. He was embarrassed that his father was one of the few fathers who never attended any football games; the boy never knew how to explain this situation to his friends. He said that the only time he saw his father was shortly after his arrival home from work and in the morning just before he left for school.

After this session it was decided to have the next meeting with Mr. A.'s two best friends, the two children, and their mother in order to identify key members for an intervention team. Before each of these sessions, Mr. A. had been notified about the meetings by his wife and told that he was welcome to attend if he agreed to treatment. It was made clear to him that treatment would consist of either inpatient therapy for four to six weeks or outpatient therapy with the use of disulfiram and regular attendance at married couples therapy.

Each time Mr. A. was notified about the meetings, and invited to come, he became very angry and said, "What business does this shrink have butting into our family affairs?" Mrs. A. replied that *she* was the patient and the psychiatrist's evaluation had shown that her husband's drinking was affecting her emotional state — that was the reason for the invitation to attend the meetings. Mr. A. showed his usual response after this angry episode by never mentioning it until the next meeting. His denial was intensified during subsequent weeks, but he also decreased his drinking for several days after each invitation to therapy. This is not an unusual sequence of events during preparation for the confrontation. The alcoholic develops the fantasy that if he or she will only cut down on drinking, the spouse will stop seeing the therapist and things can then go back to "normal."

During the third meeting, Mrs. A., the two children and Mr. A.'s two close friends were all present; we reviewed the drinking history. The two friends were surprised to learn that Mr. A. was drinking so much. However, consensual validation by the children convinced them. Then they started to recall some of the occasions when their friend had arrived at their homes slightly intoxicated; they remembered wondering why he was drinking so early in the day. During this meeting, Mrs. A. stated that she was ready to leave her husband unless he did something about his drinking problem. The children supported her statement and everyone present agreed to have a confrontation with Mr. A. We then arranged a fourth meeting with the group to prepare the list of embarrassing events that were associated with his alcoholism and to rehearse the intervention.

At the fourth meeting, I emphasized that the confrontation should consist of the attitudes of caring, nonjudgmental statements, and honesty. Each person was asked to list the episodes that had made him or her angry, embarrassed, or anxious. Since no evidence of severe depression or suicidal intent on the part of Mr. A. could be detected from the history obtained from his wife, the children, or friends, it was decided to allow Mrs. A. to arrange the confrontation on a Saturday morning at home shortly after her husband awakened. I was available by telephone in case the intervention caused unexpected reactions.

The meeting, which took place at the alcoholic's home on Saturday morning at about 8:00 a.m., was successful. The participants read their lists to avoid any angry "eye-balling." We find this technique much more comfortable for all the parties involved. Our goal is to get the alcoholic to come in for help, not to make him angry. He agreed to come in to see me, as long as his friends would no longer be involved. We arranged the meeting with Mr. A., his wife, their two children, and a couple who had successfully completed therapy in our program. I used this couple as a auxiliary therapeutic team in order to draw some of Mr. A.'s anger away from me.

During the session, I presented further educational material to Mr. A., his wife, and their children. We reviewed the genetics of alcoholism (the paternal predisposition was quite strong in his family) and discussed the meaning of the alcohol blackouts and the loss of control of drinking. The auxiliary couple, Mr. and Mrs. R., subsequently did most of the interviewing, with Mr. R. trying to get this new alcoholic patient to identify with him. Mr. R. explained that he had gone through the same type of denial and had felt furious when people asked him to seek help; he was able to present the denial process as a normal accompaniment of alcoholism. In this manner, we attempted to diffuse the anger that Mr. A. brought into therapy following the intervention.

Mr. A. was then given the choice of entering our inpatient service for four to six weeks, or entering our outpatient married couples group therapy while taking disulfiram daily at breakfast with his children and Mrs. A. present, or facing a separation from his wife and children. He chose married couples group therapy and disulfiram treatment on an outpatient basis and attended regularly for the next 12 months. At that time, he requested that the disulfiram be discontinued and ask to be terminated from group therapy, since he believed that he had made sufficient progress. During that year, his son had returned to the football team and was performing well in school; his daughter had blossomed and was relating in a very comfortable way.

The members of the group were asked to give their opinions as to whether or not they thought he was ready for discharge, and they were almost unanimous in saying that he had shown significant progress in therapy. He was now relating more openly and directly with his daughter and son, was more involved in their school and extracurricular activities, and was confiding in a more intimate way with his wife. Mrs. A. confirmed that their marriage had improved in many ways. The patient was then told that he was discharged. Both Mr. A. and his wife were also told that if there were any sign of tendency toward relapse in either behavior or alcohol intake, they should immediately call me and arrange a follow-up meeting. At this time, the alcoholic patient, his wife, and children are still doing quite well.

MR. W.: AGE IS NO BARRIER

Age is never a barrier to treatment for alcoholism. For example, a 50-year-old man called to say that he wanted to come for an interview concerning his father, a 74-year-old who had been quite successful in business, social activities, and community affairs. When I met with the son, he told me that his father, Mr. W., had been a controlled social drinker for many years until his wife had died four years earlier. The marriage had been a very happy one and had lasted for 47 years. The two sons were grown, had moved out of the house, married, and made successful careers for themselves. Mr. W., a wealthy man from a socially prominent family, had never planned adequately for his retirement or for the environmental change that occurred after his wife died. Since her death, his alcohol intake had steadily increased, to the point that he was intoxicated on a daily basis and was sometimes found drunk on the floor of his home when the children visited. They had hired a housekeeper to take care of the home and keep a careful eye on their father.

However, she was unable to control his drinking, since Mr. W. was quite skillful at hiding his liquor.

Since Mr. W.'s retirement from his job and from his involvement in community affairs, his children had noted that his episodes of depression had increased in association with his increased alcohol intake. Both sons realized that their father was still mentally competent when sober, but his drinking behavior was starting to result in erratic financial decisions involving a great deal of money. He also was starting to display some inappropriate behavior with the housekeeper, who was threatening to quit. During one of his drinking episodes at home, he fired the maid who had been working for him for the past 20 years, after arguing with her over whether or not she had taken several tomatoes from the refrigerator. This type of behavior was very different from his conduct prior to his wife's death and his increased alcohol intake. Mr. W.'s drinking was now becoming an embarrassment to the entire family.

At a second session, I met with Mr. W.'s two sons and their wives. The first part of the meeting was devoted to education on alcoholism, including the subject of denial, alcohol blackouts (the incidents with the housekeeper and maid had apparently occurred during alcohol blackouts), psychologic consequences of prolonged alcohol intake on elderly people, and possible hereditary aspects of the problem, since Mr. W.'s brother and father had also had drinking problems. It was suggested that each of the participants draw up a list of embarrassing or painful events associated with Mr. W's drinking episodes. The sons were then instructed to visit their father, tell him about this meeting and ask him if he wanted to attend the next meeting. As expected, he became extremely angry at his sons, accusing them of wanting to take over the remainder of his estate, and absolutely refused to come in and see me.

We invited Mr. W.'s three grown grandchildren to come to the third meeting, along with his sons and their wives. As the lists of drinking episodes were reviewed, it became apparent that Mr. W. had had a number of blackouts prior to his wife's death; some of these blackouts had occurred while he was driving a car and had endangered his life. At one time, he had driven a car during an alcohol blackout and could not remember where he had parked it. Another time, he had been picked up by the police for driving while intoxicated (DWI), but this charge was dropped because of his connections with prominent people in the community. Obviously, Mr. W. had been using a number of people as "enablers" to allow him to continue his heavy social drinking until he finally lost control.

From the history given by the family, it appeared that this 74-year-old man was depressed. Because I was concerned about an exacerbation of this depression during the intervention and even about the possibility of a suicide attempt, I thought it advisable to have the intervention in my office. In such cases of potential suicide, total honesty is not used with the alcoholic patient. His children told him that they wanted him to come to the medical center to see a physician for an evaluation of his high blood pressure. There was some truth behind this deception, since the patient did have high blood pressure that was probably secondary to his excessive alcohol intake. Moreover, it was our opinion that he never would have attended the intervention session if he had been told the reason for the meeting.

Mr. W. was quite surprised to see his children and grandchildren in my office at the medical school, and the intervention meeting began with a great deal of anger on his part. I took full blame for arranging the session and said that his son had come to me because he was very upset and disturbed about his relationship with Mr. W., which had been such a good one for so many years before his increased drinking. I told the patient that his children never suspected that I was going to arrange for all of them to come in for this type of intervention meeting at the time that his son first contacted me. The children and the grandchildren were very supportive and reviewed their lists of his drinking behavior in a very soft, caring manner.

This intervention session was more upsetting and initally more charged with anger than that with Mr. A. This elderly alcoholic, who had been so successful in all areas of his life, became very angry and defensive. Finally, after about a hour, he began to listen to his children and his grandchildren. In fact, he grandchildren seemed to have more impact on him with their lists of his embarrassing drinking behavior than his sons or their wives. All of them, one by one, told Mr. W. that they were going to cut off all communication with him unless he agreed to start treatment with me at that time. By the end of session, the most uncomfortable feeling that the patient expressed was severe embarrassment associated with his need for appearance and false pride. The depression apparently was secondary to the excessive alcohol intake and not a primary one; no suicidal intent could be detected. It was decided that Mr. W. would be followed in outpatient treatment, with the housekeeper administering the disulfiram on a daily basis. He readily agreed to this compromise, saying that he could never picture himself going to an "alcoholic institution." He also agreed to participate in group therapy on a regular basis and to become involved with a charitable institution that devotes its resources to educating Down's syndrome children.

In addition to this treatment regimen, family sessions with the patient, his sons, the daughters-in-law, and three grandchildren were conducted on a monthly basis for several months. The main reason for these sessions was to give the patient a pat on the back for having the courage to look at his drinking problem and to give up some of his fellow social drinkers, many of whom were hidden alcoholics. He substituted volunteer work with children who have Down's Syndrome for his social club luncheons. Later on, the patient started going out with a woman who was close to his age. At present, Mr. W. is seen every three months for a physical examination and evaluation of his Antabuse medication. In this particular case, the intervention method in an elderly man not only altered the patient's drinking habit but turned him on the road to positive behavior changes without the need for long-term follow-up psychotherapy.

MR. Y.: AN UNEXPECTED OUTCOME

A young married woman, Mrs. Y., called to say that her husband was starting to become physically abusive when he drank. During our first session, she appeared to be very anxious, tense, and shaky. Her voice was low and quivered as she related the history. She obviously was both anxious and depressed, as she had been for the last two years, resulting from her husband's excessive drinking. They had been married five years and had two children, ages one and three years.

This couple had gone steady in college for about two years, and Mrs. Y. had been aware of his occasional excessive drinking then. He had been a member of the football team and played defensive end. Mrs. Y., a tall young woman, was immediately attracted to this handsome, 6' 6", 240-pound defensive end who was the star of the football team. During football season, he was able to control his drinking fairly well and only occasionally became intoxicated on weekends after a game. During the spring semesters of college, his drinking increased and he had some occasional blackouts. During one episode, he pushed her around after she complained about his drinking. The next day he was so guilty and ashamed of his behavior that he not only apologized but remained alcohol-free until graduation the following year, when they married and he entered law school. Despite his heavy drinking, Mr. Y. graduated law school with top honors and obtained a job with a prestigious law firm.

During the first year of their marriage, Mr. Y. decreased his drinking considerably. At the end of the first year, because of his outstanding performance, he was given an unexpected promotion, which involved numerous lunch meetings with various prominent people in the city. According to his wife, his background had not prepared him for frequent social encounters with people of "high social standing." He found himself drinking two or three martinis during the lunches to feel more comfortable. His drinking increased during that year, and on occasion he came home intoxicated after having had a few drinks with some of his friends from the law firm at a bar near his office. After the birth of each of their children, his drinking decreased for two or three months and then once again increased.

During the year prior to my appointment with his wife, he had developed a daily drinking pattern of several martinis at lunch, several drinks after working hours, and several drinks at home at night. He spent less and less time with his wife and children, rarely having dinner with them in the evenings. After having a few drinks at home, he would lie down on the couch and watch T.V., go to a bar down the street for an hour or two, or go to sleep. One of his close friends had called Mrs. Y. and told her that he was worried about Mr. Y.'s drinking. He said that Mr. Y. had appeared in court twice while slightly intoxicated; on one occasion the judge had made a remark to Mr. Y. about his behavior.

I then asked his wife to invite Mr. Y.'s two closest friends to come in for our next appointment, since the children were much too young to participate in any type of intervention. She said that she was committed to leaving her husband if he did not stop drinking because the situation was becoming intolerable. I asked Mrs. Y. to tell her husband that we had had a discussion about the situation and to tell him that she was my patient because she was so nervous and concerned. She was asked to tell him that he was discussed in our conversation because of his effects on her emotional state. I also told her to request that he come to our next family meeting if he would agree to treatment, either as an outpatient or as an inpatient.

When Mrs. Y. told Mr. Y. that his two closest friends had been invited to the next session in order to offer some additional comments about the situation and to see if they validated her history he said, "Tell that shrink he has no business with my friends," but, as expected in these types of confrontations, he started to decrease his drinking. However, he did not mention anything about future meetings. It was as if he had stuck his head in the ground, surrounding himself with his denial mechanism.

During the second session, the two friends validated Mrs. Y.'s history and added some additional information about Mr. Y.'s drinking pattern at the law office and in the courtroom. They had been very much aware of his progressive deterioration during the two previous years. They had been friends with him in college and in law school and said they would do anything at all to help him. During this meeting, I educated the wife and the friends about the problem of alcoholism and the denial mechanism and reviewed the intervention techniques, including mention of the dangers of intruding on an individual's private life. I explained to the friends that Mrs. Y. was my patient and her husband's drinking was having a devastating effect on her. That was the reason for the intervention. We reviewed the goals of therapy and may plan to offer Mr. Y. the option of choosing outpatient or inpatient therapy. I explained that Mrs. Y.'s confrontations with her husband had failed in the past because the denial mechanism frequently strengthens when one person confronts the alcoholic; it is easy to defend against any one individual.

We reviewed the attitudes of being nonjudgmental, honest, and direct. I explained the necessity of their sticking with their commitment to cut off their communications and relationship with Mr. Y. or, in the case of his wife and children, to separate from him if he refused to go into treatment at that time. This separation would not be a permanent one; Mr. Y. could end it by seeking help for his drinking problem. I then asked each of them to make up a list of times Mr. Y.'s drinking behavior had made them angry, concerned, anxious, or embarrassed. I stressed that we were not judging him as a person but only evaluating the effects of his drinking behavior upon his wife, the children, and his close friends. We then scheduled a third session.

During the third session we reviewed the lists of behavior and rehearsed the final confrontation scene. Since it did not appear that Mr. Y. was depressed or suicidal, and since Mrs. Y. was extremely competent, I decided to have her conduct the intervention meeting with the two friends and her husband on a Saturday morning as soon as he awakened. I would be available by telephone during the intervention.

The following Saturday morning, he intervention was conducted with his wife and two friends sitting at Mr. Y.'s bedside. Avoiding eye contact in order to decrease any type of angry, "eye-balling" confrontation, they read their lists of drinking behavior to Mr. Y. and let him know that, even though they cared for him and loved him very much, they would have no further relationships with him until he sought help with me. He was extremely angry and at first told his wife that they could all leave. However, on second thought, he said that he would come in to see me with his wife, as long as the two friends did not attend that particular meeting. When his wife telephoned me and told me about Mr. Y's angry reaction, I decided to have one of my very competent, female medical students sit in with me for the meeting with Mr. Y., in order to diffuse some of his anger.

During the meeting with Mr. and Mrs. Y., it was quite apparent that he was extremely angry. He presented a very intimidating picture—his forbidding size and dark, staring eyes were quite frightening. For the first 45 minutes, I reviewed the lists of his drinking behavior that had been covered at the intervention, explained the problem of alcoholism, reviewed the problem of the denial mechanism, and then asked him about his decision concerning treatment.

Mr. Y. looked at me, his dark, angry eyes so intense that his wife burst out sobbing, which affected my medical student so much that she too began to cry. It was an emotionally draining experience for all of us and a frightening one for me. I had the feeling that Mr. Y. might pick me up and throw me out the window. He said, "I will stop drinking. However, I never want to see your face again. I do not like the way you entered my life, and I want you to exit from it right now. If I do drink, I will seek psychiatric help, but not from a psychiatrist that you refer to my wife." At that moment, he stood up, took his wife's hand and left the office. I was somewhat shocked but also relieved that no physical violence had occured. In thinking it over, I realized that I had made a mistake by not having an auxiliary couple present at the meeting to diffuse the anger further. I am sure that the student, a practicing physician today, still remembers the tension and fear of that meeting several years ago. As for me, I am sure I will never forget it!

One year later, Mrs. Y. called and told me that her husband was still abstinent and that their marriage had improved considerably. Mr. Y. was communicating more with her and spending more time with the children. His law practice had grown and prospered. Not only had he never resumed his drinking, but he had never gone to any therapist for help. She said, "All the marbles are falling in place, and I couldn't be happier." A subsequent three-year follow-up revealed that Mr. Y. never again mentioned my name, and Mrs. Y. never thought it would be appropriate to bring my name into their conversation. Intervention meetings can sometimes take unexpected turns and, apparently, in some cases follow-up therapy is not required.

MR. G.: AN INCOMPLETE INTERVENTION

The last case is an example of an intervention attempt which was never completed for the alcoholic but nonetheless benefited the family. The wife of the alcoholic, Mrs. G., called me for an appointment, saying that her husband was "killing himself with his drinking." During our first interview, she told me that her husband, a 60-year-old banker, had taken an early retirement at the age of 55. Prior to that time, he already had developed a moderate drinking problem, which was interfering with their communication and his relationship with their grown children. However, Mr. G. had been able to abstain for prolonged periods of time, making their existence together bearable for his wife.

Since his retirement three years before, Mr. G. spent most of his days drinking and watching television. He hardly communicated with any of the children when they visited. His high blood pressure had become more severe, but his family physician was unable to control the drinking or the blood pressure. Mrs. G. had modified her life-style by participating in many community organizations and emotionally distancing herself from the husband. They had had no sexual relations during the past five years because Mr. G. was either partially impotent or seriously hampered his sexual efforts by his drinking.

The history revealed that he had always been somewhat cold in his relationships with the children and his wife; he had always had a great deal of difficulty in saying the words, "I love you," and very rarely held or hugged the children, even when they were small. However, he was always available for advice on financial matters and always willing to give the children a helping hand when they asked him.

I asked Mrs. G. to tell her husband that we had met and that I had requested that their three grown daughters, Marge, June, and Sarah, and their son, John, come with their mother to the second session. She was also told to explain to her husband that he was welcome to come to this meeting, but only if he was willing to agree to treatment, either as an outpatient with Antabuse or as an inpatient. Of course, he became irritated and angry at his wife but quickly went back to watching television and sipping his cognac.

During the second session, the children validated much of Mrs. G.'s information. All of them agreed that their father had been a rather cold, detached individual, but they knew that, down deep inside, he truly loved them. They felt that he had always stood behind them in their various endeavors in school and in their professional lives. Mrs. G. said that she really did not know if her husband loved her anymore, and she was unsure about her feelings for him. During the session, I gave them information about the problem of alcoholism, explained the denial mechanism, and detailed the intervention technique. I told them that all of them would have to make a commitment to sever all communication and relationships with Mr. G. at the time of the intervention if he refused to come in for treatment. I said that they would have to continue this separation until he decided to obtain help for himself.

At this point, the children unanimously agreed that their father would probably never stop drinking. Mrs. G. said that she thought that the children were probably correct. She added that she was accustomed to their rather expensive style of living and, after a marriage of 36 years, it was probably too late for her to make a separate life of her own. She said that her home was the center of many of her social activities with her friends and that her husband would usually retreat to the bedroom to continue his cognac sipping when social club functions were conducted at their home. She did not want to give up the home or the social relationships, which had originally been fostered by her husband's social and financial standing in the community. At 59 years old, she felt that she would rather live with this present situation than face a new life by herself.

I could not dispute Mrs. G.'s decision and was pessimistic about the outcome. I said that, since the family was not ready for an intervention, perhaps it would be best to bring a halt to our meetings. However, at this time Marge, the oldest daughter, said, "I still believe we should give it a try. At least we'll know that we gave it a shot even though we will probably fail." The youngest daughter, Sarah, suggested, "Why don't we have a 'love-in' and at least tell Dad about our feelings in a group?" They asked if I would meet with them for one or two more sessions in order to rehearse the "love-in" and give them some confidence about expressing their feelings in a comfortable manner. They also wanted to be sure that no unexpected problems would arise. I agreed to help them with such a meeting.

During our third session, we went over a list of various types of embarrassing, angry, or anxiety-provoking behavior that each of the children and Mrs. G. had endured at one time or another. The family members all agreed that they truly believed that Mr. G. had taken an early retirement in order to allow himself more time to drink. They added some further details which made me believe that Mr. G. probably had been mildly chronically depressed most of his life. He had grown up with high family expectations and was firmly guided into the banking business by his father, who had majority ownership of the bank. Mr. G. had never been able to "do his own thing" and had assumed various types of community leadership roles because it was "expected of him." His wife and children believed that he was sick and tired of living a life he had never intended to live and that the alcohol was the only thing he enjoyed. They said that both of his parents had been strong-willed people who had bottled up their feelings, just as Mr. G. later did with his own children.

Mr. G.'s children knew that he loved them even though he was unable to express this love. They wanted a meeting with him so that they could share their feelings of concern and love within a group and could feel that they had done the right thing. Mrs. G. agreed to go along with it, as long as they did not have to threaten him with separation or make a commitment to cut off communication.

During our fourth session, we rehearsed the list of drinking behavior and how they would share their feelings of love and concern through the statements that each of the children and their mother would make to Mr. G. It was agreed that this confrontation (a real intervention never took place) would be scheduled on a Saturday morning shortly after their father awakened, before he reached the cognac bottle. I was not present at the meeting.

The day after the confrontation, Marge telephoned me and told me what had taken place. Each of them had been sitting around his bedside when he awakened that Saturday morning. They asked him to listen while they read their lists of drinking behavior which had irritated them or made them feel anxious or embarrassed in front of other people. They asked him to do something about his drinking problem and come to see me for help. He refused. Then they told him how much they truly loved him even though there was nothing they could do about his drinking problem. At this point, Mr. G. was truly touched; for the first time in many years, in fact since his mother's death, he cried. He told them that he cared for them but that he was not going to stop drinking. The four children and Mrs. G. reiterated their feelings of affection for him. They told him that they realized that he had always had trouble showing his feelings, but they knew that, "Down deep, you always loved us but just had trouble showing it. We always knew you were there when we needed you, despite your drinking."

Marge said that they all felt much better after the meeting. Even though her father still refused to get help for his drinking problem, at least she felt that she had really tried the right way, and the meeting had touched her in a very deep sense. Within the next week I received a letter from each of the other children telling me that they truly appreciated the time that we had devoted to the meetings and that they all had become much closer as a family and still had some warm feelings about the meeting which had taken place that Saturday morning. Two weeks after the confrontation, I received a letter from Mrs. G. saying that she truly believed that her husband had given up on life and had made his decision to "drink it away" before his retirement. "However," her letter said, "I do want to thank you for helping my family come together in a meaningful way. I feel closer to my children then ever before and I believe that when my husband finally succumbs to his alcohol problem, there will be no unrealistic guilt suffered by either my children or myself. It was our first truly warm family encounter, and I thank you for giving us that opportunity."

The direction that these planned interventions take is unpredictable. The technique has to be modified for each family and each patient. When conducted properly, it can bring benefits to the family members and friends even when the intervention attempt fails with the alcoholic. I am always fascinated, surprised, and emotionally rewarded whenever I become involved in this type of therapeutic endeavor.

A MODIFICATION OF THE INTERVENTION WITH ADOLESCENTS

As extensive studies of alcohol and drug use in adolescents have shown, there is a progression of drug use among adolescents, beginning with legal drugs, such as alcohol and cigarettes, leading to marijuana and then progressing to "more illegal" drugs such as LSD and heroin (Kandel, 1975; Yamaguchi & Kandel, 1984). Adolescent moderate to heavy drinkers are more likely than others to have access to marijuana, and moderate to heavy "pot" smokers have more contacts with the "more illegal" drug users and peddlers. Therefore, when attempting to treat the adolescent alcohol abuser or alcoholic, the therapist is more likely to see a polydrug abuse problem than in the middle-aged alcoholic patient.

Multiple factors are involved in the excessive use of alcohol and other drugs in adolescents: depressive symtomatology, parental use of legal and illegal drugs, underlying resentment or rebellious behavior relating to family problems, and impulsivity associated with adolescent development. The effect of peer impact on this group is immense, far more powerful then the influence of the therapist, the school, or, at times, the home environment. Therefore, it is essential to have one or two reliable, relatively "clean" peers of the young substance abuser available for the intervention. It is also important to attempt to find one or two healthy young adult models with whom the adolescent alcohol-drug abuser has a positive identification; these individuals may have a greater influence over the adolescent alcohol abuser then the family. It is also essential for these adolescents to change their peer groups after the intervention treatment has been initiated. It is almost impossible for them to stay free of drugs or alcohol if they continue to associate with their alcohol-drinking or drug-taking peers, who will have a greater influence on them than the therapist, no matter how experienced the therapist may be.

Helping the youth in treatment to find and assimilate into new peer groups is one of the most important elements of therapy with the adolescent alcohol or mixed alcohol-polydrug abuser. The initial steps in treating adolescents are to have the patients inform all of their peers as well as close relatives that they are now receiving treatment for alcohol and/or drug problems; then they must stop associating with anyone who continues to take drugs or drink excessively in front of them. It is explained to adolescent patients that anyone who continues to take drugs or drink excessively in front of them, after they have been told that the patient is seeking treatment for an alcohol and/or drug abuse problem, is inconsiderate, thoughtless, and not a real friend. The term that we use for such individuals is "creep."

OTHER INTERVENTION TECHNIQUES

In screening and intervention programs in Malmo, Sweden, the goal has been to identify heavy drinkers among healthy, middle-aged men and to intervene in their drinking habits (Kristenson et al., 1983). Since 75% of males with serum gamma-glutamyltransferase (GGT) values in the top 10% of the GGT distribution can be classified as moderate to heavy drinkers, the researchers decided that it would be feasible to use this test to influence the drinking habits of a population. In this study, all male Malmo residents in the years 1926–1933 (11,643) were invited to a planned screening program; 8,859 of these men attended the screening. The goals of this study were to attack the major middle-aged health risks related to cardiovascular disease, diabetes, and heavy drinking. All men in the top 10% of the GGT distribution were invited back for repeated analyses within three weeks. The second test was scheduled in order to validate the elevated GGT values in the population selected. A general physical exam and liver tests were performed, and the history was obtained during an interview designed to elicit detailed drinking history. Heavy drinking (more than 40 grams of alcohol per day) was acknowledged by 54% of the high GGT group and moderate drinking (20 to 40 grams per day) by another 22%. Hazardous drinking levels were concluded to be present in 76% of the intervention group, and symptoms of alcohol dependence or tolerance were found in 59% of the group considered to be heavy drinkers.

All patients were offered continuing follow-up consultations with the same physician every third month, monthly GGT tests, reinforcing contacts with the same nurse with the goal of reducing the GGT. Counseling was focused mainly on living habits. A treatment goal of moderate drinking rather than abstinence was agreed upon. Moderate drinking was tolerated as long as GGT values did not rise. The subjects were carefully informed about GGT levels at every visit and stimulated to attain normal levels. Subjects in the control group with two consecutive high GGT values were informed by letter that their tests had revealed an impaired liver, and they were told to live as usual but to restrict their alcohol beverages. They were also informed that they would be invited for subsequent liver tests after two years.

Although the GGT values in both groups were significantly decreased at the two- and four-year follow-up, the intervention group showed significantly greater improvement than the control group in the following areas: 80% fewer days sick or absent from work; 60% fewer hospitalization days; and 50% lower mortality rate. Thus, this simple biochemical intervention program with positive feedback for reducing the GGT was effective in preventing severe medical and social consequences of heavy drinking. The majority of the men consciously reduced their consumption in order to attain a lower GGT level. The surprising finding was that, although the men did not stop drinking, the counselors' prolonged individual interest and support were sufficient to maintain health and social adjustment in the majority of the cases.

Such types of biochemical intervention can be used in screening programs for large corporations, athletic teams, university faculty and students, etc. This type of biochemical intervention can be accomplished with complete confidentiality and without invasion of privacy. It may also be possible in some situations, if this type of biochemical biofeedback fails, that a therapeutic intervention, as described earlier in this chapter, can be attempted.

Use of driving records of persons convicted of driving while intoxicated (DWI) can provide another type of intervention approach. Some studies of DWI records have shown that the average time interval between conviction of driving under the influence of alcohol decreases with each subsequent arrest and conviction (Maisto et al., 1979). In this group of subjects with repeated DWI convictions, we see a marked increase in alcohol abuse and a significant deterioration in driving habits. The initial DWI conviction with a recommendation by the court for treatment and/or education on alcohol abuse and alcoholism can provide an opportunity for a therapeutic intervention with family and friends. If the courts utilize their discretion in the sentencing of these offenders, the recommended sentence can mandate the involvement of the family as part of the follow-up treatment. With this judicial backing, it is then possible for alcohol counselors to initiate intervention meetings with the families and friends as described in the earlier section of this chapter.

It is my opinion that intervention techniques are not being fully explored at the present time; within the community, we have many opportunities to attack the problem of alcoholism during its early phases. Education of school faculties about the availability of this technique for adolescent alcohol abusers may result in early interruption of drinking problems. The use of intervention techniques by private industry as well as by the legal and public school systems could result in saving substantial numbers from needless pain and suffering. However, it should be emphasized that this technique requires trained professional personnel and the consent of key family members.

REFERENCES

Berglund, M. (1984). Suicide in alcoholism. *Archives of General Psychiatry, 41*, 888–891.

Carlen, P. L., Penn, R. D., Fornazzari, L., Bennett, R. N., Wilkinson, D., & Wortzman, G. (1986). Computerized tomographic scan assessment of alcoholic brain damage and its potential reversibility. *Alcoholism: Clinical and Experimental Research, 10*, 226–232.

Gallant, D. M. (1982). *Alcohol and drug abuse curriculum guide for psychiatry faculty.* (pp. 19–22). Washington: DHHS Pub. No. ADM 82-1159.

Gallant, D. M., Rich, A., Bey, E., & Terranova, L. (1970). Group psychotherapy with married couples: A successful technique in New Orleans alcoholism clinic patients. *Journal of the Louisiana State Medical Society, 122*, 41–44.

Gorman, J. M., & Rooney, J. F. (1979). Delay in seeking help and onset of crises among Al-Anon wives. *Journal of Drug and Alcohol Abuse, 6*, 223–233.

Johnson, V. E. (1973). *I'll quit tomorrow.* New York: Harper & Row.

Kandel, D. B. (1975). Stages in adolescent involvement in drug use. *Science, 190*, 912–914.

Kristenson, H., Ohlin, H., Hulten-Nosslin, M-J., Trell, E., & Hood, B. (1983). Identification and intervention of heavy drinking in middle-aged men: Results and follow-up of 24–60 months of long-term study; with randomized controls. *Alcoholism: Clinical and Experimental Research, 7*, 203–209.

Lemert, E. M. (1965). The appearance and sequence of events in the adjustment of families to alcoholism. *Quarterly Journal of the Studies of Alcoholism, 26*, 594–604.

Maisto, S. A., Sobell, L. C., Zelhart, P. F., Connors, G. J., & Cooper, T. (1979). Driving records of persons convicted of driving under the influence of alcohol. *Journal of Studies on Alcohol, 40*, 70–77.

Petersson, B., Kristenson, H., Krantz, P., Trell, E., & Sternby, W. H. (1982). Alcohol-related death: A major contributor to mortality in urban middle-aged men. *Lancet, 2*, 1088–1090.

Truax, C. B., & Carkhuff, R. R. (1967). *Toward effective counseling and psychotherapy: Training and practice.* Chicago: Aldine Press.

Yamaguchi, K., & Kandel, D. B. (1984). Patterns of drug use from adolescence to young adulthood: Predictors of progression. *American Journal of Public Health, 74*, 673–681.

CHAPTER 7

Medical Consequences
of Alcoholism

ALL PROFESSIONAL PERSONNEL in contact with alcoholics must be aware of the medical consequences of this illness. Since various alcohol-induced physical illnesses may complicate the psychologic evaluation, even nonmedical therapists must develop a base of knowledge that will enable them to know when medical consultations are necessary. No other frequently encountered illness can significantly impair so many organ systems of the body. It is not my intention to review all of the significant details of each of the alcohol-related medical illnesses, but I will describe some of the medical symptoms that can confuse or interfere with the psychological evaluation and/or treatment of the alcoholic patient. The signs and symptoms of alcohol intoxication and overdose are listed in Table 7.1.

EFFECTS OF ETHANOL ON THE NERVOUS SYSTEM

The Syndrome of Alcohol Idiosyncratic Intoxication

The criteria for the diagnosis of this disorder stress the behavioral changes displayed by patients while under the influence of a relatively small amount of alcohol and considered to be unusual or atypical behavior for them. The lay diagnosis of "alcoholic blackout" and the *DSM-II* diagnosis of Pathological Intoxication had been assigned to this category despite the fact that these episodes may also occur under the influence of large amounts of alcohol. This diagnostic category may have important legal implications when the patient has committed a criminal offense during these unusual episodes associated with the ingestion of alcohol.

The "alcoholic blackout" is defined as a period of time that occurs while

TABLE 7.1
Signs and Symptoms of Alcohol Intoxification and Overdose

SIGNS	SYMPTOMS	DIAGNOSTIC AIDS
Mild to moderate intoxification impaired attention poor motor coordination dysmetria ataxia nystagmus slurred speech prolonged reaction time flushed face orthostatic hypotension hematemesis stupor	*Mild to moderate intoxication* alcohol on breath loquacity impaired judgment inappropriate behavioral responses inappropriate emotional responses euphoria dizziness blurred vision	In low dose intoxication, blood alcohol level is about 100 mg% or higher (If level is greater than 300 mg% and patient is alert and relatively well-coordinated, then this highly tolerant person may be an alcoholic and experience withdrawal symptoms as the blood level decreases.)
Severe intoxication and overdose respiratory rate decreased bruises or scars from analgesia and lacks coordination shock coma	*Severe intoxication* irrational angry outbursts with violent acts progressively sluggish responses to environmental stimuli "dry heaves"	In high dose coma, the blood level of alcohol should be greater than 300 mg%. Otherwise, the etiology of the coma may not be alcohol. Diabetic acidosis and hypoglycemia may be easily ruled out.

From Gallant, 1982.

the patient is drinking moderately or heavily which he cannot recall when he becomes sober. The alcohol amnestic disorder, as defined in *DSM-III-R*, is not an appropriate category for the "alcoholic blackout," since this disorder requires both short-term memory impairment (inability to learn new information) and long-term memory impairment (inability to remember information which was known in the past). In the process of obtaining a carefully detailed history, it is not unusual to find that the amnestic behavior involves merely routine, insignificant speech or actions that the patient cannot recall. However, those incidents in which the patients become assaultive or violent are so impressive to the interviewer that many therapists believe that the typical incident of an "alcoholic blackout" involves very peculiar or very unusual behavior. When one sees a patient during an "alcoholic blackout," it is impossible to determine if this is an episode for which he or she will be amnestic the next day. In fact, some patients actually appear less intoxicated during these episodes.

It should be emphasized that, although the patients are responsible for attaining the state of intoxication in which this type of amnestic behavior occurs, they are not truly responsible for their actions or words during the actual period. The patient who has a previous history of violent behavior during an "alcoholic blackout" (i.e., pathological intoxication or alcohol idiosyncratic intoxication), is much more likely to repeat this behavior during another blackout. Psychotic behavior can also occur during these blackouts. The therapist who is unaware of the history of alcohol intake may misdiagnose these patients as schizophrenics and prescribe neuroleptic drugs, which can further confuse the diagnosis and be potentially harmful to the patients. In episodes of pathological intoxication, there is a very high incidence of abnormal electroencephalograph tracing (EEGs) during the period of dangerous behavior (Maletzky, 1978).

In an extensive evaluation of 220 alcoholics admitted to a treatment program, it was found that 43% had a history of psychotic symptomatology, usually during heavy alcohol or drug use and usually associated with a prior history of antisocial problems or drug abuse (Schuckit, 1982). The severely abnormal episodic behavior displayed by some of these patients during alcoholic consumption can be confused with other neuropsychiatric diagnoses, such as temporal lobe epilepsy, schizophrenia, and drug intoxication. Complaints of numbness, cerebellar dysfunction with ataxia and slurring of speech, nausea, and diaphoresis can all be seen with phencyclidine (PCP) intoxication as well as with alcohol intoxication. Therefore, careful elicitation of drug history as well as urine survey for PCP may be necessary, particularly in young intoxicated patients who enter the emergency room or the therapist's office with potentially assaultive or suicidal behavior.

If aggression or extreme anger is part of the patient's clinical presentation during this rather sudden behavioral change, the therapist should regard the patient as dangerous and approach him as carefully as he would any totally incompetent and potentially violent individual. The guidelines for handling for this type of situation follow:

1. Never disagree with the patient about anything he says. An individual who is on the verge of an explosion can be set off by any discord in the environment.
2. Use your voice and body movements as therapeutic tools. The voice should always be calm and soft; speech should be a slow monotone with no sudden changes of pitch. Motor movements should be kept to a minimum and initiated very slowly. In this way, both voice and movement can serve as calming instruments of therapy.
3. Try to initiate a personal, familiar relationship by using the patient's first name in a calm and friendly manner (realizing that only such an unusual type of situation requires this familiar and nonprofessional approach).

4. Remember that there is little likelihood of violence while a dialogue is going on. During the conversation, try to find out personal facts about the patient, such as the names of one or two people to whom he feels close and for whom he has positive feelings. If this type of information can be elicited, the next step is to attempt to get his permission to telephone them in order to bring someone with a positive affective charge in contact with the patient. The longer the conversation progresses, the less chance there is for violence. Also, encouraging the patient to verbalize about positive affective relationships in the past or to talk to a close friend or relative on the telephone may help bring him out of this partial *temporary* amnestic episode by recalling familiar events.

Alcohol Withdrawal Syndrome

This syndrome develops after cessation of or reduction in prolonged heavy ingestion of alcohol, followed within several hours by a coarse tremor of the hands, the tongue, and the eyelids, accompanied by such symptoms as nausea, vomiting, weakness, diaphoresis, fast heart rate, anxiety, and irritability. Similar symptoms can be caused by a low blood sugar or diabetic acidosis. Some individuals with a familial or essential tremor who use alcohol in an effort to obliterate the tremor may be misdiagnosed as having this alcohol withdrawal syndrome. The alcohol withdrawal tremor is coarse and arrhythmic. The familial or benign essential tremor is rhythmic, usually at a rate of 4 to 10 per second, and worsens with fatigue, extreme cold, and social stress. Many alcoholic patients who increase alcohol consumption to control this essential tremor show an impressive positive personality change after the tremor has been inhibited by appropriate medications such as propanolol (Inderal).

The signs and symptoms of alcohol withdrawal are detailed in Table 7.2. As noted in Table 7.2, more severe signs and symptoms of withdrawal are seen in the syndrome of Alcohol Withdrawal Delirium (delirium tremens): clouding of consciousness, difficulty in sustaining attention, disorientation, possible epileptic-like seizures, and possible hallucinations with lack of insight. These symptoms usually occur within the first several days after complete cessation of drinking or reduction of extremely heavy alcohol ingestion. These signs and symptoms indicate the need for immediate medical consultation and hospitalization. With adequate treatment, these symptoms should disappear by the end of the first week or the beginning of the second week.

The visual hallucinations usually associated with this type of delirium

Alcoholism

TABLE 7.2
Signs and Symptoms of Alcohol Withdrawal

SIGNS	SYMPTOMS	DIAGNOSTIC AIDS
Alcohol Withdrawal		
Mild to moderate signs malaise or weakness muscle tension	*Mild to moderate symptoms* fluctuation of symptoms during the course of a day	EEG showing bursts of high amplitude slow waves with random spikes
tremor hyperreflexia	irritability anxiety and agitation	electrolyte depletion hypoglycemia may be present
elevated blood pressure tachycardia diaphoresis hyperacuity of all sensory modalities flushed face	overalertness extreme fatigue disturbance of sleep- wakefulness cycle anorexia vomiting headache diarrhea expressions of strong craving of alcohol	association of high laboratory values commonly found in alcoholics (e.g., macrocytosis, elevated levels of uric acid, SGPT, GGT, GGPT, alkaline phosphatase, bilirubin and triglycerides) without any other known cause
Alcohol Withdrawal Delirium		
Severe withdrawal signs respiratory alkalosis with hyperventilation	*Severe withdrawal symptoms* incoherent speech global confusion with clouding of consciousness	
fever grand mal seizures	illusions hallucinations with lack of insight	

From Gallant, 1982.

may be quite impressive, and auditory hallucinations are found to occur more frequently than expected when a careful detailed history is obtained. If the clinician is unaware of the relative frequency of auditory hallucinations in this syndrome, he may mistakenly diagnose the patient as having another type of psychosis. One also has to be aware that the illusions and hallucinations which frequently occur in the Alcohol Withdrawal Delirium may be masking head trauma, metabolic abnormalities, or space-occupying lesions. In one study of this type of delirium, 13 patients referred to a psychiatric clinic in a delirious state after prolonged intoxication were found to have chronic subdural hematomas (Reisner, 1979). Details of the criteria for hospitalization and treatment of this withdrawal syndrome are reviewed in Chapter 8.

Alcohol Hallucinosis

Diagnosing alcohol hallucinosis can be very confusing if there is no history of alcohol intake and if there are no family members available to give the history. The patient usually shows an affect that correlates with the type of hallucination, and there is no clouding of consciousness as in the delirium tremens syndrome. These symptoms may be quite dramatic, and the patient can be misdiagnosed as a schizophrenic if there is no adequate history available, as is frequently the case in a hospital emergency room. An evaluation of the hallucinations of functional psychotics and alcoholics found a higher incidence of auditory and taste hallucinations in the functional group (Deiker & Chambers, 1978). In regard to visual, olfactory, tactile, and sexual aspects of the hallucinatory experiences, there were no significant differences between the two groups.

Usually, the onset of this type of withdrawal syndrome occurs within the first week after cessation of drinking. The patient presents a history of many years of heavy drinking prior to the initial episode; the average age of onset is approximately 40. The diagnosis should not be applied to patients who have had prior psychotic episodes unrelated to alcohol or drug intake. Even when paranoid delusions as well as hallucinations are present, the patient has to have a clear sensorium before a definitive diagnosis can be made.

The development of these hallucinatory symptoms is due solely to the phenomenon of alcohol withdrawal and should not persist beyond two weeks. Follow-up evaluation of these patients should not show any evidence of a trend toward development of a chronic hallucinatory process (Gallant, in press).

The Protracted Withdrawal Syndrome (PWS)

Although the protracted withdrawal syndrome is not listed in *DSM-III*, it has been adequately described in the literature (Gallant, 1982; Kissin, 1979). Symptoms attributable to the protracted withdrawal syndrome include such physiological variations as respiratory irregularity, labile blood pressure and pulse, impairment of slow-wave sleep, decrease in cold-stress response, persistence of tolerance to sedative effects, and tremor. Symptoms of frustration and irritability resulting from deficits in problem-solving, complaints of spontaneous anxiety, depressive episodes for no apparent reason, and even transient psychotic reactions have been reported in relation to this syndrome, which persists in some patients after the acute withdrawal syndrome has terminated. Similar signs and symptoms have been reported by other authors and labeled with the alternate term, "alcoholism-induced subacute organic mental disorders" '(Grant et al., 1979, 1984).

Reported biochemical changes associated with this protracted withdrawal syndrome have included diminished tryptamine metabolism and lowered norepinephrine and testosterone levels. This syndrome has been described as lasting anywhere from one to several months. To diagnose this syndrome, the therapist should be certain that the patient did not have a combination of these symptoms prior to alcohol abstinence. All other possible metabolic, physiological, or psychological causes for these behavioral and emotional abnormalities must be eliminated before making the diagnosis of protracted withdrawal syndrome.

It appears that the syndrome of mild to moderate acute alcohol withdrawal, as well as those of severe withdrawal (see Table 7.2), can gradually blend into the protracted withdrawal syndrome or what has been called the subacute organic mental disorder (SOMD). In one important study, the authors reported a long-term investigation of alcoholics in relation to onset and recovery from alcohol-induced central nervous system (CNS) dysfunction (Grant et al., 1984). The investigators examined 204 subjects consisting of 3 subgroups: (1) 71 recently detoxified inpatient alcoholics with a mean duration of abstinence of four weeks (RD group); (2) 65 long-term abstinent alcoholics with a mean abstinence of 3.7 years (L-T group); and (3) 68 non-alcoholic volunteers matched on the basis of age and education with the recently detoxified alcoholics (V group). There were no significant differences between the two alcoholic groups except for the duration of abstinence. The extended Halstead-Reitan Neuropsychologic Test Battery was used, and the clinical ratings were performed without knowledge of the subject's assignment.

The results showed that the RD alcoholics were significantly more impaired in problem-solving and learning than the other two groups. Older subjects in all three groups had significantly more difficulty with these two areas and also with attentiveness and speed of information-processing. Thus, two factors, independent of each other, aging and brief duration of abstinence among alcoholics, appeared to contribute to deficient neuropsychologic functioning. These findings conflict with the concept that alcoholism impairment is related to a premature aging mechanism. Review of the medical histories showed that a head injury was as accurate a predictor of impaired neuropsychologic performance as a recent history of drinking. The L-T group was almost indistinguishable from the V group.

These data strongly suggest that, between the resolution of the acute alcohol abstinence syndrome (about three to four weeks) and the plateau of improvement which may not occur until after one year or more of abstinence, there indeed does exist a slowly resolving alcohol-related subacute organic mental disorder (SOMD), which Kissin has called the protracted withdrawal syndrome. In view of these findings, the therapist should move slowly in treating such patients. Abrupt confrontation therapy should be avoided until cognitive abilities show maximal improvement. Instead, during this stage emphasis should be placed on the therapeutic approaches that contribute to a trusting relationship with the patient.

In addition to the physiologic and behavioral changes already described, the patient may show increased irritability and impatience with family members and friends. These patients often complain of fatigue and lowered stress tolerance. Some patients can panic, believing that they are slipping back, and then suddenly resort to the use of alcohol in an attempt to alleviate these symptoms. Complaints of emotional lability are not unusual. Forgetfulness occurs with periods of loss of concentration, and minor problems become major crises. Some members of AA call these types of symptoms "a dry drunk." There is a high level of distractibility, and the patient may be unconsciously setting himself up for a return to alcohol because of these symptoms, feeling that sobriety results in misery. The symptoms of this syndrome may be one of the reasons why the failure rate with alcoholic patients is so high during the first six months after they are discharged from inpatient rehabilitation centers.

The best therapeutic approach for this problem is a fully detailed explanation to the patient and the family. This helps them to accept these symptoms as a *normal part of the withdrawal phase of alcohol.* Understanding that these disturbing symptoms are temporary can help the alcoholic to accommodate to the discomfort and maintain abstinence and can help the family to provide more informed support. The therapist has to remember that during this state the patient is unlikely to be able to make any adequate plans concerning the future; he is present-oriented and impulsive with a low frustration tolerance. It is important to emphasize to the patient that such emotional and physical reactions during this phase are not unusual; the recovering alcoholic will do well as long as he realizes that these symptoms are not a sign of relapse or psychological illness.

Alcoholics Anonymous (AA) can be of tremendous help at this time. Many members of AA have experienced similar symptoms in the past and may help the patient realize that this "dry drunk" is just a transient phase of recovery. Including the spouse in marital therapy or couples group therapy, as well as in Al-Anon, is crucial during this phase. It is essential for the spouse and family to understand the implications of these symptoms and to be in a position to help the patient modify them.

Use of psychopharmacologic agents during these periods may cause uncomfortable reactions such as anticholinergic (dry mouth, confusion, constipation, etc.) or sedative side effects. These may further confuse the patient.

The existence of the PWS points out the importance of evaluating the neuropsychological impairment of the alcoholic patient before initiating any treatment plan. Even mild impairment of judgment or cognition can seriously interfere with both psychotherapy and the administration of medications such as Antabuse, particularly if the impairment is not evident to the therapist or the patient. Inexpensive and readily available neuropsychological evaluation measures may be just as helpful as more costly computerized tomography (CT) for the evaluation and formulation of a treatment plan for the alcoholic patient (Graff-Radford et al., 1982).

The Reversibility of Alcohol-induced Organic Mental Disorder

Before discussing alcohol-related irreversible organic mental disorders, let me emphasize the reversibility of the alcohol-induced organic brain damage. As shown by the investigational data obtained from research into the SOMD, problem-solving and learning may continue to improve for as long as one year or more after the patient becomes abstinent (Grant et al., 1984). Therefore, early diagnosis of brain damage in an alcoholic should not necessarily carry a pessimistic prognosis. Not only can improvement be expected in clinical cognitive deficits, but computerized tomographic (CT) scan assessment of alcoholic brain damage can usually show the reversibility of the atrophy caused by chronic excess of alcohol intake.

In one study, follow-up CT scans showed brain density increasing in as short a period as four weeks in newly abstinent alcoholics (Carlen et al., 1986). The cerebral atrophy reversed in some subjects with maintained abstinence. Computerized assessment of the cerebral spinal fluid (CSF) volume, which correlates with cerebral atrophy and mean cerebral density, showed a *decreased* CSF volume and increased cerebral density with abstinence maintained for four weeks. Carlen et al. cited three other reports of similar results showing that impairment on long-term memory tasks improved in association with the increase in cerebral density. The fact that many alcoholics show some reversibility of these deficits with maintained abstinence over such a short period of time should be encouraging to all alcoholic patients and their families. It does appear that many of the psychologic deficits secondary to the brain damage will show improvement over a period of months, if there are no medical complications such as high blood pressure or diabetes.

Misdiagnosis of alcoholism in the aged can lead to tragic consequences. Without an adequate history and examination, temporary alcohol-induced episodes of confusion and amnesia may be difficult to distinguish from senile dementia and may result in unnecessary institutionalization. Not only do elderly people metabolize alcohol less efficiently, but frequently they are also taking other medications which may potentiate and prolong the sedation-confusion reaction to alcohol.

Alcohol-Related Irreversible Organic Mental Disorders: Diagnosis and Management

The alcohol amnestic disorder is one of the syndromes that indicates the presence of permanent brain damage. It is categorized by anterograde and retrograde amnesia, with *fairly good preservation of other intellectual abilities.* The diagnosis formerly known as Korsakoff syndrome falls in this group; it is characterized by more severe anterograde amnesia than retrograde amnesia. If patients are using a great deal of denial about their drinking or other problems prior to the onset of this discrete neurophysiological dysfunction, they may then try to deny their memory defects in a rather pathetic way. For example, the patient may make an inappropriate guess about the month or year to try to cover up a memory deficit. While trauma and anoxia as well as cerebral accidents can cause this type of syndrome, the most common cause is alcoholism. The major pathology appears to be in the diencephalon or mesial temporal structures (Gallant, 1982). There is no clouding of consciousness as in delirium and intoxication, and no general loss of intellectual abilities as in dementia associated with alcoholism or Alzheimer's disease.

Dementia associated with alcoholism is another alcohol-induced type of brain damage which is usually considered irreversible. However, some improvement can occur with prolonged abstinence. The state of consciousness, as with the alcohol amnestic disorder, is not clouded in this chronic organic mental disorder. The prognosis of alcoholic dementia is obviously better than that of senile dementia of the Alzheimer type (SDAT), which is one of *progressive* deterioration. Also, unlike Alzheimer's, this syndrome usually does not include aphasia. In association with moderate to severe amnesia, functional deficits are somewhat more specific, with constructional difficulty in drawing, stick design, and copying geometric designs. If the alcoholic dementia patient is able to maintain abstinence, it is not unusual to see some improvement occurring as late as six months to a year after he has initiated his sobriety. The same observations are valid for the alcohol amnestic disorder. In some studies, the degree of impairment appears to be associated with the duration of drinking history, whereas in other studies the impairment seems to relate more directly to the quantity of recent consumption (Grant et al., 1984; Parsons, 1977).

The types of brain damage in the alcoholic dementias are more widespread than generally thought. In an evaluation of the extent of alcoholic brain damage in Ireland, it was estimated that 2,000 or more of approximately 6,000 alcoholic admissions to Irish psychiatric hospitals each year have brain damage (Draper, 1978). If this percentage were applied to hospitals in the United States, then more than 10% of all psychiatric admissions (33% of which are for alcoholism) each year would have neuropsychological impairment as a result of alcohol abuse. Early brain damage must be recognized by the therapist and the family and treated appropriately or else relapse will almost certainly occur as a result of impaired judgment. Draper has described such patients who remain untreated: "Even when sober and indeed when abstinent, these cases will be responsible for more traffic accidents, more personal injury, more industrial accidents, poorer work performance, especially on skilled tasks or problem solving, than their nondamaged colleagues."

Understanding the nature and degree of impairment can help the therapist establish realistic guidelines and goals for the patient in order to avoid early failure in treatment. The type of neuropsychological impairment in dementia associated with alcoholism, as measured by such tests as the Halstead Category Subtest and Picture Arrangement, indicate a deficit in ability to adapt to new situations and new abstraction problems (Grant et al., 1984). Therefore, vocational rehabilitation and other aspects of therapeutic guidelines should not involve any marked departure from the patient's former occupation or social habits.

An invaluable aspect of the treatment of the organic mental disorder is helping the patient and the family to recognize the problem and meaning of alcohol-induced brain damage. It is important for them to realize that many of the organic mental changes may be reversible with time, abstinence, and adequate nutrition. They must be given an optimistic viewpoint and appropriate instructions on management of the patient's daily behavior while he or she is waiting for some of the organic symptoms to resolve. Short training sessions concentrating on visual-motor coordination can be performed on a daily basis. Since the patients have problems with attention span, these sessions should probably not last more than 20 minutes, but they can be repeated twice daily. Abstract thinking tasks, such as creating three-dimensional figures and abstracting from categories, should be included in these training sessions. For memory tasks, the use of mnemonics can be a most useful technique for patients displaying moderate to marked memory impairment.

Use of the following procedures to help the patient develop routine habits has proved to be very helpful: Encourage the patient to get out of bed at the same time every day, eat meals at the same time every day, and try to maintain the same schedule, including sleep time, every day. In addition, have the patient keep a little notebook in a shirt or skirt pocket with a schedule of appointments for that day, times for telephone calls, times for social engagements, and professional or work schedules. The patient should be encouraged to use these notes to compensate for the short-term memory deficit, the major problem seen in most patients with alcohol-induced brain damage when they are admitted to a rehabilitation program.

An example of this treatment regimen is shown by the following case. Mr. S. was an outstanding land-lease lawyer who was involved in many important oil exploration contracts. Despite the fact that his combination of alcoholism and diabetes had seriously interfered with his recent memory, his note-making habits developed in training sessions enabled him to maintain his very large and profitable law practice after discharge from our alcoholism rehabilitation unit. His knowledge of the law, which he had acquired many years before and practiced over and over again in courtroom settings, helped him to remain one of the most skillful lawyers in his area, despite the fact he could not remember to whom he had talked on the phone one hour before. On a 12-month follow-up with Mr. S., his recent impairment showed marked improvement. In this case, as in all such instances of alcohol-induced brain damage, we emphasized to the patient and the family that the prognosis was quite good.

The peripheral nerves are frequently damaged as a consequence of chronic excessive alcoholic intake. It is estimated that 20% of alcoholics have peripheral neuropathy (Edmondson, 1980). Usually the alcohol-induced peripheral neuropathy is bilateral and somewhat symmetrical; it appears to involve the feet and legs more commonly than the hands and arms and may go unnoticed by the patient during the early stages since vibratory sense may be mildly impaired without obvious discomfort. The development of the neuropathy *is usually slow*, extending over a period of months. The nerve involvement usually begins in the feet and is manifested by unusual sensations or paresthesias, numbness, sensitivity to pressure, and sometimes unusual burning pain in the bottom of the feet. This sensory involvement can then be followed by motor weakness in which the patient may even develop a foot drop. The peripheral muscles in the legs can be somewhat atrophied when the neuropathy has been present for a relatively long period of time. Sense of position of the feet and legs in space is impaired and reflexes are decreased or absent. The patient can develop an ataxic gait.

Although autonomic nervous system involvement may be present with paralysis of the urethral and rectal sphincters, this type of unusually severe nervous system involvement in secondary alcoholism is rarely seen at the present time (Freund, 1983). These peripheral neuropathies are usually associated with nutritional deficiencies, which may be manifested as discoloration in the skin and cracking or fissures at the corners of the mouth.

There is some variance in the reporting of the incidence of peripheral neuropathies in alcoholics (Freund, 1983). One possible explanation is that some of these studies have been performed on skid-row alcoholics, whereas other studies have been reported on admissions to neuropsychiatric hospitals. In addition, research evaluations of the incidence may be associated with more meticulous examinations and reports than the usual examination of a skid-row alcoholic on admission to a correctional institution. The incidence has probably decreased since enriched bread with vitamins was introduced in 1940 in the United States (Freund, 1983). In addition to the toxic effects of alcohol on the nerve tissue, it is possible that chronic deficiencies of thiamine, pantothenic acid, and pyridoxine may further contribute to the development of this syndrome. Although it usually takes several months for the neuropathy to improve significantly, this syndrome should respond well to alcohol abstinence and vitamin B therapy. In some cases the deficits may be permanent, with mild residual effects present even after several years of abstinence.

It is not unusual to see an alcoholic patient with middle-aged onset of diabetes mellitus and an associated peripheral neuropathy. With this particular type of patient, it is difficult to say whether the diabetes or the alcoholism has caused the neuropathy. Such neuropathy is more likely to be associated with permanent residual deficits.

At times, some very anxious alcoholic patients may have a panic disorder or an episode of hyperventilation with associated symptoms of numbness and tingling in both feet and/or hands, flushes, trembling, and possibly other symptoms, such as shortness of breath, tachycardia with palpitations, chest pain, and dizziness. If the patient complains of numbness around the lips, then it is more likely to be an episode of hyperventilation or panic disorder than neuropathy. A careful neurologic examination should rule out peripheral neuropathy, and 30 to 60 seconds of voluntary hyperventilation may replicate the symptoms of panic disorder.

EFFECTS OF ETHANOL ON OTHER ORGAN SYSTEMS

The diagnosis of *alcoholic liver disease* is used for those pathologic lesions of the liver that are a consequence of excessive use of ethanol and that cannot be attributed to any other etiologic agent. In the United States, the most widespread form of hepatitis is caused by alcohol (Senior, 1985/1986). The clinical symptoms of alcohol hepatitis are nausea and/or vomiting, mild to moderate discomfort or pain in the right upper abdominal area, loss of appetite, occasional fever, and possible jaundice (Van Thiel, 1983). The hepatitis may last from one or two weeks to several weeks. This disease can actually worsen even after the alcohol intake has stopped and may progress for several weeks before starting to improve; the development of additional symptoms after drinking has stopped may confuse the patient about the causative role of alcohol. Mild forms of this disease may be present in the absence of any symptoms except laboratory findings or a mild to moderate increase in liver enzymes (SGPT, SGOT, GGT). Mild, repeated episodes of alcoholic hepatitis may not be recognized, and the patient may develop cirrhosis without having had any diagnosed episodes of hepatitis. Each of these episodes of hepatitis may resolve, leaving the liver with only slight damage; it is the repeated episodes that can result in the cirrhotic liver.

A frequently asked question is, "Can social drinkers develop alcoholic hepatitis?" The answer is yes (Senior, 1985/1986). Each one of us differs in our susceptibility to developing organ damage in response to various environmental toxins. Thus, some alcoholics may have many years of heavy drinking without any clinical or laboratory evidence of liver damage, whereas other excessive drinkers may develop liver damage after only a few years of moderate to heavy drinking. The prevalence of alcoholic cirrhosis among all confirmed alcoholics is only about 10 to 15% at any given time (Senior, 1985/1986).

The fatty liver is less serious than alcoholic hepatitis and can occur in almost any individual who drinks alcohol heavily for even a few days. The liver enlargement is a result of swollen liver cells containing fat globules and water. This type of liver pathology is reversible and may completely disappear after alcohol intake is stopped. The fatty liver does not directly lead to cirrhosis. It is the alcohol hepatitis phase that can lead directly to a cirrhotic liver. However, if the excessive alcohol intake is interrupted and there is permanent abstinence, then the majority of patients with alcohol hepatitis will not develop cirrhosis. Use of liver enzyme tests such as the GGT as a way of confronting the patient may be useful. As discussed in Chapter 6, use of this liver enzyme test in a screening intervention program was very successful. Medical approaches for the treatment of alcohol hepatitis, including use of steroids such as cortisone, have not been shown to be of benefit when evaluated in controlled research investigations.

Once cirrhosis of the liver has been definitely diagnosed, then the patient faces the possibility of increased portal vein pressure, with resultant dilation of the esophageal veins, which could rupture with profuse bleeding. In typical examples of cirrhosis, collagen within the liver becomes sclerosed; this sclerosis may connect the central areas of adjacent lobules, developing into what is called centrolobular cirrhosis, but nodules do not develop (Edmondson, 1980). In advanced cirrhosis, the liver is usually smaller than normal size; it is hard, nodular, and has been called the "hobnail liver." It is these patients who are most likely to die of hemorrhage from the esophageal varices, particularly since the bleeding time is prolonged because of a lack of vitamin K, secondary to the liver damage. In other cases, the hemorrhage may be complicated by hepatic encephalopathy with resultant hepatic coma. In these cases, the prognosis is extremely poor.

There is some controversy about the treatment of the esophageal varices. Recommendations have varied from the use of propanolol (a beta adrenergic blocker which can lower the intrahepatic pressure) to sclerosing the veins, to shunt surgery (e.g., a portal-caval shunt, another method for lowering the pressure within the liver). Additional information about the details of alcoholic liver disease can be found in the articles by Edmondson (1980) and Senior (1985/1986) and in the *Cecil Textbook of Medicine* (Beeson et al., 1984).

Excessive alcohol intake is the most common cause of *pancreatitis* seen in large charity hospitals (Edmondson, 1980). Acute alcoholic pancreatitis tends to occur in younger male alcoholics. The pain of alcohol pancreatitis can be very severe; sometimes acute attacks lead to chronic pancreatitis. In very severe cases, the pain may become an almost constant symptom. This pain may radiate to the back between the shoulder blades and is sometimes partially relieved by sitting up. Various pancreatic enzymes, including amylase and lipase, are elevated in both the blood and urine. The 24-hour urinary amylase may remain somewhat elevated for one week after serum amylase has returned to normal. When both lipase and amylase tests are performed, 80% of the patients with pancreatitis have positive test results (Edmondson, 1980). Continued attacks of pancreatitis will result in further destruction to the pancreas and a deficiency of insulin with resultant hypoglycemia. Other complications, such as a pseudocyst or abscess of the pancreas, may require surgery.

Although excessive alcohol use can cause an alcoholic *cardiomyopathy* with heart failure and a high mortality rate for this illness, it has been shown in large-numbered studies that there is an inverse relationship between alcohol intake and coronary heart disease, which is a different pathologic entity from the cardiomyopathy. A seven-year prospective evaluation of 11,121 males, 35 to 62 years of age, concluded that: "Consumption of alcohol appears to be inversely related to incidence of coronary heart disease morbidity and mortality, but not to risk of dying" (Kozararevic et al., 1980). In this study, in contrast to the coronary artery heart disease findings, there was a positive correlation between frequency of alcohol consumption and deaths from stroke associated with hypertension, accidents, and violence. The strongly positive association of alcohol consumption with elevated high-density lipoprotein cholesterol may help to explain the apparent lower rate of myocardial infarction in drinkers as compared to abstainers.

Myopathies of the peripheral skeletal muscle can occur in some excessive drinkers; usually the skeletal muscles involved are the thigh muscles, which may be tender, can atrophy, and are associated with a laboratory finding of elevated serum creatine phosphokinase (CPK). In those hospitalized patients who have an acute form of the myopathy with tender muscles, the symptoms may be replicated with an associated increase in CPK by the administration of several beers.

Peptic ulcers of the stomach and duodenum occur quite frequently among alcoholics. In one clinical study, 23% of skid-row alcoholics had peptic ulcers (Ashley et al., 1976).

The association between *hypertension* and alcohol consumption has been recognized for many years (Gallant, 1981b). In one well-controlled study the investigators were able to show a direct association between alcohol intake and rise in blood pressure in volunteer male subjects, who were divided into high and low alcohol intake groups (Puddy et al., 1985). In this excellent study, it was shown that an 80% reduction in alcohol intake was associated with significantly lowered systolic and diastolic blood pressure. In subjects who had previously drunk a minimum of 210 ml of absolute ethanol per week (average of three drinks per day), systolic blood pressure was reduced by 1.1 mm Hg for every 100 ml reduction in ethanol intake. The study provided firm evidence that blood pressure elevation is a direct effect of long-term alcohol consumption by demonstrating a significant fall in blood pressure when normotensive men substituted a low alcohol beer for their normal "moderate" drinking habits.

These data emphasize the necessity of obtaining a meticulous history of alcohol consumption in every hypertensive patient. With reduction or elimination of alcohol consumption, the blood pressure may return to normal limits in many patients, thereby avoiding antihypertensive drug therapy. These data appear to be even more significant when evaluating the association between alcohol and hemorrhagic strokes. The risk of such a stroke is more than doubled for light drinkers compared to nondrinkers, and nearly tripled for those considered to be heavy drinkers (Donahue et al., 1986). This significant increase in hemorrhagic strokes in excessive drinkers may be associated with an increase in blood pressure and a decrease in magnesium, which can occur secondary to heavy alcohol ingestion.

The effects of excessive drinking on the *reproductive system* in both males and females have been demonstrated in a number of publications (Edmondson, 1980; Gallant, 1982; Little & Sing, 1986; Nagy et al., 1986). The well-known fetal alcohol syndrome, which includes intellectual, neurologic, and behavioral abnormalities as well as structural deficiencies such as microencephaly and facial deformities of the eyes, nose, chin, and mouth, is relatively rare compared with the number of low birthweight offspring of alcoholic mothers. Recently an association between the father's drinking and low infant birthweight was reported (Little & Sing, 1986). Since definite cytological abnormalities have been described in the sperm of alcoholics as compared to controlled cases (almost 30% fewer normal sperm cells, abnormal coil-tailed sperm, immature testicular cells, and amorphous cells), we may speculate that some of these cytologic semen anomalies could result in low birthweight or other teratogenic abnormalities (Nagy et al., 1986).

In animal research, prenatal alcohol exposure has been shown to influence the later expression of non-reproductive sexually different behaviors in males and females. In rats, prenatal alcohol exposure may change some types of female behavior to male behavior in maze-learning and saccharin preference (McGivern et al., 1984).

While it is important to be aware of developmental behavioral and structural changes in the offspring of both male and female alcoholics, abnormal changes in the offspring of alcoholics should not be automatically attributed to excessive alcohol intake. Such blaming may place unnecessary guilt on the parents. For example, children of mothers with the biochemical illness of phenylketonuria (PKU) closely resemble children diagnosed as having the fetal alcohol syndrome (FAS). The typical mid-facial hypoplasia, short palpebral fissures, diminished to absent philtrum, short upturned nose, low birthweight, and retarded central nervous system development all have been described in some of the offspring of PKU mothers (Gallant, 1981a; Lipson et al., 1981). Although the therapist may be impressed by the characteristic FAS anomalies of prenatal and postnatal growth deficiency, CNS dysfunction, particular pattern of facial characteristics, and major organ system malformations, he or she should obtain a carefully detailed description of the mother's medication intake, genetic-metabolic history, and ethanol intake before making a definitive diagnosis.

The *skin* is an organ that may give useful signs in the diagnosis and possibly even the treatment of chronic alcoholism. Frequent injuries with bruises or cigarette burns due to drowsiness may be symptoms of alcohol misuse. Middle and later stages of alcoholism may be associated with evidence of acne rosacea (dilation of vessels with thickening of skin), palmer erythema with red blanching, vascular spider nevi, and evidence of poor nutrition with inflammation of the lips. Having a patient look directly in the mirror and confronting him with the cause of these skin changes may enable him to take a good honest look at himself.

Other organ systems that can be affected by chronic excessive intake of alcohol are the hematologic, the endocrine, skeletal, and even the salivary glands. For details on the effects of alcohol on these organ systems, the reader should consult the article by Edmondson (1980) and the *Cecil Textbook of Medicine* (Beeson et al., 1984). The effects of alcohol on the immune system, including the direct immunosuppressive action of alcohol, as demonstrated by studies showing the depression of natural killer cell activity and lymphocyte transformation, is described in the monograph by Petrakis

(1985). In this monograph, the relationship between alcohol abuse and acquired immune deficiency syndrome (AIDS) is discussed in some detail. Present knowledge of alcohol's potentially damaging effects on cell-mediated immunity, as well as its disinhibiting effects on behavior, justify our warning patients with AIDS against using alcohol at intoxicating levels.

Alcohol may promote carcinogenesis and is a risk factor for many types of cancers. Investigators have now reported associations between alcohol consumption and increased risk of cancers of the mouth, pharynx, larynx, esophagus, liver, pancreas, stomach, thyroid, colon, rectum, breast, and malignant melanoma; these alcohol-related cancers account for approximately 3% of all cancer deaths (Podolsky, 1986). Alcohol may contribute to carcinogenesis through the following mechanisms: (1) contact-related local effects; (2) carcinogenic effect of cogeners such as flavorings, chemical compounds, and fermentation contaminants; (3) effect on DNA metabolism; (4) resultant effects of nutritional deficiencies; (5) effects on induction of microsomal enzymes that may activate carcinogenicity; (6) effects combined with hepatitis B virus; and (7) immunosuppressive effects (Lieber et al., 1986; MacGregor, 1986).

In summary, alcoholism, directly or indirectly, may cause damage to every organ in the body. This fact should never be overlooked by anyone involved in the treatment or research of alcoholic patients.

REFERENCES

American Psychiatric Association (1987). *Diagnostic and statistical manual of mental disorders (3rd ed.-R)*. Washington, DC: Author.

Ashley, M. J., Olin, J. S., & le Riche, W. H. (1976). Skid-row alcoholism a distinct sociomedical entity. *Archives of Internal Medicine, 136*, 272–278.

Beeson, P. B., McDermott, W., & Wyngaarden, J. B. (1984). *Cecil textbook on medicine.* Philadelphia: W. B. Saunders.

Benzer, D., & Cushman, P. (1980). Alcohol and benzodiazepines: Withdrawal syndromes. *Alcoholism: Clinical and Experimental Research, 4*, 243–247.

Carlen, P. L., Penn, R. D., Fornazzari, L., Bennett, R. N., Wilkinson, D. A., Phil, D., & Wortzman, G. (1986). Computerized tomographic scan assessment of alcoholic brain damage and its potential reversibility. *Alcoholism: Clinical and Experimental Research, 10*, 226–232.

Deiker, T., & Chambers, T. E. (1978). Structure and content of hallucinations in alcohol withdrawal and functional psychosis. *Journal of Studies on Alcohol, 39*, 1831–1840.

Donahue, R. P., Abbott, R. D., Reed, D. M., & Yano, K. (1986). Alcohol and hemorrhagic stroke. *Journal of the American Medical Association, 255*, 2311–2314.

Draper, R. J. (1978). The extent of alcoholic brain damage in the Republic of Ireland. *Journal of the Irish Medical Association, 71*, 356–360.

Edmondson, H. A. (1980). Pathology of alcoholism. *American Journal of Clinical Pathology, 74*, 725–742.

Freund, G. (1983). Neurologic diseases associated with chronic alcohol abuse. In B. Tabakoff, P. B. Sutker, & C. L. Randall (Ed.). *Medical and social aspects of alcohol abuse.* (pp. 165–186). New York: Plenum Press.

Gallant, D. M. (1981a). Phenylketonuria and fetal alcohol syndrome. *Alcoholism: Clinical and Experimental Research, 5*, 575-576.

Gallant, D. M. (1981b). Alcohol consumption: Effects on incidence of myocardial infarction. *Alcoholism: Clinical and Experimental Research, 5*, 345-346.

Gallant, D. M. (1982). Psychiatric aspects of alcohol intoxication, withdrawal and organic brain syndrome. *In J. Solomon (Ed.). Alcoholism and clinical psychiatry* (pp. 141-162). New York: Plenum Pub. Co.

Gallant, D. M. (in press). Treatment of alcohol related organic mental disorders. In *Treatment of psychiatric disorders*, Washington, DC: American Psychiatric Association.

Graff-Radford, M. R., Heaton, R. K., Earnest, M. P., & Rudikoff, J. C. (1982). Brain atrophy and neuropsychological impairment in young alcoholics. *Journal of Studies on Alcohol, 43*, 859-868.

Grant, I., Adams, K., & Reed, R. (1979). Neuropsychological abilities of alcoholic men in their late thirties. *American Journal of Psychiatry, 136*, 1263-1268.

Grant, I., Adams, K. M., & Reed, R. (1984). Aging, abstinence, and medical risk factors in the prediction of neuropsychologic deficit among long-term alcoholics. *Archives of General Psychiatry, 41*, 710-718.

Kissin, B. (1979). Biological investigations in alcohol research. *Journal of Studies on Alcohol, 8*, 146-181.

Kozararevic, D. J., Nojvodic, N., Dawber, T., McGee, D., Racic, Z., & Gordon, T. (1980). Frequency of alcohol consumption and morbidity and mortality. *Lancet, 1*, 613-616.

Lee, K., Moller, F., & Hardt, F. (1979). Alcohol-induced brain damage and liver damage in young males. *Lancet, 2*, 759-762.

Lieber, C. S., Garro, A. J., Leo, M. A., & Worner, T. M. (1986). Mechanisms for the relationship between alcohol and cancer. *Alcohol World: Health & Research, 10*, 10-17.

Lipson, A. A., Yu, J. S., & O'Halloran, N. T. (1981). Alcohol and phenylketonuria. *Lancet, 1*, 717-718.

Little, R. E., & Sing, C. F. (1986). Association of father's drinking and infant's birth weight. *New England Journal of Medicine, 314*, 1644-1645.

MacGregor, R. B. (1986). Alcohol and immune defense. *Journal of the American Association, 256*, 1474-1479.

Maletzky, B. M. (1978). The alcohol provocation test. *Journal of Clinical Psychiatry, 39*, 407-411.

McGivern, R. G., Clancy, A. N., Hill, M. A., & Noble, E. P. (1984). Prenatal alcohol exposure alters adult expression of sexually dimorphic behavior in the rat. *Science, 224*, 896-898.

Nagy, F., Pendergrass, P. D., Bowen, D. C, & Yeager, J. C. (1986). A comparative study of cytological and physiological parameters of semen obtained from alcoholics and non-alcoholics. *Alcohol & Alcoholism, 21*, 17-23.

Parsons, O. A. (1977). Neuropsychological deficits in alcoholism. Facts and fictions. *Alcoholism: Clinical and Experimental Research, 1*, 51-56.

Petrakis, P. L. (1985). *The effects of alcohol on the immune system.* Washington: NIAAA Working Document No. 85-02.

Podolsky, D. M. (1986). Alcohol and cancer. *Alcohol World: Health & Research, 10*, 3-9.

Puddy, I. B., Berlin, L. J. Vandongen, R., Rouse, I. L., & Rogers, P. (1985). Evidence for a direct effect of alcohol consumption on blood pressure in normotensive men. *Hypertension, 7*, 707-713.

Reisner, H. (1979). Das chronische subdurale Hamatom—Pachymeningeosis haemorragica interna. *Nervenarzt, 50*, 74-78.

Schuckit, M. A. (1982). The history of psychotic symptoms in alcoholics. *Journal of Clinical Psychiatry, 43*, 53-57.

Senior, J. R. (1985/1986). Alcohol hepatitis. *Alcohol Health and Research World, Winter issue*, 40-47.

Van Thiel, D. H. (1983). Effects of ethanol upon organ systems other than the cental nervous system. In B. Tabakoff, P. B Sutker, & C. L. Randall (Eds.). *Medical and social aspects of alcohol abuse.* (pp. 79-132). New York: Plenum Press.

CHAPTER 8

Management of Acute Alcohol Intoxication and Alcohol Withdrawal (Detoxification)

NONMEDICAL AS WELL AS MEDICAL personnel may be called upon to diagnose a state of severely acute intoxication or withdrawal in an alcoholic patient and to make a prompt, appropriate referral of the case. The two following case histories illustrate the importance of identifying this patient.

MR. D.: QUESTIONING FIRST ASSUMPTIONS

The first case is that of a 42-year-old alcoholic, Mr. D., who arrived with his wife in the office of a psychiatric social worker who specializes in treating patients with substance abuse problems. She had been treating this couple for five months and had finally succeeded in getting Mr. D. to begin Antabuse medication two weeks before the present visit. A contract had been arranged between the therapist and the couple whereby Mr. D. agreed to ingest the Antabuse "ground up" in half of a glass of water. According to Mrs. D., he had been faithful to the contract and had been taking the Antabuse in front of her every evening after dinner.

Mr. D. told the social worker's secretary that he was having problems with nausea, vomiting, malaise, and some diarrhea. The secretary automatically assumed that Mr. D. was having withdrawal symptoms from alcohol and suggested that Mrs. D. take her husband to a social detoxification center located in the neighborhood. As they were leaving, the secretary decided to interrupt the social worker, who was with another patient at the time, since she felt that she was not knowledgeable enough to make a final decision. The social worker came out to see Mr. and Mrs. D. and reviewed the history. Mrs. D. was certain that her husband had not had a drink in the past two weeks and had been taking his Antabuse on a regular basis. The social worker, aware that alcohol withdrawal symptoms almost always appear within the first seven days after abrupt cessation, reviewed the symptoms that had occurred in the last two weeks since Mr. D. stopped drinking. Both Mr. and Mrs. D. agreed that he had developed some mild anxiety and agitation in association with some insomnia which had lasted for about three to four days after cessation of alcohol. However, during the past 10 days, he had shown no evidence of any other significant problems until the development of the symptoms of nausea, vomiting, malaise, weakness, and diarrhea three days prior to this visit.

Feeling comfortable about her opinion that Mr. D. was not developing withdrawal symptoms at this stage of abstinence, the social worker phoned the internist whom she had consulted for initiating the Antabuse with Mr. D. She described the symptoms to the internist, who requested that she send Mr. and Mrs. D. over to his office at that time. He subsequently made a diagnosis of infectious hepatitis, which was related to raw oysters that Mr. D. had eaten several weeks prior to the onset of this recent illness. In this case, although the patient's life would not have been threatened by a misdiagnosis or a referral to a detoxification unit, he was able to receive rapid medical care without an unnecessary delay at a social detoxification unit, where the setting might have further obscured the diagnosis.

MRS. A.: DANGERS OF DELAYED TREATMENT

The second case involved one of our patients, Mrs. A., who relapsed into her former drinking habits without the knowledge of clinic personnel. We obtained the following history from one of our psychiatry residents about two weeks after her admission the hospital. Mrs. A. had come to the emergency room with the odor of alcohol on her breath; she had symptoms of anxiety and irritability, a tachycardia of 110, fever of 101° F, excessive sweating, and some nausea. The nurse in the emergency room concluded that Mrs. A. probably had influenza. The nurse and Mrs. A. had some type of minor argument, and the nurse decided that Mrs. A. should wait for the emergency room physician until he had attended several other patients. In fairness to the nurse, it should be noted that he was not aware that Mrs. A. was a severe alcoholic who had been drinking very heavily and had abruptly run out of her supply of alcohol the prior evening. Also, he was probably not concerned about the possibility of withdrawal since he had detected alcohol on her breath.

Several hours later, Mrs. A. was still sitting in one of the waiting rooms by herself when she had a "grand mal" seizure. She subsequently went into status epilepticus and was thrashing on the floor when the emergency room physician first saw her. She was immediately transferred to the neurology ward and the convulsions were controlled. Subsequently, Mrs. A. was transferred to psychiatry for follow-up treatment. Although Mrs. A. is now doing well, the case history does illustrate the potential dangers of delayed treatment for alcohol withdrawal and the importance of emergency room and alcohol treatment personnel's recognizing the signs and symptoms of this medical problem.

MANAGEMENT OF ACUTE ALCOHOL INTOXICATION

Many individuals remember a number of negative experiences with alcoholics. These experiences can contribute to an unconscious negative attitude toward alcoholic patients, particularly if they have the odor of alcohol on their breath when they are initially encountered, and may interfere with the development of an adequate therapeutic relationship (as suggested by the action of the nurse in the case of Mrs. A.). In most cases of mild alcohol intoxication, it is essential for the therapist to remember that her/his attitude will be the most important factor in determining whether or not the patient will seek follow-up therapy. The therapist must show concern for the patient's welfare, be nonjudgmental, and be honest in all statements to the patient. Although intoxicated patients may reveal some of their innermost feelings, these feelings are usually expressed inappropriately. Any anger or defensiveness on the part of therapist may result in the patient's rejecting follow-up therapy. A firm but kind therapeutic approach, even when the intoxicated patient is acting in an obnoxious manner, offers the patient the possibility of developing a trusting relationship—the key to future constructive efforts in follow-up treatment.

It is not usually necessary to admit a conscious intoxicated patient to a hospital. Close observation should be sufficient after other causes of intoxicated behavior have been ruled out. The patient should be placed on his or her side with the face down in order to avoid aspiration of vomitus.

In more serious cases of alcohol intoxication, when the patient is semicomatose or comatose, hospitalization is required since immediate steps may be necessary to sustain the airway, assure a regular respiratory rate, and maintain the circulatory system. Not only is the blood alcohol concentration useful as a diagnostic aid, but the osmolality may be of some help, for it is known that a blood alcohol concentration of 100 mg% increases the serum osmolality by 28 to 30 milliosmols per kg of water. If the osmolality is normal or only slightly increased, alcohol intoxication can be excluded as the cause of coma (Redetzki, 1977). High serum osmolality correlates with a high blood level of alcohol. The clinician should be aware that significant respiratory depression and death have occurred at concentrations of blood alcohol as low as 400 mg%.

In comatose patients who show impairment of respiration on admission, several emergency steps can be initiated while waiting for the results of the laboratory tests. In order to rule out severe hypoglycemia, 50 ml of 50% glucose solution can be given intravenously with 100 mg of thiamine. If the patient's skin shows needle marks indicative of narcotic drug use, the administration of naloxone in a dosage of 0.4 mg to 2.0 mg intravenously, repeated at two- to three-minute intervals, two or three times, may prove to be lifesaving.

The use of gastric lavage and activated charcoal is not indicated on a routine basis unless the ingestion of alcohol has taken place shortly before the patient's admission to the emergency room. Since alcohol is rapidly absorbed, these procedures are not necessary. However, if the blood level of alcohol is greater than 600 mg%, hemodialysis may be useful in patients with impaired liver function. The use of analeptics is of no value.

MANAGEMENT OF THE ACUTE WITHDRAWAL SYNDROMES

Alcohol withdrawal is defined in *DSM-III-R* as cessation of or reduction in prolonged (several days or longer) heavy ingestion of alcohol, followed within several hours by coarse tremor of the hands, tongue, and eyelids and at least one of the following: (1) nausea and vomiting; (2) malaise or weakness; (3) autonomic hyperactivity (e.g., tachycardia, sweating, elevated blood pressure); (4) anxiety; (5) depressed mood or irritability; and (6) orthostatic hypotension.

Mild to Moderate Alcohol Withdrawal

For the majority of patients displaying the syndrome of alcohol withdrawal, outpatient office treatment may be sufficient and one need not resort to hospitalization. The blood alcohol can be used as one of the more reliable guidelines for making a decision to place the patient in a social alcohol detoxification unit with specialized care, or to refer him to a medical ward for more intensive treatment of severe withdrawal symptoms, or to follow the patient at home with proper supervision. For example, if the alcohol level is 250 to 300 mg% and the patient appears to be alert and not dysarthric, then the physician should be on guard for the possible appearance of withdrawal symptoms as the blood alcohol level decreases. In this type of patient, the tolerance for alcohol is too high and suggests chronic alcohol abuse with an increased predisposition to develop withdrawal symptoms upon cessation of the alcohol.

In one study, only 45 of 564 patients (8%) of acute alcohol outpatient admissions required hospitalization (Pattison, 1977). In another extensive study of alcohol detoxification, fewer than 10% required medical detoxification; the remainder of the 1,024 patients in the study received nondrug detoxification (Whitfield, 1980). Seizures occurred in only 1%, hallucinations in 3.7%, and delirium tremens in fewer than 1%. However, 8% of the original sample did require medical referral to a hospital emergency room for further evaluation. Whitfield's treatment team was specially trained to deal with nondrug detoxification and instructed on how to "talk the patient down" and give him reality orientation in a therapeutic manner. Thus, the use of benzodiazepines was required in under 10% of the entire patient population. Many physicians refer patients to inpatient facilities where they are automatically placed on medication; this step makes it difficult to withdraw them later from the sedative hypnotics. If Pattison's and Whitfield's patient populations are representative of alcoholism populations in general, then it would not be an exaggeration to say that the majority of alcoholic patients should be able to withdraw from alcohol without the use of habituating minor tranquilizers.

One may help the patient to decrease the intake of alcohol with family aid and the use of a short-acting hypnotic for sleep for the next five to seven days (e.g., chloral hydrate). Muscle relaxation and deep breathing exercises may help the patient to decrease his discomfort as he goes through mild withdrawal (McFarlain et al., 1976). Other relaxation techniques, such as reality orientation, the use of mild, pleasurable, sensory stimulations such as appropriate music, the company of friends and relatives, attempts to keep the patient active, and reassurance may also be of help to the patient during this uncomfortable phase. In this way, it may be possible to substitute psychologic management for the automatic pharmacologic approach used by some detoxification units.

Thiamine, 50 to 100 mg per day, in addition to multivitamins and folic acid, 1 to 3 mg per day, should be given to all patients experiencing mild to severe alcohol withdrawal, orally for patients in the mild to moderate stages, and intramuscularly (i.m.) or intravenously (i.v.) for hospitalized patients with poor gastrointestinal absorption or those who are in a severe stage of withdrawal. Short-term administration of high dosages of vitamins should not result in any serious side effects. Shortly after the patient's blood alcohol reaches zero, disulfiram (Antabuse) should be seriously considered unless there are definite medical contraindications.

If the patient has a combination of symptoms during the withdrawal stage that are too uncomfortable to tolerate, hydroxyzine or a benzodiazepine may be used on a temporary basis. The drug should be administered by a relative or friend in order to be sure that the patient does not misuse it. Of course, the more severe the signs and symptoms of withdrawal, the more difficulty the patient will experience in abstaining from alcohol and the more frequently he should be seen at the office. It is not unusual for us to have patients come to the clinic on a daily basis when they begin taking disulfiram. We may give them only enough tranquilizers to last until they return to the clinic the next day. Dependency-producing medications such as benzodiazepines should not be used for more than one to two weeks because patients with problems of alcohol abuse are more likely to misuse these tranquilizers as well.

Among the safer agents to use on a *temporary* basis for sleep are sedative antihistamines, paraldehyde, and benzodiazepines. If emesis occurs, prochlorperazine, 10 mg i.m., can be used to control it on a temporary basis. The oral dosage of chlordiazepoxide for the outpatient management of withdrawal symptoms should not have to exceed 150 mg daily or not more than 30 mg of diazepam per day. If higher dosages are necessary, this usually means that the withdrawal symptoms are worsening and the patient may have to be placed on a detoxification unit or hospitalized.

If the patient has a past history of convulsions during withdrawal from alcohol, the drug of choice is one of the benzodiazepines, since they have anticonvulsive as well as sedative properties. In addition, with the oral administration of these agents, a peak blood level can be obtained within four to seven hours, whereas it takes a longer period of time with phenytoin (Dilantin). However, as Whitfield stressed, reassurance and reality orientation are the basis of the therapeutic approach for withdrawal symptomatology. The time required for the practicing physician to deal effectively with the alcoholic outpatient is not wasted because proper early treatment may decrease the number of repeat visits to the office or hospital for recurrences of the alcoholism and its medical complications.

Whitfield (1980) proposed the following procedures as standing orders for social detoxification in the ambulatory patient undergoing alcohol withdrawal:

1. Diet and fluids as desired (regular diet).
2. No restraints.
3. Vital signs every four hours.
4. History and physical examination by a physician or physician assistant within 24 hours of admission to the center.
5. Thiamine 100 mg, folate 1 mg by mouth daily.
6. Multiple vitamins by mouth daily.
7. Tylenol, antacid as needed.
8. No psychoactive drugs.
9. Provide a nonthreatening, positive environment.
10. Keep patient active, as tolerated.
11. Reality orientation, reassurance and respect in abundance.

12. Call physician or take patient to emergency department in hospital as indicated.

If the patient continues to drink sporadically during this outpatient treatment of the mild to moderate alcohol withdrawal syndrome, it may be necessary to institute inpatient detoxification even though the patient may not be experiencing severe withdrawal symptoms. From a therapeutic viewpoint, it may be necessary to interrupt the self-destructive cycle of heavy drinking followed by withdrawal symptoms, which are then relieved through resumption of alcohol intake.

Severe Alcohol Withdrawal (Alcohol Withdrawal Delirium)

Diagnostic criteria for alcohol withdrawal delirium include a clouding of consciousness, difficulty in sustaining attention, disorientation to present circumstance, and autonomic hyperactivity associated with tachycardia, sweating, and elevated blood pressure. These symptoms occur within one week after the cessation of or reduction in heavy alcohol ingestion. With adequate treatment, these symptoms should disappear by the end of the first week and surely by no later than the beginning of the second week. If untreated, the mortality rate may be as high as 15% (Dubin et al., 1986). A diagnostic problem may occur with the emergency room patient if the history of alcohol intake is unknown and there is no family available for information. Such diagnoses as schizophrenia, schizophreniform disorder, other psychotic disorders, or dementia can be confused with this diagnosis if the history of alcohol intake is lacking.

If the diagnosis of alcohol withdrawal delirium is correct, then immediate hospitalization is indicated, since the diagnosis infers that the patient is unable to care for himself and is seriously ill. The criteria for hospital admission of alcohol withdrawal patients are given in Table 8.1, which is modified from audit criteria for acute alcoholism admissions (West, 1978).

The temporary use of benzodiazepines may be of considerable help in alcoholics who have experienced recent alcohol withdrawal convulsions because these compounds possess anticonvulsant activity as well as sedative properties. If the patient is suspected of having a moderate amount of liver damage, the most appropriate benzodiazepines may be oxazepam or lorazepam, since they do not require hydroxylation by the liver and, therefore, do not accumulate. Chlordiazepoxide, diazepam, and chlorazepate are all metabolized in the liver and can accumulate in the patient who has a fair degree of liver damage, particularly since these agents have relatively long half-lives. Hydroxyzine is the safer sedative from the viewpoint of dependence, but its anticholinergic activity may confuse the patient if the drug is admin-

TABLE 8.1
Criteria for Hospital Admission of Alcohol Withdrawal Patients

	ELEMENTS	EXCEPTIONS	INSTRUCTIONS AND DEFINITIONS FOR DATA RETRIEVAL
	Diagnosis		
	1. (a) Psychomotor agitation and tremors or		Psychomotor agitation = shakes
	(b) Hallucinations		Acute intoxication = blood alcohol 150
	(c) Delirium or		mg/100 ml
	(d) Seizures		
	Admission		
J U S T I F I C A T I O N	2. (a) Acute intoxication or stage I with other disease or injury or	2 (A) Admission criteria, if not noted on	Stage I = psychomotor agitation, tachycardia
	(b) Stage II, III, or IV acute withdrawal syndrome	ER record, may be found on progress notes,	(pulse > 100) Temperature > 100° F tremulousness,
	(c) Acute intoxication with history of stage II, III, or IV withdrawal symptoms	history, physical, and discharge summary	sweating, hypertension (BP > 160/100)
			Stage II = above with hallucinations
			Stage III = above with delirium (disorientation)
			State IV = above with seizures or history of seizures
			Either the stage number or the symptoms may be recorded
	Above to be noted on ER/AC record		
	Treatment-Stages I-IV and acute intoxication		
	3. Sedatives and		
	4. Therapy		
	5. No restraints	5 (A) Restraints in stage III	Sedatives include the use of benzodiazepines
	6. Anticonvulsants if stage IV	if threat to self or others	Therapy (individual counseling, group therapy, Alcoholics Anonymous meeting) criteria met if any of the above is ordered and nurses' notes document participation

(continued)

TABLE 8.1
Continued

ELEMENTS	EXCEPTIONS	INSTRUCTIONS AND DEFINITIONS FOR DATA RETRIEVAL
OUTCOME Discharge status 7. Ambulatory and 8. All psychoactive drugs (sedatives) discontinued and 9. On solid diet 10. Mortality 11. Length of stay 5-10 days	11 (A) Complications below	
INDICATORS Complications 12. Dehydration	Critical preventive and responsive management I. V. fluid replacement	Dehydration as documented in record
13. Hyperpyrexia	Hypothermia machine, fluids	Hyperplexia = temperature > 104° F
14. Renal shutdown	Fluids, steriods(?), hypothermia machine	Renal shutdown = no urinary output
15. Esophageal hemorrhage	Blood replacement, portocaval shunt or sclerosing of veins or beta blocker treatment	Gastric hemorrhage = any vomiting of blood
16. Gastric hemorrhage	Blood replacement if hematocrit below 30	
17. Pancreatitis	Antibiotics, pain medication	

Modification of West, 1978.

istered in high dosages. Unlike the benzodiazepines, it has no anticonvulsant properties. The adequate use of sedative/hypnotic therapy for severe withdrawal symptoms, good nursing care, absence of restraint, a well-lighted room, and use of thiamine and multivitamins can help to alleviate the symptomatology.

The use of antipsychotic agents or neuroleptics for the withdrawal syndrome is questionable since these agents can lower the convulsive threshold, potentiate orthostatic hypotension, and cause uncomfortable atropine-like side effects. Some alcoholic patients receiving neuroleptics have been reported to develop prolonged unconsciousness (Holzbach & Buhler, 1979). These compounds can potentiate seizure activity, whereas benzodiazepines control and prevent the development of withdrawal seizures.

The dosage range for benzodiazepines should vary with the duration and intensity of the alcohol consumption prior to withdrawal, the weight of the patient, and other pharmacokinetic variables for which data are available. Although patients who present with high blood alcohol levels usually experience more severe withdrawal symptoms than patients with relatively low blood levels, these observations are not consistent. Exceptions may include patients who have experienced severe withdrawal symptoms following previous drinking episodes or those who have developed intercurrent illnesses during the present withdrawal stage. In mild to moderate cases of the alcohol withdrawal syndrome without delirium, the dosage of oxazepam may vary from 15 mg, q.i.d., to 30 mg, q.i.d.; the dosage of chlordiazepoxide from 25 mg, q.i.d., to 50 mg, q.i.d.; the dosage of diazepam from 5 mg, q.i.d., to 15 mg, q.i.d. In severe cases of the alcohol withdrawal syndrome with delirium, a dosage of oxazepam as high as 45 mg, q.i.d., may be needed; the dosage of chlordiazepoxide may have to be as great as 100 mg, q.i.d.; and a dosage of diazepam as high as 25 mg, q.i.d., may be required.

In one double-blind comparison of lorazepam and diazepam in the treatment of patients displaying mild to moderate alcohol withdrawal symptoms, 6 mg of lorazepam showed no significant differences in efficacy compared to 30 mg of diazepam, except for a significant drop in blood pressure in the diazepam-treated patients. Lorazepam is a benzodiazepine with a relatively short half-life compared to diazepam; thus, it may be simpler and more predictable in its pharmacologic effects for patients presenting the alcohol withdrawal syndrome (O'Brien et al., 1983). Another double-blind study evaluated chlordiazepoxide, maximum dosage of 300 mg daily, versus halazepam (Paxipam) in dosages as high as 480 mg daily, in 80 hospitalized alcohol patients in acute withdrawal from alcohol. Halazepam appeared to be equivalent to chlordiazepoxide in controlling symptoms in this patient population (Fann et al., 1986).

In another randomized, double-blind clinical trial of patients with alcohol withdrawal symptoms, a beta blocker (atenolol) was compared with placebo (Kraus et al., 1985). The atenolol patients, compared with patients receiving placebo, had a significant reduction in the mean length of hospital stay and required significantly less concomitant benzodiazepines than the placebo group. This study concluded that atenolol is a helpful adjunct to the use of benzodiazepines in the treatment of patients with alcohol withdrawal syndrome. However, because of the lack of anticonvulsant effects, it would be inadvisable to use a beta blocker alone for the treatment of acute alcohol withdrawal symptomatology. Another potential problem with the beta blockers is that they may potentiate the hypoglycemia that can occur in the first 36 hours after ingestion of large amounts of alcohol by malnourished alcoholics (Gallant, 1982). Since alcoholics seem to have an increased incidence of chronic obstructive pulmonary disease as well as cardiomyopathy, precautions about the use of beta blockers should be further emphasized. Clonidine, an alpha adrenergic agonist, has also been found to be effective in suppressing the symptoms and signs of alcohol withdrawal (Manhem et al., 1986); however, it is ineffective in controlling seizure activity.

It is extremely important to decrease and then discontinue the benzodiazepines prior to discharge from the hospital. It appears that those patients discharged on benzodiazepines are more likely to either become habituated to the medication or else return to alcohol (Gallant, 1982). An interesting analogy of this experience has been reported in mice. After chronic involuntary administration of alcohol, mice have been shown to have an increased tendency to continue self-administration of the alcohol when offered free choice between alcohol and tap water (Deutsch & Walton, 1977). Diazepam administered during the period of withdrawal served to maintain the alcohol self-administration. Without diazepam, the tendency toward self-administration of alcohol returned to control levels. The similarity of the examples in mice and human subjects concerning the return to alcohol consumption after using diazepam as a means of withdrawal is noteworthy.

Concerning the s.c. or i.m. use of benzodiazepines, the clinician should be aware that compounds such as chlordiazepoxide and diazepam are poorly absorbed. For example, 50 mg of oral chlordiazepoxide results, within two hours after ingestion, in plasma levels which are significantly higher than those following a 50 mg, i.m. dose administered to an abstinent patient (Perry et al., 1978). If the patient is vomiting profusely and unable to tolerate oral medication, then the use of i.m. lorazepam or prochlorperazine is indicated, along with possible use of prochlorperazine, 25 mg, as a suppository. It should be stressed that i.v. infusions should be used only in patients who are definitely dehydrated from excessive vomiting or diarrhea. Even in these cases, the clinician has to be cautious with glycogen-depleted patients who may be thiamine-deficient, since the patient may be converted to Wernicke's encephalopathy by a glucose infusion which would require additional utilization of thiamine. These patients should be weighed daily in order to evaluate their hydration state.

If the patient has had a recent history of alcohol withdrawal seizures or another type of seizures, the use of benzodiazepines possessing effective anticonvulsant activity is indicated. Since diazepam is rapidly absorbed after oral ingestion, a safe anticonvulsant blood level is more rapidly reached with this medication than with phenytoin (Dilantin). In addition, experimental studies in animals suggest that phenytoin may be less effective than diazepam in the treatment of alcohol withdrawal convulsions (Gessner, 1979). In both animal and human research related to alcohol withdrawal seizures, diazepam has been shown to be a most effective anticonvulsant (Guerrero-Figueroa et al., 1970). When seizures develop or are present on admission to the hospital, diazepam may be given i.v. at a dosage of 10 mg over a period of one to two minutes and then repeated until seizures cease, but no more than a total of 30 mg should be administered over a period of 15 to 20 minutes. The diazepam should be administered slowly in order to avoid laryngospasm. If this effort fails, then i.v. amobarbitol can be given at a rate of 100 to 150 mg per minute unless respiration is compromised. At that point, anesthesiology assistance may be required for a systemic induce- ment of muscle relaxation with succinylcholine and ventilation.

MANAGEMENT OF ALCOHOLICS WHO ARE
MULTIPLE DRUG ABUSERS

Increasing numbers of patients abuse habituating drugs in association with alcohol (Sokolow et al., 1981). The combined alcohol-barbiturate pa- tient presents an additional medical problem in the treatment of withdrawal since he or she is more likely to have seizures. A fairly reliable method of calculating the dosage of medication to be used during withdrawal in this type of patient is a substitution of 15 mg phenobarbital for one ounce of 100 proof alcohol. Administration of 200 mg pentobarbital may help the physi- cian to determine the extent of physical dependence. The appearance of ataxia with slurred speech at this dose suggests that the patient is not severe- ly physically dependent and should not require a very large dosage of the long-acting barbiturate for withdrawal purposes. If the patient is addicted, a relatively safe procedure for barbiturate addiction has been detailed (Robin- son et al., 1981). Phenobarbital is administered at a dose of 120 mg every hour until the patient develops three of the five following symptoms: dy- sarthria, ataxia, nystagmus, confusion, and drowsiness. The urine is main- tained at a pH of less than 6.5, which slows the excretion of phenobarbital, allowing the patient to follow a "smooth" withdrawal from the combination alcohol-barbiturate drug addiction. In a series of 54 cases, not one convul- sion developed with the use of this technique (Robinson et al., 1981).

In another study of combined alcohol-benzodiazepine addiction in 25 alcoholics admitted for detoxification, this type of patient was observed to experience a withdrawal syndrome atypical for alcoholics. These withdrawal symptoms started anywhere from two to ten days after abrupt discontinua- tion of drugs and were characterized by more psychomotor and fewer autonomic nervous system signs than usual in alcohol withdrawal (Benzer & Cushman, 1980). The timing and the nature of the specific symptoms in this combined sedative addiction resembled benzodiazepine withdrawal. When this withdrawal syndrome was diagnosed, the investigators used a sedative tolerance test with oral pentobarbital, 200 mg orally (p.o.) and 100 mg p.o. hourly until signs of sedation were evident, i.e., ataxia, slurred speech, nystagmus, or somnolence. The dosage of pentobarbital required to produce an objective effect varied from 400 to 800 mg. Treatment with oral pheno-barbital (30 mg for every 100 mg of pentobarbital required) was then institu-ted in divided dosages, and tapered, usually at the rate of 5% daily. If a dose reduction of more than 5% per day was attempted, there was a recurrence of withdrawal symptoms. In this investigation, the treatment with gradual ta-pering of oral barbiturates after a sedative tolerance test was effective. Since many alcoholics use benzodiazepines as well as alcohol, clinicians treating alcoholics should be alert to the possibility of a combined benzodiazepine-alcohol addiction, and these patients should be closely monitored for two weeks after the alcohol and the benzodiazepines have been discontinued.

Stimulants or euphorigenic agents, such as cocaine or amphetamines, combined with alcohol may result in a facilitation of withdrawal seizures if use continues during the first few days of withdrawal from alcohol. Routine urine drug screens of these patients should enable the physician to clarify the confusing clinical picture.

Because of the widespread use of alcohol in our society, both physicians and laymen are frequently too hasty in attributing unusual behavior or difficulty with coordination to alcohol. It is important to obtain a careful history and perform a meticulous examination of these patients as the odor of alcohol may lead to incorrect presumptions. However, once the diagnoses of acute alcohol intoxication or withdrawal is confirmed, prompt referral of the patient should result in successful treatment, since the medical manage-ment of these patients is relatively easy. The rapid response to treatment should be rewarding to the clinician.

REFERENCES

American Psychiatric Association. (1987). *Diagnostic and Statistical Manual of Mental Disor-ders (3rd Ed.-R)*. Washington, DC: Author.

Benzer, D. & Cushman, P. Jr. (1980). Alcohol and benzodiazepines: Withdrawal syndromes. *Alcoholism: Clinical and Experimental Research, 4*, 243-247.

Deutsch, J. A. & Walton, N. Y. (1977). Diazepam maintenance of alcohol preference during alcohol withdrawal. *Science, 198*, 307-309.

Dubin, W. R., Weiss, K. J., & Dorn, J. M. (1986). Pharmacotherapy of psychiatric emergen-cies. *Journal of Clinical Psychopharmacology, 6*, 210-222.

Fann, W. E., Orochofsky, V. C., Leslie, C. N., Cephus, P., & Crabtree, W. B. (1986). A trial of two benzodiazepines in acute alcohol withdrawal states. *Current Therapeutic Research, 40*, 218-224.

Gallant, D. M. (1982). Psychiatric aspects of alcohol intoxication, withdrawal, and organic brain syndromes. In J. Solomon (Ed.). *Alcoholism and Clinical Psychiatry*. New York: Plenum.

Gessner, P. K. (1979). Treatment of the alcohol withdrawal syndrome. *Substance Abuse, 1*, 2-5.

Guerrero-Figueroa, R., Rye, M. M., Gallant, D. M., & Bishop, M. P. (1970). Electrographic and behavioral effects of diazepam during alcohol withdrawal in cats. *Neuropharmacology, 9*, 143-150.

Holzbach, E., & Buhler, K. E. (1979). Die behandlung des delirium tremens mit haldol. *Nervenarzt, 49*, 405-409.

Kraus, M. L., Gottlieb, L. D., Horowitz, R. I., & Anscher, M. (1985). Randomized clinical trial of atenolol in patients with alcohol withdrawal. *New England Journal of Medicine, 313*, 905-910.

Manhem, P., Nilsson, L. H., Moberg, A-L., Wadstein, J., & Hokfelt, B. (1986). Alcohol withdrawal: Effects of clonidine treatment of sympathetic activity, the renin-aldosterone system, and clinical symptoms. *Alcoholism: Clinical and Experimental Research, 9*, 238-243.

McFarlain, R. A., Mielke, D. H., & Gallant, D. M. (1976). Comparison of muscle relaxation with placebo medication for anxiety reduction in alcoholic inpatients. *Current Therapeutic Research, 20*, 173-176.

O'Brien, J. E., Meyer, R. E., & Thoms, D. C. (1983). Double-blind comparison of lorazepam and diazepam in the treatment of the acute alcohol syndrome. *Current Therapeutic Research, 34*, 825-830.

Pattison, M. E. (1977). Management of alcoholism in medical practice. *Medical Clinics of North America, 61*, 797-809.

Perry, P. P., Wilding, D. C., & Fowler, R. C. (1978). Absorption of oral and intramuscular chlordiazepoxide by alcoholics. *Clinical Pharmacology and Therapeutics, 23*, 535-541.

Redetzki, H. N. (1977). Ethanol intoxication. In B. H. Rameck, & A. R. Temple (Eds.). *Management of the poisoned patient*. Princeton, NJ: Science Press.

Robinson, G. N., Sellers, E. M., & Janacek, E. (1981). Barbiturate and hypnosedative withdrawal by multiple oral phenobarbital loading dose techniques. *Clinical Pharmacology & Therapeutics, 28*, 71-76.

Sokolow, L., Welte, J., Hynes, G., & Lyons, J. (1981). Multiple substance use by alcoholics. *British Journal of Addiction, 76*, 147-148.

West, J. W. (1978). A medical audit of acute alcoholism and chronic alcoholism. *Alcoholism: Clinical and Experimental Research, 2*, 287-291.

Whitfield, C. L. (1980). Nondrug detoxification. In C. Whitfield (Ed.). *Phenomenology and treatment of alcoholism*. New York: Spectrum.

CHAPTER 9

Inpatient Rehabilitation Treatment

PROBLEMS IN EVALUATING SUCCESS RATES OF ALCOHOLISM REHABILITATION PROGRAMS

MANY STUDIES OF ALCOHOLISM treatment fail either to follow the patients for a long enough time or to use reporting sources (e.g., spouses) other than the patient. Because reporting by alcoholics has been shown to be undependable, any study of treatment success which does not employ urine assays for alcohol at random intervals bears an additional degree of unreliability (Orrego et al., 1979).

Another problem in evaluating treatment success differences among various alcohol treatment units (ATUs) was described in a study by Ettore in 1984. In a survey of 24 ATUs in Great Britain, significant differences were found among these units in most areas of evaluation and treatment. A comparison of admission requirements revealed that an assessment interview was required by all of the 24 ATUs, but a medical examination was a requirement in only 18 of these units. A patient had to be sober on admission in only 12 of these units and had to agree to some type of treatment contract in 13 units. Only nine units required a meeting with the patient's family. Reasons for admission refusal were as follows: "actively psychotic" (17 units); "not motivated for treatment" (14 units); "does not recognize that he/she has a problem" (12 units); "has a court case pending" (eight units); and "serious physical deterioration" (six units). With such different admission requirements, the patient populations may vary considerably; such variations could account for the significant differences in treatment successes after discharge from these ATUs.

It has been reported in a number of studies that treatment success rates

119

will greatly depend upon the type or subgroup of alcoholic patient admitted to the ATU, as well as upon the quality of the treatment program. In well conducted, controlled studies of various subgroups of alcoholics treated in the same program, it has been shown that "revolving-door alcoholics" or "skid-row alcoholics" have success rates in abstinence and social adjustment of less than 10%, even with intensive treatment and social and occupational help. Other subgroups of alcoholics, who have been defined as "criminal alcoholics" and "alcoholics who are married, employed, and involved with their spouses in follow-up therapy" have success rates varying from 50% to 70% in abstinence and social and economic adjustment at 12-month and 24-month follow-up evaluations. For this reason, before comparing the efficacy of different alcoholism treatment programs, it is essential to obtain data on the percentages of each of these alcoholic subgroups admitted to the programs (Brisolara et al., 1968; Gallant et al., 1968; Gallant et al., 1970; Gallant et al., 1973).

Treatment modalities and treatment goals also varied greatly among the British inpatient units Ettore studied. Although group therapy was the most widely applied technique, it was used as a primary modality in only half of the units. Physical exercises, social skills training, assertion training, and individual psychotherapy were "rarely ever used." Review of medication use showed that antidepressants, antianxiety agents, and hypnotics were each prescribed in slightly more than half of the ATUs, with varying percentages of inpatients receiving these drugs. One-third of the units used controlled drinking as a treatment modality, a greater number than would be expected in the United States, which may correlate with the less frequent use of AA on inpatient units in Great Britain.

Other problems in evaluating the efficacy of alcoholism treatment programs result from differences in treatment goals and definitions of treatment success. While some studies consider only total abstinence for a certain period of time as success, other studies evaluate status of abstinence at different periods of the follow-up, and still others may use days of abstinence prior and after treatment in association with quantity of absolute alcohol consumed before and after inpatient treatment (Edwards et al., 1977; Fuller & Williford, 1981; Gallant, 1979, 1982; McCrady & Sher, 1983; Miller, 1978). Some studies have included various types of measuring instruments for social and economic success as well as abstinence; others have concentrated only on abstinence (Gallant et al., 1973).

In addition to the differences in treatment modalities offered by various alcoholism treatment units, the duration of inpatient therapy is another important variable. In one study comparing patients undergoing short-term inpatient therapy from 5 to 15 days and those having a significantly longer inpatient treatment experience, the latter group showed significantly greater improvement in employment and reduction in alcohol use (McLellan et al., 1982).

The spouse's involvement is another important variable. In one study comparing inpatient treatment with "advice," the husband and wife were treated separately by different therapists (Wright & Scott, 1978). Another study revealed that the success rate increased significantly when the wife was actively involved in joint counseling sessions in both the inpatient and follow-up treatment (Gallant et al., 1970). In addition, the type of follow-up therapy has an obvious bearing on the final success rate and may be more important than the variety of treatment modalities offered by the inpatient alcoholism rehabilitation service.

In sum, when studying the efficacy of alcoholism inpatient treatment programs, researchers should consider the following variables:

- the subgroups of alcoholics, such as skid-row or criminal alcoholics or those with primary versus secondary alcoholism;
- the subgroups of alcoholics with associated psychiatric problems such as major depression or bipolar depression;
- definitions of success in terms of abstinence;
- quantity of absolute alcohol consumed;
- frequency of drinking;
- definitions of success in social and economic facets of the patient's life;
- definitions of the various treatment modalities that are offered to the patient in the study;
- balancing of groups in relation to duration of alcoholism, quantity consumed, genetic history, social and economic background;
- availability of spouse;
- type of therapy offered in follow-up treatment.

Since most studies to date have not considered all these factors, the early Rand study reporting that treatment of alcoholism is not significantly better than "no treatment" should not be regarded as conclusive (Armor et al., 1978).

DESCRIPTION OF THE ALCOHOL AND DRUG ABUSE UNIT (ADU) TREATMENT PROGRAM

Considering all of the problems in evaluating the quality and efficacy of alcoholism inpatient rehabilitation programs, it is apparent that there is no ideal treatment setting which has been shown to be significantly better than the others. Nonetheless, it is productive for the reader to have a detailed description of an inpatient treatment program, including its criteria for admission, physical plan, treatment goals, admission procedure, and various treatment modalities employed. I have chosen to describe our alcohol and drug abuse unit (ADU) at Southeast Louisiana Hospital, which received the Gold Award from the American Psychiatric Association achievement awards board in 1984 in "recognition of an exceptional 25-year alcoholism program including treatment, research, and training." Our treatment program, which offers a variety of efficacious treatment modalities for various subgroups of alcoholic patients, is detailed in the following sections (Gold Award, 1984; Gallant et al., 1968; Gallant et al., 1970).

Criteria for Admission and Exclusion

The criteria for admission to ADU are rather flexible. However, based upon our experiences during the past 25 years of operating the ADU service, certain guidelines are used. Patients with a primary diagnosis of schizophrenic disorder are not considered suitable for our treatment program, since the group therapy sessions at times involve a considerable amount of confrontation and direct criticism. We have found that patients with severe primary thought disorders are much too fragile to cope with this type of confrontation. Such patients become more alienated and suspicious of the treatment environment, subsequently isolating themselves, which leads to a negative experience rather than a positive treatment response. These patients require adequate treatment for their thought disorders before therapy for alcoholism is instituted. Thus, we offer consultation for schizophrenic patients on other psychiatric units of our hospital grounds, but we do not transfer these patients to our ADU service.

Another criterion for exclusion is having been discharged from our treatment program during the previous two years; we do not believe that a patient will benefit from the same treatment program within such a short period of time. Since most of such treatment failures usually did not keep their outpatient clinic appointments after they were discharged from the ADU service, we refer them directly to our outpatient alcoholism clinics. If a patient has completed our treatment program on two different occasions, we do not accept him for a third admission unless there are some very unusual circumstances. For example, if the patient has had a prolonged period of abstinence with good social and economic adjustment following each of two previous admissions and subsequently relapsed as a result of severe environmental stresses, a third admission would then be considered.

We do not necessarily exclude those with "poor motivation"; in fact, we believe that adequate inpatient rehabilitation treatment should help to stimulate the motivation of a patient who may have been referred to us because of a driving while intoxicated (DWI) charge or some other alcohol-related legal offense. An organic mental disorder is not a reason for exclusion, since many organically impaired patients show considerable improvement in their mental status within several weeks after admission to the inpatient service. These patients may, however, require a longer duration of treatment than other patients. Thus, we have very few criteria for exclusion.

There are some patients who definitely require inpatient rehabilitation. For instance, recently we admitted a 24-year-old patient who was orphaned at two years old and reared in 12 foster homes from the age of three until he was 14. Many of these foster parents were farmers who used the child to work in the fields without any concern for his education. The boy ran away when he was 14 years old. He had never developed any sustained relationship with anyone in his environment and showed a realistically paranoid distrust of the world. It would have been impossible to develop a trusting therapeutic relationship with this patient in an outpatient alcoholism program, seeing him once or twice weekly. Such a patient requires an intensive, healthy inpatient experience in a setting where he can learn to trust a number of the staff and patients. Living in a warm, accepting environment for six or seven weeks may enable the patient to learn how to relate in a comfortable way and modify his isolated, paranoid mistrust of the world.

There are many patients who may do quite well in outpatient therapy without inpatient treatment. If the patient faces losing his or her job because of a four-week stay in the hospital or if a patient shows intense motivation about treatment with a spontaneous request for Antabuse and sincerity about keeping clinic appointments, then outpatient treatment may be the appropriate choice. If this individual subsequently fails in outpatient treatment and is unable to maintain sobriety, then admission to an inpatient program should be seriously considered and probably is warranted. At present, we have no predictor items to indicate which patients will do well in therapy without inpatient rehabilitation treatment and which patients require such treatment. However, if a patient is definite about his request for inpatient alcoholism treatment, we almost always go along with his wishes, as long as his motivation seems sincere and is not simply a manipulatory move to avoid a legal problem or a gross abandonment of some social or business responsibility.

Description of the Physical Plant

A physical plant that has been specifically designed for an inpatient alcoholism rehabilitation program is one of the three essential elements for adequate treatment. (The other two components are a well-trained staff and a variety of treatment modalities offered to the patient.) Location of a rehabilitation treatment program on a specific floor of a general hospital restricts the patient's physical freedom and limits his access to a number of physical activities. The cost of the rehabilitation unit located in the general hospital is frequently somewhat higher than that of "free-standing" units because the overhead expenses are shared with other treatment services such as the surgical specialties. Limited physical space complicates treatment of alcoholics on a rehabilitation unit within a general hospital. In close quarters even cigarette smoking, a habit which is quite prevalent among alcoholics and extremely difficult for many of them to stop while they are in treatment for their alcoholism, is a problem for nonsmoking patients and staff. Having had the opportunity to be medical director both of alcoholism rehabilitation units within a general hospital setting and of a free-standing rehabilitation unit on the grounds of a psychiatric hospital, I have no doubt that it is much easier to maintain good patient and staff morale on a free-standing unit than within a general hospital setting.

Our alcohol and drug abuse unit is a one-story structure located on the grounds of the Southeast Louisiana State Hospital in Mandeville, Louisiana. Occupying a portion of the northwest quadrant of the hospital, the unit consists of six buildings situated in a spacious woodland setting and connected by covered walkways. The overall structure resembles a motel. The ADU service consists of the main building, two buildings for men's bedrooms (24 beds), one building for women (eight beds), one occupational therapy building, and a building with offices for three social workers. On the grounds nearby, there is a covered patio with a barbeque pit and picnic tables. Patients share the use of the hospital's gymnasium, auditorium, tennis court, ballfield, miniature golf course, and swimming pool. Although it is part of a psychiatric hospital with a total bed capacity of approximately 600 patients, the ADU service is a separate, geographically distinct treatment unit.

The main building of ADU consists of a large dayroom with an open fireplace for winter evenings and air conditioning for the summer. This dayroom is used for ward meetings, family meetings, AA meetings, and Al-Anon meetings. It is furnished with approximately 40 comfortable chairs, a piano, pool table, table tennis, television, record player, radio, several table games, and card tables. The main therapeutic function of this dayroom is the social intermingling of patients and their families. This building also houses the nurses' station, the psychiatrist's office, the secretary's office, a small kitchen, and ladies' and men's restrooms.

The patients' bedrooms are well ventilated and bright with natural lighting. There are two beds to a room with a bathroom between each two bedrooms. The patients have lockers for their clothes, a dressing table with mirrors, night tables and chairs. They are encouraged to take responsibility for maintaining their own living quarters. The occupational therapy room is equipped with arts and crafts, tools, and material for the patients' use. This is a small building with an adjoining storeroom for equipment. All rooms allow views of the outdoors and overlook a tranquil, rural scene. Patients with physical disabilities have access to all of the buildings on the ADU since the entire unit is on the ground level.

The average daily cost per patient on the ADU service (excluding utilities) is less than half the average national cost of approximately $95.00 per day. One of the reasons for the relatively low cost of this program, which has treated over 7,000 patients and trained thousands of medical students, nurses, social workers and others involved in alcohol and drug abuse, is that each of the staff members has been trained to perform multiple tasks. For example, our psychiatric aides have received extensive training and supervision in group therapy, and one of our licensed practical nurses has not only received training on the inservice program but has also enrolled in several courses at the School of Social Work at Tulane. She is now doing full-time therapy with our patients and is considered to be an excellent therapist. Our occupational therapist has been trained to conduct assertion group therapy and shows educational films to our patients and staff; he also films patients performing role-playing exercises in assertion group and replays these films for the patients to enhance their social skills and self-confidence. The medical director, who spends two full days a week on the unit, is available seven days a week for 30-minute ward rounds by telephone, assuring continuity of treatment by one physician (except for vacation time) and resulting in financial savings and a low budget for this program. The help of AA and Al-Anon members, who give their services free, also contributes to the relatively low cost for this program. Weekly AA and Al-Anon meetings are an integral part of the treatment program, and all patients are urged to begin reading the "Big Book" before discharge (*Alcoholics Anonymous, 3rd edition*, 1976).

Goals of Treatment

When the patient meets the psychiatrist for the first time at a "staffing" or history-taking session (the technique of group staffing will be discussed in the next section), the goals of treatment are defined by the psychiatrist as follows:

We have five major treatment goals for the patients and five major treatment goals for our staff. Having stopped your alcohol intake is only the first step in this type of rehabilitation approach. This present state of abstinence or sobriety now enables us to work with you on the following treatment goals:

(1) To evaluate your weaknesses and your problem areas which lead you into drinking or interfere with the quality of your life, and to help identify strengths that you have not been using in the past. We want you to start eliminating some of these problems and weak points while you are on our unit and start using your strengths in order to be able to abstain from alcohol and to improve the quality of your life.

(2) To understand yourself better. We want you to be able to comprehend fully the use of the denial mechanism, the psychologic means which all of us may employ at one time or another but which is present to a severe degree in someone with a drinking problem. This mechanism allows you to minimize or deny the fact that you have had a problem with drinking or deny the effects that your drinking problem has had upon the people around you. We want you to be aware of the many ways you can fool yourself and thus lead yourself back to drinking and interfere with the enjoyment of life.

(3) To understand from the very beginning of therapy that it is absolutely essential to follow up in treatment at the alcoholism clinic nearest your home for at least 12 months after discharge. You should attend this clinic once a week in addition to using AA for yourself and Al-Anon for your families and close friends. Almost all our patient failures are those who drop out of treatment during the first eight to twelve months. We can almost guarantee you that if you make every clinic visit for the next year after discharge, you will do well, not only with abstinence but also in other areas of your life.

(4) To learn how to enjoy life without the use of alcohol, not only after you leave the inpatient service but while you are on our service. This goal may be the most important one. Treatment should offer many opportunities for enjoyment, and we would consider our efforts a failure if you do not have some good laughs while you are with us. At the same time, you should be able to develop a feeling of value as a worthwhile human being. This feeling should be an emotional one and not just an intellectual insight. The more you enjoy yourself without alcohol and the more worthwhile you feel as a human being, the more you have to lose if you go back to drinking.

(5) To inform your friends and your relatives that you are now receiving treatment for alcoholism. This is an essential goal. The patient who covers up his admission to ADU out of a sense of embarrassment or pride usually ends up as a treatment failure. If you start treatment covering up your request for help, you tend to cover up in other areas. This can be quite dangerous when it comes to alcoholism and the denial mechanism. Friends or relatives who continue to drink heavily or become intoxicated in front of you after you've told them that you have sought help through treatment should not be considered your friends. They are being thoughtless and inconsiderate. It is impossible for somebody with a drinking problem to sit around and continuously watch other people drink and become intoxicated. Eventually, either you'll join in with these individuals or you'll have to leave them. If you are living with someone who has a drinking problem, that person will have to seek help immediately or the both of you may go down the drain together.

Not only do we have treatment goals for the patients, but we also have treatment goals for our staff. We, too, have to participate in an active way and not just play the "talking game." These five treatment goals all revolve around the development of TRUST, which is the most important element that exists among all human beings, not just between the therapist and the patient. These five goals are:

(1) We have to show each one of you that we are professionals and are knowledgeable about the diagnosis and treatment of alcoholism and related psychiatric problems.

(2) We have to show you that we are always listening to you, even though we do not always agree with everything that you tell us. If at any time during the next four to six weeks you feel that we are being too impulsive and prejudging too quickly, you have to let us know immediately—we do make mistakes.

(3) We have to show each one of you that we can be totally honest and admit our mistakes during the open ward meeting. If we cannot be honest with you, how can we expect you to be open and honest with us?

(4) We have to present a nonjudgmental approach and be able to show you that we are treating you and not judging you. If you feel that we are judging you or moralizing about your behavior, then the development of a trusting relationship will be impossible.

(5) Our most difficult goal is to show each one of you that we care about you as an individual, not just as one patient among 25 or 30. We have to show you that we care about you as a person; that is what each one of us wants to feel when somebody is treating us. In order to accomplish this difficult goal, we purposely give you a card with office and home telephone numbers of six of our key staff members: our nurse, our aftercare coordinator, our three therapists, and the medical director. We want you to feel free to call us at home or at work 24 hours a day, either when you are on pass from the hospital or later on after you are discharged. We particularly want you to call us if there is a crisis; we would like to have the opportunity to help settle the crisis on the phone rather than have you wait until your next clinic visit. We hope, when you have this card in your wallet or purse, you'll feel our personal concern for you.

If all of these five goals come together so that you feel that we know what we are doing, that we are listening, being honest with you, not judging you, and have a personal concern and interest in you, then a trusting relationship should develop and something good should happen in treatment.

In our experience, patients rarely abuse the availability of our staff's telephone numbers; the emotional response of our patients and their families to this approach enhances both their trust and their comfort and security on the ADU service. In using this approach, we are telling the patients that we are involved not only with their sobriety but also with the quality of their lives.

Our treatment experiences as well as research findings over the past 25 years have led us to select abstinence as a more realistic goal than controlled drinking. The reasons for selecting the goal of abstinence are as follows:

(1) The majority of our patients have a positive family history of alcoholism; this fact particularly applies to our male patients, whose fathers often have had drinking problems. Male offspring with a patrilineal history of alcoholism may have a genetic enzyme susceptibility to alcohol. Accepting a

treatment goal of controlled or "responsible drinking" in these patients can be disastrous after their discharge from an inpatient rehabilitation unit.

(2) The recent significant increase in polydrug abuse makes it much more difficult for young alcoholics to say no to drugs even if they have only had one or two drinks of alcohol. It is much easier to abstain from all drugs, including alcohol, so one has a clear head at all times.

(3) Recent research has shown how difficult it is for alcoholics to become successful controlled drinkers (Edwards, 1985; Helzer et al., 1985). Helzer et al. conducted a five-to-seven-year outcome study of 1,289 diagnosed alcoholics treated between 1973 and 1975. In this study, the interview team contacted an informant who was likely to know the subject's drinking behavior for verification of the self-report. This step is absolutely essential, since previous studies have shown considerable underreporting of alcohol consumption by alcoholic patients (Duffy & Waterton, 1984; Orrego et al., 1979). In Helzer et al.'s extensive study, only 1.6% of the surviving subjects met the criteria for moderate drinking; an additional 4.6% alternated between moderate drinking and abstinence. Only 15% had become totally abstinent while two-thirds of the subjects were classified as "continued" alcoholics. Although controlled drinking as a treatment modality was not employed with any of these patients, the results were disappointing enough to confirm our opinion that *when a staff is responsible for a very large number of alcoholic patients in a state treatment program*, abstinence should be the only practical goal, and controlled drinking should be utilized only as a research tool.

In Edward's investigation of a prior study which had reported that seven out of 93 alcoholic addicts achieved controlled drinking, his evaluation showed that only two had achieved trouble-free social drinking. At this time, as Glatt (1986) has stated, "Abstinence is the only generally viable alternative to continued alcoholism." However, this does not rule out the possibility that a subgroup of alcoholics, without a genetic family history but with psychologic factors contributing toward abuse of alcohol, may be able to control their alcohol intake with trouble-free periods of social drinking. It should also be emphasized that behavioral self-control training (BSCT) in alcoholics, when conducted by experienced therapists, can produce significant improvement on drinking measures (Miller et al., 1980). This technique employs the goals of controlled drinking instead of abstinence.

Admission Procedure

Each patient has a urine drug screen on admission. Since our ADU service does not have a detoxification unit on the grounds of the hospital, a patient who has a positive drug screen and a history indicating recent heavy alcohol or drug intake is referred to a detoxification unit and subsequently transferred back to the ADU. Before admission, patients are notified in the clinic interview that the ADU does not have a detoxification unit.

If the patient has a negative drug screen in the outpatient clinic which subsequently becomes positive on the day of admission to the ADU, that patient is referred back to the clinic until the urine is drug-free (except for the marijuana metabolite THC, which can last in the urine for three to five weeks; then only a decrease in concentration is required before readmission). After the urine is drug-free, the patient then is readmitted to the ADU service. These patients do not require detoxification, since their alcohol/drug intake occurred only between the time they were seen at the clinic and the time they arrived at the ADU service.

It is almost impossible at the present time to conduct an adequate rehabilitation program without performing urine drug screens, since approximately 40% of our alcoholic patients and as many as 46% of patients in other primary alcoholism treatment programs have an additional drug problem in association with the alcohol abuse (Sokolow et al., 1981). The incidence of polydrug abuse in association with primary alcoholism is more common in our younger patients. Ignoring this problem could result in undermining the treatment goals of the alcoholism program by introducing a patient who may contaminate a number of the other patients with drug use on the grounds of the hospital. This routine drug screen is also conducted each time a patient returns from a visit off the grounds of the hospital. We have found the procedure to be extremely helpful in encouraging our patients to decrease their use of drugs other than alcohol. In our experience, if the patient gets "high" on one drug, he or she is more likely to have trouble saying "no" to alcohol; it also holds true that the patient who takes one or two drinks of alcohol then has more difficulty saying "no" to other drugs.

At the time of admission, the patient is greeted by one of our staff members and a member of the patient committee who is in charge of welcoming new patients. In this way, the patient is not kept waiting for a long period of time before being assigned to a bedroom, and the anxiety about hospitalization is significantly decreased.

Our treatment orientation is what some individuals call a "cafeteria" approach, with emphasis on choosing different modalities to suit the patient's individual needs, rather than administering the same treatment to every patient. All patients are asked to participate actively in the evaluation of their psychological problems and the formulation of their treatment plans. They are asked to share responsibility for completing forms such as a self-assertiveness inventory, rating scales of anxiety and depression, and an 82-item fear-survey questionnaire. This enables us to obtain as complete a history as possible. These forms, which are completed by the patient during the first 48 hours after admission (unless the patient is still having some mild withdrawal symptoms), are available for the psychiatrist during the group staffing or group intake session.

In addition to this active participation in the self-evaluation, the patient participates in individual and group therapy. Group therapy sessions are scheduled four times weekly, with an alternative session on Saturday morning without the therapist. This allows the patients freedom to ventilate some problems which they may be inhibited from talking about in front of the therapist. In addition to individual and group therapy, the patients are also involved in assertiveness training, social skills training, behavior modification (when indicated for such problems as phobias or anxiety and tension), marital and family counseling, occupational and recreational therapy, and meetings with our clergy. An extensive medical evaluation is performed on each patient and treatment for specific medical problems is instituted when indicated. AA and Al-Anon meet weekly with our patients on the unit. The lecture material involves both didactic and experiential teaching films on both alcohol and associated problems of drug abuse. A United Fund agency, the Committee on Alcohol and Drug Abuse, sends its chief executive officer to present additional didactic material at least once weekly. (See Tables 9.1 and 9.2 for an outline of the lecture topics and film presentations.)

TABLE 9.1
Videotapes for Patient Treatment and Staff Education

Orientation to ADU*
Goals of Treatment for Patients and Staff*
Protracted Withdrawal Syndrome*
The Use of Medications in Treatment of Alcoholism (Includes Antabuse)*
Pot
The Nightmare of Cocaine
My Brother's Keeper
Alcohol and Drug Abuse Among Physicians*
Chalk Talk With Father Martin
12 Steps
Personality Disorders*
Crisis Intervention*
Schizophrenia—Signs and Symptoms With Patient
Demonstrations
Foster Brooks on Problem Drinking (16mm. film)
Secret Love of Sandra Blaine
A Slight Drinking Problem
A Time for Decision
About Addiction

*Copies of these films can be obtained by writing to Mr. Jim Ponds, ADU, Southeast Louisiana Hospital, Mandeville, LA 70448. Information about ordering the remainder of the films can also be obtained from Mr. Ponds.

TABLE 9.2
Lecture and Discussion Topics for Inpatients

The discussion sessions have been designed to give patients an overview of alcohol use and alcoholism. The lectures are intended as catalysts to the therapists' efforts in individual and group treatment sessions. Because of the frequent dual involvement of alcohol and other drugs, drug abuse and related dependency problems are included in the discussion sessions.

1. ETHYL ALCOHOL

I. *Types of alcohols*
   A. Varieties
   B. Common types
      1. Methyl
      2. Ethyl
   C. Uses
      1. Anesthetic
      2. Plastics
      3. Commercial uses
      4. Consumption
II. Ethyl alcohol
   A. Production
      1. Fermentation
         a. Grapes—Wine
         b. Grains—Beer and mash
         c. Molasses—Rum
   B. Types of drinks
      1. Beer
         a. Strength
      2. Wines
         a. Types
         b. Strength
      3. Hard Liquor—Spirits
         a. Distillation
            (1) Mash—Gin and Whiskey
            (2) Wine—Brandy
            (3) Fermented molasses—Rum
         b. Meaning of "Proof"
            (1) Percentage
            (2) Origin of word
   C. Food value
      1. Incomplete food
         a. No value in proteins, carbohydrates, vitamins, minerals, fats
      2. High in calories
         a. Jigger of whiskey—80-100 calories
         b. Highball—80 + mixer or about 150 calories
         c. Cocktail—210 calories
      3. Energy Source
         a. 1 gram sugar—4 calories

(continued)

TABLE 9.2
Continued

---

        b. 1 gram of protein—4 calories
        c. 1 gram of alcohol—7 calories
        d. 1 gram of fat—9 calories
   D. Depressant
      1. Chemical cousin of ether
      2. Depressant drug
        a. Opposite of stimulant
        b. Some people can become addicted
      3. Similarity with other addictive drugs
   E. Absorption
      1. Factors involving absorption
        a. Exposing the myths of absorption prevention
          (1) Cream
          (2) Butter
          (3) Oil
      2. Oxidation process
          (1)Ethyl alcohol
          (2) Acetaldehyde
          (3) Acetic acid
          (4) Acetyl coenzyme A
      3. Antabuse in relation to oxidation
      4. Erroneous techniques of elimination
        a. Coffee
        b. Walking
        c. Cold Shower
III. *What happens when we drink*
   A. Effects on sensorium
   B. Factors involved
      1. Weight
      2. Food in stomach
      3. Rapidity of consumption
   C. One or two drinks
      1. Blood level
        a. .02%
      2. Sensorium affected
      3. Behavior affected
        a. Inhibitions
        b. Judgment
      4. Conduct
        a. Shyness removed
        b. Fears eliminated
        c. Job problems
        d. Social problems
   D. Three or Four drinks
      1. Blood level
        a. .06%

(continued)

TABLE 9.2
Continued

2. Sensorium affected
3. Behavior affected
   a. Reaction time
   b. Coordination
4. Conduct—taking chances
E. Five or Six Drinks
   1. Blood level
      a. .10%
   2. Sensorium affected
   3. Behavior affected
      a. Vision
      b. Speech
      c. Balance
   4. Conduct
      a. Thick tongue
      b. Vision blurred
      c. Making contact with ignition
      d. Automobile accidents
      e. Fatalities
F. Eight or Nine Drinks
   1. Blood level
      a. .16%
   2. Sensorium affected
   3. Behavior affected
      a. Walking
      b. Standing
   4. Conduct
      a. Swaying
      b. False security and relaxation
      c. Danger of injury
G. Twenty or more drinks
   1. Blood level
      a. .40%
   2. Sensorium affected—anesthetic effects
   3. Behavior affected—degree of consciousness
H. Twenty-five or more drinks—large quantities in gulp
   1. Blood level
      a. .50% or higher
   2. Sensorium affected
      a. Respiratory depression
      b. Cardiac effects
I. Oxidation and elimination time (within hour)
   1. One drink—1 hour
   2. Three drinks—4 hours

(continued)

TABLE 9.2
Continued

3. Five drinks—6 hours
4. Eight drinks—10 hours
5. Twenty drinks—26 hours
J. Tests for intoxication
K. Tolerance
L. Hangover

2. TYPES OF ALCOHOLICS

Perhaps many of us are here with the impression that we do not belong on the unit. You might think that you are just a "little bit alcoholic." Being "a little bit alcoholic" is like being a "little bit pregnant." Either you are or you are not.

How much you drink, how frequently you drink, whether you get drunk or not, are only a part of the problem. How alcohol affects your life is the most important question.

I. *Types of alcoholics*
   A. Primary
   B. Secondary
II. *Classification of alcoholics (Jellinek)*
   A. Alpha—psychological dependence
   B. Beta—physical complications due to drinking
   C. Gamma
      1. Gross drinking behavior
      2. Condition worsens
      3. Loss of control
      4. Addiction
   D. Delta—inability to abstain
   E. Epsilon—spree drinker—may be able to use the denial mechanism in a more subtle way than other alcoholics
   F. Plateau drinker—characteristics exhibited
III. *Follow-up treatment*
   A. What occurs when we return home
      1. Happy and smooth return
         a. Need for follow-up
         b. Reason for success
         c. What drinking can do
      2. Rough return
         a. Need for follow-up
         b. What drinking can do
         c. Things can always be worse

3. DEVELOPMENT OF ALCOHOLISM

I. *Life*
   A. Compared to cauldron
      1. Tension producers
         a. Domestic, financial, vocational

(continued)

TABLE 9.2
Continued

     (1) Ambitions
       (2) Frustrations
       (3) Failures
       (4) Resentments
       (5) Anxieties
       (6) Isolation
   2. Well-adjusted Life
     a. Eliminated tensions
       (1) Social activities
       (2) Family
       (3) Church
       (4) Hobbies
       (5) Hopes
       (6) Goals
       (7) Money
       (8) Work
       (9) Alcohol
II. *The problem drinker and alcoholic*
  A. Gross drinking behavior
  B. Blackouts
  C. Gulping and sneaking drinks
  D. Antisocial behavior
  E. Loss of friends and jobs
    1. Social life
     a. Friends avoid him
     b. No social contact—important avenue of tension escape blocked
  F. Protecting supply of alcohol
  G. Loss of control
    1. Mark of an alcoholic
    2. Hopes for present and future blurred—no motivation
  H. Alibi system
    1. Rationalization
    2. Denial
  I. Drinking alone
    1. Family on the rocks
    2. Communications
     a. Difficult situation—lack of understanding
     b. How non-alcoholic is affected
    3. Family
     a. Separation
     b. Divorce
  J. Tremors—minor withdrawal
  K. Hospitalization
    1. Medical assistance costly
    2. Drinks in grandiose style

(continued)

TABLE 9.2
Continued

       3. No pleasure out of money
       4. Financial problems
       5. Debts
   L. Unreasonable resentments
   M. Rock bottom
       1. Analyzed
       2. Only escape for tension is alcohol
   N. Collapse of alibi system
       1. Admit defeat and continue to drink
       2. Admit defeat and seek help
   O. Alcoholism is treatable
III. *Road back*
   A. Open avenues to cauldron of life
       1. Clinic
          a. Physical help
          b. Mental or psychological help
          c. Social help
       2. Spiritual help
       3. Alcoholics Anonymous—fellowship
       4. Opening allows tension to escape
   B. Block out alcohol
       1. Alcoholism is "incurable"
       2. Alcoholism requires total abstinence
       3. House burning—put out flames—then seek reason
       4. Powerless over alcohol
   C. Rehabilitation
       1. Sobriety is first step
       2. All areas of life must be readjusted or put in functioning order
          a. Social life
          b. Family
          c. Church
          d. Hobbies
          e. Hopes
          f. Goals
          g. Money
          h. Work
   D. Team approach
       1. Physician
       2. Psychiatrist
       3. Social worker
       4. Psychologist
       5. Clergy
       6. Other therapists—fellow alcoholics
   E. Aim
       1. Self-respect
       2. Normal living
       3. Usefulness in society
   F. Referral aids

(continued)

TABLE 9.2
Continued

4. WHY PEOPLE DRINK

I. *Attitudes about drinking*
  A. Prohibition
  B. Puritanical
  C. Religious
II. *Why people drink*
  A. Prevalence of alcohol
  B. Reasons for drinking
    1. Taste
    2. Toast
    3. Relax
    4. Euphoria
    5. Have fun
    6. Escape
III. *Why problem drinkers drink—excuses given*
  A. I owe everybody
  B. It's the only way I can relax
  C. It's my nerves
  D. It's my mother-in-law
  E. Nobody understands me
  F. It's hereditary with me
  G. My job gets me down
  H. If you want to be successful, you have to entertain
  I. I'm a very sick man
  J. I can take it or leave it alone
  K. It helps me think
  L. I'm all right as long as I stick to beer
IV. *What's your reason or excuse for drinking?*
  (see Figure 9.1)

5. PHYSICAL COMPLICATIONS (Part I)

I. *Diseases*
  A. Reversible
  B. Irreversible
II. *Common complications suffered by problem drinkers*
  A. Medical complications
    1. Heart; blood pressure and "strokes"
    2. Kidney and bladder
    3. Stomach
      a. Gastritis
      b. Ulcers
      c. Perforated ulcer
    4. Peripheral neuropathies

(continued)

TABLE 9.2
Continued

---

    5. Brain damage
    6. Types of liver damage—development
    7. Other medical complications
    8. Skin manifestations of alcoholism
  B. Nutritional problems
    1. Alcohol—poor food
    2. Malnutrition
    3. Drinking—no eating
      a. Caloric intake
      b. Diseases and effects
    4. Vitamin needs
    5. Vitamin deficiencies
  C. Withdrawal
    1. Shakes
    2. Hallucinations
    3. DT's

6. PHYSICAL COMPLICATIONS (Part II)

  I. *Fetal alcohol syndrome*
    A. Suspicions concerning abuse
    B. Animal studies
    C. Malformations, etc., with ethanol group
    D. Human subjects—description and research data
  II. *Smoking*
    A. Content of cigarettes
    B. Effects on lungs
    C. Effects on heart
    D. Effects on other organ systems

7. OTHER DRUGS OF ABUSE

  I.*Philosophy of drugs*
    A. Good and bad use
    B. Legal and illegal use
    C. Addiction vs. dependence
  II. *Why people take drugs*
    A. Feel comfortable
    B. Feel accepted
    C. Peer pressure
    D. Escape
    E. Cope with tensions and pressures
    F. Other
  III. *Causes of drug abuse and addiction*
    A. Cope with pressures

(continued)

TABLE 9.2
Continued

   B. Use to cope with pain and illnesses
   C. Use to seek pleasure
   D. Availability
   E. Physical and mental makeup
   F. Social factors
   G. Continued use regardless of reasons
   H. Peer pressure
   I. Other
IV. *Classification of drugs*
   A. Depressants
      1. Barbiturates
      2. Alcohol
      3. Heroin
      4. Methadone
   B. Stimulants
      1. Amphetamines
      2. Nicotine
      3. Methamphetamines
      4. Cocaine
   C. Hallucinogens
      1. LSD
      2. Mescaline
      3. Volatile substances
   D. Marijuana
   E. Review of each classification as pertinent to drug
      1. Identification of drug
      2. Signs of use
      3. Dangers
      4. Withdrawal (when relevant)
V. *Life and drugs*
   A. Alternatives to drugs
   B. Natural high

8. CHAPLAIN LECTURES

Emphasizes the spiritual needs of patients in relation to helping other individuals (e.g., AA, volunteer work, etc.). Discussions are based on defining moral behavior as preserving the dignity of self and others and on the moral obligation to preserve life.

9. BEHAVIOR MODIFICATION LECTURES

A series of lectures on various treatment modalities such as muscle relaxation, breathing, and role playing with stress reduction exercises.

"Sure you do! There is not a case on record of a man who drank his way out of debt. . . . Figure out what and whom you owe and make up your mind to pay it all off—and start paying—and watch your self-respect boom. It may work. . . . "

"You mean, of course, collapse. . . . This is unavoidable in an alcoholic. No matter how long he's been sober, one drink is enough to start the cycle. . . . He relaxes on the street, in doorways, in gutters. . . . Just don't relax your resistance to suggestion."

"You said it, brother! There are no nerves so frayed as those of a bottle baby. . . . I wouldn't deny a man a drink, but nerves—that's something else. When liquor is what you need to keep you normal, my friend, you're in sore need of a doctor. . . . "

"Why, the old hay bag! What a ferocious, meddlesome, insufferable fiend from the pit she is. . . . She's also been your best excuse for over 2,000 years. . . . But give her a chance, son. . . . Don't blame her for sniping. After all, she is somebody's mother."

FIGURE 9.1
What's Your Excuse?

"The sorry part of this excuse is that you get to believe it yourself. It sounds so convincing. . . . You don't need understanding, you need treatment. . . . But settle down, most drunks wind up talking to themselves anyway. . . . "

"Talk straight, mister. I didn't hear you. Did you say you're getting your job down? Well, that's what you meant. . . . When you start drinking heavily you've changed jobs. The old man in the front office isn't your boss—Alcohol is!"

"The common cold is an alcoholic's best friend. . . . Yes, he's a sick man, but not with a cold. No germ could last in a system saturated with alcohol. . . . When you sober up, you'll feel so healthy friends will avoid you. Maybe you need new friends. . . . "

"Listen, if you were clear-headed enough to have any choice in the matter, you'd have no need even to make such a statement. . . . Ever ask yourself why you always decide to take it? . . . An alcoholic must say: 'I CAN LEAVE IT ALONE!' "

FIGURE 9.1
Continued

" . . . Great thinkers have been great drink-ers—but not for long. The only successful al-coholic is a dead one. Alcohol is a stimulant, yes, but like a drug it is depressively reaction-ary. It keeps you from acting. You only think you think."

"Well, good for beer! Only trouble is it gnaws at an alcoholic's weak spots until he switches to something stronger. That's the way I did it. . . . Beer will nickel and dime you to death. . . . No, it's not beer, baby—it's only you. . . ."

FIGURE 9.1
Continued

Group Staffing Technique

Unfortunately, in many alcoholism treatment institutions the standard process of "staffing the new patient" has acquired certain ritualistic aspects. In some programs, the psychiatrist or professional alcoholism counselor, psychologist, social workers, nurses, psychiatric aides, and sometimes visiting medical students or other hospital therapy personnel attend the staffing. In other programs, the patient may be seen alone by the counselor and then have his or her history presented in a subsequent session to other staff members. The patient, whose anxiety is already intensified by the unfamiliar environment, is expected to discuss intimate information with these strangers.

A new hospital environment frequently includes some regimentation.

restricted communication, loss of physical freedom, and the necessity of assuming a passive role in relation to an authoritarian atmosphere—all of which may unavoidably infringe upon the patient's sense of personal identity. When each patient is staffed individually, his alienation and estrangement are compounded by the realistic discomfort he suffers as the only patient among professional staff. In this atmosphere, the alcoholic patient may tend to exaggerate his denial. Moreover, his hostility toward authoritarian figures may be aggravated by the submissive role that has been assigned to him as patient.

On the ADU service, three or four patients are staffed simultaneously. The average group staffing session lasts four to four and a half hours, with one or two 15-minute breaks. This relatively long period of time with the patients allows the psychiatrist to learn more about the patients from a nonverbal point of view; simultaneously, the patients have a greater opportunity to understand and learn more about the psychiatrist. This procedure allows the staffing to be completed within three days after the patient's admission.

Prior to the staffing, the social worker's histories are reviewed, and the following essential information is noted:

- reason for requesting help;
- closest interpersonal relationship previously experienced by the patient;
- previous group experiences which may have been either very positive or negative;
- duration of alcoholism;
- severity of physical symptoms associated with alcoholism;
- evidence of a better adjustment level in the past; and
- potential family and occupational resources available to the patient while in the hospital and after discharge from the ADU.

Having already been briefed about the procedure, the patients realize that they may freely refuse to answer any questions considered too intimate for group discussion and may request that the psychiatrist or the assigned social worker reserve such questions for a private session.

This group staffing, with emphasis on group therapy techniques, permits the patients early in the course of their hospitalization to realize their ability to offer help to their fellow human beings, as well as to receive help from them. The patients are encouraged to develop an evolving awareness of self in relation to others and to develop responsibility for their group. The group staffing procedure is a very helpful start toward this goal, which is later accomplished in group therapy. In this group staffing, realistic anxiety about the present and future is discussed and are assessed within a controlled therapeutic environment.

An active, direct approach is used early in the group staffing session. The therapist's immediate goal is to induce a feeling of cohesiveness and unity within the group, thereby promoting the tendency of group members to interact. The therapist requests the assistance of the group, admitting that he or she alone cannot help the patients. Thus, we ask one of the patients present at the group staffing to ask a few questions of the patient from whom the initial history is being obtained. The patients are complimented for their ability to ask appropriate questions, and positive reinforcement is offered to stimulate this type of group interaction in which one patient assumes social responsibility for his fellow human being.

Usually we pick the patient with the most severe history of alcoholism (blackouts, delirium tremens) as the initial focus of the staffing interview. This patient is encouraged to discuss freely the early symptoms of alcoholism and subsequent addiction. The other patients are then offered the opportunity to identify their own alcoholism as in the early, middle, or late stage. The technique of "going around" is used, forcing the patients into the role of co-therapists. This technique is ego-strengthening, since it encourages patients to recognize their ability to contribute to the welfare of others. The therapist forces interaction by drawing out opinions and feelings from the patients about the problems of others. Although the alcoholic may use his or her denial mechanism expertly with the staff, he/she will have difficulty maintaining this defense in the presence of two or three other alcoholics. The ability of the group to arrive at a realistic consensus regarding the accuracy of a fellow alcoholic's drinking history provides validation for the therapist.

It is generally accepted that no typical character or personality pattern is shared by all alcoholics. However, exaggerated dependency needs and difficulty in expressing anger appropriately are quite common. These problems are probed in the middle stages of the group staffing, starting with the dynamic developmental sketch of one of the other patients. Each of the patients is asked to give an early developmental history concerning family relationship with parents, school relationships, and other interpersonal problems and psychodynamic defense mechanisms that developed prior to the alcoholism. The genetic history is carefully explored.

Common difficulties are used to foster empathy and identification among patients. The mechanism of identification helps the other patients to discuss their own problems and to offer additional information about their own early development. The denial mechanism is freely discussed at this time, and problems outside of alcoholism are mentioned in relation to this defense. The collective strength of the group allows the patients to admit some of these difficulties and adds immeasurably to their initial orientation to the group treatment program.

It is amazing how much personal, sometimes embarrassing, and very relevant information is obtained during these group staffing sessions. Some of my medical students are extremely surprised about the amount of information that we gather during these meetings; their initial reaction is, "I could never talk about myself in a group that way." However, by the end of a staffing session, not only the students but also the patients usually feel quite comfortable about all of the information elicited. The most paranoid patient is usually saved for the next-to-last or last staffing, in order to show the patient that some trust can be developed within the setting and that any information that he may not want to offer can be easily addressed in a follow-up private meeting.

At the termination of the initial staffing session, the patients are encouraged to discuss the material among themselves but cautioned not to bring information about one of the other patients into the group therapy meetings unless that patient decides to bring the material up on his own. In summary, it has been our experience that the goals of diagnosis, prognosis, and therapeutic management can be readily evaluated and achieved within a group staffing. This procedure has several advantages:

1. Early evaluation of the patient by the staff minimizes mistakes associated with the early phases of treatment.
2. This interpersonal approach permits early identification of patients with others in the group and discourages further alienation.
3. The early transference relationship among the patients can be used therapeutically during hospitalization. Assumption of the role of co-therapist early in treatment is ego-building, as the patient becomes aware of his or her ability to contribute to the welfare of others.
4. Transactions within the group quickly reveal a patient's individual personality traits, providing the therapist with an early opportunity to observe the patient's interpersonal as well as intrapsychic reactions. The therapist is then able to plan a more effective treatment program for the individual patient shortly after admission to the hospital. Moreover, the patient's ability to assume a degree of social responsibility for ward activities can be adequately evaluated by this procedure.
5. The alcoholic patient's expert use of the denial mechanism is approached effectively within the group staffing procedure.
6. The patient's suitability for individual or group therapy or both is

adequately evaluated during this early phase of hospitalization within a group staffing setting.

7. Paradoxically — and possibly even more important than the previous advantages — differences and unique characteristics in patients' personalities are more obvious to the staff and other patients when they are sitting together than when they are interviewed one by one in an individual staffing.

As of this time, no indications have been found for excluding any specific personality disorders from such a group setting. The patients have exhibited a strong positive response to this early therapeutic contact with the hospital. In fact, this group staffing session has been in use since 1962 without any negative consequences coming to our attention. The staffing procedure is considered to be a positive, realistic approach to the therapeutic management of the hospitalized alcoholic patient. (In Chapter 11, a description of a research evaluation of this group intake session in an outpatient setting will be detailed. In that research study it was shown that this type of staffing technique is not only efficacious in terms of time but was also very effective in terms of treatment success).

At the time of admission to the hospital, patients are given rating sheets to evaluate the quality of the admission procedure: how long they were kept waiting; the attitude of the people who welcomed them; and whether or not their initial questions were answered satisfactorily.

Patients are also given global rating forms to evaluate 16 different aspects of the treatment program at the time of their discharge: the evaluation of the aftercare coordinator, social skills group training, group therapy, the psychiatrist, the nursing staff, occupational therapy, activity therapy, films, the bedroom, the food, laboratory services, medical services, the program schedule, secretary, chaplains, and social workers. Since patients do not have to sign their names, they do not hesitate to express negative feelings. Such questionnaires should have a "scapegoat" item, i.e., a service which is known for its poor quality. In the case of our state hospital, as is the case with many other state institutions, the quality of the food is not as good as the quality of the treatment. Thus, if a patient grades the food as "excellent," we may pay less attention to his evaluation sheet than to those of others who are a bit more discriminating.

Group Therapy

It is important for all therapists on an alcoholism rehabilitation unit to realize that each patient will progress at a different pace in group therapy. Some patients may have significant cognitive impairment, as described in

Chapter 7 in the section on Subacute Organic Mental Disorder. They may become easily frustrated when they are expected to participate actively within a group therapy setting. Other patients, who have been abstinent for several weeks prior to admission to the alcoholism rehabilitation unit, may have no difficulties.

There are a number of other variables that affect the patient's participation in group therapy. For example, consider an individual who grew up in a family setting in which he or she was the only child, had no healthy group experiences with peers in school, failed to develop any long-term relationships, and had parents who were extremely poor in communicating with each other as well as with the child. Since such a person may have a severe distrust of the group setting, the therapist has to proceed very slowly. This patient should be seen frequently in individual counseling and learn how to trust the therapist before being placed in a group. On the other hand, therapy may proceed more rapidly with a person who grew up in a family with several brothers and sisters, had some good positive group experiences within the home and at school, and later in life married and had children. This patient should "swim" very easily within the group setting and participate actively from the very beginning of the placement in the group.

The goals of group therapy are to penetrate the patient's denial mechanism and help this individual develop a healthy living experience within the group setting. In the group meetings on the ADU service, the "here and now" approach to treatment is strongly emphasized. Honest, direct impressions of one another are consistently requested of the patients. Opinions on improvement in behavior, character deficits, constructive or destructive behavior, and attitudes towards each other are constantly sought in these treatment sessions. Some advantages of the group therapy structure are: consensual validation; raising one's self-esteem through sharing responibility by giving honest opinions about other fellow patients; modeling behaviors, such as assertion, for others in the group; and natural humor, which is more readily tapped within a group situation than in individual therapy. The therapist attempts to act as the facilitator by having the patients question each other; thus, the patients do most of the work within this type of group setting. At the same time, it is the responsibility of the therapist to promote healthy behavior within group structure and to step in if destructive behavior starts to occur.

It is important to allow the passive, isolated patient to move at his own pace at the start of treatment and to shelter the mildly brain-damaged patient. Direct confrontations with these types of individuals are definitely not therapeutic during the early phase of rehabilitation treatment. Such patients require a more supportive type of counseling. The passive patient has to learn additional social skills and assertion. There should be a social skills training or assertion group available within the same rehabilitation treatment program. Otherwise, group therapy can become a destructive experience for this patient, who may feel like a failure if he or she is never able to speak up and participate in the same way that other patients do. The brain-damaged patient should be allowed to be a passive observer of the initial group meetings. The group should be informed that this individual has had a recent, devastating alcohol binge which requires a longer phase of recovery before he/she can participate in an active fashion.

Women's Group Therapy

Every rehabilitation unit that treats both sexes should have a women's group available once or twice a week. It is not unusual for a passive, female alcoholic patient to be inhibited in group therapy or to have difficulty discussing embarrassing information in front of the male patients. We had one patient who had been sexually molested by her father and, just prior to admission, was confronted with sexual advances from her alcoholic father-in-law. She was much too embarrassed to discuss this problem in a mixed group but was able to relate the incident and ventilate her feelings in our women's group. After acceptance of her problem in the women's group, she was able to tell her husband about the problem and later to discuss the past and present sexual molestation in our mixed group, where she received good, healthy support from the group members.

In another case, a 22-year-old female patient with bulimia was far too intimidated and embarrassed to discuss these symptoms in our mixed group. However, with considerable support from our social worker, she was able to initiate discussion of this illness in the female group. The other women gave her a considerable amount of acceptance and understanding. These problems, as well as other painful and embarrassing ones such as promiscuity, are examples of why we believe that every mixed alcoholism rehabilitation unit should have a women's group as one of the routine treatment modalities.

Social Skills Training or Assertion Groups

All alcoholism rehabilitation units should have social skills training or assertion groups available for all patients, particularly those who have grown up in deprived homes or who have developed passive personality problems. As previously noted, it can be destructive to place a passive individual in group therapy without any psychological support. In fact, it has been our experience on the ADU service that some of our passive patients receive more help from their social skills training groups than from the group therapy meetings.

There are several goals for the social skills training group (SST). The patient should learn how to: express positive feelings in a comfortable manner; accept positive feelings and respond appropriately; express criticism in a constructive manner and accept appropriate criticism without feeling devastated; initiate requests for help; and say "no" to requests when this response is justified. In addition, practicing conversations during mealtimes and improving socialization phenomena can be role played within the SST group.

Patients who have particularly severe problems with assertion are asked to keep an assertion diary on a daily basis. Here they list those times when they should have spoken up and did not, those situations in which they should have spoken up and did so in an appropriate manner (so that they can pat themselves on the back in a healthy way), and those occasions when they should have spoken up but did so in a sarcastic or aggressive manner. Assertion has to be distinguished from aggression. The goal is to have patients learn how to express themselves directly, spontaneously, and honestly, without being destructive to others or to themselves. The expression of positive feelings may be role played, with compliments and such physical signs of affection as handshakes and, when appropriate, hugs.

The assertion diary is reviewed once or twice weekly. If on a particular day no incidents occur which are appropriate for the diary, the patient is requested to write, "nothing happened." In this way, we are telling the patients that they have to work on their problems on a daily basis if their social skills are to improve and if they are to learn how to enjoy life without alcohol. The diary aids the patient in bringing fresh material to the therapist and decreases the distortion of remembered events. The diary also helps patients to realize that they are responsible for their progress in therapy and that no changes will occur unless they actively participate in the treatment.

For very severe assertion problems, we may ask the patient to write down a hierarchy of situations in which assertive behavior is progressively more anxiety-provoking. The patient may then be asked to list the appropriate behavior in each situation. If the anxiety is very severe, the patient may be asked to read the description of the appropriate behavior and role play the situation within the assertion group. In the group the behavior is accepted. Only after the patient has succeeded in this phase of therapy are situations arranged so that he can try spontaneous, assertive behavior without the handwritten notes. In this manner, we try to eliminate failure and provide opportunities for success with positive reinforcement. During these exercises patients are instructed to look directly at one another. For those who feel self-conscious about looking someone in the eye, we suggest that they look first at the other person's forehead, then the left ear, the chin, and the right ear; thereby giving the appearance of looking directly at the other individual, who is not aware of this technique. Videotaping of these positive experiences with playback to the patient is an effective way of intensifying the positive reinforcement.

In addition to the various modes of therapy offered on the ADU service, a cognitive therapy approach is useful for patients who are extremely critical of themselves (Childress & Burns, 1981; McMullin, 1986). These patients are asked to keep a daily diary of incidents when they were too critical of themselves, either in their thoughts or in their feelings. They are asked to write down the incident, what they thought or felt about themselves, and the cognitive correction or realistic assessment of what they should have said or felt. For example, if the patient makes a mistake and says to himself, "Oh, what a jerk I am!" he is asked to describe the incident in his diary, write down the words that he felt or said to himself, and then write down a realistic correction such as, "Lots of people make mistakes. I also did some things correctly this past week. It is quite human to make mistakes and I am quite human." Again, as in the assertion diary, if nothing worth noting happened that day, the patient is requested to write, "nothing happened." In this way, patients are once again reminded that they have to work on these problems on a daily basis. They have to be aware of and interrupt an automatic hypercritical attitude; this may have begun in childhood but has now become a maladaptive pattern leading to depression or anxiety. The patient is given the Childress and Burns article on cognitive therapy to read and keep in his room as a reminder of the diary requirement and as an aid in defining the various types of cognitive distortions.

A social skills group is also an appropriate setting for rehearsing responses to possible symptoms of alcoholism relapse in preparation for discharge from the ADU service. In some cases, the Relapse Precipitants Inventory (RPI), a 25-item instrument which has been shown to discriminate significantly between alcohol relapsers and survivors, is used. In a study of 256 alcoholic patients, Litman et al. (1983) administered the RPI three times: after withdrawal was completed, six weeks after discharge, and six to twelve months later. Analyses of the RPI data showed three emergent factors leading to situations most likely to result in a return to heavy drinking: unpleasant mood states (e.g., "when I feel depressed or tense"); external situations and euphoric states (e.g., "when I pass a bar or feel happy"); and lessened cognitive vigilance (e.g., "when I start thinking that one drink would do no harm"). When used during the initial rehabilitation phase of therapy in the SST group, the RPI can guide the therapist in choosing the specific treatment interventions and formulating relevant follow-up support systems. Following such cues as, "when I pass a bar," or "when I feel I'm being punished unjustly," or "when there are rows and arguments at home," the therapist can design specific role plays and formulate coping mechanisms for individual patients to use after discharge from the hospital.

Family Meetings

One of the rules in treatment is to use everyone and everything available in the environment for the treatment of the patient. Thus, family meetings, when families or friends are available, are essential in treating the alcoholic patient. We have group family meetings on a weekly basis with the patients and their families sitting together. There are an average of three to five families at each of these meetings, which include the patients' spouses, parents, their teenage or adult children, friends, employers if possible, and other relatives.

These family meetings begin with the team leader's review of the five treatment goals for the patients and five treatment goals for the staff (see p. 125). The home telephone numbers of the six key staff members are handed out to each of the family members in an attempt to convey our personal interest and to gain the family's cooperation in treatment. Family members are told that they can call the therapist at any time, as long as the patient is available near the phone and is aware of the entire conversation. We cannot afford to lose the trust of the patients while we are relating to their families.

Having several families at the meeting helps them to identify with each others' problems and experiences. If the sessions are conducted properly, the families can learn from each other and share some of their hopes and anxieties. It is important for each of the families to realize that they are not alone and that they should bear no guilt for the patient's excessive alcohol intake. We regard the families as our guests and tell them that we feel fortunate that they have taken time out from work or other activities to help us treat the patient.

In earlier years, when the families were not seen in a group but alone with the patient, there was too much concern about appearances and too much defensiveness on the part of the parents or the spouse of the patient. In that setting, we had more difficulty getting the family to collaborate actively in the patient's treatment, since it was not unusual for the parents or spouse to thrust a great deal of blame upon the patient during the family sessions. Within the group family meetings identification with other families enables these relatives to see that there are many other people in the same boat. Defensiveness is less apparent, and the anger prevalent in the single family meetings is diffused. Accusations that the patient has a "weak will" or "bad morals" do not often occur within the family group setting.

Sometimes a single family session is needed. For instance, if there are some embarrassing sexual problems to review, the patient and the spouse are followed up in a private meeting. Or if any of the family members objects to the group setting, we then automatically go into a single family meeting with one of the therapists. If the family problems appear to be severe, individual family sessions are also scheduled.

The goal of these family sessions is to obtain additional information about the patient and to get the family to collaborate actively in the patient's treatment after discharge from the inpatient rehabilitation service. Family members are told that each one of us sees the world through our own eyes and that the more sets of eyes that we have available to report on the patient's history, the more accurate the data and the more help we can give the patient. It has been our experience that the families give each other a great deal of healthy support during these meetings, as well as some excellent therapeutic advice.

After this introduction, we review each patient's history obtained at the group staffing. (The patient has been given the staffing note prior to his family session and asked to delete any information that he or she considers too embarrassing or personal for this family group meeting.) In addition, parts of the psychological tests, are also reviewed during the group family session in order to validate some of the interpretations made by our psychologist.

As the history and the psychological test report are reviewed, the therapist attempts to have the family and the patient share their opinions about the information. In the great majority of cases, additional valuable information is obtained from the family, while some counseling and directions are offered to the family members. If anyone is unwittingly enabling the patient to continue his or her drinking pattern, the therapist points it out as delicately as possible and requests some changes in the "enabler's" behavior. The patient is asked whether or not he agrees with this request; invariably assent is given in a manner that is superficial but adequate enough to encourage the enabler to modify his or her behavior.

Therapeutic Use of the Psychological Report

The results of psychological testing, although widely used for diagnostic purposes and for treatment planning, are frequently withheld from the patient, lest sudden insight or a traumatic statement precipitate an emotional upset. This reasoning may be valid for certain patients, such as borderline psychotics whose anxiety might result in a breakdown of defenses if certain problems were suddenly exposed. However, it is my opinion that the alcoholic's denial mechanism must be directly confronted in a variety of therapeutic approaches. We began using the psychological test report as a therapeutic tool on our alcoholism treatment service after having achieved satisfactory results with direct confrontation in the group staffing procedure (Gallant, 1964; Jensen & Gallant, 1966). It should be noted that those patients with symptoms of subacute organic mental disorder or protracted withdrawal syndrome are not confronted in this direct way until they have adequately recovered from their alcohol-induced organic impairment (Gallant, 1984; Grant et al., 1984).

The therapeutic use of the psychological report appears to be especially efficacious for those patients who meet at least one of the following criteria: a tendency to blame others for their own shortcomings; doubts regarding their own abilities and a chronic tendency to berate themselves; obvious lack of respect for the clinical judgment of the staff; minimal awareness of their emotional problems; and severe personality problems which may interfere with rehabilitation treatment. In addition, those patients who originally denied their organic mental impairment are confronted with the testing results, but only after they have sufficiently recovered from their impairment to be able to cooperate with treatment and comprehend the testing results. These patients must be made aware of the tremendous damage caused by their alcoholism, and this confrontation is one approach which can be helpful.

Patients are given a test battery consisting of the Minnesota Multiphasic Personality Inventory (MMPI), Wechsler Adult Intelligence Scale, the Bender Visual-Motor Gestalt Test, Memory-for-Designs Test, Draw-A-Person Test, Rorschach Psychodiagnostic Test, and Sentence Completion Test. The subjects are interviewed briefly in order to establish rapport, but no background information is elicited by the clinical psychologist. If the clinical psychologist obtains too much background information, the patients then use their denial mechanism to brush aside the test results, saying that the report relied solely on the history. *These psychological reports are written in a form directly addressing the patient and technical psychiatric terminology is avoided.*

Each patient is given the option of reviewing the psychological test results during one of our group meetings or of selecting one or two other patients whom he trusts to join him in attending a private meeting with the staff at which the report will be reviewed. Patients almost always allow the report to be discussed at the group meeting. The psychiatrist slowly reads the report to the patients, who are encouraged to interrupt to make comments or ask questions. Portions of the report are discussed in detail and related to the tested patient's background and to those emotional and behavioral difficulties of which the staff and the other patients are aware (e.g., his feelings about himself, identification problems, distortions, anger, inappropriate expression of feelings, and interpersonal difficulties). If possible, interpretation of these problems is made through examples of the patient's behavior on the ward, which are pointed out by the other patients attending the session or by the ward nurse.

The following excerpts from a report which was presented to a 37-year-old married woman provide an example of a psychological test confrontation:

On the intelligence test you had an I.Q. score of 125, which shows that you have "very superior intelligence." Some of the tests show that your present functioning varies quite a bit, from superior to sometimes mediocre or even poor performance. . . . These tests suggest several reasons why you do not perform in a more stable and consistent manner, which I'll point out to you later. . . . Your high intelligence is also seen in your performance on the ink-blot test. This test, however, points very clearly to your personality problems. The way you presented your responses as well as your appearance gave me the feeling that you were playing to an audience rather than seeking help as a patient. Your perception of the ink-blots was usually accurate; you did not distort in this area. Your intelligence and imagination show a high potential for creativity and originality. Your thinking, however, lacks organization and discipline.

The most disturbing aspect of your test results is that you haven't yet realized that this extensive and rich fantasy life cannot be part of your real life. It is meaningless for your everyday adjustment, and that is why you have serious problems. Considering that you feel anxious, depressed, and have marital difficulties as well as a serious drinking problem, this whole world of "fairy tales and make-believe" becomes an escape from your problems, the same way drinking is an escape. Many of your responses on the ink-blot test repeated the same pattern; you mentioned such beings as, "baby bull moose," "little bears bouncing ice cream cones," "baby birds still in the embryonic stage," "water babies," and "little beings that have no reason to exist." All of these associations, but especially the last one, tell something important about you—that in many ways you feel like a very little girl, maybe like a child who wants to be taken care of, to be cuddled and fed. Young children are mainly concerned with themselves and their own needs, especially their needs to be taken care of and fed. If you think about the way you usually relate to people close to you, you may see that your need to take in love and affection and be taken care of by others is a bit too strong and possibly immature, like a child who may only be able to take and not give.

Never giving up these needs through the years has caused you to remain an emotionally immature person. There is evidence that you have been searching for your identity for a long time, and this must be frustrating because the role you're seeking is an unrealistic one. It appears that you know very little about yourself as a real person. For instance, you greatly misjudged your intelligence when you said that you had less than average intelligence, and this is only a minor example. In addition, you seem to see the world in extremes, such as good and bad or success and failure. There are many shades of grey between the two poles that are useful and constructive. These grey shades can be gratifying once you accept them as part of yourself.

> You might turn out to be a difficult therapy patient because there is the possibility that you might want to drop out of treatment when you become uncomfortable or anxious, or when you see your dependency needs frustrated by the therapist. It is important that you become aware of these difficulties. . . . Because of your natural intelligence and your ability to grow, you should commit yourself completely to treatment. This treatment should be the center of your life for at least the next 12 months. If you make this commitment, you'll gain a great deal from therapy and do very well.

After the reading of the report, the patient is given a copy of these results to read in private. He is asked to discuss the material with other patients and present it at the group psychotherapy sessions on the unit. Subsequent interpretations or confrontations in the group therapy sessions may refer to the psychological report and provide examples of some of the behaviors cited in it. This method is an additional, effective approach to the alcoholic patient's neurotic defenses, particularly his or her expert use of the denial mechanism. Consensual validation of the report material by the staff and other patients who are present helps the patient gain rapid insight into his or her problems.

Indications for Individual Therapy

For patients who have severe problems in trust, particularly those who grew up in an environment in which they could trust neither their father nor their mother and had negative interpersonal relationships with people outside the family, individual therapy is an absolute necessity in addition to the group setting. One should never expect such patients to participate actively when initially exposed to the group—a gathering of strangers. These patients need individual counseling and additional attention, with the goal of learning to trust the therapist who is the group leader. Otherwise, they will feel that they are being treated impersonally and rejected once again. In fact, if any patients have had very negative experiences with group situations in the past, such as family settings, school situations, teams, or other group activities, they require special individual counseling in association with the group setting. Of course, role playing with assertion techniques, first involving modeling with the therapist and later with other individuals, can help prepare the patient to speak up and be more active within a group therapy setting.

Patients who have embarrassing sexual problems such as impotence, unusual sexual identity problems, a history of being abused as a child or of having abused their own children will also require additional individual therapy.

Behavior Modification Techniques for Alcohol Abuse, Phobias, Sexual Problems, and Cigarette Smoking

Sometimes behavior modification techniques such as covert sensitization can be quite useful within an alcoholism program. With this type of technique, vivid descriptions of extremely noxious scenes, such as vomiting and nausea, are described to the patient in association with descriptions of the undesirable behavior. For example, in the treatment of an alcoholic patient who is unable to take Antabuse for specific medical reasons, the following scene can be described to him:

> As you approach the bar, you develop an uneasy feeling in the pit of your stomach. You order your [the patient's favorite drink], and as the bartender fills your glass, you feel the vomitus filling your stomach and starting to push its way up into your throat. As you lift the glass to your mouth, the vomitus starts pouring out of your mouth, through your nostrils, and into your glass of liquor as the glass touches your lips. The vomitus is a greenish yellow, and you accidently drink some of it as the alcohol enters your mouth.

This type of treatment approach requires the patient's total cooperation. For the preparation of this technique, the therapist helps the patient complete 10 or 12 index cards, each card listing a brief scene graded from 5 points to 100 points. The 5-point card represents early anticipation of the drink with some slight pleasure; each card with increasing value in points represents more pleasure, the final card (100 points) representing the patient's sipping his favorite drink and enjoying its feeling as it travels down his throat. About three or four negative scenes are used to interrupt these descriptions and help condition the patient by associating these negative feelings with the pleasurable anticipation of a drink.

The process is a rather tedious one and not as simple as it may seem. The patient is requested to practice about 10 to 15 minutes each day, starting off with the cards that have the lowest grade of pleasure, imagining the positive scene and then attempting to obliterate the pleasure of that scene by visualizing the scene on one of the negative cards. If only one negative scene is used, the patient may become saturated by the repetition of that single scene, which then loses its usefulness in obliterating the pleasurable scenes. When the patient reaches a card that contains a pleasurable scene that cannot be obliterated by the negative card, he is then requested to go back to the previous card so that he can end on a successful note for the day. If the patient is fully cooperative with the procedure, it is interesting to see the automatic negative feeling toward drinking which develops with this type of behavior modification technique. This type of covert sensitization may also be useful for patients who have sexual perversions that they would like to change in therapy. Such sexual problems are not unusual in alcoholics.

We also use other behavior modification techniques, such as systematic (hierarchical) densensitization, for patients who present other emotional problems. The classical example is fear of heights: The patient uses about 10 or 12 cards describing the fear of heights, graded from 5 points, which may represent thinking about visiting a tall building, to 100 points, which could be standing on top of a 20-story building and looking down from the ledge. In this technique, the content of the cards is almost opposite in affect to that of the cards used in covert sensitization. The patient is taught muscle relaxation techniques, relaxation breathing, and sometimes thought stoppage before using these hierarchy cards to deal with his fear of heights.

The patient is asked to work on these cards every day, to imagine the first one or two cards, allow himself to feel the anxiety, and then attempt to obliterate it with the muscle relaxation techniques or relaxation scenes that have now been incorporated into his daily mental exercise program. As the patient begins to eliminate the fear expressed on the first two or three cards, he may be asked to visit a building which has two or three stories. By the time the patient reaches the last card, he is ready for a visit (accompanied by the therapist) to a tall building. Frequently, another patient who has been able to overcome a fear of heights is asked to join this trip.

With this method, we are almost always able to help a patient eliminate this type of severe anxiety or phobic problem with heights before he or she is discharged from the ADU service. This technique enables patients to see some very specific goals accomplished in therapy. Such accomplishment enhances their self-esteem and their confidence and motivates them to challenge other anxiety-provoking problems with similar mental techniques, rather than resorting to alcohol or other drugs.

Since many of our alcoholic patients are heavy smokers, we also use behavior modification techniques for those who want to stop smoking or for those who have developed such chronic pulmonary problems as emphysema or chronic bronchitis. In addition to the routine of writing down the date, time, number of cigarettes that day, and activity at the time of "lighting up," we also employ covert sensitization techniques for insertion of negative scenes associated with the inhaling of the cigarette smoke. Although most of our patients find it more difficult to give up smoking than alcohol, we believe that it would be medically negligent for us to ignore this problem. Even when we fail to stop the patient's smoking habit, we are often partially successful by decreasing the number of cigarettes smoked daily. It is my opinion that every alcohol rehabilitation program should incorporate a nicotine abstinence program as part of the routine treatment for every alcoholic patient since there is a strong correlation between heavy drinking and heavy smoking with a resultant increase in carcinogenic and cardiovascular diseases. There is nothing more painful than seeing an alcoholic who has been sober for several years develop cancer of the pharynx, larynx, or lungs and die during the period of life that should have been the most enjoyable years for the patient and his family.

One of the best reference sources for learning the techniques of behavior modification is the book by W. Stewart Agras, *Behavior Modification: Principles and Clinical Applications.*

SPECIAL TREATMENT PROBLEMS

Treatment of Mixed Alcohol-Drug Use and of Alcohol-Related Legal Problems

Alcoholism rehabilitation units are currently facing many special treatment problems. In an important review article on multiple substance use by alcoholics, Sokolow et al. (1981) detailed the use of nonmedically prescribed drugs by 1,340 alcoholic patients in 17 New York alcoholism rehabilitation units. A shocking 46% of the patients reported use of nonmedically prescribed drugs during the 30 days before entering a facility specializing in alcoholism treatment. The drugs most frequently misused were minor tranquilizers, marijuana, sedatives, amphetamines, hallucinogens, and narcotics. Approximately 20% of the patients reported using two or more drugs in addition to alcohol during the 30 days prior to treatment. For alcoholics with drug problems other than ethanol, such as cocaine or benzodiazepine abuse, it is essential to treat these problems before the patient is discharged from the inpatient rehabilitation program or else the patient will very likely drop out of aftercare treatment and return to drinking. The technique of covert sensitization, as described in the previous section, can also be successfully employed to treat the drug problem. The goal is to condition the patient to develop automatic negative feelings whenever the drug is available. Through conditioning, the patient learns to use his brain for an aversive reaction to drugs, just as he uses Antabuse as his protection against ethanol.

Although alcohol and drug use fell markedly after inpatient treatment, the three-month follow-up interview showed that *tranquilizers remained the most commonly misused drugs in this group of alcoholics.* Drug use three months after discharge from inpatient treatment was directly related to the consumption level of alcohol. If the alcoholic was drinking 10 or more ounces per day, the probability was about three times as great that he was using drugs than if he was abstinent. A reduction in alcohol intake after treatment may be only temporary if the patient continues to use drugs at the pretreatment level, since the follow-up also indicates that multiple drug use in abstinent alcoholics may be a predictor of relapse in terms of alcohol. Therefore, patients who use alcohol in association with nonmedically prescribed drugs may require additional treatment modalities and more extensive treatment than the routine regimen offered in most alcohol rehabilitation centers.

These alcoholic substance abusers appear to be physiologically and psychologically more disabled than "pure" alcoholics; alcoholic rehabilitation centers should, therefore, revise their assessment and treatment modalities for such patients. These individuals may need a great deal of help in learning how to say "no" to drugs as well as to alcohol. In assertion group training, they need to practice their skills specifically in these areas. Many of these patients have additional emotional problems and may need extensive individual as well as group therapy. They also require more frequent urine drug screen surveys when returning to the hospital from pass and during follow-up in the clinic. The therapist who ignores the necessity for these urine screens is playing the same game of denial that the patient used prior to treatment.

Other special treatment techniques may be necessary for "criminal alcoholics" who have committed recent crimes associated directly or indirectly with alcoholism. These subjects have a much better prognosis when treatment is compulsory. One study of male criminal alcoholic parolees from Louisiana State Penitentiary at Angola, who had recently served sentences of one year or more for a major offense (e.g., auto theft, grand larceny, burglary, homicide), directly or indirectly associated with alcoholism, showed that compulsory treatment for six months or more resulted in a 70% success rate in terms of both abstinence and social and economic gains at the end of the one year follow-up (Gallant et al., 1968). This study was a controlled project, with the criminal alcoholic parolees randomly assigned to either a compulsory or a voluntary treatment group. The voluntary treatment group success rates were only 10%. Thus, there are situations in which compulsory treatment for certain types of subgroups of alcoholics may be efficacious; in other cases the same type of treatment approach may be a waste of time, for example, with such patients as the revolving-door alcoholic (Gallant et al., 1973).

When treating the alcoholic patient, we must remember the essential concept of "treating the whole individual" if we are going to help the alcoholic live a more enjoyable and meaningful life without alcohol. If we concentrate only on abstinence, we may leave a patient with other problems that can devastate not only the person but his or her family as well. An excellent example of the need to evaluate every alcoholism patient fully for emotional problems is seen in the study on alcoholism, drug abuse, and gambling conducted in a private psychiatric hospital in New York (Lesieur et al., 1986). In this evaluation of 458 patients in an alcoholism and drug dependency treatment facility, 9% of the patients were diagnosed as pathological gamblers; an additional 10% showed signs of problematic gambling. These patients showed strong evidence of emotional, financial, family, and occupational disruption, as well as illegal activity in association with the gambling, compounding the chaos induced by alcohol and/or drugs. The results showed a sex difference: 11.5% of the males and only 2% of the females were classified as pathological gamblers. Another interesting finding was seen in the family histories of the gambling-alcohol-drug patients, which revealed a significant amount of parental gambling. Gambling by siblings, alcoholism in the father, gambling prior to age 20, and "chasing losses in order to get even," were also positively correlated. It is important to evaluate obsessive gambling as a specific item in *every* alcoholic's history because this severe problem, if untreated, can lead the patient back to alcohol. Techniques such as covert sensitization, group therapy, and Gamblers Anonymous can be valuable in treating a gambling problem.

The Treatment of Affective Disorders in Alcoholics

The problem of depression in alcoholics has been much discussed in the literature, and the importance of separating primary depressions from alcohol-induced secondary depressions is recognized by most therapists in the field of alcoholism and other substance abuse disorders. One of the studies that points out the necessity of adequately treating depression in alcoholics was undertaken to assess changes in psychopathology in alcoholic subjects who remained abstinent for four consecutive years following inpatient treatment (Pettinati et al., 1982). In this study, alcoholic patients completed the Minnesota Multiphasic Personality Inventory (MMPI) while hospitalized for treatment and again after four years of follow-up. Those alcoholics who remained abstinent and functioned well in the community for the four-year period had been characterized during inpatient treatment by a significant elevation on the depression (D) scale, which then *decreased* to normal ranges at follow-up. Those patients who continued to drink periodically over the four-year period had had initial peaks on psychopathy (Pd) and hypomania (Ma) (no elevations on the D scale), which were still elevated at follow-up and therefore had not been treated adequately. An intermediate group who were mainly abstinent during the four-year period with only occasional relapses had shown initial elevations on the D and Pd scales during inpatient treatment with return to normal levels at follow-up, indicating that treatment had been somewhat successful for these particular problems. If the depression is treated adequately, long-term abstinence is more readily achieved.

Similar findings have been noted with other types of substance abusers. In Kosten et al.'s (1986) study of opioid addicts, follow-up evaluations suggested that depression and life crises are associated with decreased abstinence. These two risk factors of depression and life crises have additive effects, increasing the chances for continued drug abuse. Here again we see the need to treat the substance abuser's depression adequately prior to discharge from the hospital setting.

In one of our studies of depression in alcoholics, approximately 50% of the alcoholic patients scored within the depression range of the Self-rating Depression Scale (Zung Scale), whereas none of the control group in the same age range attained the cut-off score of 50, a score indicating moderate to marked depression. There is no doubt that there is a significant difference in the degree of depression among patients with the problem of alcoholism compared to a non-alcoholic population with similar biographical data (Wester et al., 1979). Thus, the possible presence of depression must be thoroughly evaluated and the patient treated before discharge from the treatment program.

Secondary depression is considered to be a result of the excessive drinking of alcohol, a CNS depressant drug, and the subsequent life failures associated with alcoholism. A patient with secondary depression may require careful observation during the initial phase of therapy, but should not require antidepressant medication. This type of depression usually clears after an abstinence period of three or four weeks.

Primary depression is diagnosed when the history of the alcoholic patient reveals depression which occurred prior to the onset of alcoholism or has occurred during prolonged periods of abstinence with no obvious precipitating environmental causes. Family history of depression, history of phobias in the patient or the family, or presence of the depression on the alcohol rehabilitation unit three or four weeks after admission to the unit may all lead to the suspicion of primary depression. The incidence of primary depression in alcoholics may vary according to different hospital settings; for example, the incidence of primary depression in alcoholics in Veteran Administration hospitals may be lower than in state hospital settings where female alcoholics are present in greater numbers (Schuckit, 1986; Wester et al., 1979). Since the suicide rate is dramatically higher in the alcoholic population, it is important to be able to delineate these two types of depression and treat them adequately before patients reenter the environment outside the hospital setting.

The value of the Dexamethasone Suppression Test (DST) as an aid in the differential diagnosis of primary versus secondary depression is questionable in alcoholic patients. In a study of 27 alcoholics who were administered the DST, which reflects an alteration in the hypothalamic-pituitary adrenal axis, 59% of the patients showed a positive reaction, suggesting the presence of major depression (Dackis et al., 1986). However, the positive test does not tell us whether or not the alcoholic is suffering from a primary major depression which requires antidepressant medication or from an alcohol-induced depression which may clear without medication. It appears that the DST can be positive for both primary depressions and alcohol-induced secondary depressions; few investigators and researchers in the field of alcoholism believe that 59% of all alcoholic patients have true primary depressions. Even though the alcohol-induced secondary depression may not require antidepressant medication, the patient should be carefully evaluated in order to be certain that the clinician is not misdiagnosing a primary depression as a secondary depression. While we all want to avoid needless pharmacotherapy, we also want to be certain that we do not deny the primary depressed alcoholic the opportunity of a good therapeutic response to appropriate antidepressant medication.

For alcoholic patients with bipolar affective disorders, it is absolutely essential not only to use lithium but to be certain that the patient takes Antabuse on a regular basis for a prolonged period of time. Bipolar patients have provided me with the most difficult doctor-patient relationships that I have ever encountered in my practice of psychiatry. When they stop taking their lithium, they almost always return to alcohol eventually, as they swing into either mania or depression. On the other hand, when they stop their Antabuse, they almost always discontinue the lithium and relapse into bipolar illness.

There is one case that comes to mind when I discuss this type of patient, an individual I will never forget, who clearly represents the problem in treating the combination illness of alcoholism-bipolar disorder. Many years ago, during the early days of my practice in treating alcoholics, my wife and I were scheduled to leave the country for an international meeting. On the day of departure, our kitchen caught fire and was badly damaged. My wife decided to stay behind to take care of the problems, and I left for the meeting where I was scheduled to present a paper. That evening, my wife called me, asking me where I had placed the insurance papers. At the time of the call, I had been taking a shower; I heard the phone ring and stepped out of the shower to answer it. In the middle of our conversation, the operator interrupted us and said that there was an emergency phone call from one of my patients in New Orleans. My wife and I hung up, and at that moment, Mr. R., an alcoholic-bipolar patient, came on the phone very intoxicated. In a magnificent slurring speech, he told me what a wonderful psychiatrist I was, how I had saved his life, and that he only called to thank me for everything I had done for him. He was quite obviously drunk and had stopped both his lithium and his Antabuse. I was so disturbed that I slammed the phone down and dressed myself in my new suit while I was still dripping from the shower. I did not realize that I was completely wet until I knotted my tie.

The therapist should require this type of patient to sign a contract stating that he or she will take the Antabuse and lithium on an indefinite basis, as long as there are no uncomfortable side effects. It is almost impossible for these patients to cooperate in ongoing therapy if they do not continue both medications.

OTHER SPECIAL TREATMENT GROUPS

The Elderly

With the increase in the size of the aged population, it is inevitable that the absolute number of elderly alcohol abusers will also grow, even though the incidence may not increase. In one very thoughtful paper, the problem of alcohol abuse in the aging population was reviewed (Brody, 1982). Brody's objective evaluation of the available data helps us to place this problem in its proper perspective. Using the arbitrary definition of the aged as 65 years and older, it has been estimated that there will be 32 million in this category by the year 2,000. Currently only 20% of the males over the age of 65 are working, and a devastatingly low 8% of the females in this group are employed. Forty percent of this age group have serious health problems which interfere with normal daily activities. These data suggest factors which may be responsible for an increase in alcohol use by some members of the aged population: (1) premature retirement with problems in adaptation to a new role; (2) poor health with limitation of routine activities; and (3) loneliness with increased likelihood of depression.

Reliable data about the incidence of drinking problems in the elderly residing in communities are not available at this time; estimates of alcoholism in the elderly have varied five-fold (Brody, 1982). However, most surveys do agree that there is a significant incidence of alcoholism in the aged who are hospitalized or institutionalized, the percentage varying from 10% to 15% according to different surveys. Alcoholism in the aged can lead to tragic consequences. Without an adequate history and examination, temporary alcohol-induced episodes of confusion and amnesia may be difficult to distinguish from senile dementia, which can result in subsequent chronic institutionalization. Not only do elderly people metabolize alcohol less efficiently, but frequently they are also taking other medications which may potentiate and prolong the sedation-confusion reaction to alcohol. There are indications that elderly alcoholics can respond quite well to treatment; some authors have suggested that these patients are easier to treat than other alcoholics (Brody, 1982; Gallant, 1983).

Special considerations in treating elderly alcoholics should include: scheduling daily activities including volunteer work for patients who have retired; adequate attention to the medical problems associated with the aging process which can compound alcohol-induced brain damage; and social planning for patients who are living alone.

It is not unusual for elderly alcoholics to present with brain damage secondary to long-term abuse of alcohol as well as the additive effects of the aging process. Therefore, an essential element of treatment includes helping the patients and their families understand the impairment caused by alcohol-induced brain damage. Although there is a possibility that many of the organic mental changes are reversible with abstinence, adequate nutrition, and correction of other medical problems, the therapist may have to plan special sessions to teach the patient how to compensate for the memory changes. Short training sessions concentrating on visual-motor coordination with appropriate exercises of attention span can be performed daily. Abstract thinking tasks should be included in these training sessions. In addition, helping the patient develop routine habits has proved to be very useful for the elderly alcoholic who may have some mild brain damage.

Veterans With Post-Traumatic Stress Disorder

Another special subgroup of alcoholics consists of those veterans with a combination of *alcoholism and post-traumatic stress disorder (PTSD)*. Combat veterans with a history of PTSD (flashbacks, severe nightmares of their war experiences, misdirected assaultive episodes, and startle reactions, sometimes accompanied by a great deal of guilt for having survived) have an increased incidence of substance abuse, including alcoholism (Jelinek & Williams, 1984). Alcoholism may suppress or exacerbate the PTSD symptoms. In Jelinek and Williams' study of 2,000 combat veterans of the Vietnam war, 80% had experienced alcohol-related problems during or after their combat experience.

Treatment planning must take into account the specific symptoms of PTSD as well as alcoholism. These patients should be taking Antabuse while they are working on their stress disorder. Fortunately, in most major cities in this country, there is a Vets Center staffed by veterans who have been trained in treating the PTSD; most of these veterans have experienced this syndrome before being trained as therapists. In our alcoholism treatment program at the Veterans Administration Hospital in New Orleans, alcoholism aftercare clinic visits for follow-up treatment of veterans with alcoholism are combined with the same patients' attendance at our Vets Center for specific treatment of their PTSD. We always maintain open communication lines with the staff at the Vets Center to be sure that our treatment of the alcoholism patient with PTSD is well coordinated.

Physicians

Another special patient who occasionally enters our treatment program is the physician who is disabled by alcoholism or other drugs (Johnson & Connelly, 1981). The prevalence of alcoholism among physicians is uncertain, but the treatment results are encouraging (Brewster, 1986; Gallant, 1986; Murray, 1976). In one report on the treatment of 50 doctors, a nine-month to four-year follow-up evaluation showed that 50% of the physicians under 40 years and 72% of subjects over 40 years were practicing medicine and abstinent (Brewster, 1986). Thus, it is apparent that appropriate treatment of the addicted physician can produce high success rates. Awareness of the high success rate that can be obtained when these physicians are treated during the early or middle phases of illness may prompt more frequent early intervention with and confrontation of addicted physicians by their fellow doctors before it is necessary to require suspension or licensure probation. Delayed treatment of substance-abusing physicians can result in tragedy and possibly suicide, as noted in a study of Oregon physicians who were placed on probation for 10 years after their licenses had been suspended without a requirement for therapy (Crenshaw et al., 1980).

Patients With Other Psychiatric Disorders

Occasionally a therapist comes across a schizophrenic patient who had definite, severe thought disorder problems preceding the onset of alcoholism. This patient should be appropriately treated with antipsychotic drugs in order to improve his or her thought associations, facilitate speech complexity and coherence, and enable participation in psychotherapy in a more appropriate manner. Otherwise, he will have a very difficult time being accepted on an alcoholism rehabilitation unit, since the thought disorder problems will become very obvious to most of the patients, who will tend to shy away, further alienating the schizophrenic patient and creating a negative experience for him.

There is a significant number of primary alcoholics who require psychiatric treatment, frequently including psychopharmacology, as well as abstinence. While alcoholism may be the major diagnosis and most impressive feature during their initial admission to a rehabilitation treatment program, therapeutic attempts at abstinence with a healthy social adjustment will fail if they do not receive adequate psychiatric treatment for the accompanying emotional problems. However, there is no doubt that another subgroup of primary alcoholics does exist — patients whose emotional and social problems fall into place quite easily after they attain a state of abstinence;

psychiatric treatment is not necessary for this particular subgroup of alcoholics.

Members of Minority Groups

Knowledge of patients' cultural backgrounds contributes to successful therapy. As emphasized in Chapter 4, cultural attitudes play an important role in the acceptance or rejection of alcohol (Westermeyer, 1976). A rehabilitation treatment program has to tailor the treatment to meet the needs of the individual patient. In certain minority populations, these needs are more varied. For instance, in treating Indian alcoholics reared on reservations, therapists on a rehabilitation unit would be wise not to ignore the traditional Indian strengths. If the Indian patient is to return to reservation living after discharge, then contacting a traditional medicine man or woman from the tribe and including this individual in the family sessions may enhance the chance of success in follow-up treatment (May, 1986). A survey of 40 Navajo medicine men and women found that 75% of these individuals have treated alcohol and drug misusers with considerable success (May, 1986). Since many Indians attempt to live in two cultures at the same time, treatment should seek to integrate the strengths of both systems.

Data from other research into alcoholism among minorities should also be integrated into the inpatient rehabilitation treatment techniques and used as a guide for planning follow-up outpatient therapy. In one extensive study of drinking patterns of inner-city Black American and Puerto Rican alcoholics, it was found that Puerto Rican women were significantly older at the first time of drunkenness and tended to drink at home daily more than the other groups (Fernandez-Pol et al., 1986). The transition from the traditional role of a middle-aged woman in Latin American society to a New York ghetto can result in culture shock. Thus, the changing roles of Puerto Rican females, as well as socialization problems, should be specifically addressed in group therapy and social skills training groups as part of treatment. Family therapy may be needed to address the cultural transition and a modification of the role values in the family. In this same study, a significantly higher percentage of alcoholic Black females used drinking to "make friends" and there was a definite tendency for Black alcoholics to encourage their spouses to drink. In this subgroup of alcoholics, it would be essential to teach new socialization skills and to automatically include the spouse in therapy, with the possible goal of abstinence for the spouse as well as the patient. More about these suggestions will be detailed in Chapter 11 on outpatient therapy.

To summarize the goals of an inpatient alcoholism rehabilitation treatment program, it is a setting where the alcoholic patient has a chance to stop, take a deep breath, and look at himself/herself; at the same time, it offers the patient and the staff an opportunity to become better acquainted with each other and develop a trusting relationship. By the time of discharge, patients should have gained a better understanding of themselves, be motivated to continue to work on the goal of abstinence, be determined to continue treatment with the AA and the outpatient alcoholism clinic, and should have initiated the development of a worthwhile value system. By the time of discharge, the staff should have come to understand the patient's problems in depth and established a relationship in which the patient would feel comfortable contacting them at any time a crisis develops. The staff should have been able to utilize this intensive treatment setting to establish a relationship of trust with the patient that will enhance his/her desire to continue with the therapy team in the outpatient setting.

REFERENCES

Agras, W. S. (1972). *Behavior modification: Principles and clinical applications.* Boston: Little, Brown.

Alcoholics anonymous, 3rd edition (1976). New York: Alcoholics Anonymous World Services, Inc.

Armor, D. J., Polich, S. M., & Stambul, H. B. (1978). *Alcoholism and treatment.* New York: Wiley.

Brewster, J. M. (1986). Prevalence of alcohol and other drug problems among physicians. *Journal of the American Medical Association, 255,* 1913-1920.

Brisolara, A. M., Bishop, M. P., Bossetta, J. R., & Gallant, D. M. (1968). The New Orleans revolving door alcoholic: Degree of severity of illness and financial expense to the community. *Journal of the Louisiana State Medical Society, 120,* 397-399.

Brody, J. A. (1982). Aging and alcohol abuse. *Journal of the American Geriatric Society, 30,* 123-126.

Childress, A. R. & Burns, D. D. (1981). The basics of cognitive therapy. *Psychosomatics, 22,* 1017-1027.

Crenshaw, R., Bruce, D. A., & Eraker, P. L. (1980). An epidemic of suicide among physicians on probation. *Journal of the American Medical Association, 243,* 1915-1917.

Dackis, C. A., Stucky, R. F., Gold, M. S., & Pottash, A. L. C. (1986). Dexamethasone suppression test testing of depressed alcoholics. *Alcoholism: Clinical and Experimental Research, 10,* 59-60.

Duffy, J. C. & Waterton, J. J. (1984). Under-reporting of alcohol consumption in sample surveys: The effect of computer interviewing in field work. *British Journal of Addiction, 79,* 303-308.

Edwards, G. (1985). A follow-up of a classic case series. D. L. Davis' 1962 report and its significance for the present. *Journal of Studies on Alcohol, 46,* 181-190.

Edwards, G., Osford, J., Egert, S., Gathrie, S., Hawker, A., Hensman, C., & Mitcheson, M. (1977). Alcoholism: A controlled trial of "treatment" and "advice." *Journal of Studies on Alcohol, 38,* 1004-1031.

Ettore, E. M. (1984). A study of alcoholism treatment units: I. Treatment activities and the institutional response. *Alcohol and Alcoholism, 19,* 243-255.

Fernandez-Pol, B., Bluestone, H., Missouri, C., Morales, G., & Mizruchi, M. S. (1986). Drinking patterns of inner-city Black Americans and Puerto Ricans. *Journal of Studies on Alcohol, 47,* 156-160.

Fuller, R. K., & Williford, W. O. (1981). Life table analysis of abstinence in a study evaluating the efficacy of disulfiram. *Alcoholism: Clinical and Experimental Research, 4,* 298-301.

168 *Alcoholism*

Gallant, D. M. (1964). Group staffing on an alcoholism treatment service. *International Journal of Group Psychotherapy, 14*, 218–220.
Gallant, D. M. (1979). Another look at a controversial study. *Substance Abuse, 1*, 1–5.
Gallant, D. M. (1982). *Alcohol and drug abuse curriculum guide for psychiatry faculty.* (pp. 27–31). Washington: DHHS Pub No. (ADM) 82-1159.
Gallant, D. M. (1983). Alcohol abuse in the aging population. *Alcoholism: Clinical and Experimental Research, 7*, 244–245.
Gallant, D. M. (1984). The alcoholism-induced organic mental disorder. *Alcoholism: Clinical and Experimental Research, 8*, 595–596.
Gallant, D. M. (1986). Can some alcoholics become social drinkers? *Alcoholism: Clinical and Experimental Research, 10*, 217–218.
Gallant, D. M., Faulkner, M. A., Stoy, B., Bishop, M. P., & Langdon, D. (1968). Enforced clinic treatment of paroled criminal alcoholics. *Quarterly Journal of Studies on Alcohol, 29*, 77–83.
Gallant, D. M., Rich, A., Bey, E., & Terranova, L. (1970). Group psychotherapy with married couples: A successful technique in New Orleans alcoholism clinic patients. *Journal of the Louisiana State Medical Society, 122*, 41–44.
Gallant, D. M., Bishop, M. P., Mouledoux, A., Faulkner, M. A., Brisolara, A. M., & Swanson, W. A. (1973). The revolving door alcoholic: An impasse in the treatment of the chronic alcoholic. *Archives of General Psychiatry, 28*, 633–635.
Glatt, M. M. (1986). Alcoholism. *Lancet, 1*, 1095.
Gold Award (1984). Individualized treatment for substance abusers. *Hospital and Community Psychiatry, 35*, 1141–1144.
Grant, I., Admas, K. M., & Reed, R. (1984). Aging, abstinence, and medical risk factors in the prediction of neuropsychologic deficit among long-term alcoholics. *Archives of General Psychiatry, 41*, 710–718.
Helzer, J. E., Robins, L. N., Taylor, J. R., Carey, B. A., Miller, R. H., Combs-Orme, T., & Farmer, A. (1985). The extent of long-term drinking among alcoholics discharged from medical and psychiatric facilities. *New England Journal of Medicine, 312*, 1678–1682.
Jelinek, J. M., & Williams, T. (1984). Post-traumatic stress disorder and substance abuse in Vietnam combat veterans: Treatment problems, strategies and recommendations. *Journal of Substance Abuse Treatment, 1*, 87–97.
Jensen, S. M., & Gallant, D. M. (1966). Therapeutic use of a psychological report on an alcoholism treatment service. *Quarterly Journal on Studies of Alcoholism, 27*, 717–720.
Johnson, R. P., & Connelly, J. C. (1981). Addicted physicians: A closer look. *Journal of the American Medical Association, 245*, 253–257.
Kosten, T. R., Rounsaville, B. J., & Kleber, H. D. (1986). A 2.5 year follow-up of depression, life crises, and treatment effects on abstinence among opioid addicts. *Archives of General Psychiatry, 43*, 733–738.
Lesieur, H. R., Blume, S. B., & Zoppa, R. M. (1986). Alcoholism, drug abuse, and gambling. *Alcoholism: Clinical and Experimental Research, 10*, 33–38.
Litman, G. K., Stapleton, J., Oppenheim, A. N., Peleg, M., & Jackson, S. (1983). Situations related to alcoholism relapse. *British Journal of Addiction, 78*, 381–389.
May, P. A. (1986). Alcohol and drug misuse prevention programs for American Indians: Needs and opportunities. *Journal of Studies on Alcohol, 47*, 187–195.
McCrady, B. S. & Sher, K. J. (1983). Alcoholism treatment approaches: Patient variables, treatment variables. In B. Tabakoff, P. B. Sutker, & C. L. Randall (Eds.). *Medical and social aspects of alcohol abuse.* (pp. 309–374). New York: Plenum Press.
McLellan, A. T., Laborsky, L., O'Brien, C. P., Woody, G. E., & Durley, K. A. (1982). Is treatment for substance abuse effective? *Journal of the American Medical Association, 247*, 1423–1428.
Mc Mullin, R. E. (1986). *Handbook of cognitive therapy techniques.* New York: Norton.
Miller, W. R. (1978). Behavioral treatment of problem drinkers: A comparative outcome study of three controlled drinking therapies. *Journal of Consulting and Clinical Psychology, 46*, 74–86.
Miller, W. R., Taylor, C. A, & West, J. C. (1980). Focused versus broad-spectrum behavior therapy for problem drinkers. *Journal of Consulting and Clinical Psychology, 48*, 590–601.

Murray, R. N. (1976). Alcoholism amongst male doctors in Scotland. *Lancet, 2*, 729–731.

Orrego, H., Blendis, L. M., Blake, J. E., Kapur, B. M., & Israel, Y. (1979). Reliability of alcohol intake based on personal interviews in a liver clinic. *Lancet, 2*, 1354–1356.

Pettinati, H. M., Sugerman, A. A., & Maurer, H. S. (1982). Four year MMPI changes in abstinent and drinking alcoholics. *Alcoholism: Clinical and Experimental Research, 6*, 482–494.

Schuckit, M. A. (1986). Genetic and clinical implications of alcoholism and affective disorder. *American Journal of Psychiatry, 143*, 140–147.

Sokolow, L., Welte, J., Hynes, G., & Lyons, J. (1981). Multiple substance abuse by alcoholics. *British Journal of Addiction, 76*, 147–158.

Wester, R., Atchison, B., Kleinman, R., Gallant, D. H., & Gallant, D. M. (1979). A study of depression in alcoholic patients. *Journal of the Louisiana State Medical Society, 131*, 259–261.

Westermeyer, J. (1976). Predisposing factors. In J. Westermeyer, *Primer on chemical dependency.* (pp. 23–29). Baltimore: Williams & Wilkins.

Wright, K. D., & Scott, T. B. (1978). The relationship of wives' treatment to the drinking status of alcoholics. *Journal of Studies on Alcohol, 39*, 1577–1581.

CHAPTER 10

The Use of Psychopharmacologic Medications in Alcoholism

ANTABUSE (disulfiram)

A GREAT DEAL OF MISINFORMATION exists about the use of psychopharmacologic medications with alcoholic patients. Over the years, I have heard patients make such statements as, "One of my alcoholic friends tells me that Antabuse can kill you even if you don't take a drink." Having been medically responsible for administering Antabuse to more than 20,000 patients in the past 25 years, I have no doubt that the benefits of Antabuse (disulfiram) far outweigh the risks of taking this medication. I have never known of any patient dying as a result of Antabuse administration, even including those who drank alcohol while they were taking the Antabuse.

Antabuse does inhibit liver aldehyde dehydrogenase as well as dopamine beta hydroxylase (Jensen & Faiman, 1986; Major et al., 1979). The former metabolic action appears to be associated with the Antabuse-alcohol reaction (disulfiram-ethanol reaction or DER). This DER apparently results in an increase of blood acetaldehyde, which is associated with hypothermia and hypotension occurring during the DER. However, in a research study of the DER in rats, although disulfiram was shown to inhibit aldehyde dehydrogenase and increase blood acetaldehyde, the severity of the DER was not related to the level of blood acetaldehyde but appeared to correlate with blood ethanol levels. This suggests that brain dopamine and the dopamine receptor may be partially responsible for the development of the DER (Jensen & Faiman, 1986). These investigators found that pimozide, a blocker of presynaptic dopamine receptors, attenuated the DER. The exact biochemical explanation for the DER is still uncertain at this time.

The DER is associated with some unpleasant symptoms, which include flushing, increased heart rate, palpitations, and hypotension. In addition, some patients may feel an uncomfortable tightness in the chest, become nauseous, and vomit. This type of reaction makes it extremely difficult for most patients to become intoxicated because they have to wait from 4 to 14 days after the last Antabuse tablet before taking a drink; this period provides ample time for them to stop and think before they act.

Risks of Antabuse

Using a dosage of Antabuse of 250 mg, h.s., I have found it to be one of the safest compounds to administer if the patient has full information about potential side effects and the medications and foods to avoid. In addition to having the patients read the *Physician Desk Reference (PDR)*, I have them review the controlled studies that have compared Antabuse with placebo. I strongly believe that educating patients not only decreases their anxieties about various medications but also enhances their compliance with the treatment regimen. In one placebo-Antabuse, double-blind controlled study in alcoholic patients, the evaluation of side effects in 158 patients completing the study showed no statistically significant differences between the two groups, except for a greater number of complaints of sexual problems in the placebo group (Christensen et al., 1984). Surprisingly, fatigue, itching, unpleasant taste, and skin reactions were no more common in the Antabuse group than in the placebo group. However, complaints of "bad breath" did occur more frequently in the Antabuse group. The dosage of Antabuse used in the study was 250 mg, dissolved in plain soda water, taken daily for six weeks under staff supervision. The investigators emphasized the importance of using this dosage of Antabuse when performing this type of controlled evaluation.

Peripheral nerve damage, including optic neuritis, has been described, usually in association with daily doses of 500 mg of Antabuse, which is an unnecessarily high dosage.

In a study which specifically evaluated the potential liver toxicity of Antabuse, 453 alcoholism patients were randomly assigned to either Antabuse or placebo for a 12-month period (Iber et al., in press). The evaluation of drinking status included analyses of blood and urine samples, subject interviews, and *contact with household members* at regular intervals. Liver tests were performed every two months. The results showed that there was no relationship between liver test elevation and Antabuse treatment, but there was a correlation between elevated liver tests and drinking status. These results point out that there is frequent drinking by alcoholic patients which is undetected by the physician and denied by the patient: 76% of the patients were found to be drinking at some time during the study. The authors concluded that patients on Antabuse who show liver test abnormalities are usually drinking. In a previous study, one of these investigators concluded that the use of Antabuse in patients with liver disease was "safe and useful" (Iber et al., 1977).

In my clinical experience, the most important contraindication for the use of Antabuse has been an associated diagnosis of schizophrenia. We have seen a number of schizophrenic patients who have been convicted of Driving While Intoxicated (DWI) and have been placed in a court-referred treatment program with administration of Antabuse without an adequate psychiatric evaluation. The initiation of a dosage of Antabuse at 500 mg daily in these particular patients resulted in a number of psychotic reactions. Since one of the metabolic functions of Antabuse is to inhibit dopamine-beta-hydroxylase with a subsequent increase of dopamine in the brain, large doses of Antabuse (500 mg per day), or perhaps even low doses (250 mg daily), can exacerbate schizophrenic psychoses (Major et al., 1979). Therefore, it is best not to use Antabuse in this particular patient population or to use a "placebo" dose of only 62.5 mg as a reminder for the patient.

Although Antabuse has the potential to activate a schizophrenic psychosis, it has no observable mood-altering effects on nonpsychotic alcoholic patients (Goyer et al., 1984). One double-blind study of 40 alcoholic patients compared 500 mg of Antabuse versus 250 mg of Antabuse versus placebo for three weeks. The Antabuse subjects showed no significant changes in anxiety or depression as compared to the placebo group. All three patient groups showed significant improvement in the anxiety and depression scales used during the period of the study, but there were no significant differences among the three groups.

The most serious side effects I have ever seen in alcoholic patients were observed in three patients who developed mild peripheral neuropathies which appeared to be Antabuse-related and disappeared when the medication was discontinued, and one possible case of optic neuritis which showed no further progression after the cessation of Antabuse. Approximately 2 to 3% of our patients develop a slight skin rash, usually a mild, acne-type rash on the trunk or forehead and, at other times, an erythematous rash of the trunk. This rash is responsive to hydrocortisone cream and usually does not reappear if the routine daily dosage of 250 mg of Antabuse is reduced to 125 mg.

Occasionally, the patient may complain of a bad taste in the mouth or mild tension headaches. Approximately 5 to 8% of our patients develop daytime lethargy even though the medication is administered at night before sleep. With these patients, we reduce the dosage to 125 mg, h.s.

When performing weekly liver enzyme studies on patients who were admitted with hepatic damage, we have observed a mild to moderate increase in these liver enzymes in five patients who were taking Antabuse while abstinent on our inpatient service. We did not observe the development of severe liver damage in any of these patients. Stopping the Antabuse resulted in a return of the liver enzymes toward normal baseline values, and reinstituting the Antabuse at 125 mg did not result in a recurrence of elevation of these enzymes.

Drug interactions with Antabuse may occur when patients are receiving concurrent treatment with several compounds. Antabuse can inhibit the metabolism of phenytoin and coumarin, resulting in higher levels of both these compounds. The simultaneous administration of Antabuse and metronidazole (Flagyl) can result in confusional states. At present, there is no definite proof of teratogenic or carcinogenic activity associated with Antabuse administration.

Benefits of Antabuse

During my 25 years of experience as medical director of two alcoholism inpatient treatment programs and of the state substance abuse clinic in New Orleans, I have been extremely impressed by the value of Antabuse. On innumerable occasions, patients, after some discouraging experience, have said to me, "If it were not for Antabuse, I would have drunk that day." On other occasions, after having achieved some goal and wanting to celebrate, patients have often told me, "We were all having such a great time that evening that I would have drunk with my friends if it were not for Antabuse." The former case occurs more frequently and has made me realize what an invaluable help Antabuse has been to many of my patients.

There are some excellent, well-controlled, scientific investigations which show the effectiveness of Antabuse and objectively confirm my subjective experiences. The efficacy of Antabuse has been demonstrated in a number of studies, including an evaluation of 128 alcoholic males by Fuller and Williford (1980). In this study, 128 alcoholic males were assigned randomly to one of three treatment groups: (1) 500 mg of disulfiram (Antabuse) daily for one week followed by 250 mg daily for one year; (2) 1 mg of Antabuse daily as a control for the implied threat of illness from the Antabuse-alcohol reaction (DER); and (3) nondrug medical care. All three groups received counseling. Motivation was equal among the groups since all patients in the study had requested Antabuse. The results showed statistically significant therapeutic gains for both medication groups (the 500/250 mg and the 1 mg Antabuse) as compared to the control group. Fuller and Williford used a life-table analysis which evaluated the effects of alcoholism treatment over time. This method provides information about the number of additional months of abstinence (as compared to end point analysis) which may delay or even prevent occurrence of tissue damage to various organs. This study also showed that the threat of taking Antabuse may be more therapeutic than the action of the drug itself.

In another study (Fuller et al., 1986), a controlled, blinded evaluation of Antabuse in 605 alcoholics randomly assigned to 250 mg, 1 mg, and placebo, the 250 mg Antabuse group showed a significant reduction in drinking days as compared with the other two treatment groups during a 52-week follow-up. There were no significant differences among the groups in total abstinence. However, the significant decrease in number of drinking days in the 250 mg group ($p = .03$) indicates that Antabuse treatment can reduce the medical complications and death rate associated with alcoholism.

The efficacy of an outpatient program of mandatory, supervised Antabuse therapy for patients who wish to remain "connected" to the clinic was shown in another study (Sereny et al., 1986). Of those patients who had previously continued to drink while attending the clinic, approximately 60% who agreed to this mandatory regimen achieved significant periods of sobriety. It is clear, then, that Antabuse increases the therapeutic success rates of patients who are very difficult cases, as well as the average alcoholic patients who are treated in an outpatient setting.

Despite these objective data, the use of Antabuse is still controversial among some professionals and laymen, who call it a "crutch" and believe that the patient should not "lean" on any medication. At the other end of the continuum, it is felt that all alcoholics should use Antabuse indefinitely, since this drug is less toxic than alcohol and there is no reason to avoid it unless the individual is going to drink. It has been stressed throughout this book that there are many different approaches available for treating alcoholics; Antabuse is one useful adjunct to many of these treatment modalities. A number of studies of Antabuse have shown that the use of this medication as an addition to other treatment modalities helps to increase the abstinence rate significantly (Gallant, 1982a).

It is important to be certain that the following three essentials of informed consent are present before giving a patient a medication such as Antabuse: (1) ability of the patient to understand the information; (2) the state of voluntariness; and (3) information about the major risks and benefits. It is particularly important to explain to patients that individuals prone toward schizophrenic or psychotic reactions are more likely to develop adverse psychological reactions to Antabuse.

Antabuse can be used not only to produce an adverse reaction to drinking alcohol but also as a symbol of the patient's commitment to treatment. In some treatment programs, patients' taking Antabuse can also be symbolic of their commitment to their families. In our treatment approach, the spouse is asked to participate actively in the treatment program by administering

Antabuse to the alcoholic (Gallant, 1982a). In this case, the patient is taking Antabuse in order to decrease the spouse's daily anticipatory anxiety about the patient's drinking and to eliminate false accusations of having "sneaked a drink." Another positive approach is the use of Antabuse with the emphasis that it is an insurance policy rather than a "crutch." The patient's reactions to the suggestion help the therapist estimate the degree of denial and noncompliance in a treatment program. If a patient agrees to take Antabuse and then discontinues the medication secretly, this act signifies that patient's extreme denial. Compliance can be determined by testing the urine for diethylamine, a metabolite of Antabuse (Fuller & Neiderhiser, 1981).

Antabuse-like Drugs

Carbamide (Temposil), not yet available in the United States, is another agent that inhibits hepatic aldehyde dehydrogenase (Ald DH), causing increases in blood acetaldehyde levels after ethanol administration. Carbamide's acetaldehyde dehydrogenase inhibition peaks at one to two hours after administration and is reversible. The duration of the carbamide-induced inhibition is less than 24 hours, whereas Antabuse-induced inhibition lasts several days; Antabuse's onset of effect is 12 hours, which is much slower than carbamide's (Sellers et al., 1981).

Inhibition of Ald DH by either Antabuse or carbamide results in similar physiologic changes, including tachycardia, tachypnea, palpitations, shortness of breath, and nausea or vomiting. The intensity of these changes depends on the dosages of Antabuse or carbamide and the quantity of ethanol. However, there are differences between carbamide and Antabuse, since carbamide produces fewer side effects. This compound does not inhibit dopamine-beta-hydroxylase (DBH); it is, therefore, much safer for schizophrenics whose psychoses may be activated by an increase in dopamine levels. In addition, carbamide does not inhibit the metabolism of phenytoin (Dilantin) and may therefore be a more appropriate drug to use in alcoholics who are taking Dilantin to control their seizures.

The great majority of Antabuse-ethanol or carbamide-ethanol reactions present no life-threatening risks to the patient (Sellers et al., 1981). Nevertheless, reactions should be managed in the emergency room. Severe hypotension is one serious side effect requiring emergency measures. If arrhythmias occur, they should be treated symptomatically with other supportive measures. Although recommendations for the use of vitamin C and intravenous Benadryl have been made by some clinicians, there have been no controlled double-blind evaluations of these compounds and no evidence of efficacy in aborting the Antabuse-ethanol or carbamide-ethanol reaction.

There are other therapeutic agents that can produce uncomfortable Antabuse-like reactions associated with alcohol ingestion, such as flushing, tachycardia, and hypotension. These compounds include cephalosporins, some oral hypoglycemic agents, and metronidazole (Flagyl). However, these agents have not been found to be of any practical use in the treatment of alcoholism. The reaction to metronidazole appears to be too mild to be a deterrent, and this compound has shown evidence of carcinogenic activity in studies of chronic, oral administration in mice and rats. Prolonged administration of metronidazole is not recommended in humans.

LITHIUM

The role of lithium in the treatment of affective disorders has been well established, and the relationship between affective disorders and alcoholism has been noted (Gallant & Simpson, 1976; Reynold et al., 1977). However, the value of lithium in treating alcoholics is as yet difficult to confirm. A review of 61 published studies of lithium in alcoholics revealed that the inadequacies of these studies ranged from lack of controls to inadequate definitions of the problems under investigation (McMillan, 1981). According to McMillan, none of the controlled studies reviewed used both a standard classification for alcoholism and acceptable diagnostic nomenclature for the affective disorder which was being simultaneously evaluated. Just as important, some of the controlled studies failed to document the genetic alcoholic variables and other relevant biographical data which could influence subsequent drinking episodes as well as response to psychopharmacologic medications. In some of the lithium studies, only an arbitrary quantitative score on a psychological rating depression scale, such as the Beck, was considered to be acceptable for including "depressed" patients in the study; very few attempts were made to separate patients with primary affective disorders who were using alcohol to obliterate the dysphoria from primary alcoholics who had developed depression secondary to chronic excessive alcohol use and its accompanying life-style. Except for a brief two-week study, there was an absence of well-controlled evaluations of lithium versus a standard MAO inhibitor or tricyclic antidepressant. It may well be that any antidepressant drug has the ability to decrease not only the primary depression in a secondary alcoholic but also the accompanying excessive alcohol intake in such patients.

There is one interesting placebo-controlled, double-blind study of the effects of lithium treatment on experimental ethanol intoxication in detoxified alcoholics. In this study (Judd & Leighton, 1984), the experimental population consisted of 35 inpatient male alcoholic volunteers, whose ages ranged from 24 to 55 years; each had been diagnosed as alcoholic by two independent research psychiatrists using two standardized diagnostic criteria for alcoholism. Each subject had to meet criteria for both diagnostic systems and be classified as gamma alcoholic (Jellinek's classification) before admission to the study. The subjects were also assigned psychiatric diagnoses by using the Schedule for Affective Disorders and Schizophrenia Life-time Version/Research Diagnostic Criteria (SADS-L/RDC). Of the 35 patients, 16 were assigned diagnoses of primary affective disorder. All subjects had to be alcohol and drug-free for a minimum of 21 days before starting the study.

Judd and Leighton's double-blind study was a split-half crossover design with a randomized presentation of lithium and placebo. The medication and placebo periods were 14 days each. The mean serum lithium level on experimental testing days was 0.89 meq/liter (range = 0.7–1.55 meq/liter). Each subject had identical, standardized testing sessions at baseline, after lithium, and after placebo administration. The subjects completed a pre-ethanol test battery before receiving 1.32 ml/kg of 95% ethanol in orange juice, which was administered in four divided doses over 60 minutes. Blood alcohol measurements were obtained 10 minutes after consumption of the ethanol; the subjects were then asked to complete the post-ethanol test battery. The blood alcohol levels during the experimental sessions ranged from 70 to 153 mg/100 cc with a mean of 104 mg/100 cc.

The results of this study showed that 14 days of lithium maintenance therapy had a significant effect on alleviating the subjective experiences of confusion, intoxication, and the desire to drink that is produced by ethanol in alcoholics. On cognitive testing, lithium appeared to interfere with rapid calculations and short-term attention but did block ethanol's negative effect on the Minnesota Clerical Test, a test of sustained attention. It may be that lithium therapy produces a qualitatively and quantitatively different ethanol-induced subjective experience for the alcoholic, with a subsequent decrease in desire to continue drinking.

Considering these data, I believe that it is important now to initiate and complete similarly well-controlled long-term evaluations of lithium in the treatment of alcoholism, using the same types of standardized diagnostic criteria for alcoholism and other psychiatric illnesses and appropriately balancing the drug-placebo groups for genetic background, available human support systems, and primary affective illness. These protocols should include plans for adequate follow-up and evaluation of the dropouts. Such investigations will have to consider carefully the appropriate number of patients to be included in these studies in order to obtain significant results, since the dropout rate for alcoholics in long-term investigations is relatively high. Although the data from Judd and Leighton's study support the concept that lithium maintenance may be a useful therapeutic modality in the management of a subgroup of alcoholics, it would be a mistake to initiate widespread use of lithium in alcoholics until more data are available.

THE ROLE OF ANTIDEPRESSANT AGENTS

One of the most difficult and important diagnostic problems facing therapists in the field of alcoholism is the delineation of primary versus secondary depression in patients presenting the syndrome of alcoholism. If the clinician can elicit a history of DSM-III-R diagnostic criteria for major depression-recurrent type or bipolar disorder *preceding* the onset of alcoholism or a history of an affective disorder occurring during sustained periods of abstinence, then he/she can confidently assume that the patient has a diagnosis of primary affective disorder as well as a diagnosis of alcoholism. An early childhood history of separation anxiety, phobic behavior, or panic disorder may also lead the physician to suspect the presence of an underlying primary depression. However, inadequate histories given by alcoholics and difficulties in dating the initial onset of loss of alcohol control and the initial development of depression interfere with the reliability of the diagnostic classification, particularly for individuals who developed their problems of alcoholism and depression during their teenage years.

The type of inpatient setting may influence the incidence of the diagnoses of primary alcoholism and primary depression. On inpatient rehabilitation units such as those operated by the Veterans Administration, male patients outnumber female patients by ratios as large as 10 or 20 to 1. Since major depression is more prevalent among female patients, we would expect a much higher incidence of this diagnosis in alcoholics admitted to private or state alcoholism rehabilitation programs.

The importance of a family history of depression as a factor in separating primary from secondary depression in alcoholics is uncertain. While one survey found no significant differences in the incidence of a family history of affective disorder between these two alcoholic depressive subgroups, published data do suggest that careful, extensive family histories may contribute to a more reliable diagnostic classification of primary and secondary depression (Akiskal et al., 1979; Schuckit, 1983). Primary affective illness may be differentiated from secondary affective reactions by the following historical data:

1. occurrence of a hypomanic or manic reaction to antidepressant medication;
2. family history of bipolar illness;
3. family history of affective illness in two or more consecutive generations.

Although only one-third of those with primary affective illness present such biographical data, the diagnostic specificity was 95% in one study (Akiskal et al., 1979). If the dexamethasone suppression test (DST) is positive after the alcoholic has been abstinent for four or more weeks, then the diagnosis is more likely to be a primary illness (Dackis et al., 1983). However, the DST appears to be positive in only about 35% to 40% of the cases diagnosed as major depression.

The diagnosis of a primary major depression usually indicates the need for antidepressant medication as well as counseling for the treatment of this particular alcoholic patient. Undertreatment of major depression is more likely to result in subsequent relapse of the alcohol problem and possible future suicide attempts (Pettinati et al., 1982).

There are no controlled data which show any commercially available antidepressants to be more efficacious or less toxic than another antidepressant for use in those alcoholics presenting major depressive episodes. Liver sensitization can occur with the tricyclics, and hepatotoxicity has been associated with monoamine oxidase (MAO) inhibitors, but the incidence appears to be relatively low in alcoholics who do not initially present severe liver pathology. The most common mistakes in the use of antidepressants are prescribing too low a dosage for too short a period of time and premature discontinuation of the medication once an adequate therapeutic response has occurred. It appears that MAO inhibitors may be somewhat superior in efficacy to tricyclics in patients presenting a great deal of anxiety in association with depression and in atypical depression associated with hypersomnia, overeating, and panic disorder (Gallant, 1986).

Family data collected on alcoholics with depression should include careful historical information about the existence oi agoraphobia, panic disorder, and depression in the family. In addition, if a close relative has shown a good therapeutic response to a specific antidepressant, then that same medication should be tried in the alcoholic with a major depressive episode. Patients with panic disorder, especially agoraphobics, show relatively good therapeutic responses to MAO inhibitors.

Some of the antidepressant agents, such as doxepin and amitriptyline, can be used for hypnotic purposes in alcoholic patients. The sedative side effects of these antidepressants, used at relatively low dosages of 50 mg hs or 100 mg hs, have proved to be quite helpful in some alcoholics who have a history of chronic insomnia. These medications are not habit-forming, and it is easy to discontinue them after the patients have developed adequate sleeping habits. I am extremely hesitant, and in fact feel very negative, about using benzodiazepines or other habit-forming medications as hypnotics to enable alcoholic patients to sleep comfortably *after* they have completed detoxification.

In summary, it is my opinion that some patients may use alcohol to obliterate the pain and discomfort of major depressive episodes, as well as of panic disorder, and thus develop a second major psychiatric illness of alcoholism. However, if the depressive symptomatology is secondary to excessive alcohol intake and the accompanying life failures, then the depression should be alleviated within a period of several weeks as abstinence continues; these patients require no specific psychopharmacologic intervention for their depressive symptomatology.

USE OF ANXIOLYTIC AGENTS

Anxiolytic efficacy is the ability of a medication to cause a significant reduction in the psychologic and somatic symptoms of anxiety without hampering the patient's cognitive processes and manual dexterity. The medication should not interfere with the recovery of the alcoholic patient, who may be likely to abuse a habit-forming drug such as a benzodiazepine. Ideally, the compound should produce neither high dose tolerance nor normal dose dependence withdrawal symptoms; thus, it should be suitable for prolonged use without any undue risks.

On our alcohol and drug unit at Southeast Louisiana Hospital, approximately 20 to 25% of the patients still experience moderate to marked anxiety after the acute withdrawal phase has been terminated (Gallant et al., 1969; McFarlain et al., 1976). The availability of an appropriate anxiolytic would enable many of these patients to reduce the level of their anxiety so that they could more rapidly participate in insight psychotherapy techniques. However, the tendency of alcohol and drug abusers to misuse benzodiazepines prevents us from utilizing these compounds. Our main treatment approaches for reducing anxiety in the alcoholic population involve various types of cognitive and psychotherapeutic techniques and behavioral therapies.

The use of benzodiazepines and other antianxiety compounds for the treatment of alcohol detoxification was described in Chapter 8. After the stage of detoxification has been completed, dependency-producing medications such as benzodiazepines should not be used for more than one to two weeks, for patients with problems of abuse are likely to misuse these tranquilizers. Small sedative doses of doxepin or amitriptyline may be used for alcoholic patients with chronic insomnia and oral prn doses of hydroxyzine (Atarax, Vistaril) for occasional episodes of anxiety or agitation. However, it should be stressed that the treatment of anxiety in alcoholic patients should never be confined solely to drugs; there are many nonpharmacological, environmental therapeutic modalities, such as various types of anxiety-reducing psychodynamic, cognitive, and behavioral techniques. Some of these techniques were described in Chapter 9. It is important to realize that such psychologic therapies may do more to build confidence than medication, since the patient can give credit for improvement to himself rather than to a pill. In addition, the common side effects of the benzodiazepines, such as daytime somnolence, muscle weakness and fatigue, motor incoordination, cerebellar symptoms of nystagmus, dysarthria and ataxia, and occasional disinhibition of anger, may all interfere with the alcoholic's attempts to maintain abstinence. In one evaluation of the differential effects of diazepam (Valium) and pentobarbital on mood and behavior, diazepam produced a greater increase in subjects' hostility with a concomitant deterioration in social behavior (Griffith et al., 1983).

An often underestimated side effect of the benzodiazepines (BZ) is a decrease in performance of cognitive tasks and manual dexterity. This may not be noticed by the patients. In a placebo crossover evaluation of flurazepam (Dalmane) 30 mg, hs, for three weeks in 12 patients with sleep problems, Oswald (1979) showed that on all tests of mental concentration and manual dexterity, flurazepam (which has a half-life of 80 to 100 hours) impaired performance all day long. Ability to sustain alertness for one hour (to listen for the randomly distributed bleeps of 400 msec duration among 1,800 msec slightly longer bleeps) was significantly impaired by the second week of drug administration and even more so in the third week ($p < 0.005$). The subjects' self-ratings indicated that they perceived the impairment at the end of the first week but completely failed to recognize the impairment during the third week, suggesting that they had accommodated to their cognitive impairment. The potential danger of accommodating to these effects and not being aware of them is obvious.

In a sleep study evaluation of lorazepam, a benzodiazepine with a relatively short half-life of approximately 12 hours, Scharf and Jacoby (1982) described an anterograde amnesia and hangover effect occurring the day after the first drug night. These subjects reported amnesia for daytime events after the first drug night; improvement was first noted by the third night. A number of other benzodiazepines have been reported to induce anterograde amnesia. This side effect could pose serious problems, particularly for alcoholic patients who are in learning situations important to therapy or to their jobs.

These benzodiazepine-induced cognitive deficits in ability to sustain alertness, associated with daytime sedation and fatigue, may interfere with the treatment of affective disorders in some patients. In a double-blind evaluation of moderate to severely depressed inpatients with primary affective disorder, all of whom were receiving adequate doses of tricyclic agents, half were randomly assigned to 20 mg diazepam daily and half to placebo. The results of the Beck Depression Inventory indicated that the addition of diazepam retarded the improvement of the patients who were taking the tricyclic antidepressants. Caution is advised in treating severely depressed patients with diazepam or other benzodiazepines (Bowen, 1978).

Withdrawal symptoms associated with cognitive deficits, severe anxiety and agitation, paresthesias, and insomnia have occurred after only six weeks of "normal dose" benzodiazepine therapy. In one study (Murphy et al., 1984), 40 patients were randomly assigned to diazepam, mean daily dose of only 11.4 mg, or buspirone (a new anxiolytic), mean daily dose of 7.7 mg, for six or twelve weeks. There were four drug groups: two groups withdrawn from active medication after six weeks and the other two withdrawn at twelve weeks. Placebo was substituted in blind fashion for those patients whose active medication was terminated after six weeks. Withdrawal of diazepam at six weeks produced a marked increase in symptoms of anxiety, agitation, difficulties with concentration and paresthesias. These symptoms usually develop within three to five days after discontinuation of a benzo-diazepine with a long half-life such as diazepam or flurazepam.

Beta blockers have been used for reduction of the target symptomatology of anxiety and tension in alcoholics (Gallant et al., 1973). These compounds are not habit-forming, but, as noted in Chapter 8, may have side effects that can precipitate asthmatic attacks in patients who have a history of bronchial asthma and obstruction and may interfere with myocardial contractility in patients who have developed an alcoholic cardiomyopathy. In our (Gallant et al., 1973) double-blind study of hospitalized, volunteer, chronic alcoholic patients with the target syndrome of "anxiety and tension," a dosage of propanolol, 120 mg daily, was compared with placebo during a four-week study period. Despite a significant placebo response in this particular inpatient population, there was a statistically significant improvement in the global ratings of the propanolol (Inderal) group at the 0.05 level, as compared with the placebo group. The side effects in this study were unusually mild and infrequent. One patient in the propanolol group developed a bradycardia of 56, which necessitated maintaining the maximal dosage at 80 mg daily, and one patient in the placebo group developed mild somnolence. No other clinical laboratory abnormalities were observed or reported. However, this study showed no significant differences in the psychologic test scales that were used; therefore, these conflicting results would indicate only that further studies of beta blockers should be conducted in severely anxious patients who have completed their detoxification.

THE ROLE OF VITAMINS

Alcoholism produces multiple nutritional deficiencies, as well as the organic abnormalities described in Chapter 7. When an alcoholic population is evaluated for specific types of nutritional deficiencies, such as zinc, magnesium, and various vitamin deficiencies, it is not unusual to find a sizable proportion with one or more of the nutritional deficits. Most researchers and clinicians in the field agree that supplemental thiamine (vitamin B_1) should be administered to all patients who have a history of chronic alcoholism. While a considerable percentage of normal subjects have low tissue thiamine status, alcoholics with poor diets are even more likely to be lacking in adequate thiamine tissue levels (Anderson et al., 1986). In severe alcoholics, immediate treatment with thiamine, 100 mg daily, can prove to be of some help and definitely is of no harm to the patient.

Thiamine treatment is the specific treatment for Wernicke's encephalopathy, a rapidly deteriorating organic mental syndrome secondary to alcoholism. This alcohol-related brain damage appears to be associated with progressive neuronal degeneration, particularly in the periventricular area of the brain. Unfortunately, it is frequently not diagnosed until death. Of 51 patients with this disease first diagnosed at autopsy, 45 were alcoholics, only seven of whom had been diagnosed as such prior to death (Harper, 1979). Many of the patients died of hemorrhage into the brain-stem, involving the cardiac and respiratory nuclei. Cerebral and ventricular atrophy was commonly found at autopsy. One major recommendation resulting from the data of Harper's study was the routine use of large doses of prophylactic thiamine in alcoholic patients, particularly those with clinical evidence of cerebral damage.

Research into the etiology of the Wernicke-Korsakoff syndrome has indicated that thiamine pyrophosphatase (TPP)-dependent transketalase activity may be decreased in patients who develop the syndrome (Blass & Gibson, 1979). It is suggested that some alcoholics may have a greater genetic-metabolic tendency than others for the development of the Wernicke-Korsakoff syndrome.

Treatment of acute Wernicke-Korsakoff syndrome can be extremely rewarding. My first contact with such a case was in the emergency room at Charity Hospital in New Orleans in 1956 when I was an intern. A patient came to the emergency room with severe ophthalmoplegia (weakness of all eye muscles with double vision and inability to focus), severe ataxia, and extreme confusion. Administration of 100 mg of thiamine i.v. resulted in the patient's showing a dramatic response within one hour, with a complete remission of the ophthalmoplegia and ataxia. It is amazing to see vitamin therapy have such dramatic effects within a short period of time.

The use of folic acid, 1 to 3 mg daily, is also recommended by some clinicians. In one study, a folate deficiency was found in the erythrocytes in 35% of the patients, in the liver of 31%, and in the serum of 28% of the alcoholic subjects. However, only 13% of these patients were anemic. Enlargement of the red blood cells may be caused by a direct toxic effect of alcohol on the developing erythrocytes as well as by a folate deficiency (Edmondson, 1980). It is interesting to note that alcoholics frequently show a relative macrocytosis without a significant anemia (38% in one study) and without abnormal folic acid and vitamin B_{12} levels (Carney & Sheffield, 1980). Only 2% of the non-alcoholic population displays this type of hemogram. Thus, a patient with a relative macrocytosis without an anemia and without a folic acid and B_{12} deficiency would only have a 5% chance of being misdiagnosed as an alcoholic. The CBC to determine macrocytosis is one of the better screening tests for chronic alcoholism.

A significant percentage of alcoholics have peripheral neuropathies with symmetrical symptoms of numbness, tingling sensations, burning sensations, and sometimes weakness in both legs. It may be that chronic thiamine deficiency, as well as pantothenic acid and pyridoxine deficiency, may be responsible for the development of this syndrome. However, since we are not sure whether one or several of these vitamin deficiencies are specific causes of development of this syndrome and we are uncertain as to what part direct alcohol toxicity plays in producing this pathology, multiple mega-B therapy is recommended for these patients.

Other diseases that may benefit from supplemental thiamine therapy include alcoholic amblyopia, characterized by blurring of vision due to central scotomas, which can develop into optic atrophy if untreated (Edmondson, 1980). Improvement has been reported in association with vitamin B supplements, but there are no controlled studies in this area; controlled data are similarly lacking in most of the other areas involving vitamin therapy of alcohol-related diseases. In many cases, it is difficult to delineate the damage that is produced by alcohol and that produced by vitamin deficiencies secondary to chronic alcohol intake with malnutrition. However, vitamin and mineral supplements will seldom be harmful to alcoholic patients. Because of the occasional episodes of night blindness and reports of alcoholic amblyopia, vitamin A therapy and zinc supplements have been recommended by some clinicians. On our alcohol and drug abuse (ADU) service, the routine orders include daily thiamine, 100 mg, mega-B vitamins, and a multivitamin supplement. This vitamin therapy is continued throughout the patient's stay on the unit and then maintained for several weeks in the clinic. Although there is no scientific basis for this duration of vitamin therapy, this type of short-term vitamin supplement can do no harm and may be of some slight value in patients who are still undergoing the protracted withdrawal syndrome or subacute organic mental disorder for several weeks or months following the cessation of alcohol.

All personnel involved in the treatment of alcoholic patients should be aware of the various indications for the use of psychopharmacologic medications as well as the value of appropriate vitamin and mineral therapy. I believe that there are very few contraindications for the use of Antabuse, and the research data indicate the significant benefits when an alcoholic takes this medication daily. In patients who present dual diagnoses, such as major depression or bipolar disorder or severe generalized anxiety disorder in association with the illness of alcoholism, correct use of an antidepressant or lithium or a non-habituating anxiolytic agent may enable the patient not only to remain abstinent but enhance the quality of his sober life.

REFERENCES

Akiskal, H. S., Rosenthal, R. H., Rosenthal, T. L., Kashgarian, M., Khani, M. K., & Puzantian, V. R. (1979). Differentiation of primary affective illness from situational, symptomatic and secondary depression. *Archives of General Psychiatry, 36*, 635–643.

Anderson, S. H., Vickery, C. A., & Nicol, A. D. (1986). Adult thiamine requirements and the continuing need to fortify processed cereals. *Lancet, 2*, 85–89.

Blass, J. P., & Gibson, G. E. (1979). Genetic factors in Wernicke-Korsakoff syndrome. *Alcoholism: Clinical and Experimental Research, 3*, 126–134.

Bowen, R. C. (1978). The effects of diazepam on the recovery of endogenously depressed patients. *Journal of Clinical Pharmacology, May/June*, 280–284.

Carney, M. W. P., & Sheffield, B. F. (1980). The hemogram in the diagnosis of alcoholism. *Journal of Studies on Alcohol, 41*, 744–748.

Christensen, J. K., Ronstead, P., & Vaag, U. H. (1984). Side effects after disulfiram. *Acta Psychiatrica Scandinavica, 69*, 265–273.

Dackis, C. A., Pottash, A. L. C., Bailey, J., Stuckey, R. F., Extein, I. L., & Gold, M. S. (1983). The specificity of the thyrotropin releasing hormone (TRH) and dexamethasone suppression test (DST) for major depressive illness in alcoholics. In *Problems of drug dependence*, NIDA Research Monograph 43.

Edmondson, H. A. (1980). Pathology of alcoholism. *American Journal of Clinical Pathology, 74*, 725–742.

Fuller, R. K., Branchey, L., Brightwell, D. R., Derman, R. M., Emrick, C. D., Iber, F. L., James, K. E., Lacoursiere, R. B., Lee, K. K., Lowenstam, I., Maany, I., Neiderhiser, D., Nocks, J. J., & Shaw, S. (1986). Disulfiram treatment of alcoholism. *Journal of the American Medical Association, 256*, 1449–1455.

Fuller, R. K., & Neiderhiser, D. H. (1980). Evaluation and application of urinary diethylamine method to measure compliance with disulfiram therapy. *Journal of Studies on Alcohol, 42*, 202–207.

Fuller, R. K., & Williford, W. O. (1981). Life-table analysis of abstinence in a study evaluating the efficacy of disulfiram. *Alcoholism: Clinical and Experimental Research, 4*, 298–301.

Gallant, D. M. (1982). *Alcohol and drug abuse curriculum guide for psychiatry faculty.* (p.30). Rockville, MD: DHHS Pub No (ADM) 82-1159.

Gallant, D. M. (1986). The use of psychotropic medications in alcoholism. *Substance Abuse, Spring*, 35–47.

Gallant, D. M., Bishop, M. P., & Guerrero-Figueroa, R. (1969). Doxepin versus diazepam: A controlled evaluation in 100 chronic alcoholic patients. *Journal of Clinical Pharmacology, 9*, 57–61.

Gallant, D. M., & Simpson, G. M. (1976). *Depression: Behavioral, biochemical, diagnostic and treatment concepts.* New York: Spectrum.

Gallant, D. M., Swanson, W. C., & Guerrero-Figueroa, R. (1973). A controlled evaluation of propranolol in chronic alcoholic patients presenting the symptomatology of anxiety and tension. *Journal of Clinical Pharmacology, 13*, 41–43.

Goyer, P. F., Brown, G. L., Minichiello, M. D., & Major, L. F. (1984). Mood-altering effects of disulfiram in alcoholics. *Journal of Studies and Alcohol, 45*, 209–213.

Griffith, R. R., Bigelow, G. F., & Liebson, I. (1983). Differential effects of diazepam and pentobarbital on mood and behavior. *Archives of General Psychiatry, 40*, 865–873.

Harper, C. (1979). Wernicke's encephalopathy: A more common disease than realized: A neuropathological study of 51 cases. *Journal of Neurology, Neurosurgery, and Psychiatry, 42*, 226–231.

Iber, F. L., Dutta, S., Shamszad, M., & Krause, S. (1977). Excretion of radioactivity following the administration of sulfur-labeled disulfiram in man. *Alcoholism: Clinical and Experimental Research, 1*, 359–364.

Iber, F. L., Lee, K., Lacoursiere, R., & Fuller, R. (in press). Liver toxicity encountered in the Veterans Administration trial of disulfiram. *Alcoholism: Clinical and Experimental Research.*

Jensen, J. C., & Faiman, M. D. (1986). Disulfiram-ethanol reaction in the rat. 1. Blood alcohol, acetaldehyde, and liver aldehyde dehydrogenase relations. *Alcoholism: Clinical and Experimental Research, 10*, 45–49.

Judd, L. L., Leighton, Y. H. (1984). Lithium antagonizes ethanol intoxication in alcoholics. *American Journal of Psychiatry, 141*, 1517–1521.

Major, L. F., Lerner, P., & Ballenger, J. L. (1979). Dopamine-beta-hydroxylase in the cerebrospinal fluid: Relation to disulfiram-induced psychosis. *Biological Psychiatry, 14*, 337–344.

McFarlain, R. A., Mielke, D. H., & Gallant, D. M. (1976). Comparison of muscle relaxation with placebo medication for anxiety reduction in alcoholic patients. *Current Therapeutic Research, 20*, 173–177.

McMillan, T. N. (1981). Lithium and the treatment of alcoholism: A critical review. *British Journal of Addiction, 76*, 245–258.

Murphy, S. M., Owen, R. T., & Tyrer, P. J. (1984). Withdrawal symptoms after six weeks' treatment with diazepam. *Lancet, 2*, 1389–1390.

Oswald, I. (1979). The why and how of hypnotic drugs. *British Medical Journal, 1* 1167–1168.

Reynold, M. C., Merry, J., & Coppen, A. (1977). Prophylatic treatment of alcoholism by lithium carbonate: An initial report. *Alcoholism: Clinical and Experimental Research, 1*, 109–111.

Scharf, M.B., & Jacoby, J. A. (1982). Lorazepam: Efficacy, side effects, and rebound phenomena. *Journal of Clinical Pharmacology and Therapeutics, 31*, 175–179.

Schuckit, M. (1983). Alcoholic patients with secondary depression. *American Journal of Psychiatry, 140*, 711–714.

Sellers, E. M., Naranjo, C. A., & Peachey, J. E. (1981). Drugs to decrease alcohol consumption. *New England Journal of Medicine, 305*, 1255–1262.

Sereny, G., Sharma, V., Holt, J., & Gordis, E. (1986). Mandatory supervised Antabuse therapy in an outpatient alcoholism program: A pilot study. *Alcoholism: Clinical and Experimental Research, 10*, 290–292.

CHAPTER 11

Outpatient Treatment

As we have seen in Chapter 9, there are many problems in evaluating treatment success rates of both inpatient and outpatient alcoholism rehabilitation programs. However, the specific type of follow-up therapy employed has an important bearing on the final success rate; some treatment modalities that may enhance the success rate will be reviewed in this chapter (Fuller et al., 1986; Gallant et al., 1966; Gallant et al., 1970; Sereny et al., 1986).

THE INTAKE OR INITIAL HISTORY-TAKING

Most community or state outpatient clinics are understaffed and overburdened with a large number of new applicants and a heavy treatment caseload. Nevertheless, a screening interview of the new applicant by a psychiatric social worker, followed by an "individual" intake interview by the psychiatric consultant, is standard in many of these clinics. This technique of gathering information may be feasible or practical in a private clinic, but the inflexibility of this procedure results in a large waiting list of patients after their initial telephone contact for an appointment with a community, county, or state substance abuse clinic. This inability of the clinic to meet the immediate needs of patients is a major cause of the high dropout rate in mental health clinics, including alcoholism clinics. It is understandable that many patients see this delay in treatment as overt rejection or lack of concern. In addition, "first appointments" scheduled for individual intake sessions with a social worker result in a further waste of valuable time for an understaffed clinic, since approximately 15–30% of these patients do not keep the initial appointment (Abrahams & Enright, 1965; Korner, 1964). Paradoxically, we have overburdened treatment programs with staff members waiting in their offices for patients who do not appear.

A review of our New Orleans alcoholism clinic's procedures over a nine-month period confirmed the need for a more realistic assessment approach to the patient's first clinic appointment (Gallant et al., 1966). Of 377 alcoholic patients who were required to wait no more than 48 hours for their first appointments, 323 patients (86%) kept their scheduled appointments; of 155 patients who had to wait from 48 to 144 hours for the first appointments, 108 patients (69%) kept the appointments; and of 37 patients who had to wait more than seven days for their first appointments, only 17 (46%) came to the clinic. These data show a significant increase in the dropout rate as the time interval from telephone contact to scheduled appointment is increased beyond 48 hours ($x^2 = 32.14$; $p < .001$). This delay results not only in untreated patients but also in scheduled clinic staff hours which are unfilled, with therapists waiting for patients who never appear.

The dropout rate is a serious problem for all understaffed mental health clinics, but particularly for an alcoholism treatment clinic, because it is unusual for the dropout alcoholic patient to have a spontaneous remission after he or she fails to follow through with treatment plans. In an attempt to remedy this situation, our clinic adopted a group intake procedure for the first clinic contact. Using this procedure enables us to see a large number of applicants for their initial intake sessions within 36 hours of the telephone request for an appointment. However, before beginning this procedure we decided to evaluate the efficacy of this group intake approach in order to be certain that we were not introducing an inefficient treatment modality.

Methodologic Procedure for Evaluation of the Group Intake Technique

The New Orleans Substance Abuse Clinic is the only state clinic in the city that offers outpatient treatment to the patient with symptomatic alcoholism. This clinic accepts any patient who has a major problem with alcoholism, excluding only those with overt psychotic illnesses; they are referred to the mental health centers. An average of 800 to 1,000 new patients visit the clinic yearly, and the monthly caseload averages between 600 and 800 cases. The number of personnel budgeted for the clinic is insufficient to meet the demands of this heavy caseload. Group therapy (singles, couples, and women's groups) is the main treatment technique. Individual counseling is reserved for those alcoholic patients who have severe emotional and/or psychological problems which must be treated if the patient is going to maintain sobriety.

In this research endeavor, the group intake sessions were scheduled for two and a half hours duration, three days weekly. Six patients who had requested appointments (usually by telephone) were randomly selected for each session. A similar number was assigned to the individual intake sessions, which consisted of taking the standard history, including chief complaint, presenting symptoms, past history, and developmental family history. The interviewer attempted to establish a therapeutic relationship. The same therapists conducted both the group sessions and individual intake sessions in order to decrease the variables when comparing the efficacy of these two initial treatment approaches.

Of the six patients assigned to the group intake, usually four or five kept their appointments. They were not notified about the group procedure until they arrived at the clinic, since the group intake session was considered to be a routine aspect of the treatment program. The family members accompanying the patient were invited to sit in the back of the room during the group meeting. During the session, questions were occasionally asked of the family members about certain responses the patient made in the group. This session is a modification of the group staffing procedure on the inpatient rehabilitation unit, which was described in Chapter 9.

The four or five new patients were led into the office and introduced to the therapist and to each other. The patients (and any family members who were present) were briefed about the types of treatment available in the clinic and its associated inpatient service. It was explained that they were free to refuse to answer any questions considered too intimate for group discussion and could request that the interviewer reserve such questions for a private session. The immediate goals of the therapist were to obtain a brief history from each patient and to induce a feeling of cohesiveness and unity within the group. The patient who appeared likely to have the most typical history of alcoholism (blackouts, delirium tremens, history of post-alcoholic convulsions) was selected as the initial focus of the session. This patient was encouraged to discuss freely the early and later symptoms of alcoholism. The other patients were then offered the opportunity to identify with some of these symptoms of alcoholism. The technique of "going around" was employed, enabling the patients to assume the role of co-therapist during this first clinic contact. This technique builds confidence as it enables patients to share responsibility for others. This contribution is particularly noticeable when a patient who obviously requires hospitalization on the alcoholism inpatient service resists the interviewer's recommendation for hospitalization. Invariably the other patients present come to the aid of the therapist and try to convince the patient that he or she should seek hospitalization.

The patients' responses to the group intake session were consistently impressive. The therapist fostered interaction by drawing out opinions and feelings from the patients regarding the problems of other patients in the group. Although the alcoholic can use the denial mechanism expertly with the therapist in a one to one relationship, he has difficulty maintaining this defense in the presence of four or five other alcoholics. Often the group was able to arrive at a realistic consensus regarding the accuracy of a fellow alcoholic's drinking history and to provide consensual validation for the therapist.

In the middle phase of the group session, the exaggerated dependency needs of alcoholics and their difficulty in expressing anger appropriately, even when they are sober, was discussed. At this point the attention shifted to one of the other patients whose developmental history was obtained. As group members found that they shared the same difficulties, empathy and identification grew among them. The denial mechanism was freely discussed, and problems other than alcoholism were mentioned in relation to this defense. The collective strength of the group allowed the patients to admit some of these difficulties and added immeasurably to their initial orientation to the group treatment program.

At the end of the session, the therapist arranged disposition to either inpatient treatment or continuation of clinic treatment, with recommendations for one of the following modes of treatment: patient group therapy, marital couples therapy, women's group therapy, or individual sessions in preparation for group therapy. During this research project, all patients from each group intake were referred to the same ongoing treatment group in the clinic to encourage the development of cohesiveness. Transactions within the group during the intake quickly revealed the patients' personality traits, providing the interviewer with an early opportunity to view their interpersonal and intrapsychic reactions. This technique enables the therapist to plan an effective treatment program for the patients shortly after their admission to the clinic.

Patients have generally exhibited a strong positive response to this initial group intake. When a patient is seen in an individual intake session, his alienation and estrangement are sometimes compounded by the realistic loneliness he suffers as a new patient in a strange treatment setting. In such an atmosphere, he may tend to exaggerate his denial mechanism. The interpersonal approach of the group intake session seemed to permit early identification of patients with others in the group and to discourage further alienation. In addition, the alcoholic patient's expert use of the denial mechanism was approached effectively within the group intake procedure.

Results of the Group Intake versus Individual Intake Sessions

My optimistic expectations of this flexible adaptation of the group process to the clinic intake sessions was supported not only by the consistent, positive responses and memories of those patients who subsequently talked about their initial contact with the clinic, but also by objective evidence. Pertinent data on the value of group intake were provided by comparing the dropout rates at the second scheduled session of patients in the two groups. Of the patients referred for a second visit to the clinic after a group intake session, 31 of 49 (63%) kept their appointments, whereas only 28 of 61 patients (46%) referred after individual intake returned for their second clinic visit. Although these data do not show a statistically significant difference between the two intake procedures with respect to percentage of patients who drop out following the intake interview, there appears to be a definite trend ($x^2 = 3.3$; $p < 0.10$) in the direction of fewer dropouts following the group intake session. It should be emphasized that both the individual and group intake sessions were conducted by the same personnel (two psychiatrists and two psychiatric social workers). One hundred forty-seven patients who requested hospitalization and were accepted by the clinic for admission to the hospital were not included in this study, since they presumably had a significantly greater motivation to return to the clinic for admission to the inpatient service (98% of these patients returned for the second visit).

The standard clinic intake session with individual alcoholic patients appears to be less efficient and possibly less therapeutic than the group intake. The goals of diagnosis and therapeutic management are more easily evaluated and achieved within a group intake session. This procedure has several additional, subjective advantages:

1. The group approach appears to permit early identification by the patients with others in the group and discourages alienation.
2. The patient's assumption of the role of co-therapist early in clinic treatment is ego-strengthening, as the patient becomes aware of his ability to contribute to the welfare of others.
3. Transactions within this group setting quickly reveal the patient's interpersonal as well as intrapsychic reactions.
4. The alcoholic patient's expert use of the denial mechanism is approached more effectively within the group intake setting.
5. The patient's comfort or lack of comfort within the group setting is more adequately evaluated for future group therapy during this initial phase of treatment.

The comparative review of the individual and group intake sessions revealed the following objective advantages:

1. Economy of clinic staff time is achieved because the procedure eliminates the wasted hours of cancelled appointments by new clinic patients.
2. If properly utilized, the group intake session can contribute consid-

erably to reducing the dropout rate, since it permits an understaffed clinic to see patients in an extended session within 36 hours after the initial request for an appointment. Data has been presented to show that the dropout rate increases significantly if the patients have to wait more than 48 hours for their first scheduled appointment.

3. A review of the number of patients returning for a second clinic visit following individual sessions versus group intake sessions revealed a trend in favor of the group intake procedure ($p < 0.10$).

Treatment Choices

There are many patients who do quite well in outpatient therapy without inpatient treatment. After the group intake or individual session, decisions are made regarding continued outpatient therapy or referral to an inpatient program. Many variables are considered, some of which are more relevant to the patient's life situation and available human support system than to the specific psychologic and medical indications for inpatient therapy. For example, if the patient has been threatened with loss of his job if he leaves it for a four- or six-week stay in a hospital, then necessity may dictate initial outpatient therapy. On the other hand, if the patient has failed in a number of attempts at outpatient therapy and is unable to maintain sobriety, then admission to an inpatient rehabilitation program has to be seriously considered, even though that hospitalization may result in the patient's losing his job. There are no predictor items to indicate which patients will do well in therapy as outpatients and which patients need to enter an inpatient rehabilitation program.

At the end of group or individual intake session, the goals of therapy are reviewed. In addition to the five treatment goals described in Chapter 9 (p. 000), we also discuss the goal of abstinence. Most of our patients know a little about the debate surrounding abstinence versus controlled drinking as a treatment goal. This debate will probably never be satisfactorily resolved. We review some of the research data with our patients and discuss the strong and the weak points of each of the research projects which have evaluated abstinence or controlled drinking as the final goal for the alcoholic patient.

A recent study by the Addiction Research Foundation in Toronto emphasized the disadvantages of imposing the goal of abstinence on "problem drinkers" (Sanchez-Craig & Lei, 1986). In this study, 35 patients were randomly assigned to an abstinence group (AB) and 35 patients to a controlled drinking group (CD). The six-month follow-up results showed that the "lighter" drinking group had a better chance of becoming moderate drinkers after treatment than the "heavier" groups. While no significant differences between the AB or CD groups were found in the "lighter" group, the "heavier" drinking subjects assigned to the CD groups were more successful in accomplishing the treatment goals of "success," as defined in the study, than those "heavier" drinking patients in the AB group.

How do we reconcile Sanchez-Craig and Lei's findings with the results of another recent study, which reported that only 1.6% of 393 patients were successful moderate social drinkers three years after discharge from hospital settings (Helzer et al., 1985)? We inform our patients about the shortcomings of both studies. In the study by Sanchez-Craig & Lei, the patient population was diagnosed only by the amount of alcohol ingested, based solely on the patient's reports. There were a number of shortcomings in this particular study: The patients appeared to be early, young problem drinkers with an average age of only 35 years; genetic history of alcoholism was unknown; follow-up was only six months; collateral reporting was vague; and adversive compounds such as Antabuse were not offered the abstinence (AB) group. In the study by Helzer et al., which had such a pessimistic outcome, 40% of the patients did not participate in formal alcohol rehabilitation programs, the social support systems were inadequate, and controlled drinking was never used as a treatment modality for these patients.

We also review the longest reported follow-up study of a program of controlled drinking, which showed that "sooner or later" all of the alcoholics who had learned a controlled drinking technique had either begun to drink again with loss of control or had decided to stop drinking altogether (Ewing & Rouse, 1976). The follow-up period ranged from 27 to 55 months.

We explain to our patients that perhaps a subgroup of "early alcoholics" or problem drinkers without family histories of alcoholism exists, a group that might do well with a controlled drinking therapeutic technique. However, until the shortcomings of the previously mentioned studies are eliminated in future research, it would be irresponsible and inappropriate for us to use controlled drinking as a therapeutic goal in a treatment program. In our staff meetings, we tell our personnel that the treatment goals of abstinence or controlled drinking are not mutually exclusive. On a practical basis, when we encounter heavy drinkers who refuse total abstinence as a goal, we do attempt to seduce them into treatment by offering controlled drinking, with a contractual understanding that, if that fails, then the patient will agree to take Antabuse with abstinence as the goal.

COUPLES GROUP PSYCHOTHERAPY

Readers should turn to Chapter 9, p. 146, for a review of group therapy goals, women's groups, social skills training, and assertion groups. All outpatient programs should have a women's group available for discussing material that is too embarrassing, painful, or threatening for a mixed group, as well as social skills group for those shy or severely inhibited individuals who require additional psychological support and encouragement.

We have also found that couples group therapy can be quite helpful for alcoholics who are living with a spouse or a long-term companion. Outcome evaluations of couples group therapy have shown this technique to be efficacious (Blinder & Kirschenbaum, 1967; Gallant et al., 1970; Leichter, 1962). In our 18-month follow-up evaluation of 118 couples, the success rate, which included significant economic and social gains as well as *total* abstinence, was approximately 60% (Gallant et al., 1970). The success rate in this particular follow-up evaluation would have even been higher if decreased or controlled drinking had been included as a "success." Only three of the 118 couples were considered to be permanently separated at the time of the final interviews, a smaller number than expected in view of the national average divorce rate.

In the treatment of patients with alcohol abuse or dependence, it is absolutely essential to incorporate all of the human resources that are available to the patients. The patient's spouse can be very important in treatment. Since each one of us sees the world through our own eyes, it would be unwise to accept totally the view of the world that the alcoholic presents in the therapy sessions. The goals of the group psychotherapy technique with couples are: (1) penetration of the patient's severe denial in association with the goal of abstinence; and (2) helping the spouses improve their relationship.

The couples groups meet every week for two hours or every two weeks for four hours. The group that meets biweekly includes patients whose work schedules do not permit them to visit the clinic every week. Each group consists of six to seven couples and is open-ended. Each couple spends from one to three years in the group, depending on the severity of the intrapsychic and interpersonal problems. In the group meetings, the "here and now" approach to problems is strongly emphasized. Couples are consistently asked to give their honest, direct impressions and opinions of other patients in the group. The technique closely resembles the group therapy approach described in Chapter 9 (p. 146). Opinions about improvement in behavior, character deficits, constructive or destructive behavior, and attitudes toward spouse are freely given in the treatment sessions.

Some of the following observations from my experience may explain the success of the couples group approach:

1. The spouse of the alcoholic helps to keep "pulling" the patient back to treatment, and the dropout rate is lower as a result. The patient cannot say, "I'm the only who is trying in my marriage."
2. There is a common goal of abstinence to unify the group. The

primary goal is to start the couple working on their marital problems, but sobriety is required for this goal.

3. In some cases, the therapist uses the spouse to administer disulfiram to the patient when it is considered to be psychologically sound.

4. The therapist obtains a more realistic view of the patient's home life by seeing some of the marital interactions in the group. Habitual nonverbal communications between the partners (smirks, grimaces, clenched fists, etc.) allow the therapist and the group to see the feelings and mood behind the verbal interchanges. Thus, the therapist and the group can refuse to accept the distortions of either husband or wife, thereby helping to break neurotic patterns.

5. The dependent or narcissistic needs that may have attracted the partners to each other can now be faced and treated in an open manner.

6. The couples group approach enables the alcoholic patient to develop personal freedom and decrease defensiveness. For example, an extremely dependent, alcoholic wife may be given permission to speak up to her dominating husband in the group. In other situations, the unhealthy guilt of the spouse and passive acceptance of the alcoholic can be decreased; for example, the group's support may enable the patient's wife to set limits and to force him to give up his denial when he realizes that this is the "last time around."

7. With both partners present, minor bickering is eliminated in the group and their basic problems are faced directly. Without the group, minor bickering between the patient and the spouse can persist, each mate forever complaining to the therapist about the other.

8. Homework assignments or behavioral tasks—setting specific periods of time aside for communication, planning various leisure activities together, or expressing mutual affection at home—can be proposed with both partners present, allowing little room for distortion. These homework assignments can be positively reinforced by the group.

The patient and spouse should be treated together as a couple to prevent a recurrent neurotic disequilibrium. For example, as the male alcoholic makes progress in therapy and starts to take on his appropriate responsibilities, the wife must be aware of this change and allow him to resume his role in the home. If the wife is deprived of the opportunity of participating with her husband in treatment, then the therapist, as well as the patient, could misinterpret her attitude and classify her as a castrating, dominating, or controlling wife. This distortion by therapists and patients has already filled the literature with the classical picture of the alcoholic's wife who has a need to keep her husband in a submissive role. This generalization, on close examination and in treatment of these couples, is usually untrue and misleading. Most wives of alcoholics are only too happy to give up inappropriate roles which were thrust upon them by an alcoholic husband who could not sustain his responsibilities. Another example that demonstrates the need for the spouse of the patient to participate in treatment is seen in the case of the wife who resolves some of her intrapsychic emotional problems and becomes more sexually aroused. If she is married to a man who has feelings of sexual inadequacy and occasional impotence, his excuse for faulty performance is now gone and complete impotence can develop.

Most of the couples attending group therapy also use AA and Al-Anon for help with abstinence. However, even with this support, there are relapses. If the alcoholic resumes drinking, a contract is then drawn up, stating that the patient's spouse will administer disulfiram, suspended in water, daily. The agreement states that disulfiram is a symbol of the alcoholic's commitment to his or her family as well as to treatment. Thus, the patient is taking disulfiram in order to decrease the spouse's daily anticipatory anxiety about the patient's drinking and to eliminate false accusations of having "sneaked a drink." It is emphasized that disulfiram is an insurance policy rather than a "crutch." The patient's reaction to this suggestion provides one way of estimating the degree of his or her denial and noncompliance in therapy.

There are exceptions to using couples group therapy as a routine technique. If one of the spouses is overtly psychotic, the mental illness will become quite conspicuous in the couples group and further alienate the couple. If the children have secondary psychological problems, then family therapy should be used in addition to the couples therapy sessions. If there are acute, embarrassing sexual problems that are threatening to disrupt the relationship, then it is absolutely essential to see the couple in private sexual counseling as well as in the couples group, since the group may not have reached a stage where such personal problems can be explored openly. Outside of these few exceptions, we routinely prepare couples for group therapy and start the group sessions as soon as orientation has been completed.

Case Histories of Couples Therapy

MR. B.: ADJUSTING TO ABSTINENCE

The first case history emphasizes the importance of having the alcoholic patient's spouse involved in the same therapy setting in order to understand the changes that the patient is undergoing during abstinence.

A 48-year-old alcoholic male, Mr. B., had been married for 20 years to a woman who had originally been appropriate in the way she asserted herself with both family and friends. However, over the years, as her husband's drinking increased, Mrs. B. had to assume more responsibility, not only for raising the children, but also for managing the family finances. Mr. B., although an extremely conscientious accountant, became very irresponsible and squandered financial resources during his episodes of drinking. Not only did he gamble more money than he could afford, but he also went on outrageous buying sprees. At first he refused to discuss his drinking, but eventually he allowed his wife to take over the financial management of the household. As the years went by, she assumed more and more responsibility for the checkbook and other financial holdings of the family.

Before beginning couples therapy, Mr. B. had completed an inpatient alcoholism treatment program. He was already taking disulfiram regularly at the family dinner time in order to allay some of his wife's and children's anxieties about his drinking. In the couples group setting, the subject of sharing responsibility for disciplining the children and managing household finances was discussed. Mrs. B. naturally expressed some anxiety about turning the checkbook over to her husband, in view of his past history of financial irresponsibility. Some of the other wives in the group talked about how difficult it had been for them to return to sharing financial responsibility with their husbands after they had become abstinent. One of the wives told Mrs. B., "As long as he's taking the Antabuse, there should be no realistic worry. Also, if you're going to trust the marriage, you might as well trust it all the way until he proves you wrong. How long can you go on questioning the situation without undermining your own confidence in him as well as his confidence?" Similar comments from other spouses of alcoholics in the group helped Mrs. B. make a decision about sharing responsibilities for the checkbook with her husband. She was able to see behavioral changes in him, not only at home but within the group setting, and was able to understand that her anxiety about giving up some of the responsibility was quite normal.

In the couples group therapy session one month later, Mrs. B. started talking about how wonderful it was ". . . not to have to carry the world around on my back." She went on to say, "Looking back, I'm only too happy to have someone share all these troubles with me; it's actually a pleasure to have someone worry with you."

MRS. C.: IMPORTANCE OF HAVING SPOUSE AVAILABLE

Mrs. C., a 39-year-old alcoholic, was a very passive, dependent woman with a dominating, aggressive husband. At the time of their marriage, she had been an extremely attractive woman; her appearance had been one of the reasons her husband had wanted to marry her. Mr. C. was a very aggressive, hard-driving businessman who put a great deal of value on appearance. To keep his self-esteem intact, he had to possess a beautiful wife, drive foreign cars, wear expensive clothes, and be seen in the best restaurants. Whenever Mrs. C. attempted to assert herself in an appropriate manner, he would clamp down rather aggressively, which only increased her nonassertiveness, which had developed during her childhood with an overbearing father and a weak mother.

She did quite well as far as abstinence was concerned, but the group therapy sessions revealed that she still had difficulties in asserting herself with her husband. In a series of several sessions, some of the female spouses in the couples group expressed direct opinions to Mr. C. He accepted these appropriately, much to Mrs. C.'s surprise. In addition, there was a free discussion of his appearance-oriented value system, which had only undermined his wife's confidence; she could no longer keep up the youthful, attractive appearance that she had presented at the time of their marriage. During a couples therapy session, one of the other wives asked Mrs. C. to tell her husband directly about her need for him to give an opinion concerning her personality characteristics as well as her appearance. Much to her surprise, he started to talk about her honesty and sincerity, something he had never done in private. The "here and now" approach helped her speak directly to her husband about their current problems. The task was much more easily accomplished than if she had been asked to go home and question him about his value system. This successful experience within the group setting resulted in immediate positive reinforcement from other members of the group and also enabled Mrs. C. to see that her husband could respond to appropriate, direct comments. This helped her overcome some of her unfounded fears of his anger.

During another session, one of the other wives in the group directly disagreed with Mr. C.'s opinion about a local political figure. Much to his wife's amazement, Mr. C. did not respond in an angry way to this confrontation; in fact, he appeared to be somewhat flexible in his thinking. Some of the other members in the group pointed out that she was allowing past interactional patterns between her and her husband to influence her behavior in the present. These advantages — staying in the "here and now," consensual validation, correction of neurotic distortions between the couple, and available modeling experiences within the group — add psychotherapeutic efficacy to this particular technique.

There are many reasons for treating marital partners in the same group and in a direct and open manner. If there is any relationship in which honesty and openness are essential, it is the marital experience. In fact, treatment of the husband and wife by separate therapists can magnify the distortions and misunderstandings between the partners, possibly bringing about a separation or divorce because of the unrealistic treatment structure. With different therapists, each one is encouraged to discuss marital problems without the partner's being present. This can be interpreted by some outsiders as "acting out" in relation to the marriage. Projection of blame and responsibility, which is a neurotic pattern in many marriages, can be treated only with both parties present. With the exception of the specific exclusions mentioned previously, I feel strongly that couples group therapy with alcoholics who are living with their spouses is the treatment of choice.

FAMILY THERAPY

Family therapy in the outpatient setting is the continuation of the inpatient family meetings described in Chapter 9 (p. 151), but not all families need ongoing family therapy in the outpatient treatment program. While an ideal treatment plan would include family members of all alcoholics, limitation of staff time makes this goal an impractical one. It may, however, be possible to include some families in multiple family group therapy in aftercare (Lansky et al., 1978). At times family therapy involves not only the spouse and the children but also the patient's parents or in-laws. By necessity, we limit ongoing family therapy to severe family problems, where it is absolutely essential to intervene in the intrafamilial pathology. These family problems include: physical abuse or sexual abuse of the children; severe psychological disturbance or psychiatric pathology in one or more of the children; a pattern of delinquency in one or more of the children; strongly suspected early onset of alcohol or drug abuse in the offspring; violent arguments between the husband and the wife as a pattern of the marriage; and other especially severe psychological disturbances within the family setting.

Psychodynamics of the Alcoholic's Family

Although there is no consistent family system or psychologic pattern that develops within families of alcoholics, the therapist working with alcoholics should be aware of a number of maladaptive behavioral patterns common to such families. The alcoholic has a profound effect on family members and other individuals closely associated with the family. Psychologic reactions to the alcoholic can vary considerably among different family members, depending partially on the alcoholic's behavior while sober as well as drinking and partially on the family member's psychological state. However, there are some psychological roles which are frequently assumed within the alcoholic family; these can be observed by the therapist during the interview sessions. Such roles include the "chief enabler," the "family hero," the "scapegoat," the "lost child," and the "mascot," or "the baby," as described by Anderson and Liepman (1984).

The "chief enabler" is usually the spouse or parent of the alcoholic. In the early years of the patient's alcoholism, his wife may frequently enable him to cover up his drinking problem by making excuses to his employer such as, "He is sick today and cannot go to work," or she may continue to threaten to leave the alcoholic because of his drinking but never follow through with this threat. In another situation, it may be the parent who consistently pays for the legal damages incurred by a son's or daughter's drinking behavior. Sometimes the enabler will attempt a confrontation but inevitably fail by yelling and shouting at her spouse: "Your drinking is ruining our family! You show no concern for us!" Repeating these accusations frequently enables the alcoholic to claim that his wife drives him to drink with her constant nagging. Sometimes, this type of spouse will seem to be a "bad guy," while her pleasant (alcoholic) husband, who is always doing favors for the neighbors but not for her, appears to be a "nice guy" married to a shrew. In exploring the dynamics of the family, it is essential to evaluate the possible existence of an enabler.

Children are almost always hurt by the behavior of the alcoholic in a family. While repression of anger frequently occurs, we see many situations in which the child develops a tremendous amount of ambivalence toward the parent. There are many cases in which the father is verbally and/or physically brutal with the child and then tries to compensate for his guilt by the child buying toys and luxury items. This type of father may even "mellow out" as the years pass; then the child feels even more guilt when he or she expresses anger towards him. In this situation, it is important for the therapist to be able to show the child that it is normal to be angry about the parent's drinking behavior without judging or moralizing about that parent as a person. Emphasis on the drinking behavior and not on the total human being sometimes helps to decrease the guilt and allow expression of appropriate anger.

It is not unusual to see the oldest child assume the role of the "family hero," who may develop into a perfectionist (Anderson & Liepman, 1984). Realizing the pressure on the sober parent and unable to do anything about the other parent's drinking, this firstborn may start assuming adult responsibilities by preparing the dinner for the intoxicated mother or driving the father home from a bar; eventually this child becomes another parent in the house. Feeling inadequate and insecure under the tremendous pressure of assuming adult responsibilities, these individuals may become overly self-critical and attempt to control every aspect of their lives. Sometimes they overcompensate by trying to do their school work or job in a perfect manner. Often the wife of the alcoholic tends to place all of her future hopes on the eldest child and may set extremely high goals of accomplishment for the child; when the son or daughter falls short of those goals, harsh criticism results. This type of pressure can result in such children growing into adults who are successful in their professional or business careers but never satisfied with their accomplishments.

Frequently we see a child who is the "scapegoat" within the family setting. Such children are unable to live up to the accomplishments of the oldest child. Frequent comparisons may be made between them and the oldest sibling by the frustrated (sober) parent; sometimes these "scapegoats" may even be subjected to such comparisons by their school teachers. Constant failure and school problems may become part of their early life patterns. Attempting to stay away from family affairs and becoming involved with peers who are rebellious may contribute to additional failures. These children are filled with frustration, anger and rebellious behavior. They tend to have the triad of GIN: the G stands for associating with alcohol or drug peer groups; the I represents impulsive behavior (such individuals do not stop and think before they act); and the N stands for nonconforming or rebellious behavior.

Scapegoated children are almost certainly fated to end up with drinking and/or drug problems in early or late adolescence. Then the scapegoating becomes relatively easy for the family; everyone can target their anger and frustration upon this child. I have actually seen cases in which the mother vented her frustration and anger on the adolescent with an alcohol and drug problem rather than on her husband with a 25-year history of alcoholism. By concentrating on this adolescent alcohol- or drug-seeking child, the family members can increase their denial and minimize the seriousness of the father's drinking problem. Such adolescents have been admitted to my alcoholism rehabilitation treatment program as "the problem" in the family, with the alcoholic father designated as a supposed helper. Family sessions may be extremely frustrating because it is very difficult to change the focus of the family's frustrations or anger from the child to the adult alcoholic within the family setting. Without family therapy, both the father and the adolescent alcoholic or drug user are bound to deteriorate further.

Younger children in the family may be neglected since the main concerns and frustrations of the family have been directed toward the older siblings or the alcoholic parent. These "lost children" may be unpredictable in their behavior. Some of them rebel because they feel neglected and emotionally deprived; many of them attempt to gain attention through various delinquent behavior or substance abuse; some withdraw into an autistic pattern associated with excessive eating and poor self-image.

The youngest child in the family, who has been called the "mascot" or the "baby," may develop the same type of behavior patterns seen in the lost or isolated child or may be able to relieve the tension in the home, since he is the least threatening person within the family structure.

All of these family roles are modified according to the varying patterns of behavior displayed by the father or mother when the parent is sober or drinking. I have seen some families in which the angry, sometimes violent father caused such frustration and resentment within the family that most of the siblings not only ended up with chronic depressions but also developed problems with poor self-image and an excessive need for love or affection which they never received at home.

DR. F.: AN ERRATIC FATHER

Dr. F., an alcoholic father who was a physician, provides a good example. When he returned home from the office after a few drinks, he sometimes snatched the food from one of the children's plates, saying that he deserved first chance at the food since he worked so hard. At other times after drinking, he verbally devastated his daughters by calling them "whores" or made fun of their physical appearance, despite the fact they were quite attractive. When he was sober, the same father coddled and overprotected and spoiled the children with expensive gifts.

Later, I saw one of the daughters in treatment after she had married. Each time she attempted to criticize her father in therapy, she broke down and started crying because she felt so guilty when she remembered some of the nice things he had done for her. The patient unfortunately had a continuing emotional attachment to her father as well as to the family. She felt guilty about not being able to help her mother stabilize the family problems. She still missed the childhood that she had never had and had confused feelings of anger about the emotional deprivation she had suffered as a child. Even though she was an attractive person and very talented artistically, she had tremendous feelings of inadequacy and insecurity. Her emotional attachment to the past interfered with her marriage; she was unable to offer her husband total intimacy and trust because her childhood experience of her father's erratic behavior made it difficult for her to trust any men in her adult life. This type of emotional attachment to the primary family has been described by Brown and Beletsis (1986).

Guidelines for Family Therapy

After obtaining the background and details of the family history, I ask the families to observe very strictly the three following treatment guidelines:

1. Never bring up past behavior when dealing with present problems. There are certain words that we try to eliminate from our language in therapy. Such words as "always" or "never" or similar words that the family has used to remind each other of past mistakes are eliminated from the treatment vocabulary. For example, it is not unusual for a woman to say to her husband "You are *always* saying

'yes' to your friends and 'no' to me." This wording only enables the alcoholic patient to increase his denial mechanism, since he is usually able to bring up at least one time when he paid more attention to his wife than to a friend. Another example is a remark from a daughter to her father: "You *never* pay attention to my school work or ask me how I am doing." Such a comment only opens the door for father to remind her of the time he signed her report card and reviewed her grades. In addition, talking about the past with such words as "always" or "never" only increases the anger of the confrontation and frequently blocks an increase of insight or understanding by either participant in the discussion.

2. Keep verbalizations in the present tense and offer options when confronting each other within the family setting. Refer to the specific, current behavior. A wife may say to her husband, "I put on this new dress this evening just for you. Marge complimented me at the party, but you *never* compliment me." This use of the past only makes the husband angry or defensive; then he searches his memory to find some trivial compliment that he may have given her several weeks before. If, instead, she only asks him, "Did you notice my new dress tonight?" or "What do you think of this new dress?" his response may be positive rather than defensive. A second example: A man asks his wife to see a particular movie with him. She responds, "You are *always* the one who decides where we go." A more appropriate response would be, "We can see that movie this evening, but I would like to select one next Tuesday or Wednesday." Offering him options, she is able to assert herself appropriately and "share" the decision. It has been my experience that when family members restrict their remarks to the behavior that has just occurred, the anger never gets too intense or destructive and the individuals involved are able to confront each other more appropriately. Competition or proving that one is right and the other is wrong always results in everyone within the family losing.

3. Never use any of the information brought out in the family meeting as weapons for criticism or intimidation at home.

Case Histories of Family Therapy

THE K. FAMILY: FATHER AND SON ALCOHOLICS

My first contact with the K. family was with the 22-year-old son, Paul, who was referred to our alcoholism inpatient rehabilitation unit. On admission, Paul presented a history of a very dominating, overbearing father who also had a drinking problem. Supposedly, Mr. K. had stopped drinking about two years prior to Paul's admission, but Paul said that his father was still occasionally "sneak drinking." Paul described his mother as a passive woman who covered up her husband's drinking problem. Paul's younger sister, Jane, was described as a loving, caring person. His older brother, Sam, 28, was a perfectionist who apparently looked down on Paul and blamed him for the family problems.

Paul's alcoholism history started when he was 14 years old. At that time, he occasionally sneaked beer and sometimes liquor from his father's bar in the house. Paul's drinking increased considerably during the subsequent years in high school, and he was already having blackouts by the time he graduated. Much of his drinking was peer-related. At that time, his father was also drinking very heavily and displayed explosive behavior during some of his drinking episodes. On several occasions, Mr. K. hit his wife. Paul's attempts to intervene ended in physical fights with his father. During those years, Sam was attending college and visited home only during vacations. Jane avoided family conflict and never really challenged her father.

Paul's drinking episodes resulted in two driving while intoxicated (DWI) charges and two arrests for assault episodes that occurred in a bar. After high school graduation, Paul remained in the household and worked in his father's business, a firm that serviced offshore oil rigs. Even when they were both sober, Paul and his father had many disagreements. Mr. K. could never admit that he was wrong and was very skillful at finding and pointing out all of his son's faults. Of course, during Paul's drinking episodes, he did make a number of mistakes at work and missed several days while drying out at home. Finally, Mr. K. fired him. Paul then went to work for a trucking company. During the two years prior to admission to the unit, Paul had worked at three different jobs, with no more than four or five months at any one job.

During our first family session on the alcohol rehabilitation unit, Mr. K. told me, "I'm fed up with Paul. This is his last chance. He has already gone through two other treatment programs." Mrs. K. sat passively, occasionally nodding her head. At times she grimaced as if she were disagreeing with her husband, but she denied any differences of opinion when asked about her facial expressions. Paul's sister, Jane, showed more healthy concern for the patient and told us that their father had recently been drinking. The older brother, Sam, let us know that he had a very responsible position with a law firm and that Paul was an embarrassment to him. However, as this initial family session progressed, Sam did show some positive feelings for Paul and at the end of the session talked about his love and concern for him. It was decided that we would have some additional family meetings since Paul was going to be living at home after discharge from the hospital because he had no financial resources to pay for his rent while looking for a job. By the time of discharge, Paul did manage to obtain employment with a local moving company.

During our first family session with these five people, Mr. K. dominated the initial part of the meeting with constant criticism of Paul. Mrs. K. remained passive. I then asked the family to follow some rules at home which might help communication within the family. At first, Mr. K. objected, "I'm the leader of the household and I pay the rent. I can't have someone else lay down rules for me to follow at home." Fortunately, both Jane and Sam spoke up and said that Mr. K. should give this treatment a chance. Much to our surprise, Mrs. K. then said to her husband, "Joe, why don't you give the doctor a chance to help us? Nothing else that we have done has been of any help to Paul." Mr. K. then nodded his head in acquiescence but became sullen. I then said, "All I would like the five of you to do is to direct yourself to the present situation. Let's leave out the words 'always' and 'never' and the expression 'every time.' Also, concentrate on criticizing or approving present behavior in a very specific way in order to avoid going back to the past." All of them agreed to follow these guidelines as much as possible.

During our second session, Jane told me that a violent argument had occurred between Paul and his father at home. Paul had returned home from work with dirty shoes and had made some slight dirt tracks on the carpet. As soon as Mr. K. noticed the soil, he yelled out, "Paul, you are *always* messing up things. You're 22 years old and still come in like a teenager." Paul became very defensive and angry. He had been taking Antabuse daily and had been totally abstinent since his discharge from the hospital, while his father was still occasionally drinking at home. At the time of the confrontation, Mr. K. had a drink in his hand and Paul responded, "How can you accuse me of messing up when you have been messing up with booze *all your life*! Look at you with the drink in your hand!" Of course, both Paul and his father had failed to follow the guidelines; both brought up past behaviors. We then carefully reviewed the rules. Mrs. K. spoke up at that point and said, "It looks like you both broke the rules and look what happened. I think that the doctor has a good idea." Jane and Sam agreed with her and both of them gave her a hug, providing valuable approval for her appropriate assertiveness. At the end of the session, Mrs. K. was beaming, but her husband was still quite angry about the situation. However, he did agree to give the guidelines another chance. As the session ended, when Paul walked out of the room first, his father started to say, "Paul you're *always* walking in front . . ." and then he smiled. We all laughed and I said, "There goes the past again."

During the next session at the clinic, we discussed Paul's drinking problem and how it enabled others to focus on Paul as the scapegoat and to avoid discussing some of their own problems. Mrs. K. said that she had been the chief enabler for Paul by covering up for him, paying for his traffic fines, helping him with his legal problems, and trying to overprotect him. Jane told her mother that she thought she showed courage in this admission; Sam also complimented his mother. At that time, Sam talked about his own attitude toward Paul in the past, his criticism of his younger brother, and his having never given the boy a compliment. He said he realized that Paul had looked up to him as the older brother and perhaps he had let him down.

At this point, Paul started to cry, which was a shock to all of us. He said, "I don't know why I'm crying. Maybe it's because I'm starting to get a feeling that I *do* have a family. Maybe I should have known this all along." At that point, Mr. K.'s eyes filled with tears, but he did not say anything. I said to Mr. K., "You seem to be a little bit sad—do you have tears in your eyes?" He shook his head in denial, but his three children and his wife all noticed the sad expression on his face. It was a rather moving moment for the family.

I then told them that they all had some more homework to do. Giving *homework instructions* or *behavioral tasks* to family members encourages them to work on their problems on a daily basis. I explained that we could not solve their problems solely through therapy sessions once or twice week-ly and stressed that the most important hours in treatment are the many hours between our meetings. I emphasized that the treatment sessions only make us aware of the problems that have to be solved; the family has to work on these problems during those very important hours between our meetings. At the end of this meeting, I asked all of the family members to keep a daily diary on the guidelines that I detailed for them. I wanted them to write down in the diary each time that words were used that went back to the past and generalized the problems in a unrealistic way. I also asked them to set up "fine box" in which they would place a dollar each time they used words such as "always" or "never." They all agreed to this contract. Contracting is regarded as an important part of these homework assignments.

At the next session, the family brought in the fine box, which contained $12.00. Seven of the dollars came from Mr. K., $3.00 from Paul, and $1.00 each from Mrs. K. and Jane. Since Sam was not living in the home, there were fewer chances for him to get caught in the trap of using the past against one of the other family members. We reviewed each of the incidents that resulted in a fine. Since each of the family members was keeping an individual diary, the material was fresh and not distorted as much as it would have been if we had relied on their memories of the incidents.

In subsequent family sessions, Mr. K. agreed to start taking Antabuse after the family pointed out that he made fewer mistakes about the past when he was sober. They also pointed out to him that it would be of help to

Paul, who had been trying to stay abstinent while his father was drinking in front of him.

Over several more sessions, a modification of roles developed in the family. By this time, Mrs. K. was speaking up frequently and appropriately. At my request and the urging of her children, she had signed up for an assertiveness training group in our clinic and was progressing rapidly. She told her husband that she wanted to start sharing responsibility for the checkbook and he agreed. Mr. K. had begun inviting Paul to join him at the Saints football games and said, "This will be the first time we have watched the Saints sober and will remember what took place when we get home. We might even remember the score." They all had a good laugh at this statement. Sam added, "Perhaps you both would be better off drunk if you're going to have to watch the Saints play." The laughter increased, and it was quite obvious that Mr. K. was now changing his role in the family from that of a dominating, defensive man to someone who was willing to share responsibility with his wife and also admit some mistakes that he may have made. Mrs. K.'s moving out of her passive, enabling role was obviously an important element in her husband's shift.

Paul, the "scapegoat," was becoming more of a "hero," since he had been abstinent for a relatively long period of time and his performance at work had resulted in a promotion. This shift in role would have been difficult to achieve within a patient group therapy setting without the family's presence. In fact, it would have been difficult to accomplish these goals if we had placed Mr. and Mrs. K. in a couples group and Paul in a singles group. We needed the support of the other two children to confront and validate some of Mr. K.'s behavior and to encourage Mrs. K. to become more open and direct about her feelings within our meetings.

THE L. FAMILY: ALCOHOLISM, MARITAL DISCORD, AND CHILD ABUSE

In the L. family, the three young sons had been verbally and physically abused for a number of years by their alcoholic father. Mr. L., a 44-year-old professor at a local university, was married to a 42-year-old woman who was a professor in another department of the same institution. Mr. L.'s drinking behavior had deteriorated during the past five years. He had been requested to see me for an evaluation and recommendation for treatment by the chairman of his department. He had received several previous warnings and now had been informed that he would be asked to leave the department unless he committed himself to ongoing treatment. Therefore, he was not a totally voluntary patient. During our first session, I met with Mr. L. and his wife and reviewed his drinking history. Mrs. L. had threatened to leave her husband unless he sought help for his drinking problem. There was no doubt that his drinking problem was severe; both he and his wife agreed that he had been verbally and physically abusive to the children during some of his drinking episodes. The three children were Junior, age 12, James, 10 years old, and George, who was 8. Both parents claimed that George was impossible to control and that sometimes physical discipline was the only method that seemed to "put the child in line temporarily." Junior was doing quite well in school and was apparently ignoring his father's drinking problems as well as his parents' marital problems. The middle son, James, was in constant battles with George and, of course, George was always the loser.

It was my impression that the three children were approaching emotional crises in their lives, and I thought it best to involve them in the subsequent family meetings.

During our second meeting, which included the parents and the three children, Junior and James began a vicious verbal attack on George right in front of their parents and me. They talked about George's aggressive behavior and how he disobeyed his parents and his two older brothers. They mentioned that George was often involved in fights at school, as well as at home. Mr. and Mrs. L. nodded their heads in agreement as the two older boys talked about George's problems. In the middle of the session, George ran out of the room. I asked my secretary to follow him. Shortly afterwards, she returned and told me that he had decided to sit in the lobby to avoid the remainder of our session. Toward the end of our meeting, Mr. L. said jokingly that perhaps it was George who had driven him to drink. It was apparent that George was the "scapegoat" for the family; they focused on his misbehavior instead of on their own problems.

In addition, the session revealed a tremendous competitive struggle between Mr. and Mrs. L. Both of them were professors at the same university, but Mrs. L. had progressed much more rapidly in her research and teaching than her husband. In fact, she was developing a national reputation through her published papers; he had published only six papers and had not yet received tenure. Recently, the chairman of Mr. L.'s department had discussed the possibility of dropping him from the faculty because of his lack of publications. Mr. L. was facing the loss of his job, not only because of drinking but also because of his poor performance.

During our third session, the intellectual battle between Mr. and Mrs. L. became even more obvious. She said to her husband, "If it hadn't been for your drinking, your job wouldn't be in any danger. You could have been publishing more frequently." He replied, "If you had spent more time with the children, which you should have done, you wouldn't have progressed so rapidly. I've ended up being the babysitter while you've been busy publishing." The three children fidgeted while these comments were thrown back and forth between the parents. Junior looked out the window and seemed to ignore the tension, while James discreetly pinched George, who proceeded to fight back. At that point, I spelled out specific guidelines, saying that there would be no physical fighting and no shouting between either the parents or the children.

It was now obvious that family therapy was essential and that we could not solve the children's problems by seeing only the parents in couples therapy. I told Mr. L. that the only way to handle this type of treatment setting was by having him completely stop drinking. I explained that I realized that his drinking was not causing all of these problems, but I felt that it would be impossible to modify the situation and bring some type of psychological balance back into the family unless he had a clear mind and could provide a role model for the children. I also pointed out that he had already developed some moderate liver damage and that his blood pressure was moderately high, secondary to the excessive alcohol intake.

He agreed to try to abstain from alcohol. I then asked him to make a contract with me, agreeing to start taking Antabuse on a regular basis if he were unable to stay completely abstinent during the following weeks. He agreed. I asked the children if they thought that their father would be able to give up alcohol; Junior and James said that they did not know, but George said that he was sure that his father could stop drinking. This response surprised me, but later I realized that George might have been using an opportunity to disagree with his brothers.

I gave homework assignments to Mr. and Mrs. L. similar to those discussed in the K. family case. These instructions included not using the past and confronting each other only with specific behavior which had just occurred. I cautioned them against using information elicited during therapy as tools against each other.

During the next session, I confronted Mr. and Mrs. L. with the power struggle that was going on between them and asked the children's opinions about some of the differences between the parents. Junior and James both felt that their parents' disagreements about problems or issues that occurred at the university resulted in anger about various events that took place in the home. Mr. L. was obviously feeling somewhat castrated by his wife's success at the university and also having some similar feelings at home, where he thought that his children respected his wife more than they respected him. We had a "go-around" with the children about their opinions concerning their father and mother, and all three children agreed that they were more likely to listen to their father when he was sober than to their mother, who apparently had less control of her anger. They said that Mrs. L. would sometimes yell at them rather than speak calmly, whereas their father had a soft but firm way of disciplining them. The boys' statements provided beautiful positive reinforcement for Mr. L.'s continued abstinence. At first Mrs.

L. could not accept what the children were saying but she did agree to think it over.

At the end of this session I added some additional guidelines, requesting that Mr. and Mrs. L. not take home with them their differences of opinion at the university and that James and Junior agree to share some time with George on separate occasions, since George always appeared to be the "odd man out" when the three children were together. In this way I hoped to decrease some of the sibling competition and pairing off, which usually resulted in George's becoming the scapegoat. In subsequent sessions, George's behavior dramatically improved. The parents reported that he was no longer in trouble at school, where earlier he had been having many fights in class. He was developing better control of his anger and of himself. Junior seemed to be more involved in the family setting and less detached. In fact, he was starting to bring friends home to visit overnight; he had never done so before. All of these positive changes in behavior were pointed out to Mr. and Mrs. L., since it is important to give approval as soon as healthy behavior occurs.

Although we could have managed Mr. and Mrs. L.'s marital problems in couples therapy and probably could have decreased the competitive animosity between them, I do not think that the "spin-off" therapeutic effects would have enabled the children to modify the angry interaction among themselves or between them and their parents. In particular, it would have been extremely difficult to modify George's severe behavior problem at school. His hyperactive, aggressive activities had almost resulted in the principal's requesting that the parents transfer George to another school. Thus, family therapy provided the means to step in early in the course of the children's problems and may have prevented more serious psychological problems in the three sons.

Multiple Family Group Therapy

As noted earlier in this section, limited staff time prevents us from using family therapy in all cases which may require some type of family intervention. However, when the family structure is out of balance in terms of the roles of the parents and the various problems of the children, some type of family therapy can be of significant help. Multiple family group therapy may then be considered as an option (Lansky et al., 1978). This approach enables various individuals within each family to identify with members of other families and may help some of the participants become less defensive, as they realize that there are other people in the same predicament. Identifying with members of other families who are in similar positions or roles may help an individual to be more open about his or her own problems.

As with family therapy, multiple family group therapy usually is dominated during the early phases by some members of the family blaming others for the problem. It is not unusual to see some of the husbands band together against the wives or vice versa. In the same manner, the children in a group may attempt to follow a similar pattern in blaming their parents for some of their behavioral problems at home or in school. However, as these sessions progress, more basic problems surface, and the openness of the setting allows for realistic identification. For example, the child who has had to assume adult responsibilities in caring for the alcoholic mother or father is able to relate very readily to a child from another family who has had to assume a similar role. The "scapegoat" child may find that he is not alone in the world and can easily see how some of the other children have been used as an excuse by family members to avoid dealing with their own problems. Similar identification can develop among the parents in the families.

These multiple family group therapy sessions may include three or four families, depending upon the size of each family. It is unwise to have more than 15 people attending such a group session. This type of multiple family group meeting requires at least two hours or more of therapy time.

OTHER SPECIAL TREATMENT MODALITIES

Programs for Homosexuals

In any geographical area with a relatively large homosexual population, it is necessary to have a gay counselor in the alcoholism clinic. If there are a large number of gay alcoholics, a group therapy setting should also be available for them. Although the ideal goal for all alcoholics is to be able to integrate themselves into a heterogeneous culture and to enjoy their chosen life-styles, it is important for alcoholic patients entering treatment to have a feeling that the therapist accepts and is "in tune" with them. Many of our gay patients request a gay counselor after their initial interviews at the clinic. We explain to these patients that such a counselor is available and that the ideal treatment includes attending both our gay and heterosexual groups in order to avoid unnecessarily restricting themselves solely to cultural subgroups. I believe that gay alcoholics can receive more comprehensive treatment this way and develop a better understanding of themselves as well as of the world in which they live. The availability of a gay therapist is also important to educate the clinic staff about gay problems and sensitivities (e.g., social stigma and the particular emotional problems of patients who have AIDS). The dates and times of the gay AA meetings should be made available to the staff and the patients; gay AA sponsors should be in frequent contact with the clinic.

Spanish-speaking Patients

In cities with a relatively large Hispanic population, such as New Orleans, New York, Miami, and Los Angeles, it is important that the clinic have a therapist whose primary language is Spanish. The initial history-taking or intake session is the most important meeting that takes place between the patient and the clinic staff. The more rapidly and easily the patient begins to feel comfortable within the clinic setting, the more likely the patient is to return and become involved in a successful treatment endeavor. Communities with a large Hispanic population usually have one or more Spanish-speaking AA groups in the area. Sponsors from these AA groups should be in frequent contact with the clinic and available for these patients.

Sexual Abuse and Dysfunction

Other treatment modalities that should be incorporated into a community alcoholism clinic include counseling for various types of sexual problems. In our treatment program, it is not unusual to encounter alcoholic families in which the alcoholic father has been sexually abusing one or more of the children for several years. In addition to reporting these problems to the child abuse authorities and youth services representatives, the alcoholism clinic staff should include a therapist who is experienced in managing sexual problems. This therapist should coordinate the family's treatment program with the child abuse authorities. It is important not to fragment the treatment of such a family by having more than one agency involved in the ongoing therapy. The parents and the children should be treated within the same setting, although the abused child should also be seen in individual therapy sessions.

Another frequently encountered sexual problem is impotence in male alcoholics. This is usually managed in private couples therapy sessions with one of our therapists. Progressive relaxation exercises, avoidance of early performance failure, prolongation of ejaculation exercises, etc., with modifications of the Masters and Johnson (1970) approach, are utilized for these couples. When sexual performance has improved, the couples are then encouraged to discuss in the group therapy sessions some of the events which led to the sexual problem. Often, this helps other patients in the group therapy meetings feel less inhibited about discussing sexual problems which may have seemed too embarrassing to reveal.

Approaches to Compliance

When treating alcoholics, the therapist and the clinic staff sometimes have to modify treatment approaches according to the patient's ability to comply. For example, if a patient has one or more drinking episodes after discharge from the inpatient rehabilitation unit, we may institute compulsory ingestion of Antabuse following a breathalyzer test. The patient is requested to come to the clinic on Mondays, Wednesdays, and Fridays for a 250 mg dose of Antabuse, or on Mondays and Thursdays for a 500 mg dose of Antabuse. If the patient is able to drink after taking these dosages of Antabuse without having an alcohol-Antabuse reaction, then the dosages may be slightly increased. We have found this approach to be particularly successful with middle-aged and elderly alcoholics who are living alone with little family support. They actually use these visits to the clinic for Antabuse to socialize with our nursing staff and other patients. As noted in Chapter 10, the efficacy of mandatory, supervised Antabuse therapy for patients who wish to remain within the clinic treatment setting has been demonstrated in an impressive study (Sereny et al., 1986).

Other types of authoritative approaches include blood or urine alcohol screens or urine drug screens, along with strong suggestions to the patients that screening tests will be performed. A recent study demonstrated that self-reporting of alcohol consumption, even in nonalcoholics, is extremely unreliable and that reliability can be increased by suggesting to the patients that laboratory tests will be conducted to determine the validity of their statements (Lowe et al., 1986). In Lowe et al.'s evaluation, 220 pregnant women attending a maternity care clinic were randomly assigned to two study groups to determine if signing a permission form which stated that blood and urine tests would be conducted for alcohol or drugs increased the accuracy of self-reports of alcohol consumption. The majority of these women were in the first trimester of pregnancy. The following statement was included on the informed consent form at the time of the first examination of the experimental group: "I agree to allow lab tests to be performed on samples of my blood and urine. These tests will be used to improve ways of identifying legal drug use. This will not require additional blood or urine." The subjects were told that the tests would confirm their self-reported alcohol consumption.

The results showed a significant difference ($p < 0.025$) between the control group and those women who were told that their self-reported alcohol consumption would be confirmed by physiological tests. Only 14% of the self-report group said they used alcohol during the current pregnancy, whereas 27% of the "supposed physiological test" group reported consumption of alcohol during pregnancy.

This type of information should be available to all professionals who treat alcoholics and to other professionals such as obstetricians. As cited at the beginning of Chapters 2 and 9, there are multiple reports in the literature indicating the unreliability of self-reporting of alcohol intake without confirmation by close relatives or significant others. Although all therapists want to believe their patients and want to trust the data that they obtain from alcoholic patients, it is unwise to rely totally on self-reports of alcohol consumption—not only the reports of alcoholics but also those of other individuals who may believe that their consumption of alcohol is not acceptable behavior for cultural or physical reasons, such as pregnancy. The occasional screening of urine for disulfiram metabolites after informing the patient that this procedure is sometimes used may also help to enhance compliance with disulfiram (Fuller & Neiderhiser, 1981).

USING THE CLINIC DURING THE WAITING PERIOD BEFORE ADMISSION TO A REHABILITATION UNIT

Although it has been established that a delayed period of time between telephone contact and first clinic visit results in a significantly higher drop-out rate, the significance of the waiting period between discharge from a detoxification unit and admission to a rehabilitation treatment center is not now known. There is a general opinion among staff personnel treating alcoholics that an extended waiting period before admission to an inpatient rehabilitation center is a serious disadvantage for the patient. However, this has not been confirmed.

In one evaluation of the effects of the extended waiting period, Eriksen (1986) compared two inpatient treatment groups during the first four weeks after discharge from the rehabilitation unit. One group had been admitted immediately after detoxification; the other group was scheduled for two clinic visits during a four-week waiting period before admission. All subjects in the study had been informed of the standard rule of the rehabilitation unit: They would lose their opportunity for inpatient treatment if they were drunk on the day that they were to be admitted.

The 17 patients who were evaluated in Eriksen's study had been voluntarily admitted to a detoxification unit and subsequently had applied for the inpatient rehabilitation program. These patients were randomly assigned to a waiting list group (eight patients) or to the inpatient unit (nine patients). The group of patients on the waiting list were told that they had to wait an "unspecified" period of time before they could be admitted to the unit, due to "lack of capacity." During this waiting period, they were asked to fill in a short, daily self-report concerning four behaviors during the seven days prior to the scheduled clinic visit: drinking behavior; work history; sleeping at home the night before the follow-up evaluation; and use of disulfiram. Appointments were scheduled for two weeks later; at that time the self-reports were reviewed and they were asked to continue the self-reports and return in two weeks.

At the second appointment, after a total of a four-week waiting period, they were informed that they could then enter the inpatient program. Only two subjects elected to enter the inpatient program at that time; the remaining patients were instructed to fill in the daily self-reports for three months and were given outpatient clinic appointments on a monthly basis. The two patients from the four-week waiting list who were admitted to the inpatient program were subsequently seen monthly for three months after discharge and requested to complete the same forms.

The average stay of the nine members of the inpatient group who were admitted immediately after detoxification was 47 days (range 29–72). This group was asked to complete the same self-reports during the first three months after discharge.

An evaluation of all of the self-rating results showed that the only significant difference between the two groups was that the waiting list group had more disulfiram ingestion days ($p < 0.05$). Abstinence success was disappointing in both groups: Four of eight subjects on the waiting list drank the first day after discharge from the detoxification unit, and five of nine patients in the rehabilitation group drank on the first day after discharge. There were a number of shortcomings in this study of which the investigator was aware: The population studied was a select alcoholic subgroup with a severe drinking background consisting of an average of two previous admissions to inpatient units and requiring inpatient detoxification before entering the study; the number of patients in each group was too small and the failure rate was too high for statistical comparison; only four subjects had their self-reports confirmed by "significant others"; and the original motivation of the waiting list patients for taking disulfiram may have been enhanced by the knowledge that they had to be sober when they received the notice that they were accepted for the inpatient program.

Despite these experimental deficiencies, it appears that in this select subgroup of recently detoxified alcoholics whose illness could be classified as severe, a four-week waiting period (using daily self-reports and Antabuse) before admission to a rehabilitation program results in no more serious consequences than if these subjects are immediately admitted from a detoxification center. If these results are replicated in future studies with a larger number of patients, then this waiting time could be justified as a screening period for assignment of patients to the most suitable outpatient and/or inpatient treatment modalities.

USE OF OTHER COMMUNITY RESOURCES

Alcoholics Anonymous (AA) is, of course, the chief community resource for all alcoholics. To help the reader understand the historical background of AA, I recommend a delightful, interesting history recorded in the book, *Dr. Bob and the Good Oldtimers.* Because of the tremendous impact that AA has had on the public acceptance and treatment of alcoholism, it is important for all personnel interested in the problem of alcoholism to read some of the literature and become familiar with the 12 steps and the 12 traditions. In Chapter 5 of the book, *Alcoholics Anonymous* (1976), the 12 steps are listed as:

1. We admitted we were powerless over alcohol—that our lives had become unmanageable.
2. Came to believe that a Power greater than ourselves could restore us to sanity.
3. Made a decision to turn our will and our lives over to the care of God as we understood Him.
4. Made a searching and fearless moral inventory of ourselves.
5. Admitted to God, to ourselves, and to another human being the exact nature of our wrongs.
6. Were entirely ready to have God remove all these defects of character.
7. Humbly asked Him to remove our shortcomings.
8. Made a list of all persons we had harmed, and became willing to make amends to them all.
9. Made direct amends to such people wherever possible, except when to do so would injure them or others.
10. Continued to take personal inventory and when we were wrong promptly admitted it.
11. Sought through prayer and meditation to improve our conscious contact with God as we understood Him, praying only for knowledge of His will for us and the power to carry that out.
12. Having had a spiritual awakening as the result of these steps, we tried to carry this message to alcoholics and to practice these principles in all our affairs.

The following 12 traditions are guidelines for the functioning of AA:

1. Our common welfare should come first; personal recovery depends upon AA unity.
2. For our group purpose there is but one ultimate authority—a lov-

ing God as He expresses Himself in our group conscience. Our leaders are but trusted servants; they do not govern.
3. The only requirement for AA membership is a desire to stop drinking.
4. Each group should be autonomous except in matters affecting other groups or AA as a whole.
5. Each group has but one primary purpose — to carry its message to the alcoholic who still suffers.
6. An AA group ought never endorse, finance or lend the AA name to any related facility or outside enterprise, lest problems of money, property and prestige divert us from our primary purpose.
7. Every AA group ought to be fully self-supporting, declining outside contributions.
8. Alcoholics Anonymous should remain forever nonprofessional, but our service centers may employ special workers.
9. AA, as such, ought never be organized; but we may create service boards or committees directly responsible to those they serve.
10. Alcoholics Anonymous has no opinion on outside issues; hence the AA name ought never be drawn into public controversy.
11. Our public relations policy is based on attraction rather than promotion; we need always maintain personal anonymity at the level of press, radio and films.
12. Anonymity is the spiritual foundation of all our Traditions, forever reminding us to place principles before personalities.

In addition to a variety of AA groups, including "agnostic" AA groups, "nonsmoking" AA groups, Spanish-speaking groups, gay groups, and even young AA groups for people in their adolescent years or early twenties, there are associated groups, such as Al-Anon for relatives and friends of alcoholics. Al-Anon is a very healthy supportive group which emphasizes that the wife and other family members are not responsible for the patient's drinking and stresses that they must go on leading their own lives even if the alcoholic continues to drink. Al-Ateen is the support group for the teenage children of alcoholics. Some of these children have already developed the problem of alcoholism; others are coping with the emotional trauma of living with an alcoholic father or mother.

Adult Children of Alcoholics (ACA) is another group whose numbers have rapidly increased during the past decade. Since 10 to 15% of the population over the age of 18 years have a problem with alcoholism at some time during their lives, a tremendous number of people have lived with alcoholic fathers or mothers. Talking out their problems with others who grew up in similar households enables these adult children of alcoholics to realize that they are not alone and to learn various techniques of decreasing the pain of the past and becoming more involved in the future.

The value of AA cannot be overemphasized. Even with the recent expansion of alcoholism treatment facilities, the importance of AA can only increase in the future. There will never be enough professionals available to treat all of the alcoholics in this country. And, since the emotional and psychological problems of alcoholics continue for prolonged periods of time following abstinence, it would be impossible for clinic staffs or treatment teams to follow alcoholics in therapy settings as long as they require. De Soto et al. (1985), for example, used the Symptom Check-list 90 with 312 abstinent alcoholics (163 males and 149 females). This revealed high levels of symptomatology, not only during the early months of abstinence but later on. Such items on the scale as depression, anxiety, thought process problems, difficulty in making decisions, trouble in remembering things, "feeling blocked in getting things done," and trouble concentrating continued to show improvement for two years or more and, in some cases, up to five years after the beginning of abstinence. Such studies show that AA can be extremely helpful to the alcoholic during the early and later stages of abstinence. In fact, alcoholics should make a commitment to AA for an indefinite period of time after they have been discharged from an outpatient clinic or treatment center.

Despite all of the importance I place on the value of AA, it should be pointed out that an extensive review of the literature led to the conclusion that the efficacy of AA has not yet been proved (Glaser & Ogborne, 1982). Research on the efficacy of AA is severely hampered by the voluntary, informal, and anonymous nature of its structure. To enhance the validity of a study of the success of AA, Glaser and Ogborne proposed using multiple data points before and after the subjects enter AA, obtaining a detailed history at initial assessment and administering the laboratory tests, psychologic, social, and economic measurements on a monthly basis for an extended period of time. A randomized control group chosen from the same intake population could be referred for outpatient counseling or some other type of potentially positive psychosocial reinforcement group. Attrition problems and self-selection into other programs could be statistically accounted for in this type of randomized controlled study. AA sponsors could be utilized to help those patients assigned to AA to become affiliated and could assist in recording the frequency of AA attendance. Such a study could be accomplished with preservation of anonymity and confidentiality. If a series of studies of this type were conducted in multiple settings with different patients, then the reliability and construct validity of the outcome measures could be more adequately assessed.

AA has been and continues to be the dominant treatment modality for the illness of alcoholism; the total number of individuals who have been actively involved in AA is estimated to be in the tens of millions. Nevertheless, although most of us in the field of alcoholism believe that AA works, we still do not have accurate scientific data about the degree of efficacy or the type of patient who is likely to do better in AA than some other type of treatment modality.

Other community resources for alcoholics include both federal and state vocational rehabilitation treatment programs (for which most alcoholics are eligible once they have entered a treatment facility), Family Services, Traveler's Aid, and, of course, half-way houses, both public and federally funded. In most cities, there are half-way houses conducted by religious organizations as well as by the state and federal agencies. People associated with the treatment of alcoholics should be aware of the availability of these community resources, since it is not unusual for many alcoholic patients to have lost a significant part of their human support systems by the time they go into treatment. These half-way facilities frequently lack adequate funding and are sometimes in relatively poor structural condition, but they serve a very valuable purpose by offering the patient a temporary residence while he is in outpatient treatment or waiting for admission to an inpatient rehabilitation program.

The staff of an alcoholism outpatient clinic has to be constantly geared to using everything and everyone available in the environment to help the alcoholic patient. The spouse, other family members, employer, friends, and other key people in the environment can be extremely helpful in treatment. The therapist should be continually asking, "What human support system can I enlist in the treatment of this particular patient?" The therapist has to be flexible, innovative, and persistent in finding various community support systems for this patient. Resources such as AA, Al-Anon, and Al-Ateen should always be kept in mind. Use of sponsors from AA, awareness of various types of half-way residences for alcoholics, and knowledge of other community resources such as the Golden Age Club, singles groups associated with various churches, and senior citizens' clubs will enable the therapist to treat alcoholic patients more adequately and enhance their enjoyment of sobriety.

REFERENCES

A.A. General Service Conference-approved Literature (1980). *Dr. Bob and the Good Oldtimers*. New York: Alcoholics Anonymous World Services, Inc.

Alcoholics Anonymous-3rd Edition (1976). New York: Alcoholics Anonymous World Services, Inc.

Abrahams, D. & Enright, J. B. (1965) Psychiatric intake in groups: A pilot study of procedures, problems, and prospects. *American Journal of Psychiatry, 121*, 170–174.

Anderson, R. C. & Liepman, M. R. (1984). Chemical dependency and the family. In M. R. Liepman, R. C. Anderson, J. V. Fisher (Eds.). *Family medicine curriculum guide to substance abuse*. (8-1 to 8-34). Kansas City, MO: Society for Teachers of Family Medicine.

Blinder, M. G. & Kirschenbaum, M. (1967). The technique of married couples group therapy. *Archives of General Psychiatry, 17*, 44–52.

Brown, S. & Beletsis, S. (1986). The development of family transference in groups for the adult children of alcoholics. *International Journal of Group Psychotherapy, 36*, 97–114.

DeSoto, C. B., O'Donnell, W. E., Allred, L. J., & Lopes, C. E. (1985). Symptomatology in alcoholics at various stages of abstinence. *Alcoholism: Clinical and Experimental Research, 9*, 505–512.

Eriksen, L. (1986). The effect of waiting for inpatient alcoholism treatment after detoxification. An experimental comparison between inpatient treatment and advice only. *Addictive Behaviors, 11*, 380–397.

Ewing, J. A. & Rouse, B. A. (1976). Failure of an experimental treatment program to inculcate controlled drinking in alcoholics. *British Journal of Addiction, 71*, 123–134.

Fuller, R. K., Branchey, L., Brightwell, D. R., Derman, R. M., Emrick, C. D., Iber, F. L., James, K. E., Lacoursiere, R. B., Lee, K. K., Lowenstam, I., Maany, I., Neiderhiser, D. H., Nocks, J. J., & Shaw, S. (1986). Disulfiram treatment of alcoholism. *Journal of the American Medical Association, 256*, 1449–1489.

Fuller, R. K., & Neiderhiser, D. H. (1981). Evaluation and application of a urinary diethylamine method to measure compliance with disulfiram therapy. *Journal of Studies on Alcohol, 42*, 202–207.

Gallant, D. M., Bishop, M. P., Stoy, B., Faulkner, M. A., & Paternostro, L. (1966). The value of a "first contact" group intake session in an alcoholism outpatient clinic: Statistical confirmation. *Psychosomatics, 7*, 349–352.

Gallant, D. M., Rich, A., Bey, E., & Terranova, L. (1970). Group psychotherapy with married couples: A successful technique in New Orleans alcoholism clinic patients. *The Journal of the Louisiana State Medical Society, 122*, 41–44.

Glaser, F. B., & Ogborne, A. C. (1982). Does A.A. really work? *British Journal of Addiction, 77*, 123–129.

Helzer, J. E., Robins, L. N., Taylor, J. R., Carey, B. A., Miller, R. H., Combs-Orme, T., & Farmer, A. (1985). The extent of long-term drinking among alcoholics discharged from medical and psychiatric facilities. *New England Journal of Medicine, 312*, 1678–1682.

Korner, H. (1964). Abolishing the waiting list in a mental health center. *American Journal of Psychiatry, 121*, 1097–1100.

Lansky, M. R., Bley, C. R., McVey, G. G., & Brotman, B. (1978). Multiple family groups as aftercare. *International Journal of Group Psychotherapy, 28*, 211–224.

Leichter, E. (1962). Group psychotherapy with married couples: Some characteristic treatment dynamics. *International Journal of Group Psychotherapy, 12*, 154–163.

Lowe, J. B., Windsor, R. A., Adams, B., Morris, J., & Reese, Y. (1986). Use of a "bogus pipeline" method to increase accuracy of self-reported alcohol consumption among pregnant women. *Journal of Studies on Alcohol, 47*, 173–175.

Masters, W. H., & Johnson, V. E. (1970). *Human sexual inadequacy*. Boston: Little, Brown.

Sanchez-Craig, M. & Lei, H. (1986). Disadvantages to imposing the goal of abstinence on problem drinkers. *British Journal of Addiction, 81*, 505–512.

Sereny, G., Sharma, V., Holt, J. & Gordis, E. (1986). Mandatory supervised Antabuse therapy in an outpatient alcoholism program: A pilot study. *Alcoholism: Clinical and Experimental Research, 10*, 290–292.

CHAPTER 12

Prevention

PRIMARY PREVENTION

I BELIEVE THAT PRIMARY PREVENTION, whose goal is to decrease the occurrence of alcohol abuse and alcoholism, is more important than secondary prevention, which will be discussed later in this chapter. Appropriate use of primary preventive measures can result in a significantly greater decrease in alcohol-related morbidity and mortality; also, over a long period of time, it may be significantly less expensive than secondary or tertiary preventive methods. The targets for primary prevention include not only alcoholism itself but also alcohol-related medical injuries and deaths. Since a significant number of problem drinkers are found among the individuals charged with driving while intoxicated (DWI) or driving under the influence (DUI), and since many of these convicted DWI offenders are referred to alcoholism clinics or treatment programs for educational classes on alcohol use, it seems appropriate to include such alcohol-related problems within the context of primary prevention.

It should be emphasized that there are very few controlled evaluations of primary prevention in the field of alcoholism and alcohol abuse. The majority of the available data is derived primarily from retrospective studies or comparisons of current incidence with data from previous years. However, some reviews of the data show very strong trends that should not be ignored. The following sections on legal and educational approaches review these data.

Taxation Policies

Taxation may be the most powerful tool available to reduce alcohol-related deaths and injuries and illnesses associated with alcoholism. Since the national data consistently show an annual death rate from alcohol-related motor vehicle accidents of 25,000 human beings or more every year and since prospective studies have shown that excessive alcohol use is the major cause of death in urban middle-aged men, it is incumbent upon the federal government to set forth public health policies designed to reduce alcohol use (Petersson et al., 1982; Richman, 1985). From 1951 to 1985, federal taxes on alcoholic beverages were not raised. As a result, there was a sharp decline in the real price of alcohol beverages compared to staple items such as milk and bread. Taxation of alcohol beverages as a public health measure has been a politically sensitive subject. However, many researchers in the field of alcoholism believe that alcohol taxes and laws regulating the minimum drinking age may have a much greater impact than expensive national and local education efforts in reducing alcohol-related morbidity and mortality (Gallant, 1982).

An important review of alcohol taxation data demonstrated that such taxes, if properly used, can be a very effective public health policy instrument (Cook, 1982). Cook reviewed four separate studies which showed that the consumption of alcohol decreases as a result of tax increases. The alcohol taxes and cirrhosis mortality rates in 30 states for the period of 1960–1974 were evaluated. Although the cirrhosis mortality rate is not a direct gauge of the current percentage of alcoholics in the population, it does appear to be a good indicator of heavy drinking for one or two decades. There were 38 instances in which one of the states had increased its liquor tax by substantial amounts (greater than $.24 per gallon). Analysis of the data showed that there was a greater reduction of cirrhosis mortality (probability of 0.072) in states which had raised their liquor taxes than in other states in the same year. Thus, the concept that cirrhosis mortality is *not* affected by liquor tax increases can be rejected at the 0.02 confidence level. In another study of the same 30 states, using a parametric estimation technique, Cook showed that a one-dollar increase in state liquor tax for each proof gallon would reduce the state's cirrhosis mortality rate by 1.9%. Extending his application of this statistical method, the author predicted that doubling the U.S. federal liquor tax would reduce the nation's cirrhosis mortality rate by 20%. Since the long-term reduction in cirrhotic mortality rates resulting from a tax increase would exceed the initial reduction, these estimates do not take into account the full beneficial effects of such a tax policy.

Cook's analysis agrees with other studies that relate to the "distribution of consumption model," which is one of the major hypotheses for reducing alcohol-related illnesses. This model states that the availability of alcohol beverages has a direct effect on the total level of alcohol consumption in a population and a subsequent indirect effect on the incidence and prevalence of alcohol-related damage. The *price* of alcohol relative to total income is considered to be the most important factor in influencing total alcohol consumption and is the major component of availability that can be managed by public health or governmental controls (Popham et al., 1978). However, the results of another study which used the model of distribution of consumption provided statistical evidence that government policies restricting the *retail availability* of alcohol beverages can also reduce the per capita rates of alcohol consumption, thereby reducing the level of alcohol-related mortality and morbidity (Rush et al., 1986).

Not all investigators accept the distribution of consumption model, and some study results show a deviation from this model. Ornstein (1980), in a review of the literature, reported that the consumption sensitivity to price changes varied across beverages with the following results: (1) An increase in the price of distilled spirits leads to a proportional or greater than proportional decrease in distilled spirits consumption. (2) However, an increase in the price of beer leads to less than proportional decline in beer consumption. And (3) the results about wine were too unreliable to offer any conclusions.

When discussing taxation and alcohol consumption, it is important to analyze the relationship between per capita alcohol consumption and morbidity. A study of alcohol-related hospital admission rates gives added importance to the previously discussed taxation and alcohol consumption data. Poikolainen (1983) evaluated the admission rates for five alcohol-related diseases (cirrhosis of the liver, pancreatitis, alcoholism, alcohol psychosis, and alcohol poisoning) in 11 Finnish provinces during the years from 1969 to 1975, a period of rapid increase in alcohol consumption. In 1968, one year prior to the enactment of a liberal new alcohol law, the per capita consumption was 2.9 liters of pure alcohol, as compared to 6.2 liters in 1975. Since the data evaluated successive years and the observations were not independent, product-moment correlation coefficients were calculated for mean value, both between the studied years and between the provinces. With the exception of alcohol poisoning, positive correlations were found between alcohol consumption and hospital admission rates for all of the alcohol-related diseases under investigation during the study period of 1969–1975.

The findings of Poikolainen's study also support the "distribution of consumption" hypothesis, with the increase in per capita alcohol consumption occurring more among the heavier drinkers. If the increase in per capita alcohol consumption had been due mainly to moderate drinkers and abstinent individuals who joined the ranks of the drinkers, then no significant changes in alcohol-related morbidity would have occurred. When it is realized that there is now adequate documentation that consumption of distilled spirits decreases proportionally or somewhat more than proportionally as result of tax increases, these findings become even more significant. Since an increase in per capita consumption is associated with a concomitant increase in heavy consumers, it then becomes apparent that significant federal and state tax increases on alcohol would be a worthwhile public health measure to decrease the development of alcohol-related diseases and hospital admission rates. Data indicate that the heaviest drinkers would justifiably pay 40–50% of these taxes (Cook, 1982).

Another benefit of a significantly increased federal excise tax on alcohol and the subsequent decrease in total alcohol consumption would be an associated decrease in violent deaths. A study of trends in alcohol consumption and violent deaths suggests that a fairly strong increase in rates of alcohol-related violent deaths correlated with an increase in alcohol consumption (Skog, 1986). The violent deaths evaluated in the study were those associated with falling, drowning, motor vehicle accidents, marine transportation accidents, alcohol poisoning, suicide and homicide. Although violent deaths not related to alcohol decreased in the same time period, there was a significant increase in alcohol-associated violent deaths. The increase was particularly significant among males, a group in which the incidence of violent, alcohol-related deaths increased from 8% in the early 1950s to approximately 15% in the late 1970s.

The argument against a significant increase in federal excise taxes on alcohol claims that such a tax would decrease the amount of alcohol purchased so much that the overall loss of taxes would increase the budget deficit. This argument has been fostered by people not only in this country but also in other countries, such as Poland. Although official figures in Poland show that about 3 million Polish people get drunk daily and 1.2 million are absent from their jobs on any given day because of drunkenness, the government is hesitant to impose harsh restrictions and price increases on liquor to reduce consumption (UPI release, 1986). The sale of liquor is a significant source of national income in Poland; in 1985, the Poles spent half as much on liquor as they did on food. However, this argument neglects the money which would be saved in hospital costs, loss of work days, and early death of productive citizens. Therefore, many people believe that a significant increase in alcohol excise taxes not only is a sensible way to reduce a country's budget deficits but can also be of significant benefit to the health of its citizens.

Driving While Intoxicated (DWI or DUI) laws

Unfortunately, there are very few adequate studies of alcohol-related fatal automobile crashes (Richman, 1985). In 15 states where investigations of fatal crashes were thorough, 85% of the involved drivers had measurable blood alcohol levels (BALs). It is estimated that of the more than 44,000 motor vehicle fatalities in the U.S. in 1981, alcohol was involved in 50 to 55% of those accidents (Fell, 1982). The data indicate the BALs in drivers involved in fatal crashes tend to be appreciably higher than in those involved in less serious crashes. It is even higher in drivers involved in single car crashes.

In a study of alcohol-related accident rates, a clear time pattern emerges: The rates are highest in January and February, about 40% higher than during the summer months; the rates are higher on Saturdays and Sundays, with eight times as many accidents between midnight and 4:00 a.m. as between 4:00 a.m. and 8:00 a.m.; and the statistics show lower rates Mondays through Fridays (Joksch, 1985). It is noteworthy that there is also an association between the time of accident and the age of the driver; the accident rates for 15-19-year-old drivers are 150 times higher on Saturdays between midnight and 4:00 a.m. than on Thursdays between 8:00 a.m. and noon (1,300 times higher for single car accidents). Of course, such environmental factors as weather conditions, traffic, and light conditions account for some of these time patterns, but most of the differences are due to driver factors, including the effects of alcohol (Joksch, 1985). Joksch also presents data showing that the risk of being caught by the police for driving while intoxicated or under the influence of alcohol is only about 1 : 1,000 or less.

These data emphasize the cultural acceptance of driving and drinking as long as one does not get caught or become involved in an accident. The chance of death, the ultimate penalty for drunk driving, is only 1 in 30,000 miles of driving while under the influence of alcohol (Voas & House, 1983). With these odds, the psychological mechanism of denial becomes an important part of the driving and drinking problem. I've been told by some alcoholics that they thought that if they did have an automobile accident, the relaxant effects of alcohol might decrease the severity of the injury; actually, controlled laboratory studies using animal models indicate that alcohol exacerbates the injurious effects of trauma. In one study, an analysis of data for more than 1,000,000 drivers involved in motor vehicle crashes indicated that the drinking driver was more likely to suffer serious injury or death compared with the nondrinking driver, even after the effects of injury-related variables such as safety belt use, type of vehicle damage, vehicle speed, driver age, and vehicle weight were taken into account (Waller, 1986).

In view of these data, there is no doubt that alcohol misuse results in a significantly increased risk of accidents, with a tremendous loss of lives. Approximately 250,000 Americans die every decade because of drunken driving. In fact, the risk of accidents for those with blood alcohol concentrations over 160 mg% is 21 times higher than if they had not been drinking (Allsop, 1966).

Many of the present laws are adequate for protection of the public from the drunken driver. However, many people in the field of alcoholism, including myself, have time and time again seen drunken drivers evading the laws, either through their attorneys' skillful use of legal technicalities or through judges' failure to fulfill obligations to the letter of the law regarding drunken driving. We have seen many individuals who have been convicted for drunken driving for the third time allowed to pay a fine and attend an outpatient clinic for follow-up treatment without any requirements for public service or a jail sentence. The courts are understaffed and unprepared for this relatively large number of drunken driving offenders, and the probation supervision of these individuals is inadequate in many areas. Even though a Gallup Poll indicated that 77% of all Americans support mandatory prison sentences for drunken drivers, even first offenders, it is a rarity when this sentence is imposed unless a traffic fatality has occurred. Even in vehicular homicide cases, is not unusual for the offender to receive a fine and probation and no jail term.

Many different types of strategies have been proposed in order to curb the drunken driver. The following recommendations, which have been made by the Mothers Against Drunk Drivers (MADD), are inexpensive policies that would decrease alcohol-related deaths if they were carried out consistently on a national basis:

1. Newspapers should print the names and addresses of citizens whose licenses are revoked after a drunk-driving accident.
2. Surprise roadblocks should be routinely set up so that police can spot drunk drivers.
3. A red license plate should be issued for those individuals convicted of driving while intoxicated, in order to warn the people in back of them.
4. Police should be given the power to suspend a drunk driver's license on the spot until the person appears in court.
5. Breath-testing devices should be placed in bars and restaurants so that patrons can check their blood alcohol levels.
6. Citizens should organize car pools on a routine basis to provide rides home for people who are intoxicated. In addition, car pools can be organized before leaving home for the evening with the provision that one individual will not drink at all and be the driver for the evening.
7. Courts should levy fines and fees on drunk drivers to pay for driving instruction programs. In addition, the fines and fees should be sufficient to cover the educational costs of instructing children in

the public school system about the use and misuse of alcohol and how to use alternatives to alcohol when socializing.

The community organizations involved with the drunken driving problem are listed in the MADD brochures and can be obtained from the cultural information service of the National Broadcasting Company (1983).

The National Council on Alcoholism (NCA) recommendations on drinking and driving are described in Table 12.1.

It is important to note that alcohol-related vehicular accidents are not only a serious problem with automobiles but also play an important role in the shipping industry, the piloting of airplanes, and in railroad traffic. In 1983, the Federal Railroad Administration (FRA) published rules to protect public safety (National Transportation Safety Board, 1986). These rules include the following recommendations:

1. Mandates post-accident toxicological testing for employees involved in certain accidents and incidents.
2. Gives the railroads the authorization to test employees in reasonable course situations.
3. Mandates that the railroads will provide treatment and rehabilitation for employees with the problem of substance abuse.
4. Mandates that railroads will conduct pre-employment drug screens on candidates who drive in covered service.

These guidelines were established in a workshop on performance related to alcohol and other drugs in transportation and indicate the growing national awareness of the tragic impact of alcohol abuse on transportation fatalities.

Minimum Drinking Age

There is a consistent correlation between minimum legal drinking age and traffic morbidity and mortality rates in younger people with high blood alcohol concentrations at the time of the accident (Cohen, 1981; Wagenaar & Douglass, 1980). Young people are not only less experienced drivers but also less experienced drinkers. In addition, the normal development of adolescence includes some impulsivity with occasional poor judgment and some problems with self-restraint. When drinking occurs in this particular age group, we see an increased probability of serious accidents associated with alcohol.

In 1972, Michigan reduced the minimum legal drinking age from 21 to 18 years. A five-year follow-up report by the University of Michigan Highway

TABLE 12.1
Policy Recommendations on Drinking and Driving*

PREAMBLE

A significant percentage of drinking drivers are suffering from the disease of alcoholism. Identification and treatment of persons with alcoholism are critically important for the individual, his or her family, and society. The National Commission Against Drunk Driving in its December 1985 publication, "A Progress Report on the Implementation of Recommendations by the Presidential Commission on Drunk Driving," noted that those alcohol-impaired drivers who are problem drinkers or alcoholics are responsible for nearly one-third of all alcohol-related fatalities. These drinkers are more likely to have BAC levels substantially above the 0.10 level.

The National Council on Alcoholism also recognizes the severe consequences to the health and safety of the American public as a result of persons driving under the influence of alcohol.

Therefore, the National Council on Alcoholism endorses the following initiatives and policies as necessary components of a comprehensive strategy to reduce the incidence of drinking and driving and its tragic consequences for individuals, families and the society at large.

ALCOHOLISM TREATMENT

The National Council on Alcoholism encourages alcoholism treatment as an integral component of all policies, strategies and laws which address drinking and driving. Without treatment of the underlying disease there is no feasible means of reducing the number of repeat offenders.

Any legislation which imposes penalties for drinking and driving should also include provisions for alcoholism treatment.

Local jurisdictions should develop procedures for pre-sentence investigations, in conjunction with alcoholism treatment professionals and volunteers. The pre-sentence investigation process should include screening for identification of alcoholism and other problem drinking, and referral to treatment.

When possible, city/county law enforcement agencies should transfer blood alcohol level testing to the local detoxification facility. This will enable alcohol/drug professionals to interact with the driver in order to begin a process of education or intervention, if required in addition, detoxification services may be provided at the point of blood alcohol level determination.

There should be a provision for monitoring compliance with the law and ensuring the availability of high quality treatment and rehabilitation programs, in accordance with state-established standards.

State insurance commissioners should require and/or state legislators should enact legislation requiring health insurance providers to include coverage for treatment and rehabilitation of alcohol and other drug dependent persons in all health insurance policies.

Workshops/seminars for local employers to educate them on the cost benefits of a comprehensive alcohol/drug insurance program should be offered by NCA affiliates and other alcohol/drug constituency organizations.

LAW ENFORCEMENT

All states should adopt a law making .05 BAL/BAC as per se illegal for driving, as recommended by the American Medical Association.

*National Council on Alcoholism, Inc.   (continued)

TABLE 12.1
Continued

Each state should establish an "implied consent" statute which provides that all licensed drivers have consented to tests of blood, breath or urine to determine alcohol concentration.

Prosecutors should not plea bargain DUI/DWI charges to non-alcohol-related offenses, because this practice tends to inhibit the detection and treatment of the alcoholic driver.

States should require mandatory alcohol testing of all drivers fatally injured, where there is probable cause to suspect alcohol involvement, all drivers involved in a fatal or serious personal injury crash.

PREVENTION

The strategic framework for NCA's prevention efforts emphasizes the need for environmental, cultural and social changes regarding the use of alcohol. Key educational initiatives coupled with public policy measures which affect the preceptions of appropriate alcohol use as well as availability of alcohol are critical components of an effective prevention strategy. NCA views public policies which control the availability of alcohol to high-risk populations or to individuals in high-risk situations as necessary ingredients in a comprehensive effort to reduce drinking and driving related accidents and to ultimately make drinking and driving socially unacceptable. These policy measures include:

States should cooperate in establishment of a national legal drinking age of 21 for the purchase and public possession of all alcoholic beverages.

State and local governments should prohibit consumption of alcoholic beverages in motor vehicles and prohibit possession of open alcoholic beverage containers in passenger compartments of motor vehicles.

Each state should enact "Dram Shop" laws that establish liability against any person or establishment which sells or serves alcoholic beverages to an individual who is visibly intoxicated or who is under the legal drinking age.

Consideration of access to transportation other than private automobiles should be part of any decision to award licenses to serve alcoholic beverages.

Taxes on alcoholic beverages should be increased, and should be equalized by percentage of alcohol content across the beverage classes to reduce consumption, especially by young people.

States should enact laws prohibiting the sale of alcoholic beverages at gasoline stations.

EDUCATION

General

Public information campaigns should continue to be developed on the state and national levels, in cooperation with the private sector, to focus on alcoholism, alcohol use and misuse, and their correlation with highway safety and other alcohol-related problems.

State and federal efforts should include information on alcoholism treatment and rehabilitation in their public education campaigns related to enforcement of drinking and driving legislation.

Editorial boards and media trade associations should encourage their associates and members to communicate to the public regularly about alcohol use and its relationship to highway safety and other alcohol-related problems.

(continued)

TABLE 12.1
Continued

Broadcast and print media should portray alcoholism, alcohol use and their relationship to highway safety and other alcohol-related problems in a responsible manner and, when appropriate, use program content to communicate with the public about alcohol-impaired driving and other alcohol-related social and health consequences.

Education should be encouraged for bartenders and other servers of alcoholic beverages (including social hosts and hostesses) about safe serving practices, prevention of harm to a person who is alcohol-impaired, and responsibilities under the law.

PROFESSIONAL

Each state should have a program for training criminal justice personnel, including police officers, probation officers, judges and both prosecution and defense attorneys, concerning alcoholism and other alcohol-related problems.

Medical schools and associations should give high priority to alcoholism and alcohol use and misuse in their curricula and organizational agendas. Physicians should be encouraged to educate their patients about alcohol, and the interactions between alcohol and other drugs, especially as they affect driving.

Professional education for all health and human service workers should include appropriate information about alcoholism and other alcohol-related problems.

Private Sector Organizations, Including Corporations, Industry, Trade Associations, Labor Organizations and Civil, Fraternal and Social Organizations

Implement employee assistance programs to deal with alcoholism problems.

Develop and disseminate policy statements regarding the use and misuse of alcohol, and alcohol's relationship to highway-related deaths and injuries and other social and health problems, including the appropriate role of alcohol at company-sponsored functions.

Become active advocates and participants in local, state and national endeavors to reduce driving under the influence, alcoholism and other alcohol-related problems.

Youth

Development of school curricula concerning alcohol's effects on the body and its relationship to highway safety and other health and social problems. Curricula should employ a life-style/risk reduction approach to alcohol use aimed at changing youthful behavior related to alcohol-impaired driving as well as other alcohol-related health and social problems.

Athletic and other youth organizations should include information on the effects of alcohol and other drugs on the body and mind with the aim of reducing risks associated with youthful involvement in drinking and other alcohol-related problems.

Drivers

Driver education programs should include information on alcohol, its effects on the body and the impact of alcoholic consumption upon driving abilities and effects of withdrawal syndrome on attitude, capabilities, coordination and judgment.

Driver licensing manuals should stress the relationship of alcohol and other drugs to highway safety and include information on penalties for arrest and conviction of DUI/DWI offenses.

(continued)

TABLE 12.1
Continued

Driver's license examinations should include questions to determine applicants' knowledge of the relationship of alcohol and other drugs to highway safety and their understanding of laws governing such conduct.

RESEARCH

Support for research on the impact of alcoholism treatment on reducing the recidivism rate for DUI/DWI offenders.

Support for research on female drinking and driving to determine the likelihood of arrest and conviction as well as the percentage of problem drinkers in this population—with a comparison with a male group.

Support for research on the relative impacts of alcohol control measures, including a 21 drinking age, open container laws and increases in alcohol taxes, on reducing drinking and driving.

Support for continuing research on blood alcohol levels and their relationship to impaired driving in a number of specific target groups, including women, youth and alcoholics.

Support for research on alcohol media messages including public service announcements, alcohol-related program content and alcohol advertising, and their impact on attitudes and behavior related to drinking and driving.

Support for research on the efficacy of drinking and driving-related warning labels on alcoholic beverages as a way to educate and influence decision-making regarding drinking and driving.

Support for continuing research on the interactive effects of alcohol and other drugs on driving.

Support for research on the efficacy of a data system which tracks individuals between the criminal justice and alcoholic/drug treatment systems to determine if individuals who received treatment are later cited for DUI/DWI and to identify individuals who have multiple alcohol-related arrests but have never received any form of treatment.

Safety Institute showed a 132% increase in the 18-to-20-year-old drinking drivers involved in fatal accidents and a 217% increase in the same group who were involved in nonfatal personal injury accidents; during this same five-year follow-up period, the number of 18-to-20-year-old licensed drivers increased by only 9% (Wagenaar & Douglass, 1980).

Similar observations were reported when Ontario, Canada lowered the drinking age from 21 to 18 years. The number of alcohol-related automobile accidents in the 15-to-19-year-old group increased by 75%, whereas there were no significant changes in the other age groups (Smart, 1981). These data show a "drifting down" effect which indicates that decreasing the drinking age to 18 years probably provides increased drinking opportunities for those who are younger than 18. In association with these findings, Smart also cites data which indicate that lowering the minimum drinking age probably led to 29 additional deaths in Michigan, 28 in Ontario, and 13 in Wisconsin during the first year that the Canadian and U.S. laws were in effect. In addition, studying the increase in alcohol abuse in young people in association with changes in the legal drinking age, Smart reported that the increase in drinking was greatest in the categories of most frequent use; the number of students drinking four times per month or more almost doubled (from 12.7% to 23.3% of the population), whereas there was no increase of students drinking only once a month. The results of this study suggest that lowering the legal drinking age has a substantial impact on increased drinking and alcohol purchases, particularly in bars and taverns.

Among the most impressive data supporting a minimum drinking age of 21 years is the experience in Michigan after the drinking age of 21 years was reestablished in December, 1978 (Wagenaar & Douglass, 1980). This change resulted from a grass-roots movement by educated laymen, knowledgeable about the disastrous effects of the 18-year-old minimum drinking age, who formed a group called "Coalition for 21." Their successful effort had been strongly opposed by an interesting coalition of groups, such as the alcohol beverage industry, the Bar Owners' Association, vocal college students, and some state representatives. Only one year after the legal drinking age was again raised to 21 years, alcohol-related traffic accidents in the 18-to-20-year-old group were reduced by 30%; the fact that there were no significant changes in the other groups eliminated other variables which might have influenced the data.

The alcohol-related traffic accident and mortality rate for the 18-to-20-year-old group has shown a continued decrease since this last report. The National Highway Traffic Safety Administration has estimated that approximately 700 lives were saved in 1984 by the efforts of 44 states which had mandated a minimum drinking age above 18 years. The agency administrator also stated that if all 44 of these states had a minimum drinking age of 21 years, an additional 400 lives could have been saved (National Highway Traffic Safety Administration, 1986). It was further noted that in 1981 young adults under the age of 21 years composed 23.6% of alcohol-related fatalities, although this age group represented only 10% of the total number of licensed drivers.

The Insurance Institute for Highway Safety's Report, perhaps the most comprehensive study available, includes data showing that a state can expect an average of 28% decline in drinking-related driver fatalities if the minimum drinking age level is raised from 18 to 21 years (Curry, 1981).

Important additional data relating to the problem of young drinking drivers have been cited by other authors. In a presentation at a meeting of the American Medical Society on Alcoholism and Other Drugs, it was demonstrated that motor vehicle accidents are the leading cause of death among persons 15 to 24 years of age; 44 per 100,000 died in fatal crashes in 1980 (Malin & Harford, 1982). Malin and Harford further reported that national surveys estimate that one out of every four senior high school students is at risk for an alcohol-related accident each year. With this type of data available to us, how can one argue for maintaining the minimum drinking age at 18 years? Such laws merely increase the accessibility of alcohol beverages to an age group which is still inexperienced and impulsive in its drinking and driving habits. Despite all of the problems involved in enforcing a minimum drinking age of 21 years, legislators would still be neglectful and illogical to pursue a policy that recommends maintaining the minimum drinking age at 18 years.

When we advocate a higher minimum drinking age, we must cite other realities. The national statistics on drunken driving and fatal accidents do not reflect the full extent of the problem because some police officers allow drivers to leave the scene without being tested for alcohol abuse. Of 32,000 drivers who survived accidents involving fatalities in 1984, more than 75% left the scene without being tested for alcohol abuse (Sherman, 1986). More than 25% of the 25,582 drivers who were killed in accidents were not tested for blood alcohol concentration. The same report also stated that national statistics have actually underestimated the involvement of repeat offenders in drunken driving deaths and that approximately 27% of repeat offenders were driving without a valid license at the time of the accident. Thus, there are cases in which enforcement of the law is not consistent and other cases in which gross disobedience of the law results in additional deaths. Nonetheless, the data suggest that rigid and firm application of the laws on drunken driving and minimum drinking age is likely to be of significant help to the young segment of our population.

In a Council Report by the American Medical Association, the following policy recommendations for safe driving were:

1. public education urging drivers not to drink;
2. adoption by all states of 0.05% blood alcohol levels as per se evidence of alcohol-impaired driving;
3. 21 years as the minimum legal drinking age in all states;
4. adoption by all states of administrative driver's license suspension in driving under the influence (DUI) cases;
5. encouragement for the automobile industry to develop a safety module that thwarts operation of a motor vehicle by an intoxicated person (Council on Scientific Affairs, 1986).

Educational Approaches

Early education is generally considered the major primary preventive approach to adolescent drinking. However, educational efforts in this area are frequently neither scientifically organized nor designed with self-evaluating systems to determine the efficacy of the approach. In one investigation of a group of 12- and 13-year-old students, three instruments were used: the Alcohol Consumption and Social Class Questionnaire; the Counseling Form of the Tennessee Self Concept Scale (TSCS); and the Alcohol Knowledge Test (Butler, 1982). The 388 students evaluated were separated into three groups: abstainers, infrequent drinkers (fewer than two drinks per week), and frequent drinkers (an average of two or more drinks per week). The TSCS yielded nine scores of self-esteem and one score of self-criticism. Using the 35-item Alcohol Knowledge Test, high and low knowledge groups were determined by using the upper and lower 27th percentiles.

The results showed that 63.9% of these early adolescents were abstainers, 18% were infrequent drinkers, and 18.1% were relatively frequent drinkers. There were no significant sex differences in relation to alcohol consumption in this age group. Most importantly, no significant differences in alcohol consumption were found between the high and low knowledge groups for either boys or girls. The differences were significant only in higher scores on the Behavior and Physical Self-concept sections of the TSCS for the abstinent group.

The shortcomings of this study, such as the arbitrary designation of "frequent drinker" if the adolescent consumed two or more drinks per week, prevent reaching any definite conclusions about the values of self-concept and knowledge of alcohol in relation to alcohol consumption in this particular group. However, these data do suggest that knowledge about alcohol consumption in this age group does not significantly reduce drinking, whereas personality antecedents to alcohol use, such as self-confidence about physical appearance and social skills, may be associated with decreased alcohol consumption by teenagers. Such studies emphasize the need to devise protocols that are designed to evaluate possible correlations between alcohol consumption and self-concept and between consumption and knowledge about alcohol before instituting an educational program on alcohol and drug abuse.

These data agree with the findings of other studies which report a correlation between the expectations that alcohol improves social skills and the development of problem drinking (Smith et al., 1986). These researchers reported that the two expectations which best predicted teenage drinking problems were: (1) alcohol enhances social behavior; and (2) alcohol improves cognitive and motor functioning. Increased drinking problems were also associated with opinions that alcohol would improve sexual activity, increase arousal, and promote relaxation. In this study, questionnaires were administered to 553 seventh and eighth grade students, ages 12 to 14 years. The data indicated that the more strongly adolescents believed that alcohol enhanced their social skills and cognitive-motor functioning, the more they were drinking one year later. The replication of such findings in other studies would indicate that the educational steps for prevention should concentrate on methods to improve self-image and self-concept as tools to enhance the self-esteem of these young people.

Parents as well as school authorities have an obligation to help their children prepare for the problems of maturing in our complex society. Although parents have the right, as well as the responsibility, to require certain standards of conduct from their children in their home environment, these same parents also have the obligation to serve as positive role models in their own drinking behavior. The National Federation of Parents for Drug-Free Youth (NFP) has a strong anti-alcohol and anti-marijuana orientation. This organization takes the position that illegal drinking by minors should be prohibited but that it is up to the parents if they wish to permit their teenager to drink socially at home. The goal is to encourage teenagers to develop pride in their ability to abstain from alcohol and other drugs.

The Parents' Resource Institute for Drug Education (PRIDE) at Georgia State University provides educational resources and instructional material and conducts annual conferences which provide current information on alcohol and drugs. One of the points repeatedly emphasized by such organizations is the belief that children may actually be harmed by the failure to teach them what is permissible and what is not, leaving them without guidelines as they develop. It has been estimated that there are as many as 5,000 chapters of concerned parents attempting to cope with teenage alcohol and drug use (Cohen, 1984).

In association with parental education and self-help groups, the school system must also play an important role in prevention of alcohol misuse by adolescents. Classroom discussion should emphasize peer approval for abstinence, as well as disapproval of drinking habits. An adolescent's perceptions of peer and legal sanctions may influence his or her drinking patterns. In a study by Burkett and Carrithers (1980), a combination of expected legal sanctions and peer disapproval was a strong deterrent in 90% of the nondrinkers, of whom 69% feared legal sanctions and 81% feared peer disapproval.

The role of the media in affecting the use of alcohol is still uncertain. In one study of fifth and sixth grade children, the subjects were randomly assigned to experimental and control groups (Kotch et al., 1986). The experimental group saw television programs in which the principal characters were shown drinking alcoholic beverages in some scenes; these episodes were eliminated in the programs viewed by the control group. Parents' drinking and other television-watching at home were similar for both groups. Immediately after viewing the television programs, the children completed questionnaires on alcohol attitude and expected use. The boys who saw the film with drinking were significantly more likely to respond that the good things about alcohol were more important than the bad things. In the control group, the boys felt that harmful and good effects were equally important. There were no significant differences noted between the experimental and control groups of the girls. This short-term study did not evaluate subsequent drinking behavior; further research of the media effects on drinking habits is necessary before we can make any definitive conclusions about the impact of television on drinking behavior. This area of prevention is extremely important because it appears that the prevention of early involvement in legal drugs may have significant effects on reducing the subsequent use of marijuana and other illicit drugs (Yamaguchi & Kandel, 1984). At this time, data suggest that preventive efforts are more effective for all drugs if they are targeted at reducing the first use of the drugs, rather than on decreasing use among adolescents and adults who have already become users.

The therapeutic effects of educational programs for drinking drivers are also uncertain. In one evaluation of the short-term effects of an educational program for drinking drivers who had been arrested, 122 subjects were randomly assigned to an eight-hour educational safe-driving program or to a no-education group (Scoles & Fine, 1977). Pretest and post-test scores showed no significant differences between these two groups in the measures of amount of absolute alcohol consumed daily and in physical and behavioral symptoms of heavy drinking. Although the between-group differences during the 30-day follow-up period were not significant, there was a decrease in alcohol consumption and improvement in behavior in both groups, which suggested that these positive changes were associated with the arrest process and not the educational program.

In a survey of changes in legislation and public education efforts to decrease drinking and driving accidents, the question was again raised about the value of publicity and education affecting public attitudes and subsequent reduction in driving accidents (Editorial, 1978). Although this survey concluded that education may or may not have more impact than short-term publicity, the data did indicate that fear of detection was still the best deterrent. However, massive and consistent educational and publicity efforts in the Scandinavian countries apparently have resulted in significant reductions in drunken driving mortality and morbidity. Information from public opinion polls in Scandinavian countries on the severity of drunken driving provided the following information: In Denmark, drunken driving was not only considered to be inexcusable but almost equated in severity with rape; in Norway, drunken driving was considered to be a more severe offense than house-breaking; and in Sweden drunken driving was considered a more serious offense than assault, fraud, or burglary (Hauge, 1978). Thus, it is possible for education to influence public attitudes and opinions about a problem that causes so many deaths and permanent injuries.

To change public attitudes and behaviors, it is first necessary to educate the educators. The attitudes of future physicians and other health care professionals concerning the promotion of public health is important, since the beliefs of these influential members of society affect the way they practice their profession and advise patients. In one study of the 1983 class of freshman medical students, only 5% of the group smoked cigarettes (a significant decrease compared with data from 1974), but 80% of the group reported using alcohol at least twice weekly, with 16% consuming an average of more than six alcohol drinks each time they drank (Maynard et al., 1986). In this same study, an attitudinal questionnaire showed that the students rated alcohol intake in moderation or abstinence as a much less important health-promoting factor than nutrition, sleep, or exercise. In another study of psychoactive substance use among medical students, 12% of the sample reported daily use of one or more substances during the month prior to the study (Maddux et al., 1986). Before the study, 91% of the students had used alcohol; 23%, marijuana; 19%, opioids; 17%, benzodiazepines; 8%, cocaine; and 8%, amphetamines. The same denial mechanisms used by some of these students to allow themselves to continue their drug use may also result in their minimizing the seriousness of alcohol or other drug use by their future patients.

It is important that more information about the damaging effects of alcohol on young people, even in relatively small doses, as well as the overall harmful effects of heavy alcohol consumption, be disseminated in a meaningful way. The present methods of informing the public are obviously deficient. For example, the data about neuropsychologic decrements as a function of alcohol intake in young male students is relatively unknown even among professionals. In a study by Parker et al. (1980) of 45 male university students, mean age of 22.6 years (S.D. ± 2 years), it was shown that cognitive decrements in abstraction and word meanings were significantly associated with the amount of alcohol consumed per occasion; the average amount of alcohol ingested per event was in the range of only 40–50 mg of absolute alcohol. The tests were conducted on days following alcohol ingestion, when the subjects were alcohol-free. The scores on the standard cognitive tests were inversely related to the quantity of alcohol consumed on each occasion and not to the frequency of drinking episodes. The alcohol intake actually accounted for approximately 25% of the variance in test scores. It should be stressed that even slight losses in intellectual function can be important to young people when they are in learning or testing situations or in a setting which requires adequate eye-hand coordination.

The American Medical Society on Alcoholism, considering such data as detailed in Parker et al.'s study, has issued a statement in support of labeling alcohol beverages which contain more than 24% alcohol with the following notice: "Attention: Consumption of alcoholic beverages may be hazardous to your health" (Galanter, 1980). In addition to labeling, it has been suggested that messages concerning the cancer risks associated with alcohol be presented in health promotion programs (Houghton et al., 1986). Promotion of health as a realistic benefit of decreased alcohol consumption may help to decrease the denial that some people exhibit in believing that alcohol is necessary to enhance their ability to relate in social situations.

It is important that the audiovisual materials used are appropriate for groups in which the literacy rate is low but the cancer risk associated with heavy alcohol intake is high. Preventive efforts are often lacking in areas where public interest is low and public health support measures are inadequate. For instance, the high mortality and morbidity rates associated with alcohol use in American Indians has still not received enough public attention and support (May, 1986). Education about early developmental problems which might lead to misuse of alcohol is negligible in most American Indian communities, and rehabilitation programs are inadequate.

Although the dangers of alcohol-related problems in pregnancy have received a tremendous increase in publicity during the past decade, primary prevention is still not sufficient. Recent birth data show that the fetal alcohol syndrome is now the leading cause of mental retardation, even more common than Down's syndrome or spina bifida (Abel & Sokol, 1986). Such impressive data must be made available to the public at large through all forms of the media.

SECONDARY PREVENTION

The primary emphasis of secondary prevention of alcoholism is early case-finding. All professionals in the field of mental health should learn the early symptoms and signs of substance abuse. If the therapist is alert to the early signs and symptoms, he or she may have the opportunity to intervene while the patient's social support system is still intact. Professionals should be encouraged to make routine use of screening questionnaires, such as the MAST or the Diagnostic Questions for Early or Advanced Alcoholism (see Tables 5.1 and 5.2 in Chapter 5).

Legal Approaches for Early Case-finding

Screening the driving records of persons convicted of driving while intoxicated (DWI or DUI) is one legal approach for detecting early cases of alcohol and drug abuse and preventing future problems. These simple data, which are available in most communities, can have important therapeutic implications for early prevention. The average time span between DWI convictions progressively decreases with each conviction, increasing the likelihood of a disastrous car accident (Maisto et al., 1979). Compulsory treatment of such traffic violators may be helpful in some cases, if the duration of the sentence is long enough to work out the subject's initial anger over being forced to accept therapy and if the sentence provides harsh penalties for noncompliance (Gallant et al., 1968; Inge, 1979).

It has been shown that the practice of using breathalyzer tests on the day of pretrial evaluation of a DUI subject has identified a number of offenders whose drinking behaviors require alcoholism treatment. In one study of breathalyzer tests administered to 500 DUI offenders on the day of their scheduled presentencing evaluations, positive blood alcohol levels were found in 132 (26.4%) of the subjects (Scoles et al., 1986). These individuals were more likely to be diagnosed as having alcoholism disorders, had higher blood alcohol levels at the time of their arrests, and had a history of higher alcohol intake than subjects who did not have positive blood alcohol levels on the day of their presentence evaluation. This obvious loss of control over drinking behavior indicates the need for alcoholism treatment, as well as the necessary legal penalties. In addition to the breathalyzer tests and the previously mentioned alcoholism questionnaires, other screening tests and questionnaires are available for use in courts and related social agencies, such as probation units (Dubach & Schneider, 1980; Hoffman et al., 1974; Morse & Heest, 1979; Woodruff et al., 1976). These screening efforts could also be utilized in child abuse cases, spouse beatings, and other possible court-related substance abuse problems. This type of early case-finding within the legal system can be quite productive, since it is likely that the court will have the legal power to incorporate treatment into its sentence.

It is interesting that many persons who drive while under the influence of alcohol are willing to report it when questioned. In a random telephone survey of 1,492 adults, at least 18 years old, the question was asked, "During the past four weeks, how many times have you driven after having perhaps too much to drink?" (Anda et al., 1986). Surprisingly, 7.5% of all these respondents (95% confidence interval = 5.9% to 9.1%) and nearly 33% of all men 18 to 24 years of age reported driving while under the influence of alcohol at least once in the month prior to the survey. Almost half of those who reported driving while impaired had done so on two or more occasions in the previous four weeks. Extrapolating from these data, it is estimated that during this four-week interval, 5,000 (approximately 8%) of the 6,300,000 adults in the state of Michigan, where the study was conducted, drove while impaired and that there were over 1,000,000 episodes of alcohol-impaired driving during that month. Using police data on drunken driving arrests during that same year of 1982, it was estimated that the risk of being arrested during an episode of alcohol-impaired driving was only 4 in 1,000. Considering these data, it would have required at least 1,000,000 police-hours monthly to arrest all of these impaired drivers.

Obviously, law enforcement can never be an adequate method of preventing alcohol-related car accidents, although it is an important component of this effort. Multiple strategies, such as continuous public education efforts beginning with young children during their early school years, stricter enforcement of DWI or DUI laws, labeling alcohol beverages about the hazards of use, enforcing laws that prohibit sales of alcohol to intoxicated customers and those under the age of 21, and more frequent use of the media for public health statements on the hazards of alcohol use, are needed. In addition, the data published by Anda et al., which indicate that a considerable number of individuals are willing to report incidents associated with impaired driving, should encourage all professionals and paraprofessionals in the field of health delivery services to question, identify, and counsel those individuals who drink and drive.

Use of Social and School Agencies
for Early Case-finding

In families with histories of child abuse, spouse battering, or other types of extreme violence, such as rape or assault, it is not uncommon to find the problem of alcoholism (Baehling, 1979; Gershon, 1978; Johnson et al., 1978; NIAAA, 1980). All health care personnel should understand that treating only the end result of an alcoholism problem, such as medical management of a battered child or spouse, is not proper treatment. It is essential for personnel who treat victims of domestic violence to develop liaison arrangements with alcoholism counselors. It is not unusual to meet a spouse who has been experiencing violence or witnessing alcohol-related problems for many years without ever having sought help. The passive acceptance and denial of the battered wife or the mother of an abused child of an alcoholic are similar and frequently found within the same family setting. As Rogan has said, "When alcoholism counselors and those who work in the area of domestic violence do not understand how frequently the two problems are associated, or if they fail to recognize the impact that such dual affliction has on their clients, they may miss an important opportunity to intervene in the cycle of abuse" (1985/86). Identification of the offender and *assurance* that this person receives follow-up treatment in order to avoid future violence are the moral responsibility of all health personnel.

Alcohol-related violence frequently includes a drinking *victim* as well as drinking offender. In one study of the social victims of alcohol abusers, the victims tended to resemble "problem drinkers" found in general population surveys in several ways: They tended to be young, single, in lower socioeconomic groups, frequent and/or heavy drinkers, and worried about their own drinking (Fillmore, 1985). In this particular study, the evidence was clear that heavier and more frequent drinking on the part of the victims placed them at increased risk for suffering the consequences of other people's drinking behavior. Women were more vulnerable in general, especially so if they were exposed to social situations in which heavy drinking took place, if they were living with heavy drinkers, or if they themselves were heavy frequent drinkers. If strategies are to be developed to prevent or decrease alcohol-related victimization, blaming the victim or the victimizer will not help us to adequately understand or treat these problems.

Secondary prevention is also important for the geriatric population. In this patient group, certain signs and symptoms, such as repeated falls, episodic confusion, and self-neglect, may be indicators of underlying drinking problems. Professional or paraprofessional personnel working in retirement homes or areas where large geriatric populations reside should be aware that it is not unusual for some patients to start abusing alcohol late in life (Wattis, 1981). In some cases, close relatives who abuse alcohol themselves may be enabling the elderly patient to drink.

At the other end of the chronological continuum, the incidence of alcohol abuse and misuse has been a serious problem among adolescents for the last several decades. One practical tool for defining alcohol misuse and alcoholism-like illnesses in the adolescent population is the Adolescent Alcohol Involvement Scale (Mayer & Filstead, 1979). This scale can be used to measure the degree of alcohol misuse in a community school. Understanding the extent of the problem is essential before a community initiates primary or secondary preventive interventions. Secondary prevention of alcoholism in this age group must focus on early identification of the problem; education of the parents, peers, and school system; and the need to have abstinent peer groups available for the young alcoholic to turn to when asked to give up his or her former drinking friends.

It is also important for us to be aware that some patient populations may have a high percentage of alcoholics; a higher index of suspicion for the problem should be present when treating such populations. For example, even after controlling for sex, age, income, education, and marital status, veterans over 35 years of age who are less educated and have a lower incidence of marriage show a significantly higher prevalence of alcohol abuse than nonveterans from similar backgrounds (Boscarino, 1981). Such information may be particularly useful for alcoholism counselors working with veterans or with the armed forces personnel.

Medical Approaches for Early Case-finding

Medical data such as that published by Rosett and his colleagues (1980) reinforce the importance of medical secondary prevention or early case-finding. For instance, as a consequence of significantly reducing the alcohol intake in 25 pregnant women who drank heavily, there was less growth retardation among their offspring at birth than among the offspring of 44 women who continued to drink heavily. Thus, early case findings in pregnant alcoholic women can serve as secondary prevention for low infant birthweight and possible subsequent impaired motor and mental development (Streissguth et al., 1980).

Routine blood alcohol screening in hospital emergency rooms can reach a significant number of alcohol-abusing patients who present with other complaints, for example, 63% wtih trauma and 23% with vague neuropsychiatric complaints in one study (Rund et al., 1981). Personnel in hospital emergency rooms must be constantly alert to the alcoholism problem if they are to determine an adequate treatment follow-up strategy for every patient seen.

Other secondary preventive medical interventions, such as the use of questionnaires for population surveys, knowledge of early signs and symptoms of alcohol abuse, and use of specific laboratory tests for detecting alcohol abuse in general populations are described in Chapter 5.

Since the lifetime prevalence of alcohol abuse or dependence in the general population over the age of 18 years is 11% to 16%, the need for more adequate primary and secondary preventive measures is evident (Robins et al., 1984). The preventive measures described here should be considered only the initial steps in the campaign to reduce the morbidity and mortality rates caused by this nationwide disaster affecting all segments of American communities.

REFERENCES

Abel, E. L. & Sokol, R. J. (1986). Fetal alcohol syndrome is now leading cause of mental retardation. *Lancet, 2*, 1222.
Allsop, R. E. (1966). Alcohol and road accidents: A discussion of the Grand Rapids study. Report No. 6, Harmondsworth, Road Research Laboratory.
Anda, R. F., Remington, P. L., & Williamson, D. F. (1986). A sobering perspective on a lower blood alcohol limit. *Journal of the American Medical Association, 256*, 3213.

Baehling, B. W. (1979). Alcohol abuse as encountered in 51 instances of reported child abuse. *Clinical Pediatrics, 18*, 87–91.

Boscarino, J. (1981). Current excessive drinking among Vietnam veterans: A comparison with other veterans and non-veterans. *The International Journal of Social Psychiatry, 27*, 1–11.

Burkett, J. R. & Carrithers, W. T. (1980). Adolescents' drinking and perceptions of legal and informed sanctions. *Journal of Studies on Alcohol, 41*, 839–853.

Butler, J. T. (1982). Early adolescent alcohol consumption and self-concept, social class, and knowledge of alcohol. *Journal of Studies on Alcohol, 43*, 603–607.

Cohen, S. (1981). The one vehicle accident. *Drug Abuse & Alcoholism Newsletter, 13*, 1–3.

Cohen, S. (1984). Parent power. *Drug Abuse & Alcoholism Newsletter, 13*, 1–3.

Cook, P. J. (1982). Alcohol taxes as a public health measure. *British Journal of Addiction, 77*, 244–250.

Council on Scientific Affairs (1986). Alcohol and the driver. *Journal of the American Medical Association, 255*, 522–527.

Curry, B. (1981). Road deaths raise doubt about teen-age drinking. *Times Picayune*, New Orleans, December 23.

Dubach, U. C. & Schneider, J. (1980). Screening for alcoholism. *Lancet, 2*, 1374.

Editorial: (1978). Drinking and driving accidents—does education help? *British Medical Journal, 2*, 1352–1353.

Fell, J. C. (1982). Alcohol involvement in traffic accidents: Recent estimates from the National Center for Statistics and Analysis. *U.S. Department of Transportation, Publication No. DOT HS-806-269*, Springfield, VA., National Technical Information Service.

Fillmore, K. M. (1985). Social victims of drinking. *British Journal of Addiction, 80*, 307–314.

Galanter, M. (1980). Young adult social drinkers: Another group at risk? *Alcoholism: Clinical and Experimental Research, 4*, 241–242.

Gallant, D. M., Faulkner, B., Stoy, B., Bishop, M. P., & Langdon, D. (1968). Enforced clinic treatment of paroled criminal alcoholics—1 year follow-up. *Quarterly Journal of Studies on Alcohol, 29*, 77–83.

Gallant, D. M. (1982). Prevention of substance abuse within a community. In D. M. Gallant, *Alcohol and drug abuse curriculum guide for psychiatry faculty*. (pp. 41–44). DHHS Pub No. (ADM) 82-1159.

Gershon, L. W. (1978). Alcohol-related acts of violence: Who is drinking and where the acts occurred. *Journal of Studies on Alcohol, 39*, 1294–1296.

Hauge, R. (1978). *Drinking and driving in Scandinavia*. Oslo: Scandinavian University Books.

Hoffman, H., Loper, R. G., & Kammeier, M. L. (1974). Identifying future alcoholics with MMPI alcoholism scales. *Quarterly Journal of Studies on Alcohol, 35*, 490–498.

Houghton, J. F., Romano, R. M., & Podolsky, D. M. (1986). Alcohol and cancer prevention awareness. *Alcohol Health & Research World, 10*, 44–47.

Inge, E. C. G. (1979). An analysis of personality change in twice-convicted drunk drivers undergoing psychotherapy. Ph.D. dissertation on University Microfilm No. 8013264, United States International University.

Johnson, S. P., Gibson, L., & Linden, R. (1978). Alcohol and rape in Winnepeg, 1966–1975. *Journal of Studies on Alcohol, 39*, 1887–1894.

Joksch, H. C. (1985). Review of the major risk factors. *Journal of Studies on Alcohol, Supplement No. 10*, 47–53.

Kotch, J. B., Coulter, M. L., & Lipsitz, A. (1986). Does televised drinking influence children's attitudes toward alcohol? *Addictive Behaviors, 11*, 67–70.

Lundberg, G. D. (1986). Let's stop driving after drinking and using other psychoactive drugs. *Journal of the American Medical Association, 255*, 529–530.

Maddux, J. F., Hoppe, S. K., & Costello, R. N. (1986). Psychoactive substance use among medical students. *American Journal of Psychiatry, 143*, 187–191.

Maisto, S. A., Sobell, L. C., Zelhart, P. F., Connors, G. J., & Cooper, T. (1979). Driving records of persons convicted of driving under the influence of alcohol. *Journal of Studies on Alcohol, 40, 70*–77.

Malin, H., & Harford, T. (1982). Ecological factors and fatal highway accidents among teenagers and young adults. Abstract from NCA/AMSA/RSA Meeting in New Orleans, December.

May, P. A. (1986). Alcohol and drug misuse prevention programs for American Indians: Needs and opportunities. *Journal of Studies on Alcohol, 47*, 187-195.

Mayer, J., & Filstead, W. J. (1979). The adolescent alcohol involvement scale: An instrument for measuring adolescents' use and misuse of alcohol. *Journal of Studies on Alcohol, 40*, 291-300.

Maynard, L., Goldberg, R., Ockene, J., Levy, B., Howe, J., & Dalen, J. (1986). Behaviors and attitudes among medical students concerning cigarette smoking and alcohol consumption. *Journal of Medical Education, 61*, 921-922.

Morse, R. M., & Heest, R. D. (1979). Screening for alcoholism. *Journal of the American Medical Association, 242*, 2688-2690.

National Broadcasting Company Viewer's Guide (1983). Mothers Against Drunk Drivers: The Candy Lightner Story. March 14.

National Institute on Alcohol Abuse and Alcoholism Information and Feature Service. (1980). Alcoholism cited in domestic violence cases. June 9.

National Highway Traffic Safety Administration (1986). Higher drinking ages saved 700, study says. *Commercial Appeal*, Memphis, Tenn., March 5.

National Transportation Safety Board (1986). Railroad Programs. Workshop on Performance Guidelines Related to Alcohol and Other Drugs in Transportation, January 16-17, (p. 40).

Ornstein, S. I. (1980). Control of alcohol consumption through price increases. *Journal of Studies on Alcohol, 41*, 807-818.

Parker, E. S., Birnbaum, I. M., Boyd, R. A., & Noble, E. P. (1980). Neuropsychologic decrements as a function of alcohol intake in male students. *Alcoholism: Clinical and Experimental Research, 4*, 330-334.

Petersson, B., Kristenson, H., Krant, P., Trell, E., & Sternby, W. H. (1982). Alcohol related deaths: A major contributor to mortality in urban middle-aged men. *Lancet, 2*, 1088-1090.

Poikolainen, K. (1983). Increasing alcohol consumption correlated with hospital admission rates. *British Journal of Addiction, 78*, 305-309.

Popham, R., Schmidt, W., & De Lint, J. (1978). Government control measures to prevent hazardous drinking. In J. A. Ewing, & B. A. Rouse (Eds.). *Drinking: Alcohol in American society — Issues and current research*. (pp. 239-266). Chicago: Nelson-Hall.

Reichler, B. D., Clement, J. L., & Dunner, D. L. (1983). Chart review of alcohol problems in adolescent psychiatric patients in an emergency room. *Journal of Clinical Psychiatry, 44*, 338-340.

Richman, A. (1985). Human risk factors in alcohol-related crashes. *Journal of Studies on Alcohol, Supplement No. 10*, 21-31.

Robins, L. N., Heltzer, J. E., Weissman, M. M., Orbaschell, H., Gruenberg, E., Burke, J. D., & Reiger, D. A. (1984). Lifetime prevalence of specific psychiatric disorders in three sites. *Archives of General Psychiatry, 41*, 949-958.

Rogan, A. (1985/86). Domestic violence and alcohol: Barriers to cooperation. *Alcohol Health and Research World, 10*, 22-27.

Rosett, H. L., Weiner, L., Zuckerman, B., McKinley, S., & Edelin, K. C. (1980). Reduction of alcohol consumption during pregnancy with benefits to the newborn. *Alcoholism: Clinical and Experimental Research, 4*, 178-184.

Rund, G. A., Summers, W. K., & Levin, M. (1981). Alcohol use and psychiatric illness in emergency patients. *Journal of the American Medical Association, 245*, 1240-1241.

Rush, B. R., Gliksman, L., & Brook, R. (1986). Alcohol availability, alcohol consumption and alcohol related damage. I. The distribution of consumption model. *Journal of Studies on Alcohol, 47*, 1-10.

Scoles, P. E., & Fine, E. W. (1977). Short-term effects of an educational program of drinking drivers. *Journal of Studies on Alcohol, 38*, 633-637.

Scoles, P. E., Fine, E. W., & Steer, R. A. (1986). DUI offenders presenting with positive blood alcohol levels at presentencing evaluation. *Journal of Studies on Alcohol, 47*, 500-502.

Sherman, S. (1986, December 1). Drunken drivers getting away. (Crime Control Institute Report by the Associated Press). *Times-Picayune*, New Orleans.

Skog, O-J. (1986). Trends in alcohol consumption and violent deaths. *British Journal of Addiction, 81*, 365–379.

Smart, R. G. (1971). *The New Drinkers*. Addiction Research Foundation of Ontario Publication, Toronto, Canada.

Smart, R. G. (1981). The impact of changes in legal purchase or drinking age on drinking and admissions to treatment. In H. Wechsler (Ed.). *Minimum-Drinking-Age Laws*. (pp. 133–154). Toronto: Lexington Books.

Smith, G. T., Roehling, P. V., Christiansen, B. A., & Goldman, M. S. (1986, September 2). High hopes often lead teens to drink. Report by P. Young in the *Times-Picayune*, New Orleans.

Streissguth, A. P., Burr, H. N., Martin, V. C., & Herman, C. S. (1980). Effects of alcohol, nicotine, and caffeine use during pregnancy on infants' mental and motor development at eight months. *Alcoholism: Clinical and Experimental Research, 4*, 152–164.

UPI Press Release. (1986, August 13). Poland shares alcohol problems with Soviets. *Times-Picayune*, New Orleans.

Voas, R. B. & House, J. M. (1983). Deterring the drinking driver: The Stockton experience. Alexandria, VA.: National Public Services Research Institute.

Wagenaar, A. C., & Douglass, R. K. (1980). An evaluation of changes in the legal drinking age in Michigan, summary of principal findings. *The Bottom Line, 4*, 16–17.

Waller, P. F., Stewart, J. R., Hansen, A. R., Stutts, J. C., Popkin, C. L. & Rodgman, E. A. (1986). The potentiating effects of alcohol on driver injury. *Journal of the American Medical Association, 256*, 1461–1466.

Wattis, J. P. (1981). Alcohol problems in the elderly. *Journal of the American Geriatric Society, 29*, 131–134.

Woodruff, R. A., Clayton, P. J., Cloniger, C. R., & Guze, S. B. (1976). A brief method of screening for alcoholism. *Journal of Clinical Psychiatry, 37*, 434–435.

Yamaguchi, K., & Kandel, D. B. (1984). Patterns of drug use from adolescent to young adulthood: III. Predictors of progression. *American Journal of Public Health, 74*, 673–681.

Index

Abel, E. L., 238
abstinence, as treatment goal, 121, 127–28, 167, 192–93
acetaldehyde, 27–31, 44, 170, 175
acetate, 27–28
acetyl-coenzyme A, 28
acne rosacea, 102
acquired immune deficiency syndrome (AIDS), 103, 211
addiction (physiological dependency), 3, 5, 10
  barbiturate, 116–17
  non-opioid receptor systems and, 31–32
  opioid receptor systems and, 29–31
  tetrahydroisoquinoline in, 44
  see also chemical dependency
Addiction Research Foundation in Toronto, 192
adenosine receptors, 31
ADH (alcohol dehydrogenase), 27, 29–30
Adolescent Alcohol Involvement Scale (AAIS), 16–18, 241
adolescents:
  drug abuse by, 18–19, 82–83, 201, 235
  early intervention with, 82–83
  early symptoms in, 54
  education for, 234–36
  incidence of alcohol use by, 15–21, 234
  psychiatric problems in, 19–20
  secondary prevention for, 241
  traffic accidents/fatalities among, 20–21, 227
adoption studies, 42–43
advertising, by alcohol beverage industry, 42
Adult Children of Alcoholics (ACA), 217
affect, lability of, 15, 23, 93

affective disorders, treatment of, 160–63, 176–77
  see also depression
aged, see elderly
aggression, assertion vs., 149
aging, premature, 92
agoraphobia, 179
Agras, W. Stewart, 158
AIDS (acquired immune deficiency syndrome), 103, 211
airplanes, accidents involving, 227
Akiskal, H. S., 178–79
Al-Anon, 56, 58, 63–65, 93, 124–26, 130, 196, 217, 219
Al-Ateen, 217, 219
alcohol:
  blood levels of, 52, 56–59, 107–9, 114, 132–33, 170, 177, 225, 227–28, 233, 239
  carbomide reaction with, 175
  food value of, 130–31
  immune system and, 102–3
  nervous system and, 86–98
  organ systems and, 98–103
  pharmacology and metabolism of, 26–33
  price and availability of, 222–23
  reproductive system and, 101–2
  skin and, 102
  taxation and consumption of, 221–24
  testing for, 119, 213, 229, 233, 239, 242
  tolerance to, 27–31, 53, 58–59
Alcohol Abuse, Alcohol Dependence vs., 1, 3–4
alcohol amnestic disorder, 86–89, 95
alcohol and drug abuse unit (ADU), Southeast Louisiana Hospital, 122–58, 180, 184

246

Alcohol Consumption and Social Class
   Questionnaire, 234
alcohol dehydrogenase (ADH), 27, 29–
   30
alcohol hallucinosis, 91
alcoholic liver disease, 98–100
alcoholics:
   criminal, 120–21, 159
   personality characteristics of, 11, 23,
      35–41, 54, 144, 148–51, 152–55, 234
Alcoholics Anonymous (AA), 36, 56, 65, 93,
   120, 124–26, 130, 167, 196, 211–12,
   216–19
Alcoholics Anonymous (the "Big Book"),
   125, 216–17
alcohol idiosyncratic intoxication, 86–89
alcoholism, alcohol abuse:
   behavioral indicators of, 6, 8–9
   cultural factors in, 41–42, 166–67
   definitions of, 1–3, 9–11
   development of, 134–36
   diagnosis of, *see* diagnosis
   early intervention techniques for, *see* early
      intervention
   early signs of, 54–58
   genetic factors in, 11, 20, 42–45, 53,
      127–28
   incidence of, 13–21, 242
   misdiagnosis of, 88, 90–91, 111
   periodic, *see* binge drinking
   physiological indicators of, 5–7
   primary vs. secondary, 121, 134, 176
   psychological consequences of, *see* organic
      mental disturbances, alcohol-related
   psychological mechanisms in, 35–40
   selecting appropriate treatment for, 59–
      61
   sex-linked transmission of, 43
   underreporting of, 13–14, 213
alcoholism dependence, 1, 3–4, 11
Alcohol Knowledge Test, 234
alcohol poisoning, 223
alcohol psychosis, 223
alcohol-related morbidity and mortality
   rates, *see* morbidity rates; mortality
   rates
alcohol treatment units (ATUs), *see* inpatient
   rehabilitation treatment
alcohol withdrawal delirium (delirium
   tremens), 89–91, 109, 111–16
alcohol withdrawal syndrome, *see* withdrawal
aldehyde dehydrogenase (Ald DH), 27–29,
   31, 44, 170, 175
alkaline phosphatase, 57, 90
Allsop, R. E., 225
alpha alcoholism, 10, 134

Alzheimer's disease (senile dementia), 94–95,
   111
amblyopia, 184
American Indians:
   lack of prevention for, 238
   treatment for, 166
American Medical Association, 228, 233
American Medical Society on Alcoholism
   and Other Drugs, 233, 238
American Psychiatric Association (APA), 1,
   4, 122
amitriptyline, 179–80
amnesia, 86–89, 95
   from lorazepam, 181
   see also blackouts
amobarbitol, 116
amphetamines, 48, 117, 158, 237
amylase, 100
analeptics, 108
analgesic narcotics, 49
Anda, R. F., 239–40
Anderson, R. C., 199–200
Anderson, S. H., 183
anemia, 183–84
anger:
   difficulty in expressing, 144, 190
   toward family, 66, 72, 74–75, 151, 202
   of family members, 200–202
   toward therapist, 66, 71, 73, 75, 78–79,
      88–89
Antabuse (disulfiram), 27, 36, 65, 67–68,
   109–10, 123, 158, 170–75
   administered by spouse, 195–96
   alcohol interaction with, 170–71, 173, 175
   benefits of, 173–75, 185
   with bipolar patients, 162
   in case histories, 71, 73, 75, 105–6, 205–6,
      209
   compulsory use of, 213–14
   dosages of, 171–73
   impairments interfering with, 94
   onset/offset duration of, 171, 175
   with post-traumatic stress disorder, 164
   risks of, 170–73
   urine testing for compliance with, 175, 214
antidepressant drug therapy, 26, 40, 60, 120,
   161–62, 176, 178–80, 185
anxiety, 130, 180–82, 185
   in learning theory, 37
   separation, 178
anxiolytics (antianxiety agents), 49, 120,
   180–82, 185
aphasia, 95
Armor, D. J., 121
Ashley, M. J., 101
assertion diaries, 149

assertiveness training, 120, 130, 147–51, 159, 207
ataxia, 88, 97, 116, 183
atenolol, 114
automobile accidents, 13, 16, 20–22, 221–27, 231–33, 236–37, 240
autonomic nervous system, effects on, 97, 111

Babor, T. F., 50
"baby," family role of, 199, 201
Baehling, B. W., 240
barbiturates, 116–17
Beck Depression Inventory, 176, 181
Beeson, P. B., 100, 102
behavioral self-control training (BSCT), 128
behavioral modification, 130, 139, 156–58, 180
Behavior Modification: Principles and Clinical Applications (Agras), 158
Beletsis, S., 202
Benadryl, 175
Bender Visual-Motor Gestalt Test, 153
Benzer, D., 116
benzodiazepines (BZ), 30, 32, 109–17, 158, 179–82, 237
Berglund, M., 22, 24, 63
Bernadt, M. W., 61
beta alcoholism, 10, 134
beta-blockers, 32, 100, 114–15, 182
"Big Book" (*Alcoholics Anonymous*), 125, 216–17
bilirubin, 57, 90
binge drinking, 10, 15
bipolar affective disorders, 60, 121, 162–63, 178
blackouts, 44, 54–55, 71, 74, 86–89, 204
Blacks, treatment for, 166
Blass, J. P., 183
Blinder, M. G., 200
blood alcohol levels (BALs), 52, 56–59, 107–9, 114, 132–33, 170, 177, 225, 227–28, 233, 239
Bohman, M., 43–44
Boscarino, J., 242
brain, atrophy of, 63, 94
brain damage, *see* organic mental disturbances, alcohol-related
Breed, W., 42
Brewster, J. M., 165
Brisolara, A. M., 40, 120
Brody, J. A., 24, 167
bronchial asthma, 182
bronchitis, 157
Brown, S., 202
Buhler, K. E., 113

Burkett, J. R., 235
Burns, D. D., 150
Burnside, M. A., 39
buspirone, 182
butanediol, 29
Butler, J. T., 234

caffeine, 47–48
CAGE 4-item questionnaire, 50–54
cancer, 22, 65, 103, 157–58
carbamide (Temposil), 175
cardiomyopathy, 22, 100, 182
Carkhuff, R. R., 64–65
Carlen, P. L., 94
Carrithers, W. T., 235
case-finding, early, 238–42
case histories:
    of couples therapy, 196–98
    of early intervention, 70–82
    of family therapy, 202–10
    of intoxication and withdrawal, 105–7
    of psychological test confrontation, 154–55
Cecil Textbook of Medicine (Beeson, McDermott and Wyngaarden), 100, 102
central nervous system (CNS), 161
    impairment of, 58, 92
    neuronal cell adaptation in, 29–30
centrolobular cirrhosis, 99
cephalosporins, 176
cerebellar dysfunction, 88
cerebral atrophy, alcohol-induced, 63, 94
cerebral spinal fluid (CSF) volume, 63, 94
Chambers, T. E., 91
Charity Hospital in New Orleans, 183
chemical dependency:
    learning theory of, 37
    psychodynamic theory of, 37–40
    see also addiction
"chief enabler," family role of, 199–200, 206
child abuse, 2, 64, 148, 155, 199, 207–8, 212, 239–41
Childress, A. R., 150
chloral hydrate, 109
chlorazepate, 111
chlordiazepoxide, 110–11, 114–15
Christensen, J. K., 171
chronic bronchitis, 157
chronic obstructive pulmonary disease, 115
cigarettes, 47–48, 82, 157–58
cirrhosis of the liver, 10, 13, 22, 30, 42, 99, 222–23
clergy, in inpatient treatment, 130, 139
clonidine, 115
Cloninger, C. R., 43–44
cluster syndrome typologic approach, 11

cocaine, 117, 158, 237
Coffman, J. A., 31
cognitive therapy, 150, 180
Cohen, G., 30
Cohen, S., 227
Collins, M., 30
Committee on Alcohol and Drug Abuse, 130
community resources, 216–19
computerized tomographic (CT) scans, 63, 94
confidentiality, patient-therapist, 49, 66
confrontation, in early intervention, 65–82
  key attitudes in, 64–66, 68, 72, 78
  rehearsing of, 66, 69
  when to avoid, 93
Connelly, J. C., 165
consensual validation, 147, 155, 190, 198
contracts, treatment, 67–68, 105, 163, 196, 206, 209
controlled drinking, as treatment goal, 120, 126–27, 192–93
convulsions, *see* seizures
Cook, P. J., 222, 224
coronary heart disease, 100
coumarin, 173
Council on Scientific Affairs, 233
couples therapy, 130
  group, 193–99
  private, 190, 212
covert sensitization, 156–58, 160
creatine phosphokinase (CPK), 100–101
Crenshaw, R., 165
cultural background, effects of, 41–42, 166–67
Curry, B., 232
Cushman, P., 116

Dackis, C. A., 161, 185
Darvon, 49
Davis, V. E., 30-31
Defoe, J. R., 42
Deiker, T., 91
delirium tremens (alcohol withdrawal delirium), 89–91, 109, 111–16
delta alcoholism, 10, 134
dementia, alcohol related, 95–96, 163
denial:
  alcoholics' use of, 2, 11, 14, 35–37, 40, 47–48, 54, 70, 126, 143–45, 147, 175, 203, 225
  in case histories, 71–74, 77–78
  dramatic confrontation to overcome, 65
  within families, 201, 203
  in inpatient treatment, 60–61, 152–53, 155
  of memory defects, 95

in outpatient group settings, 190–91, 194–95
  by physicians, 237
  by therapists, 159
Denmark, attitudes about drunk driving in, 237
dependency, 144, 155, 190, 195, 197
depression, 23, 39–41, 49, 81, 181–82, 202
  in adolescents, 82, 202
  bipolar, 60, 121, 162–63, 178
  family history of, 178–79
  lithium treatment and, 162–63, 176–77
  loneliness and, 163
  major-recurrent, 60, 121, 178–80
  primary vs. secondary, 40, 75, 160–62, 176, 178–80
  see also antidepressant drug therapy
DeSoto, C. B., 218
detoxification, 24, 70, 108–17
  habit-forming drugs after, 179–80
Deutsch, J. A., 32, 115
Dexamethasone Suppression Test (DST), 161–62, 179
diabetes mellitus, 98
diabetic acidosis, 87, 89
diagnosis, 47–61
  criteria for, 3–9
  differential, 58–59
  interview process in, 47–54
Diagnostic and Statistical Manual of Mental Disorders (American Psychiatric Association):
  second edition (*DSM-II*), 4, 86
  third edition (*DSM-III*), 1, 3, 15, 20, 60, 91
  third edition, revised (*DSM-III-R*), 1, 3–4, 15, 60, 87, 108, 178
Diagnostic Interview Scale (DIS), 14–15
Diagnostic Questions for Early or Advanced Alcoholism (DQEAA), 54–56, 238
diaphoresis, 88
diaries, therapeutic use of, 149–50, 206
diazepam (Valium), 32, 49, 110–11, 115–16, 181
diethylamine, 175
Dilantin (phenytoin), 110, 115, 173, 175
Disease Concept of Alcoholism, The (Jellinek), 9–10
distribution of consumption model, 222–23
disulfiram, *see* Antabuse
disulfiram-ethanol reaction (DER), 170–71, 173
Donovan, J. M., 1
dopamine (DA), 30–31, 170, 172, 175
dopamine beta hydroxylase (DBH), 170, 172
Douglass, R. K., 227, 231–32

doxepin, 179–80
dramatic confrontation, *see* confrontation,
    in early intervention
Draper, R. J., 96
Draw-A-Person Test, 153
Dr. Bob and the Good Oldtimers, 216
Drejer, K., 44
drinking age, 42, 222, 227, 231–33, 240
driving under the influence (DUI), driving
    while intoxicated (DWI), 2, 54–55, 74,
    84–85, 123, 172, 204, 221
    in early case-finding, 239–40
    laws on, 224–31, 233
    public attitudes in Scandinavia on, 236–37
    see also automobile accidents
drug use/abuse, 138–39, 160–61, 201, 235–37
    multiple, 48–49, 70, 82–83, 116–17,
        128–29, 158
    progression of, 18–19, 82
    see also specific drugs
"dry drunk," 61, 93
*DSM-II; DSM-III; DSM-III-R, see
    Diagnostic and Statistical Manual of
    Mental Disorders*
Dubach, U. C., 56, 239
Dubin, W. R., 111
Duffy, J. C., 1, 13–14, 128
Dunwiddie, T. V., 31

early intervention:
    case histories of, 70–82
    importance of, 63–64
    key attitudes in, 64–66, 68, 72, 78
    techniques of, 65–70
Edmonson, H. A., 97, 99–102, 184
education, preventive, 229–30, 234–38
Edwards, G., 128
elderly:
    misdiagnosis in, 94–95
    secondary prevention for, 241
    treatment of, 73–76, 163–64
electroencephalograph (EEG), abnormalities
    in, 7, 32, 88, 90
emesis, 110
emphysema, 157
employment, interference in, 2, 11, 41, 54,
    57, 84
"enablers," of drinking behavior, 152,
    199–200, 206–7
Epidemiologic Catchment Area (ECA)
    survey, 14–15
epsilon alcoholism, 10, 134
Eriksen, L., 214
esophageal varices, hemorrhaging of, 99–
    100
Ettore, E. M., 120

euphorigenic agents, 117
Ewing, J. A., 193

Faiman, M. D., 170
families:
    cohesiveness of, 39
    early intervention involvement of, 66–82
    history of alcoholism in, *see* genetic
        susceptibility
    interference in functioning of, 2, 11, 41
    psychodynamics of, 199–202
    temporary separation from, 65
"family hero," role of, 199–200, 207
Family Services, 219
family therapy, 130, 151–52, 199–211
    case histories of, 202–10
Fann, W. E., 114
fatty liver, 30, 99
Federal Railroad Administration (FRA), 227
Fell, J. C., 225
fetal alcohol syndrome (FAS), 101–2, 138, 238
Fillmore, K. M., 241
Filstead, W. J., 16, 241
Fine, E. W., 236
Finland, taxation and alcohol consumption
    in, 223
Flagyl (metronidazole), 173
flurazepam (Dalmane), 181–82
folic acid, 109, 183–84
Freund, G., 97–98
Fuller, R. K., 120, 173–75, 187, 220

GABA (gamma aminobutyric acid) system,
    30–31
Galanter, M., 238
Gallant, D. M., 1, 11, 15, 22, 48, 61, 65, 87,
    91, 95, 101–2, 114–15, 120–22, 153, 159,
    163, 165, 174–76, 180, 182, 187–88, 194,
    222, 239
Gallup, G., 48
Gamblers Anonymous, 160
gambling, 159–60, 197
gamma alcoholism, 10, 134, 177
gamma aminobutyric acid (GABA) system,
    31–32
gamma-glutamyl-transferase (GGT), 57,
    83–84, 90, 99
gamma-glutamyl-transpeptidase (GGTP), 50,
    57, 90
gastritis, 10
gastrointestinal complaints, 54
gays, counseling for, 211–12, 217
genetic susceptibility, 11, 20, 42–45, 53,
    127–28
    to depression, 179–80
    to Wernicke-Korsokoff syndrome, 183

Gershon, L. W., 240
Gessner, P. K., 115
GGT (gamma-glutamyl-transferase), 57,
    83–84, 90, 99
GGTP (gamma-glutamyl-transpeptidase, 50,
    57, 90
Gibson, G. E., 183
Glatt, M. M., 128
"going around," 144, 209
Gold Award, 122
Golden Age Club, 219
Goldstein, J. N., 39, 54
Goodwin, D. W., 43
Gorman, J. M., 63–64
Goyer, P. F., 172
Graff-Radford, M. R., 94
Grant, I., 91–92, 94–96, 153
Great Britain, inpatient units in, 119–20
Griffith, R. R., 186
group staffing (intake):
    in inpatient treatment, 130, 142–46,
        152–53
    in outpatient treatment, 146, 189–93
group therapy, 122, 144, 146–48, 190–91
Guerrero-Figueroa, R., 32, 116
guilt, of family members, 151, 195, 200,
    202

halazepam (Paxipam), 114
half-way houses, 219
hallucinations, 89–91, 109
hallucinogenic drugs, 39, 82
Halstead Category Subtest and Picture
    Arrangement, 96
Halstead-Reitan Neuropsychologic Test
    Battery, 92
hangovers, 2, 53
    from lorazepam, 181
Harford, T., 233
Harper, C., 183
Hatcher, R., 59
Hauge, R., 237
Heest, R. D., 239
Helzer, J. E., 128, 193
hemodialysis, 108
hepatic encephalopathy, 100
hepatitis, 30, 98–99, 103, 106
"here and now" approach, 147, 194, 198
heroin, 82
Hispanics, counseling for, 212, 217
"hobnail liver," 99
Hoffman, H., 39, 239
Holzbach, E., 113
homework (behavioral tasks), in outpatient
    treatment, 195, 206, 209
homosexuals, counseling for, 211–12, 217

hospitalization:
    for detoxification, 108–13
    rates of, 57, 223–24
House, J. M., 225
hydroxyzine (Atarax, Vistaril), 109, 111–13,
    180
hyperactive addictive phenomena, 30
hyperlipemia, 28
hypersensitivity with "brittleness," 23
hypersomnia, 179
hypertension, 2, 22, 75, 79, 100–101
hypnotics, 109, 113, 120, 158
hypoglycemia, 87, 90, 100, 108, 114
hypoglycemic agents, 176

Iber, F. L., 171–72
immediate gratification, 37–38
impulsivity, substance abuse and, 39, 50, 54,
    82
Indians, American:
    lack of prevention for, 238
    treatment for, 166
individual therapy, 120, 130, 155, 190–91
Inge, E. C. G., 239
inpatient detoxification, 108–13
inpatient rehabilitation treatment, 119–67
    admission procedures for, 128–30
    admission requirements for, 119, 122–23
    average daily cost of, 125
    "cafeteria" approach to, 129
    family meetings in, 151–52
    goals of, 125–28
    group staffing in, 130, 142–46, 152–53
    outpatient treatment vs., 60, 123, 192
    physical facilities for, 123–25
    psychological testing in, 129–30, 152–55
    success rates of, 119–22
insomnia, 49, 179–80, 182
insulin, deficiencies of, 100
Insurance Institute for Highway Safety's
    Report, 232
intake (staffing) sessions, 125, 130, 142–46,
    152–53, 189–93
interpersonal relations, interference in, 2, 10,
    11, 41
intervention, 63–85
interviews, in diagnosis, 47–54
intoxication:
    alcohol idiosyncratic, 86–89
    management of, 105–8
    signs and symptoms of, 87

Jacoby, J. A., 181
Jeffries, G. H., 13
Jelinek, J. M., 164
Jellinek, E. M., 9–10, 134, 177

Jensen, J. C., 170
Jensen, S. M., 153
Johnson, R. P., 165
Johnson, S. P., 240
Johnson, V. E., 65, 70, 212
Johnson Institute, 65
Joksch, H. C., 225
Jones, B. M., 59
Jones, M. K., 59
Judd, L. L., 176–77

Kadden, R., 50
Kandel, D. B., 19, 82, 236
Kirschenbaum, M., 194
Kissin, B., 91–92
Knox, W., 35
Korsakoff syndrome, 95, 115, 183
Kosten, T. R., 160
Kotch, J. B., 235
Kozararevic, D. J., 100
Kozlowski, L. T., 36
Kraus, M. L., 114
Kristenson, H., 57, 83

lability of affect, 15, 23, 93
Lansky, M. R., 199, 210
learning theory of chemical dependency, 37
legal problems, alcohol-related, 2, 11, 123
Lei, H., 192–93
Leichter, E., 194
Leighton, Y. H., 176–77
Lemert, E. M., 64
Lesieur, H. R., 159
Lieber, C. S., 28, 103
Liepman, M. R., 27, 57, 199
life crises, 160–61
Lin, Y-J., 58
lipase, 100
Lipson, A. A., 102
lithium, 162–63, 176–78, 185
Litman, G. K., 150
Little, R. E., 101
liver diseases, 2, 28, 30, 98–100
   cirrhosis, 10, 13, 22, 30, 42, 99, 222
liver toxicity:
   of Antabuse, 171–73
   of antidepressants, 179
lorazepam, 111, 114–15, 181
loss of control, 3, 10, 44, 178, 193, 239
"lost child," family role of, 199, 201
Louisiana State Penitentiary at Angola, 159
low birthweight offspring, 101–2, 242
Lowe, J. B., 213
LSD (lysergic acid diethylamide), 82

MacAndrew Alcoholism Scale, 50
McCrady, B. S., 120
McFarlain, R. A., 180
McGivern, R. G., 102
MacGregor, R. B., 103
McLellan, A. T., 121
McMillan, T. N., 176
macrocytosis, 57, 90, 184
MADD (Mothers Against Drunk Driving), 42, 226–27
Maddux, J. F., 237
Maisto, S. A., 84, 239
Major, L. F., 172
Malin, H., 233
Manhem, P., 115
MAO (monoamine oxidase) inhibitors, 176, 179
marijuana, 19, 39, 48, 82, 129, 158, 235–37
marital couples therapy, *see* couples therapy
"mascot," family role of, 199, 201
MAST (Michigan Alcoholism Screening Test), 2–3, 50–54, 238
Masters, W. H., 212
May, P. A., 166, 238
Mayer, J., 16, 241
Maynard, L., 237
Maletzky, B. M., 88
media, influence of, 235–36, 240
Medical and Social Aspects of Alcohol Abuse (Tabakoff, Sutker and Randall), 33
medical problems, alcohol-related, 2, 4–7, 10, 11, 22–24, 42, 49, 86–103, 137–38, 242
   see also liver diseases; organic mental disturbances, alcohol-related
Memory-for-Designs Test, 153
metronidazole (Flagyl), 173, 176
Michigan Alcoholism Screening Test (MAST), 2–3, 50–54, 238
microsomal ethanol oxidizing system (MEOS), 27, 29
Miller, W. R., 120, 128
minimum drinking age, 42, 222, 227, 231–33, 240
Minnesota Clerical Test, 177
Minnesota Multiphasic Personality Inventory (MMPI), 11, 39, 50, 153, 160
minorities, treatment for, 166–67
mitochondrial enzyme delta aminolevulinic acid synthetase (ALAS), 28
modeling, in group therapy, 147, 198
monoamine oxidase (MAO) inhibitors, 176, 179
mood disturbances, 48, 54, 56
morbidity rates, 21–24, 42, 84, 100, 174, 238
   traffic, 221–24, 227, 231–32, 236

Morse, R. M., 239
mortality rates, 20–24, 42, 57, 63, 84, 100, 111, 174, 238
    traffic, 221–25, 227, 231–33, 236
Mothers Against Drunk Driving (MADD), 42, 226–27
multivitamins, 109, 113, 184
Murphy, S. M., 182
Murray, R. N., 165
Myers, R. D., 30

Nagy, F., 101–2
naloxone, 30, 108
naltrexone, 30
narcotics:
    addiction to, 160–61
    analgesic, 49
    use of, 82, 108, 158, 237
Narcotics Anonymous (NA), 58
National Broadcasting Company (NBC), 227
National Commission Against Drunk Driving, 228
National Council on Alcoholism (NCA), 1, 4–9, 53, 227–31
National Federation of Parents for Drug-Free Youth (NFP), 235
National Highway Traffic Safety Administration (NHTSA), 21–22, 232
National Institute of Mental Health, 32
National Institute on Alcohol Abuse and Alcoholism (NIAAA), 16, 240
National Transportation Safety Board, 227
Navajo, traditions incorporated in treatment of, 166
Neiderhiser, D. H., 175, 214
nerve damage, peripheral, 97, 171–72, 184
neuroleptic drugs, 88, 113
night blindness, 184
Niven, Robert, 16
nonconformism, substance abuse and, 39, 201
non-opioid receptor systems, 30–32
norepinephrine (NE), 30, 32, 92
normorphan, 30
Norway, attitudes about drunk driving in, 237
nutritional deficiencies, 97–98, 102, 138, 182–84

obesity, ethanol metabolism and, 26
O'Brien, J. E., 114
occupational therapy, 130
Ogborne, A. C., 218
Okula, S., 42

Ontario, Canada, lowering of drinking age in, 231
opioids:
    addiction to, 160–61
    receptor systems, 29–31
    see also narcotics
opthalmoplegia, 183
optic atrophy, 184
optic neuritis, 171–72
organic mental disturbances, alcohol-related, 40–41, 50, 63, 91–98, 123, 164, 183
    in inpatient treatment, 147–48, 153
    irreversible, 95–98
    reversible, 94–95
Ornstein, S. I., 223
Orrego, H., 1, 14, 36, 119, 128
Oswald, I., 181
outpatient treatment, 187–219
    Antabuse used in, 174, 195–96, 205–6, 209, 213–14
    compliance measures in, 213–14
    dropout rates in, 191–92, 214
    family therapy in, 199–211
    goals of, 192–93
    group intake in, 146, 189–93
    "homework" assignments in, 195, 206, 209
    inpatient treatment vs., 60, 123, 192
    success rates of, 146
    treatment failures referred to, 122
    waiting period before, 214–15
    for withdrawal symptoms, 108
overdose, signs and symptoms of, 87
overeating, 179
oxazepam, 111, 114

P-450, 28
pancreatitis, 2, 22, 49, 100, 223
panic disorder, 40, 98, 178–80
pantothenic acid, deficiencies in, 98, 184
paraldehyde, 110
paranoid disorders, 60
Parent's Resource Institute for Drug Education (PRIDE), 235
Parker, E. S., 237–38
Parsons, O. A., 95
passive personality, 147–50, 197, 204, 207
Pathological Intoxication, 86
patients:
    as co-therapists, 144–45, 191
    identification between, 144–45, 190–91, 211
Pattison, M. E., 108–9
peer influence, 15, 19, 42, 83, 201, 204, 235
pentobarbitol, 117, 181
peptic ulcers, 23, 101
peripheral neuropathy, 97, 171–72, 184

Perry, P. P., 115
personality characteristics, 11, 23, 35–41, 54,
    144, 148–51, 152–55, 234
Petersson, B., 22, 24, 63, 222
Petrakis, P. L., 102–3
Pettinati, H. M., 160, 179
Petty, F., 31
phencyclidine (PCP), 88
phenobarbitol, 116
phenylketonuria (PKU), 102
phenytoin (Dilantin), 110, 115, 173, 175
phobias, 130, 157, 161, 178–79
physicians, substance abuse among, 165,
    237
Physicians Desk Reference, 171
physiological dependency, *see* addiction
Pills Anonymous (PA), 58
pimozide, 170
pneumonia, 22
Podolsky, D. M., 103
Poikolainen, K., 223
Poland, taxation and alcohol consumption
    in, 224
Ponds, Jim, 130
Popham, R., 223
porphyria, 28
portal vein pressure, 99
post-traumatic stress disorder (PTSD), 164
prevention:
    primary, 221–38
    secondary, 238–42
prochlorperazine, 110, 115
Proctor, W. R., 31
"Progress Report on the Implementation of
    Recommendations by the Presidential
    Commission on Drunk Driving, A," 228
propanediol, 29
propanolol (Inderal), 89, 100, 182
protracted withdrawal syndrome (PWS), 61,
    91–94, 184
Psychiatric Evaluation Profile, 40
psychiatric patients, alcoholism in, 19–20,
    49–50, 121, 165–66, 196
psychodynamic theory of chemical dependen-
    cy, 37–40
psychological consequences, *see* organic
    mental disturbances, alcohol-related
psychological mechanisms, of alcoholism,
    35–40
psychological testing, inpatient treatment use
    of, 129–30, 152–55
psychopharmacologic agents, use of, 170–85
psychosis, 49
    misdiagnosis as, 88, 90, 91, 111
    see also schizophrenia, schizophrenics
psychotherapy, *see specific types*

psychotic behavior, during blackouts, 88
Puddey, I. B., 22, 101
Puerto Ricans, treatment for, 166
pyridoxine, deficiencies in, 98, 184

railroad industry, accidents in, 227
rebelliousness, substance abuse and, 39, 50,
    54, 82, 201
recreational therapy, 130
Redetzki, H. N., 107
Reichler, B. D., 19, 24, 57
Reich test, 50–54
Reisner, H., 90
Relapse Precipitants Inventory (RPI), 150–
    51
retirement, premature, 163–64
revolving-door alcoholics, *see* skid-row
    alcoholics
Reynold, M. C., 177
Richman, A., 222, 224
Robins, L. N., 14–15, 24, 242
Robinson, G. N., 118
Rogan, A., 240–41
role playing, therapeutic use of, 149, 155
Rooney, J. F., 63–64
Rorschach Psychodiagnostic Test, 153
Rosett, H. L., 242
Rothstein, J. D., 32
Rounsaville, B. J., 3
Rouse, B. A., 193
Rund, G. A., 242
Rush, B. R., 223
Rutstein, D. D. 29
Ryback, R. S., 57

Sanchez-Craig, M., 192–93
Sappington, J. T., 39, 54
"scapegoat," family role of, 199, 201, 205,
    207–8, 210–11
Scharf, M. B., 181
Schedule for Affective Disorders and
    Schizophrenia Life-time Version/
    Research Diagnostic Criteria (SADS-L/
    RDC), 177
schizophrenia, schizophrenics, 60, 122, 166
    Antabuse and, 172, 174–75
    misdiagnosis as, 88, 91, 111
Schneider, J., 56, 239
school agencies, in early case-finding, 240–42
Schuckit, M. A., 1, 3, 11, 15, 40, 43–44, 88,
    161, 178
Scoles, P. E., 236, 239
Scott, T. B., 121
sedative antihistamines, 110

sedative hypnotics, 109, 113, 120, 158
seizures, 89–91, 106–7, 109–13, 115–16
self-criticism, extreme, 150, 200
self-esteem, 40–41, 147, 157, 202, 234–35
Self-Rating Depression Scale (Zung Scale),
    161
Sellers, E. M., 175
Selzer, M. L., 50
senile dementia, Alzheimer's type (SDAT),
    94–95, 111, 163
Senior, J. R., 100
Sentence Completion Test, 153
separation anxiety, 178
Sereny, G., 174, 187, 213
serum glutamic-oxalecetic transaminase
    (SGOT), 57, 99
serum osmolality, 107
sexual abuse, 148, 199, 212
sexual counseling, 196, 212
sexual dysfunction, 48, 60, 79, 152, 155–56,
    171, 196, 212
SGPT, 90, 99
Sher, K. J., 120
Sherman, S., 233
shipping industry, accidents in, 227
short-term memory deficits, 97–98
shunt surgery, 100
Simpson, G. M., 176
Sing, C. F., 101
skeletal muscle, myopathies of, 100–101
skid-row (revolving-door) alcoholics, 40–41,
    98, 101
    success rates with, 120–21, 159
Skinner, H. A., 11
Skog, O-J., 224
sleep, disturbances in, 7, 90, 91, 179
sleeping pills, 48–49
SMA-6 test, 57
SMA-12 test, 57
Smart, R. G., 231–32
Smith, G. T., 234
smooth endoplasmic reticulum (SER), 27
social agencies, in early case-finding, 240–
    42
social detoxification, 110–11
social functioning, assessing, 48–50
social skills training (SST) groups, 120, 130,
    147–51, 194
Sokol, R. J., 238
Sokolow, L., 116, 129, 158
Southeast Louisiana Hospital, alcohol and
    drug abuse unit (ADU) at, 122–58, 181,
    184
Spanish-speaking people, counseling for,
    212, 217
spouse battering, 2, 64, 239–41

spouses, involvement in treatment by, 121,
    151, 174–75, 194–99
staffing (intake) sessions, 125, 130, 142–46,
    152–53, 189–93
state-dependent learning, 32–33
stimulants, 117
Streissguth, A. P., 242
strokes, hypertension-related, 100–101
subacute organic mental disorder (SOMD),
    91–92, 147, 153, 184
    see also organic mental disturbances,
    alcohol-related
substance use pattern (continued vs.
    episodic), 11
succinylcholine, 116
suicide, 13, 22–24, 40, 48, 63, 165
    depression and, 40, 179
    preventing, 66, 74–75, 165
Suzdak, P. D., 33
Sweden, attitudes about drunk driving in,
    237
Symptom Check-list, 90, 218
systematic (hierarchical) desensitization, 157

Tabakoff, B., 30–31
taxation, as prevention tool, 221–24
Tennessee Self Concept Scale (TSCS),
    Counseling Form of, 234
testosterone levels, 92
tetrahydro-β-carbolines (THBC), 30
tetrahydropapaveroline (THP), 30
therapeutic relationship, 41, 47–48, 93, 123,
    147, 167
    essential elements of, 64–65, 107, 126–27
thiamine (vitamin B1):
    administration of, 108–9, 113, 115, 183
    deficiencies in, 98, 115, 183–84
thiamine pyrophosphatase (TPP), dependent
    transketalase activity, 183
Thomas, M., 30–31, 44
THC (marijuana metabolite), 129
tolerance, 27–31, 53
    sex differences in, 58–59
tranquilizers, 158, 180
Traveler's Aid, 219
treatment:
    contracts, 67–68, 105, 163, 196, 206, 209
    delays in seeking, 63–64, 106–7
    follow–up to, 121
    success/failure rates of, 93, 119–22, 146,
    193
    see also detoxification; inpatient rehabilita-
    tion treatment; outpatient treatment
tricyclic antidepressants, 176, 179, 181–82
triglyceride, 57, 90

Truax, C. B., 64–65
trust, in therapeutic relationship, 41, 64–65,
    93, 107, 123, 126–27, 147, 155, 167
tryptamine, metabolism of, 92
Tulane Medical School, 65
12 steps, 216
12 traditions, 216–17

United Fund, 130
University Hospital Lund, 22
University Hospital of Basel, 56
University of Michigan Highway Safety
    Institute, 227, 231
uric acid, 57, 90
urine testing:
    for alcohol, 119, 213
    for Antabuse compliance, 175, 214
    for drug abuse, 128–29, 159, 213

Valium (diazepam), 32, 49, 110–11, 115–16,
    181
vascular spider nevi, 102
vehicular homicide, 226
veterans, problems of, 164, 241–42
Veterans Administration (VA) alcoholism
    program, 31
Veterans Administration Hospital in New
    Orleans, 164
Vidamantis, R., 44
videotaping, therapeutic uses of, 38–39, 150
vitamins, 182–84
    A, 184
    B, 98, 108–9, 184, *see also* thiamine
    C, 175
    K, 99–100

Voas, R. B., 225
vocational rehabilitation, 96, 219

Wagenaar, A. C., 227, 231–32
Waller, P. F., 225
Walsh, M. J., 30–31
Walton, N. Y., 32, 115
Waterton, J. J., 1, 13–14, 128
Wattis, J. P., 241
Wechsler Adult Intelligence Scale, 153
Weissman, M. M., 15
Wernicke's encephalopathy, 115, 183
West, J. W., 111
Wester, R., 39, 161
Westermeyer, J., 15, 35, 41–42, 166
Whitfield, C. L., 53, 109–11
Williams, T., 164
Williford, W. O., 120, 173
withdrawal, 10, 24
    diazepam administered during, 32, 115
    management of, 108–17
    metabolic addiction and, 30
    mild to moderate, 89–90, 108–11, 114
    of multiple-drug users, 116–17
    protracted, 61, 91–94, 184
    severe (acute), 89–90, 111–16, 180
    signs and symptoms of, 89–90
    state-dependent theory of, 32–33
women's group therapy, 148, 190, 193
Woodruff, R. A., 2, 50, 54, 239
Wright, K. D., 121

Yamaguchi, K., 82, 236

zinc supplements, 184